HANDBOOK OF DEVELOPMENTAL EDUCATION

HANDBOOK OF DEVELOPMENTAL EDUCATION

Edited by
Robert M. Hashway

PRAEGER

New York
Westport, Connecticut
London

Library of Congress Cataloging-in-Publication Data

Handbook of developmental education / edited by Robert M. Hashway.
     p.   cm.
  Includes bibliographical references (p.) and indexes.
  ISBN 0-275-93297-4 (alk. paper)
  1. Compensatory education — United States. 2. Remedial teaching —
United States. 3. Classroom learning centers — United States.
4. College student development programs — United States.
I. Hashway, Robert M.
LC213.2.H38   1990
378'.03 — dc20   90-49852

British Library Cataloguing in Publication Data is available.

Library of Congress Catalog Card Number: 90-49852
ISBN: 0-275-93297-4

First published in 1990

Praeger Publishers, One Madison Avenue, New York, NY 10010
An imprint of Greenwood Publishing Group, Inc.

Printed in the United States of America

The paper used in this book complies with the
Permanent Paper Standard issued by the National
Information Standards Organization (Z39.48-1984).

10 9 8 7 6 5 4 3 2 1

Contents

Preface   ix

1. **Liberal Arts and Sciences: A Renewed Focus for Developmental Education**
   Lawrence A. Quigley   1

   Developmental Thinking   4

   The Dynamics of Change: The Basics of Developmental Education   7

   The Fitchburg Model   14

2. **Axioms of Developmental Learning and Instruction**
   Robert M. Hashway   23

   Developmental Thinking and Learning Models   24

3. **Cognition and Developmental Education**
   Kimberly Kinsler and Andrew Robinson   53

   The Nature of Academic Competence   54

   Moderators of Competence   57

   Methodological Approaches   66

   Feuerstein's Instructional Enrichment Model   67

   Palincsar and Brown's Reciprocal Teaching of Reading   70

   Scardamalia and Bereiter's Procedural Facilitation of Writing   72

   Schoenfeld's Approach to Mathematics Instruction   74

   Comments and Conclusions   76

4. **Fostering Student Learning and Development through Effective Teaching**
   Charles S. Claxton   85

   Knowledge as Social Construction   86

   Student Learning Styles   89

   Alternative Ways of Knowing   92

   Teaching Models   97

5. **Program and Course Design Guidelines**
   Robert M. Hashway   109

   Philosophy and Development Process   110

    The Structure of Training   116

    Summary   124

6. **The Learning Center from 1829 to the Year 2000 and Beyond**
   L. Scott Lissner   127

    Learning Centers: Past and Present   129

    The Learning Center Conceived   137

    Comprehensive Systems   149

7. **College Learning Assistance Centers: Places for Learning**
   William G. White, Jr., and Mary Lee Schnuth   155

    Evolution of Learning Assistance Centers   155

    Comprehensive Components   158

    Learning Assistance Center Services   160

    College Learning Assistance Centers of the Future   166

8. **College Learning Assistance Centers: Spaces for Learning**
   William G. White, Jr., Barney Kyzar and Kenneth E. Lane   179

    College and University Planning   179

    Planning the Learning Assistance Center   182

    Conclusion   192

9. **Stress and the Developmental Student**
   George H. Roberts   197

    Classification of Developmental Students   198

    What Is Stress?   199

    The Academic Dimension of Stress   206

    The Personal Dimension of Stress   208

    Stress and the Health of Developmental Students   209

    Implications for Student Personnel Services   210

10. **Developmental Mathematics**
    Joan M. Dodway   217

11. **Reading as "Big Business" to Developmental Education**
    Gwendolyn Trotter   233

     Issues and Directions for Reading in Developmental
        Education   241

     Higher-Order Thinking Skills   244

     Competencies in Reading Minimum and Maximum Skills   247

Reading Instruction as Process 248

Collaboration for Universities/Business/Community 249

State of the Art Developmental Reading Strategies and
    Materials 250

Reading Agenda for the Twenty-First Century 252

12. Developmental Reading in College
Robin W. Erwin, Jr. 261

Definitions 264

Review of Research Findings with General Populations 265

Research Findings with Developmental Readers 269

Conclusions from Research Findings 270

Current Practices in the Delivery of Critical Reading
    Instruction for Developmental Readers 271

13. Effective Counseling
Cynthia Jackson Hammond 279

Locus of Control 288

Summary 296

14. Student Retention and Attrition in College
Patricia Hawkins Rogers 305

Retention and Attrition Rates in College 306

Retention and Attrition Theories 307

College Success Studies 310

Nonacademic Variables 314

Conclusions and Recommendations 318

15. The Developmental Educator's System of Values
Andolyn V. Brown 329

Summary 332

16. Research in Developmental Education
Kimberly Kinsler and Andrew Robinson 335

Research and Evaluation: Goals and General Principles 336

Types of Research 341

Conducting Research 344

Validity and Bias in Developmental Research 348

Research Directions in Developmental Education 353

Selected Bibliography   357

Author Index   363

Subject Index   379

About the Editor   381

List of Contributors   383

Preface

The field of developmental education, not unlike many other fields of study, is in need of mission and direction. In the *Foundations of Developmental Education* (Hashway, 1988), I traced the history of societal and political impacts upon education. We saw, in the *Foundations*, that education was subject to many conflicting political and social forces. Developmental education has been subject to the same forces.

In colleges and universities, courses called 'remedial' have been offered for decades. Facing the political and funding crises of the late 1960's thru the 1970's, educators involved in so-called remedial courses adopted a 'new' name, 'developmental education' (Clowes, 1981; Garland, 1978). That name change, they felt, gave credibility to their efforts and eased the path through legislative funding processes.

Unfortunately, those who were developing 'remedial' programs had no clear sense of purpose. Programs labeled 'remedial' ranged from basic arithmetic to calculus, reading through literature as well as chemistry, physics, history and other courses depending upon the particular institution. A subset of the field of developmental education, remediation, became identified with the entire field. The definitional uncertainty associated with remediation efforts has engulfed the entire field (Madson, 1982).

Now is the time to correct this situation.

Currently, nearly 90% of the adult population in the United States can only read safety rules, equipment instructions and write simple reports. Only seven percent of the adult population can read scientific journals and financial reports. In the next 10 years more than 40% of the adult population will be required to read scientific journals and financial reports as well as to write detailed business proposals. The evolution of the nature of business and finance will necessitates a change in the definition of functional literacy.

Increasing technological complexities have made lifelong learning a matter of survival for both U.S. employees and their employers. By 1995, manufacturers who have not assumed the responsibility for training their employees will be out of business. The American society shows signs of increasing polarization, not only between the rich and the poor, but also between the technologically elite and impoverished. Knowledge is becoming the social discriminator. A strong back and willing hands are not worth very much and will be worth less. The only way a person can compete is to be smart enough to use technology, knowledge bases, and expert systems. The worker of 1995 will not, necessarily, work harder but, will work smarter.

Society has seen the importance of developmental education. Examples of that vision have been the establishment of the Kellogg Center at Appalachian State University and the only doctoral level program in the field at Grambling State University. The Kellogg Center has focused primarily on training individuals to work in remedial centers in colleges. The Grambling doctoral program is training scholars in the field to improve practice through research. Motivated by the needs of this and the next century, developmental educators must take a broader view of their role and function.

The Broader View

Developmental education has been the mechanism for a lifelong process that offers the orderly progression of the attitudes and abilities that constitute the adult experience (Knox, 1977). Developmental learning, whether learning about psychological motives or the characteristics of various vocations, is characteristic of a healthy organism (Kidd, 1975). Developmental education is a consciousness raising process through which people become involved in the type of society that fosters autonomy and solidarity (Schiefeheim, 1982) and   attends to the fullest possible development of human talent and aims to capitalize upon strengths as well as to correct weaknesses where remediation aims to overcome academic dificiencies (Cross, 1976, 1982).

Most scholars in the field believe that developmental education is a process where adults identify their beliefs, clarify their goals and formulate an action plan (Schlossberg, Lynch and Chickering, 1989; Steltenpohl and Shipton, 1986), and is a lifelong process of self-appraisal and realignment (Cullinane and Williams, 1983; Kohlberg, 1973; Perry, 1968; Viniar, 1984). On the campus, developmental theory should form the basis of all curricular planning and the "glue" which binds students and faculty in the process of human evolution. In the workplace, developmental theory should be the foundation of personnel policy, new worker articulation strategies, employee manager relations and human development programs.

Although remediation is a component of developmental education, it is neither sufficiently significant nor important enough to be considered as encompassing the field. The nature of remediation is situationally dependent and only a very small part of the developmental process. The growth of each human necessitates that we view growth as an evolutionary experience and stages of growth as part of that evolution. Labels are needed only when a person discriminates against another person. That discrimination and its associated labels, such as 'remedial,' are counterproductive to healthy human development.

After a review of relevant literature I defined **developmental education as the process by which an organism moves from one state to another** (Hashway, 1988). *Remediation is the relativistic condition existing when the state of an organism is in discordance with the entry behaviors assumed by a particular program.* There is no new evidence to support a change in that position.

The developmental experience is the evolution of the entire human condition, not restricted to knowledge acquisition. Developmental education is not a field which focuses on a particular type of learner or a particular pedagogical technique nor does it advocate a particular set of rules or behaviors. It is a process applicable to all populations and knowledge bases recognizing the individual as a dynamic part of the learning scenario. Developmental educators advocate a process approach to education where learners are characterized in terms of specific behavioral (knowledge base and/or personality) areas, recognize learning style differences between people and within people but between subjects, multiple resources and experiences, that learning occurs at different rates at the enabling objective level and that nonmastery of enabling objectives can lead to subsequent failure at some future time, and that periodic and frequent assessment of individual progress. The developmental educator knows that learning occurs best when it is organized in terms of a multifaceted network, not in some 'lock step' fashion and takes advantage of the latest advances in technological and administrative systems. Most importantly, the developmental educator knows that the emotional state of the individual is of critical importance and provides constant reinforcement and assurnace balancing guidance and counseling practices with academic programming.

The societal need for lifelong learning experiences necessitates a focus on alternative learning settings such as industrial education centers, alternative learning centers and the education store where systems for quality assurance, research and evaluation are incorporated into the developmental learning experience. Educational development requires a research/database system approach to curriculum, service delivery, guidance and administration. This handbook has brought together the leading practitioners and researchers in the field to focus on the developmental learning agenda for the next decade.

In the first chapter Lawrence Quigley sets the stage by describing the developmental process as a holistic approach to the development of the whole person. He shows us how developmental education in college is the process of curricular integration directed toward developing an adaptable professional and goes further to describe how the process has been put into place on the college level. The remainder of this handbook is organized in terms of four thrusts: curriculum theory, learning centers, human factors research, and research methodology.

Curriculum Theory. In chapter 2, I present a synthesis of the psychological and physiological basis of human growth and development. That synthesis leads to some basic axioms for developmental learning and instruction. Subsequently, Kimberly Kinsler and Andrew Robinson describe the interplay between cognitive theories and developmental learning processes. They provide a method for the symbiosis of developmental theory and instructional practice to meet the societal demand for logical reasoners and technological problem solvers. Charles Claxton points out in chapter 4 that developmental education must focus upon students who are "strangers" to higher education. In his chapter, Claxton describes how information structures and learning styles evolve in to effective teaching and foster student learning. I end this thrust with chapter 5 on structured instructional design and delivery which describes the methodology for applying the **SMART** model and the **Developmental Pyramid** approach (Hashway, 1988) to design programs and optimize service delivery.

Learning Centers. Scott Lissner begins this thrust in chapter 6 with a review of the history of learning centers. He presents a conceptual model for learning center development. William White and Mary Lee Schnuth describe the learning center in chapter 7 as an organic growing entity. They construct a structure for future learning centers in traditional and nontraditional settings. Chapter 8 concludes this thrust by presenting physical parameters for constructing a learning center. Using the directives in that chapter, William White, Barney Kyzar and Kenneth Lane show us how to establish an environment conducive to human growth and development.

Human Factors Research. This thrust begins with chapter 9 by George Roberts where he describes the interplay between stress and development. Joan Dodway presents a survey of the history and research for teaching mathematics. Robin Erwin reviews research leading to an approach to collegiate reading instruction. Gwendolyn Trotter describes conceptual macrostructures for reading and literacy instruction in traditional and nontraditional settings and sets the agenda for the next century. Cynthia Hammond describes the problems and issues related to establishing effective counseling programs in chapter 13. Patricia Rogers summarizes the research related to attrition and retention. Chapter 15 concludes this thrust with a charge to developmental instructors and individuals who hire them to take value systems into account by Andolyn Brown. She points out that the quality of instruction is directly related to the beliefs, attitudes and values of the service providors.

Throughout this handbook, each author points out the methodological limitations of the research and the need for quality research. In chapter 15 Kinsler and Robinson inconclude a description of the constraints and methodologies which are indicative of quality research. Using their methodologies, summative and formative evaluation as well as research studies will provide the constructive feedback necessary to develop the dynamic and adaptive developmental education systems needed for human growth in the next decade.

The process of identifying contributors for this *Handbook* involved selecting leaders from the field. The first task was to identify the characteristics of a leader. I *could* have defined a leader as a well published and hence well known personality. *I defined* a leader as someone who has, in the past and is currently, involved in progressive developmental education as well as someone who can contribute new directions and perspectives. The associates I have selected are all well published professionals who are also well known in their respective areas. All are currently involved in delivering new and innovative developmental programs. It is thru their insight and creative vision that I hope we will carve a path into the next decade and beyond.

REFERENCES

Clowes, D. A. (1981). More than a definitional problem: remedial, compensatory, and developmental education. *Journal of developmental and remedial education*, 2, 8 - 10.

Cullinane, M. and D. Williams (1983). *Life, career, educational planning: A facilitator's manual.* Suffern, NY: Rockland Community College.

Cross, K. P. (1976). *Accent on learning: Improving instruction and reshaping the curriculum.* San Francisco: Jossey-Bass.

Cross, K. P. (1982). *Improving student learning skills.* San Francisco, California: Jossey-Bass.

Garland, M.(1978). Dr. Rouche, tell me...an interview with Dr. John E. Rouche. *Journal of developmental and remedial education*, 1, 5 - 7.

Hashway, R. M. (1988). *Foundations of developmental education.* New York: Praeger Publishers.

Kidd, J. R. (1975). *How adults learn.* New York: Association Press.

Knox, A. B. (1977). *Adult development and learning.* San Francisco: Jossey-Bass.

Kohlberg, L. (1973). Continuities in childhood and adult moral development revisited. In P. B. Baltes and K. W. Schare (eds.), *Life-span developmental psychology: Personality and socialization.* Orlando: Academic Press.

Madsen, D. (1982). History and philosophy of higher education. *Encyclopedia of educational research,* 4, 795 - 803.

Perry, W. G. (1968). *Forms of intellectual and ethical development in the college years: A scheme.* New York: Holt, Rinehart and Winston.

Schiefeheim, E. (1982). Would you please empty your tea chup? Epistemological aspects of developmental education, *International Review of education,* 28, 449 - 455.

Schlossberg, I. K., A. Q. Lynch and A. W. Chickering (1989). *Improving higher education environments for adults.* San Francisco: Jossey-Bass.

Steltenpohl, E. and J. Shipton (1968). Facilitating a successful transition to college for adults, *Journal of higher education,* 57, 6, 637 - 658.

Viniar, B. (1984). Adult development theory: The medium and the message. *Insight: An annual collection of articles on teaching and learning by faculty of the community colleges and state universities of New York, 1983 - 1984.* Albany: New York State Board of Regents.

HANDBOOK OF DEVELOPMENTAL EDUCATION

1

Liberal Arts and Sciences: A Renewed Focus for Developmental Education

Lawrence A. Quigley

When the history of higher education in America is written, covering the period from the 1990s into the twenty-first century, some movements in developmental education will have earned their marks as benchmarks in this process of development. Such was the lasting impact of Dewey's progressivism of the 1920s, Hutchins's *Great Books* in the 1930s and the *Red Book* revision of *General Education* under President Conant at Harvard in the 1940s. So, likewise was this venerable institution's revision and revitalization of its core curriculum in the late 1970s.

Following the leadership given by Harvard's faculty in undertaking a thorough, comprehensive review of the core requirements in a liberal arts undergraduate education, many instituions revised their course offerings and the structure of their general education programs. This was necessitated by the changing populations being served, the impact of new technologies, and the interplay of the macrocosm of the world scene upon the microcosm of academia and, vice versa, among other forces impacting on the academic marketplace.

In one case after another the focus has ultimately been placed on components in an educational program that will help develop a well-rounded person who is more fully educated and better able to relate to his or her rights and responsibilities as a citizen of this world at this critical period in the historical development of humanity. This developmental approach owes much to the emphasis on and growth of developmental psychology and its growing impact on the schemata of higher education. In an increasingly complex society, how can the individual pull together and make sense of the disparate strands of the mystery of life, rather than feal he or she is clutching at straws? One answer seems to lie in curricular emphasis on a more holistic view of life, as in the fields of medicine and ecology. This approach gives promise of being a healthful and wholesome antidote to much of the fragmentation and disintegration that riddled American higher education in the late 1960s.

As this emphasis on the individual's development in a context of strengthened societal bonds (designed so well at the elementary and secondary levels in the work of Goodland [1966] at UCLA in the 60s) continues on to the higher education level, the need for developmental models become paramount. With the increasing numbers of adult learners entering these institutions, the need becomes all the more pressing to design and deliver programs that develop the capacities of undergraduates of all ages during these critical years on campus, but which also challenge them to continue along the path of lifetime learning. In this process the import of the principles of andragogy becomes all the more significant in addressing the developmental needs of this growing population. Indeed, if cradle-to-grave and womb-to-tomb are regarded as overly comprehensive educational ranges, the spectrum of pre-K through A (adult) seems here to stay.

From a number of institutions pursuing this holistic development of programs, and concurrently of their students, this chapter presents a case study of the program design and implementation of one college's attempt to reform its general educaton program to meet the developmental education needs of its students in the 1990s and into the twenty-first century. Much remains to be done, but a solid, steady foundation has been laid, auguring well for continued, progressive growth and development of this challenging process of developmental education.

During the Summer of 1986, a group of four faculty members and the Dean of Undergraduate Studies at Fitchburg State College, Fitchburg, Massachusetts, were awarded a Summer Grant to examine and make recommendations regarding the General Education Program at the College. A certain level of frustration had set in about the quality and contemporaneity of the General Education Program, which had been a keystone of the New England Association's full ten-year approval of the undergraduate and graduate programs at Fitchburg State College 14 years earlier in 1972, during this author's tenure as Executive Vice President.

Despite some efforts to reform, reinvigorate, and redesign the general education program during the institutional self-assessment process in 1982, a vote of confidence was given to the existing program of studies in general education which comprised 60 to 64 credits, or 50 percent of the total undergraduate program. Still "the eternal discontent" of John Donne was evident among a number of faculty and administrators, seeing this body of knowledge remaining static while the rushing waves of the 1970s and 1980s were passing the college by. One essential focus of this study group, therefore, was to assess the state of the art of general education in some 100 college and universities across the nation. They assembled their findings, incorporating recommendations for the updating and upgrading of this program. In the spirit of the classical, medieval and Renaissance models of developmental education which had perdured the "touchstone of time", they labeled this new approach very directly: **The Liberal Arts and Sciences Program**. Without the appearance of any disclaimer, the committee stated its renewed purpose rather directly in these words:

> This program uses the term "Liberal Arts and Sciences" in lieu of "General Education" to emphasize to all majors that the core of their education is built upon content and skills acquired in courses in the Liberal Arts and Sciences and is intended to provide them with a Liberal, rather than a General, Education, to support and complement their specialization in a major. (Fitchburg State College Curriculum Committee, 1988)

When this proposal was referred, in accordance with its governance procedures, by the All-College Committee through its Curriculum Committee to an *ad hoc* Committee handling the proposal, much valuable dialogue and issuance of counter-proposals ensued across the campus during 1986-87, engaging the community of scholars. During the 1987-88 academic year this Proposal became the main focus of the Curriculum Committee's deliberations. Twenty-two public meetings were held, during the course of which 80 amendments to the document were put forward by members of the College community to the 22 member Curriculum Committee, consisting of 16 faculty, 3 students and 3 administrators. The renewed Liberal Arts and Sciences Program, including only 12 of these amendments, was voted by the Curriculum Committee 17 to 1, and was also recommended to the President by its parent body, the All-College Committee, 10 to 1. The President approved this new Program in May 1988 and is being implemented currently under the following seven-phase plan.

> **Phase I** (1988-1990): Establishment of Liberal Arts and Sciences Council, approval of courses for the program. Appointment of a Coordinator of the Freshman Foundation Year.
>
> **Phase II** (1989-1990): Pilot Program for the Freshman Foundation Year.
>
> **Phase III** (1990-1991): New Liberal Arts and Sciences Requirements become effective.
>
> **Phase IV** (1991-1992): Evaluation of Freshman Foundation Year. Inititation of the remainder of the cluster requirements.
>
> **Phase V** (1992-1993): Initiation of requirements of interdisciplinary courses.

Phase VI (1993 - 1994): Initiation of intermediate and advanced requirements.

Phase VII (1994-1995): Summative Assessment of the Liberal Arts and Sciences Program (Fitchburg State College Curriculum Committee, 1988).

The process for developing a consensus and a strong base of support across a campus by carefully observing a participatory process wherein each thoughtful proposal of a member of the college community was given due consideration was very important.

This later will focus primarily upon the radical reform of half of a college's curriculum, as a case study of how the vital process of curriculum redesign and implementation can truly lay the foundation for adult developmental education.

DEVELOPMENTAL THINKING

Prior to engaging in the detailed analysis of a case study, however, it is of utmost importance that this *Handbook* provide a further clarification of "developmental education," particularly as it applies to the post-adolescent or adult population to be served. In the chapter, "Higher Education as a Context for Adult Development" in his probing volume, *Dialectical Thinking and Adult Development*, Basseches (1984) has noted incisively:

> The alienation of intellect from character is a significant problem in our society, but it is not essential to the human condition; it is the product of alienation in education. It is the product of directing one's cognitive efforts toward purposes defined by teachers-for the extrinsic rewards of grades and the other perquisities of "an education"-rather than utilizing teachers to help one think about one's most personal questions, for the intrinsic reward of being able to reorganize one's life activity in a more adequate way.

Basseches (1983) has noted further that the most basic problem, as is evident in the literature on higher education considered in a developmental context is the dichotomy between "character development" and intellectual development. He judges that character is perceived as noncognitive (in contrast to being organized by ideas and thoughts) and intellectual development is all too often viewed as merely the learning of facts (rather than as the reorganization of activity). This separation is clearest in the literature on "student development."

Tollefson (1975), in his book *New Approaches to College Student Development*, notes that student development has "a positive, affirmative, educational connotation rather than the frequently negative, constricting, administrative aspect that has come to be associated with student personnel work." He further defines student development as having "a special meaning that focuses on activities undertaken for the educational benefit of the student outside the traditional purview of the professor." Such a view is typical of most of the extant literature about student development, which excludes the building of more suitable ways of cognitively organizing one's activity, classroom learning and the interaction with professors from being at the core of the process of human development. While theoreticians have capitalized on the positive impact of the term "development", few have designed any model which warrants such positive connotations.

One researcher who intended to make contributions to developmental psychology in this area was Heath (1965, 1968, 1976, 1977, 1978). He analyzes the range of changes that his subjects self-report. The categories he employs to describe "sectors" where development occurs are "intellectual functioning, self-knowledge, valuing and interpersonal relations." Such distinctions seem to imply the same dichotomy between character and intellect, as if one's self-concept, values and interpersonal relations were not structured by intellectual functioning.

One outstanding contributor to this holistic view of individual development as the aim of education was Sanford (1956, 1962, 1963, 1966, 1967). His writings and lectures continually called for the integration of in-class learning and out-of-class experience. Also, the Hazen Foundation's Committee on the Student in Higher Education (1968), comprised chiefly of student health and student affairs personnel as well as of administrators, referred in its report to "the student development approach" as geared toward "educating the whole man" and at blending social development and intellectual development. "They viewed the student as an active, caring, feeling human being rather than as a receptacle for knowledge, and they viewed the college as a social context, rather than merely as a set of classes" (Basseches, 1983).

It was Sanford who defined development as "the organization of increasing complexity" (Sanford, 1967). Some of the more sophisticated ways of understanding which do not depend on cognitive development beyond formal operations are described not only by Sanford, but also by other researchers who followed him. For example, Loevinger (1976) describes stages of ego development, Fowler (1981) classifies stages of faith development and Basseches, Hamilton and Richards (1980) identify levels of social perspective taking-all closely intertwined. In fact, the third and fourth levels of faith development and social perspective-taking of the the latter researchers generally parallel Lovinger's (1976) Confomist and Conscientious stages of ego development, respectively. As Basseches (1984) notes: "...the Conscientious stage views the self as at its best when it makes independent, responsible contributions to the maintenance and effective functioning of the society of which it is a citizen or the social movement of which it is a member." He quickly adds: "Formal operational thought, and the ability to conceptualize the abstract structure of a complex society, combined with the exposure to people from groups with varying norms, are likely to provide college students with the stimuli and the means to create Conscientious state self-concepts."

This developmental psychologist targets even higher ground than this for higher education. He raises our sights with these words

> The more difficult challenge for colleges is to promote the Autonomous ego stage and the 5B level of social perspective-taking, along with the dialectical thinking upon which such reasoning about the self and others depends. Whereas the Conscientious stage may bring with it the ability to conceptualize relatively deep stable feelings, those deeper inner feelings which are in conflict with each other and which are constantly changing require dialectical reasoning to conceptualize and express (Basseches, 1985, p. 297).

This process of dialectical thinking is essential if the student is to be freed from an indiscriminate acceptance of a particular perspective on social reality.

It was Perry's (1968) research on college students that first utilized a framework that allowed identification of structural changes in college. Most research, both before and after Perry's work, did not design a model of development as Sanford's did. In that same time period an American Council on Education study, *The Educational and Vocational Development of College Students* (Astin and Panos, 1969), studied 127,000 subjects, examining only their changes in career and educational plans and their achievement in regard to their scores on the Graduate Record Examination, and called such change and achievement ***development***.

In the literature there has been widespread use of the phrases "development of the whole person" and "student development," without the key term "development" being defined. Parker (1978) has noted incisively:

> The failure to define "development" has made it difficult to relate the general body of literature dealing with the changes in students' knowledge, values, intellectual functioning, and behaviors to "student development." On the one hand, we have no precise meaning for the term "development," and, on the other, a substantial body of knowledge of developmental

psychology has been derived without particular reference to
the field of student personnel work.

In this process of definition distinctions are helpful, but they should not
always be made mutually exclusive. Benezet (1973), for example, posits that
in the evaluation of teaching and learning, a decision must first be made as
to whether the goals of this process are academic achievement, social utility
or personal identity formation. However, when examining the person's
intellectual development in terms of the organization of the thought
processes involved in dialectical thinking, the advanced stages of ego
development must also be considered concomitantly. Basseches (1984) has
expressed this rather succinctly in these terms:

> To develop intellectually is to develop one's thinking in such a
> way that it most fully comprehends and serves the shared
> human search for truth. This should not be equated with social
> utility in the narrow sense in which it sometimes is used--to
> refer to meeting an existing society's immediate and tempor-
> ary skill needs; however, it can be equated with the goal of the
> long-term social adaptation of humanity to its environment.

What is still needed is a holistic theory of college student development
that can be used by the wide variety of professionals (including the
professors themselves) whose primary goal is student development. In
Parker's (1970, cited in Parker, 1978) view such an integrated theory would
have these five elements:

- A description of the entering students;
- a definition of the educated person;
- an identification of changes that are desirable and possible (in college);
- the identification of forces in higher education that are capable of bringing about change in students; and,
- an understanding of how such forces can be used.

THE DYNAMICS OF CHANGE: THE BASICS OF DEVELOPMENTAL EDUCATION

It shall be the aim of this *Handbook of Developmental Education* to
move this theory of human development forward by attempting to address
at various points with varying degrees of emphasis these five elements. It is
hoped that the framework for adult development presented in this volume
illustrate Parker's 4th element of student development theory and will lead
to further research which would document the circumstances under which a
wide range of types of development occurs, in comparison to those

situations in which little or no development happens. Likewise, the studies cited in this *Handbook* can well become the basis for further research efforts designed to effect specific types of developmental change.

A developmental paradigm such as this *Handbook* presents is intended to attract the attention of educators and others who work with students, to the developmental possibilities in their daily work. Still, such a model may contain the seeds of its own destruction if it is not used wisely. While educators may have a high level of confidence in their own ideas and theories of development, their actions may limit the development of their students if they do not fully interact with them. In this process, however, they must still avoid offering nothing but support for whatever a student thinks or does, rather than challenging the student to make well-considered judgements based on the more adequate knowledge gained from critical and creative thinking. This latter approach consititutes inspired teaching; it is indeed developmental learning.

Of critical importance in fostering the adult developmental process are the attitudes of the personnel providing these services to students. It is not unlikely that here also the human dynamics principle that "more is caught than taught" is in operation. The study of Widick and Simpson (1978), in fact, infers that the strengthening in teachers of attitudes supporting developmental processes and open to developmental possibilities, is more significant than actual "tracking" of students in accordance with their developmental stages. These researchers took Perry's stages of intellectual and ethical development as a schemata, and "hypothesized that students who were dualistic thinkers would need advanced organizers, a minimum of demands for independent value judgments and systematic exposure to multiple points of view, to move them toward the multiplistic positions." One major outcome of their study was that "knowing students' stages of overall intellectual and ethical development is useful in promoting learning of particular course content, but development is less well promoted by specific matching efforts than by general developmental supports" (Basseches, 1984).

It is of critical importance that this volume address, especially, Parker's 4th and 5th elements of college student development. Basseches (1984) points us in this direction when he comments:

> For an educational experience to promote development, it must challenge those structures of reasoning which the individual uses to make sense of the world. It must first engage the individual's existing structures and, with them, the individual's emotional and cognitive investment in the experience. Then it must stretch those structures to their

limits, and beyond, to the point where they are found wanting. At the same time, the experience must provide the elementary material out of which the individual can construct new, more sophisticated cognitive structures.

More concretely, Sanford enunciates the prime significance of the interaction of the student with one's environment in these pertinent observations:

> The essential point is that a person develops through being challenged: for change to occur, there must be internal or external stimuli which upset his existing equilibrium, which cause instability that existing modes of adaptation do not suffice to correct, and which thus require the person to make new responses and so to expand his personality. If the stimuli are minor or routine, the child, instead of changing, will simply react as he has before.

> It is because of their greater repertory of routine responses that students and adults do not change as readily as children. The dynamics of change, however, are essentially the same in all three groups, and if appropriate stimuli are applied, students and adults will change. We need not wait for them to "grow naturally" under conditions of comfort or protection (we would wait a long time, according to the present formulation); nor should we suppose that once people have become "mature" no more developmental change is possible.

> It follows from this same formulation that "resistance to change" does not require a special explanation; it is in the nature of the phenomenon we are studying. For example, a student entering college has a wide array of adaptive mechanisms and ways of ordering experience--mechanisms that have served him well in the past and are serving now to maintain his stability. If he is eager for new experiences, as he often is, what he anticipates is not so much change in himself as the successful testing of powers he already has. When confronted with challenging situations he first calls into play his well-tried responses; and when this structure is finally replaced, his natural inclination is to make the new structure do for all future contingencies. It is the job of the educator to keep challenging this structure in the interest of growth--a job made more difficult by the "prematurity" of many college students, who feel they already know what they want to be and how they want to live.

Unfortunately for educators, this problem of premature certainty is complicated by another. When a child is confronted with crises that are too much for his adaptive capacities, he falls back upon primitive defensive stratagems. The same thing may happen to the college student: if we propose to challenge the student and so to upset his equilibrium, we must, of course, draw a line at strain that would be so great as to cause defensive reactions to be switched in. The danger in college, however, is much less than in childhood with its peculiar combination of frustrations, conflict, and threats. In thinking about child development, many have concluded that all we need to do is protect the child from these sources of tension--a view applied indiscriminately to college students more by parents and some psychiatrists than by educators. In contrast, the theory of this chapter is that people develop when stress is great enough to challenge their prior modes of adaptation, but not so great as to induce defensive reactions. (Sanford, 1967)

The role of the academic milieu which supports optimal mismatch between existing structures and experience, while offering generally supportive features that socially affirm the individuals' integrity has been well documented in Riesman (1958), Jencks and Riesman (1968) and Moos (1979). Such an environment, which enables students to run the risks of changing their perception of things that they have previously counted on, is quite likely to enhance development.

The impact faculty members were judged to have on undergraduate students, as claimed by their students and faculty, was studied by Wilson and Goff (1975). Those faculty who preferred undergraduate teaching to research and graduate teaching were much more likely to have had an impact on the lives of students. The degree of this impact was discovered to vary directly with the quantum of effort that the faculty members put into finding out the interests of students and making their presentations more interesting. Wilson and Goff also found that students who had artistic, activist, political and intellectual orientations were more likely to become involved with faculty. Those students who were vocationally and academically oriented, though they worked the hardest at their studies, were least likely to develop intellectually. Social, political and athletic orientations were also discovered to have no correlation with intellectual development. Another finding was that students who had the chance to spend time with faculty members outside of class or to do independent work were also more likely to develop intellectually.

Delworth and Piel (1978) posit that the two factors which combine to enhance development in college are the student's coming to college with an openness to change and a campus climate supportive of change that is affirmed by other students with similar objectives. Likewise, The Hazen Foundation's Committee on the Student in Higher Education (1968) draws a direct relationship between the student's emotional involvement in the learning experience and the extent to which that experience impacts on the student's total life. This committee's recommendation is that professors make the content relevant to the "developmental tasks" with which students are dealing. Since these student populations no longer fall exclusively within the 18 - 22 year old age group, totally different approaches are needed for students of different ages. Colleges themselves must learn to apply the principles of andragogy to lifetime learners.

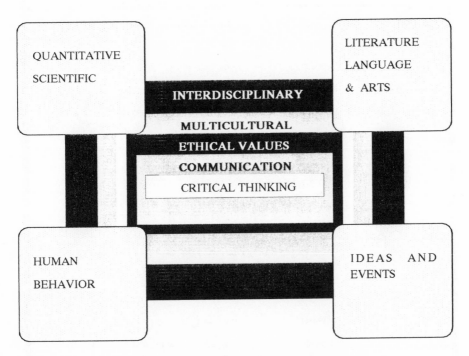

Figure 1: **Liberal Arts and Sciences**
Fitchburg State College

An important corollary to The Hazen Foundation Committee's statement about emotional engagement is that "a teacher should be aware that, in order to involve students of different ages in studying particular subject matter, the material should be related to as broad a range as possible of the developmental tasks which students might be addressing" (Basseches, 1984, p. 307). Other variables this committee states as supportive of student development include the expression of intellectual values throughout the campus life beyond the classroom and the emphasis in class on the mode of inquiry or discovery. It recommended that all methodologies be presented as subject to challenge, to the degree that they enhance the attainment of students' goals. A major conclusion that the committee reached was that truly developmental higher education was available only to an intellectual elite, and that most colleges are what they

Table 1: NELSON-DENNY TEST RESULTS

TEST SESSION	COMPREHENSION	VOCABULARY	TOTAL SCORE	READING RATE
S PRETEST C	17 (10-0)	34 (12-9)	32 (11-5)	20 (9-1)
P 1				
R 9 POST TEST D	57 (12-2)	43 (13-6)	37 (13-0)	54 (14-6)
I 8				
N 8 GROWTH	40 (2-2)	9 (0-7)	15 (1-5)	34 (5-5)
G				
F 1				
A 9 PRETEST C	31 (11-9)	41 (13-5)	35 (12-8)	22 (9-1)
L 8 POSTTEST D	53 (13-4)	50 (14-0)	50 (13-6)	46 (13-5)
L 8 GROWTH	22 (1-5)	9 (0-5)	15 (0-8)	24 (4-4)

Test scores are shown in terms of percentile equivalents (Grade Equivalents in "Years-Months" are shown in parenthesis). In the Spring of 1988, 120 students were enrolled, averaging 30 student contact hours each. In the Fall of 1988, 210 students were enrolled, averaging 22 student contact hours each.

term "2nd to 5th class schools," since they lack at least some of the conditions for effective developmental education.

One of these conditions for promoting developmental education is presenting students with multiple frames of reference-"multiple justifiable coherent ways of interpreting facts based on diverging assumptions-which can be contrasted to each other. This experience is likely to lead students to recognize the active, relativistic nature of the process of interpretation, a crucial recognition in the movement from formal to dialectical forms of cognitive organization" (Bassaches, 1984).

In addition to avoiding the danger of presenting "established facts" to students, single methods of discovery should also be avoided as much as possible. Alternative models for research should be compared and contrasted, and all modes of inquiry should be subject to question, based on how appropriately they assist in the attainment of a range of human goals. Such recognition of a wide range of modes of interpretation should help lay the foundation for the student's development as a dialectical thinker.

As students become more aware of the multiple ways of looking at problems and issues, they become better problem solvers in their own right. Through the pages of history they view the results of interaction among peoples coming from a variety of viewpoints. They learn that advances in the sciences and other areas of human knowledge occur when different perspectives so coalesce that a synergy results, producing a whole that is greater than the sum of its parts.

Indeed, "conflicting frames of reference and multiple points of view must be presented to students as facts of life, *and* as crucial moments in dialectical processes" (Basseches, 1984). These conflicts of viewpoints must be made apparent as challenges to both students and faculty alike. A premium must be placed on the struggle, the *agony* involved in searching, not only throughout the given educational experience, but also throughout one's life to seek the truth. It has been through the efforts of those who have tried and tried again, whether through their experiments or their writings, that the boundaries of knowledge have been pushed outwards.

It is also essential that the institutions of higher education provide personal support for development. As Perry (1978) has phrased this concept, educators must share "in the costs of growth". This means divesting oneself of the sure-fire "correct" answers for every question, and building a world where the true answers are those one has struggled and wrestled to attain-often leading only to further questions. Facilitators of learning must be willing to share their pain in their search to gain truth.

For if teachers hold up a bravado of confidence and comfort, students not only will have to cope with their own pain, but also with the feeling that there is something wrong with them for feeling this pain, when their teachers appear to breeze through a relativistic world so nonchalantly, so much in command. Beyond acknowledging their intellectual pain and sharing it with students, educators can actually share in students' pain, if not by holding hands, at least by holding minds. Educators will find themselves with many more opportunities to revel in the joys of their students' growth-to share the release of emancipation which occurs when the students realize new degrees of freedom-if the educators are also willing to share in growth's costs. (Basseches, 1985).

In summary, as this same developmental psychologist has synthesized these sets of issues:

...dialectical thinking is most likely to develop in educational communities in which members are (a) presented with multiple coherent frames of reference for interpreting the world; (b) invited to critically appraise various paradigmatic approaches to inquiry; (c) posed the epistemological challenge of attempting to synthesize different perspectives so that the perspectives and the people holding them may function harmoniously; and (d) supported in facing these challenges by others who both acknowledge their own pain and doubt in facing such challenges, and recognize the courage involved in taking them on. (Basseches, 1984).

It is with many facets of such a model in mind that Fitchburg State College has embarked on its renewed Liberal Arts and Sciences Program which consists of 20 courses, approximately 60 credits or two years, in disciplines traditionally recognized in the Liberal Arts and Sciences. These courses are organized into clusters that emphasize the knowledge and skills an educated person is expected to understand and appreciate, as well as to apply, in the practical business of lifetime learning. Representing the most significant and potentially transforming changes, however, are the insistence upon the development of essential, cross-disciplinary skills, the encouragement of more active teaching and learning styles, and the cultivation of intellectual habits and attitudes characteristic of liberally educated person, including the development of responsible, independent decision making.

THE FITCHBURG MODEL

A major purpose of these requirements is to assist students to develop competence in the following intellectual skills: critical thinking, writing, reading, listening, speaking, and quantifying. Students are also expected to attain a general intellectual background in the liberal arts and sciences content areas, to integrate them holistically and evaluate them intelligently, and to acquire global as well as temporal perspectives. (Fitchburg State College Curriculum Committee, 1988)

The following overview of the Fitchburg renewed Liberal Arts and Sciences curriculum reflects andragogical concepts.

- An emphasis on the development of intellectual skills across the curriculum with particular attention to critical and creative thinking and writing.
- An emphasis on teaching the modes of inquiry in the respective disciplines.
- An emphasis on the development and understanding of Ethical Reasoning within the disciplines in this curriculum and in the world at large.
- Writing requirements.
- Listening and speaking requirement.
- Health and fitness requirement.
- An intermediate and advanced requirement.
- An organization of distribution requirements which includes the following Clusters: *Quantitative/Scientific, Literature, Language and Arts, Ideas and Events,* and *Human Behavior.*
- The establishment of interdisciplinary and multicultural requirements.
- A Freshman Foundation Year.
- The creation of a Liberal Arts and Sciences Council to recommend approval for all Liberal Arts andSciences courses.
- The establishment of criteria for evaluation of courses applying for approval by the Liberal Arts and Sciences Council. (Fitchburg State College Curriculum Committee, 1988).

In this program the nine sets of fundamental skills referred to earlier are viewed as interdependent, rather than independent. For example, critical and creative thinking are closely intertwined with the processes of communication, such as reading, listening, speaking and writing. Developing critical thinking, the student evaluates the rationale and arguments presented by others and also seeks to present consistent and error-free reasoning. Employing creative thinking, s/he explores a variety of ways of interpreting a problem or issue in a broader and more meaningful context. Indeed, the student grows in the realization that effective thinking is characterized by the ability to combine both analytical, critical elements and generative, creative aspects in a flexible and appropriate manner, especially as the developmental stages of intellectual and personal growth occur.

In this context of critical and creative thinking, clear writing is developed through an emphasis on writing as process and product. The value of a campus-wide Writing-Across-the-Curriculum Committee, functioning effectively for five years before the implementation of this program, must not be overlooked in contributing to the effectiveness of the process of developing freshman and upper level writing standards and course requirements. Likewise, a professionally staffed Writing Skills Center, with a word-processing orientation, and also a concern for English-as-a-Second-Language students has been a significant catalytic element in insuring the effectiveness of this program.

Also of considerable benefit to the developmental competencies aspect of this program has been the impact made by the Developmental Reading Center during the past 14 years. Since the new library opened most of the third floor has been set aside as a Learning Skills Center. A keystone of this area of the Library has appropriately been the Developmental Reading Center. Data for students in the Spring and Fall of 1988 were summarized in Table 1.

Of key significance in the developmental education of the Fitchburg State College student is the skill area of *integrating holistically.* That component is defined thus:

> Critical to the attainment of a liberal education is the ability to interrelate and integrate knowledge. In a natural and social world which allows little easy compartmentalizing, students must learn to bring the knowledge, perspectives, and methodologies of multiple disciplines into relationship with one another; to reconcile seemingly disparate elements and achieve some degree of synthesis; to apply interdisciplinary approaches to the definition of, and solution to, complex, contemporary problems. The development of such skills cannot be left to chance. The curriculum shall include *interdisciplinary work.* (Fitchburg State College Curriculum Committee, 1988).

It is noteworthy that this curriculum for the 1990s promotes the Autonomous ego Stage and the 5B level of social perspective-taking referred to earlier by the standards it sets for evaluating intelligently and ethically, as follows:

> The ability to *evaluate intelligently,* to make judgments based on knowledge and experience, and to act humanely constitute culminating skills in a Liberal Education. Throughout their course work, students should learn to identify factors and relationships influencing particular events so that they can make informed decisions. They should become more capable of coping in creative and constructive ways with ambiguous situations. They must learn to identify differing perspectives

and to understand conflicting sides of an issue and to make decisions taking account of various interests, values, and points of view. Students should also be able to evaluate ethically, to perceive the moral and ethical issues in human actions and to formulate a set of personal principles which can be brought to bear in personal and public decision-making (Fitchburg State College Curriculum Committee, 1988).

Another critical component of this contemporary developmental education program geared toward adult learners is that the modes of inquiry or the ways of knowing be explicitly addressed in this renewed curriculum. The committee has stated its standard in these terms:

In every Liberal Arts and Sciences course, students will approach a similar set of questions although the answers will differ from discipline to discipline. Each department shall review the fundamental modes of inquiry used within its discipline(s) to arrive at the fundamental questions to be asked in its courses. Each course shall address, at least, the following questions:

1. How does this discipline formulate questions to be answered?

2. How is evidence gathered to answer the question? What counts as evidence? If evidence is not gathered, how is knowledge established?

3. How is the information obtained through research evaluated? What is the format for presenting evaluation?

4. What other disciplines present questions and evidence in similar ways?

5. How does the focus in a discipline illuminate some evidence while ignoring other questions which might be significant to a complete understanding of the question?

Possibly one of the most challenging of the required components in this Liberal Arts and Sciences Program is the emphasis on the development of ethical reasoning in the students. That element is essential in all courses, where possible. Such courses should assist the students "to translate their own observations and feelings into coherent general theories, to analyze and organize relevant data, and then, having also considered alternative and conflicting positions, to formulate clear, consistent arguments which embody a personal moral and ethical code" (Fitchburg State College Curriculum Committee, 1988).

The curricular changes in Stanford University's Western Culture program have been well-documented (Mooney, 1988). The Fitchburg Program had addressed this issue earlier, requiring each course to have a multi-cultural component, where possible, and prescribing that each student would have two of the twenty Liberal Arts and Sciences courses as strictly multi-cultural ones. The Curriculum Committee's (1988) rationale is expressed thus: "Educated men and women, who will live out the greater part of their lives in the twenty-first century, will increasingly need to interact effectively with peoples whose philosophy of life and approach to living may differ markedly from one's own. Courses which deal meaningfully with the geography, language, history, religion, art, and the societal and political organization of other cultures and sub-cultures will be among the courses appropriate to the discipline from which they are drawn."

It was judged by the designers of this contemporary curriculum that the foundation laid in the freshman year was crucial to the success of this renewed Liberal Arts and Sciences Program. Following the leadership set by programs such as the University of Notre Dame's Freshman Year of Studies, the following elements were decided upon as essential components of the Freshman Foundation Year:

- Inclusion of Modes of Inquiry and the essential intellectual skills in courses.
- A Common Theme and readings that address it.
- A Common Handbook.
- Cluster Requirements.
- An Interdisciplinary Requirement.
- A Commitment to Freshman Advising.
- A Freshman Foundation Year Plan Book.
- A Coordinator for the Freshman Foundation Year.

This College's plan for implementation of renewal called for the establishment of a Liberal Arts and Sciences Council within its All-College governance structure. That new body, broadly representative of the campus community, has been exercising assiduously the responsibility given it to review and recommend regarding all new and existing courses being proposed for inclusion in the Liberal Arts and Sciences Program according to the following criteria:

- Includes components of critical and creative thinking (gathering data, targeting

issues, identifying major conclusions, establishing hypotheses, evaluating arguments, elaborating alternatives, determining own position).
- Introduces the discipline's mode of inquiry (formulating questions in the discipline, deciding what constitutes evidence and gathering it, evaluating evidence, identifying similarities to other disciplines, determining the significant focus of the discipline).
- Emphasizes active modes of learning.
- Emphasizes speaking and listening skills via discussion/questioning.
- Emphasizes writing as a thinking process, with faculty attentin paid in evaluatin to both form and content. Courses in mathematics and the natural and physical sciences may emphasize problem-solving as a thinking process.
- Serves the non-specialist in introductory courses; exceptions may need to be made in some mathematics and science courses.
- Addresses interdisciplinary, multicultural and/or ethical concerns where possible.

This faculty did not loose sight of the fact that, to achieve such developmental goals, faculty and course development must become first order priorities. The purposes of such a Faculty and Course Development Program are to:

- Provide necessary support for faculty development and research relating to the Liberal Arts and Sciences Program.
- Provide on-going workshops for faculty on teaching models consistent with the goals of the Liberal Arts and Sciences Program.
- Continue Writing-Across-the-Curriculum efforts to assist faculty to incorporate writing for form and content within courses and to identify and develop Junior Writing requirements within the major.
- Facilitate the development of interdisciplinary courses and the inclusion and/or identification of multicultural issues within current courses.
- Facilitate the development of additional multi-cultural courses and the inclusion and/or identification of multicultural issues within current courses.
- Encourage the inclusion of ethical issues in current courses, Liberal Arts and Sciences courses, and major courses and the development of courses with a major emphasis on evaluation, judgment and decision making according to general ethical theories and/or personal moral codes.

As indicated in the seven-phase Implementation Plan described earlier, this carefully conceived Liberal Arts and Sciences Program provides a renewed focus for Developmental Education. The complexity of the developmental tasks to be accomplished in the years ahead deserves careful study by researchers. As this plan at Fitchburg State College in Fitchburg, Massachusetts continues to develop, it may well prove to be a National model of how an institution can go about the task of renewing its basic mission to its undergraduate students by applying sound principles of developmental psychology to a developmental education program designed for learners of all ages, and for lifetime learning itself.

for learners of all ages, and for lifetime learning itself.

REFERENCES

Astin, A. W. and R. J. Panos (1969). *The educational and vocational development of college students.* Washington, D. C.: American Council on Education.

Basseches, M. (1984). *Dialectical thinking and adult development.* Norwood, NJ: Ablex Publishing Corporation.

Basseches, M., S. Hamilton and F. Richards (1980). *The impact of participatory-democratic work experiences on adolescent development: a methodological report.* Paper presented at the Annual Meeting of the American Educational Research Association, Boston, Massachusetts.

Benezet, L. T. (1973). Learning what?, *New directions for higher education,* 1, 1 - 14.

Delworth, U. and E. Piel (1978). Students and their institutions: an interactive perspective. In *Encouraging development in college students,* C. Parker (ed.). Minneapolis, Minnesota: University of Minnesota Press.

Fitchburg State College Curriculum Committee (1988). *Liberal arts and sciences program.* Fitchburg, MA: Fitchburg State College.

Fowler, J. W. (1981). *School, curriculum and the individual.* Waltham, MA: Blaisdell Publishing Company.

Hazen Foundation on the Student in Higher Education (1968). *The student in higher education.* New Haven: Hazen Foundation.

Heath, D. H. (1978). A model of becoming a liberally educated and matured student. In *Encouraging development in college students,* C. Parker (Ed.). Minneapolis, Minnesota: University of Minnesota Press.

Jencks, C. and D. Riesman (1968). *The academic revolution.* Garden City, New York: Doubleday.

Loevinger, J. (1976). *Ego development.* San Francisco: Jossey Bass.

Mooney, C. J. (1988). Sweeping curricular changes is under way at Stanford as University phases out its "Western Culture" program, *Chronicle of Higher Education,* December 14, 1988, A-1, A-11 - A-13.

Parker, C. (Ed.) (1987). *Encouraging development in college students.* Minneapolis, Minnesota: University of Minnesota Press.

Perry, W. G. (1968). *Forms of intellectual and ethical development in the college years.* New York: Holt, Rinehart and Winston.

Perry, W. G. (1978). Sharing the costs of growth. In *Encouraging development in college students*, C. Parker (ed.). Minneapolis, Minnesota: University of Minnesota Press.

Riesman, D. (1958). *Constraint and variety in American education.* Garden City, NY: Doubleday.

Sanford, N. (1967). *Where colleges fail.* San Francisco: Jossey Bass.

Tollefson, A. L. (1975). *New approaches to college student development.* New York: Behavioral Publications, Inc.

The University of Notre Dame (1984). *Freshman year of studies academic guide.* Notre Dame, Indiana: The University of Notre Dame.

Widick, C. and D. Simpson (1978). Developmental concepts in college instruction. In C. Parker (ed.). *Encouraging development in college students.* Minneapolis, Minnesota: University of Minnesota Press.

Wilson, R. C. and J. G. Gaff (1975). *College professors and their impact on students.* New York: Wiley.

2

Axioms of Developmental
Learning and Instruction

Robert M. Hashway

The history of education has been characterized by a lack of leadership and fluctuating political forces as well as the lack of a sophisticated technology via which an all-encompassing theory or foundation can be developed (Hashway, 1988). Although a theoretical abyss exists, the need for a theoretical foundation is great.

McDonald (1964) has pointed out that "Education has needed a science of man." That "science of man" should serve as the foundation of the instructional process. McDonald has suggested that an educationally useful psychology of learning should be: **scientifically unimpeachable, reflective of the social characteristics of learning, accountable for developmental phenomena, promising some kind of "control" over behavior and, concerned with the individual.** Various theories have attempted to define human behavior. The theories of the stimulus-response (S-R) theorists (Hebb, 1955, 1946; Hull, 1952, 1943, 1933, 1931; Pavlov, 1927; Skinner, 1964, 1949) were the seeds of an educational movement called programmed instruction (Blyth, 1960; Coulson and Silberman, 1960; DeCecco, 1964; Edwards, 1963; Green, 1962; Holland, 1959; Hughes, 1962; Resnick, 1963; Suppes, 1964; Washburne, 1922). The S-R theories did not include dimensions of human personality. Some educational theorists contend that the myopic focus of S-R theories on narrow bands of knowledge is a serious limitation of the theory (Biggs, 1971; Bruner, 1964). Other theories are strongly associated with personality. The theories developed by Freud (1922), Maslow (1965, 1962, 1959, 1950, 1955, 1954, 1951, 1942), Maslow and Mittlemann (1951), Rogers (1963, 1955, 1947), Rogers and Dymand (1954), and others (Woodworth, 1918; Woodworth and Scholsberg, 1954) focused upon the impact of emotion on the learning process. Expectations and evidence of hypothesised underlying processes were week at best. The humanistic models lacked the scientific rigor of the S-R models.

The goal of this chapter is to form a symbiosis of these theories and lead to the genesis of a new way of looking at developmental learning and curriculum theory. That method will take into consideration the best points of both the S-R and humanistic models. The proposed theory, however, goes beyond the predictions and predictive power of both theories. I wish to describe the *"thinking"* model of learning and instruction that incorporates information processing theories and neurophysiological evidence as the processes which may take place during the learning. The "thinking" model has its roots in a classical paper by Newell, Shaw and Simon (1958) and the reader interested in the history of theory development is referred to that paper.

The "thinking" model concerns the human processing of information. Transformations are applied to the input data. The set of transformations represent logical rules which are applicable to sensory stimuli and result from accumulated knowledge, behavior patterns and experiences. The transformations transform information into particular output behaviors (rationality).

Each person has had different experiences and will behave somewhat differently to the same stimulus situation. The allowed transformations are derived from learned behavior. The "thinking" model predicts individual differences. It is a model which does not start by trying to explain modal behavior. Thinking starts at the level of the individual. The extent to which group behavior is predicted by the model is associated with the extent to which individual behavior is predictable. The thinking model does not postulate that individual differences do not exist (i.e. as the S-R model), it incorporates individual differences as a foundation of the theory.

The "thinking" model of learning and instruction is sufficiently encompassing to include pre-school as well as post-doctoral education and everything in between. The "thinking" model of developmental learning as well as the instructional design have relevance to all aspects of education.

The remainder of this chapter presents an overview of the "thinking" model and a general theory of knowledge. I will integrate implications of that model with implications for developmental learning.

DEVELOPMENTAL THINKING AND LEARNING MODELS

Regardless of whether we are designing programs for remediation or development, those programs must rest upon firm foundations. Foundations of educational programs should have their roots planted in the soil of human learning. Needs change and it is important that we use our abilities to become a self-learner. It is important that all educational programs emphasize human processes for cognitive growth and development. A chapter that concerns instruction, learning and curriculum would do a disservice to its audience without describing how the curriculum/educational philosophy it purports relates to the process of human learning and development. What is the process of human growth and development? What is the process which separates man from 'lower' life forms? Since the times of the early philosophers man has pondered that question. Only recently have neurologists, psychologists, computer scientists and educators been able to shed some light on the process of human development.

From the ashes of the theoretical and experimental furnaces of psychological, neurological and cognitive science both old and new a human information processing model has grown which explains human development (Anderson, 1980; Neisser, 1976; Norman, 1970; Posner and McLeod, 1982; Simon, 1979). Not only does it explain cognitive development it also serves as a basis for intelligent machines, artificial intelligence and expert systems.

The model is more than merely a cognitive psychology and it concerns more than just neurophysiology. The model of human growth and development is more than a mere model of information processing. Hence, we call this model the "thinking" model and the discipline which integrates psychology, education, neurology, human physiology, computer and information sciences is called **developmental learning.** It is an integration of many disciplines into the field of developmental learning that is outlined in this section.

The Activation System

A human is a system in flux, activated by information and self-perpetuating once activated. Humans are personified and, indeed, defined by the manifestation of the characteristics of a system which is catalyzed by information.

Many psychologists have postulated the existence of drives or motives to define cognitive behavior (Freud, 1922; Hull, 1952; Maslow, 1955; Rogers, 1963). Others have postulated the existence of a complexity program (Biggs, 1971). Neurological and psychological studies have localized the site of the drive for information or motivation in a an area in the brain called the **Reticular Activation System** (RAS). That RAS is the interface between the base of the brain and the spinal column. This area is active when the brain is processing information. It supplies the instruction which tells the cognitive process to go (Bloom, Lazerson and Hofstadter, 1985; Hebb, 1955; Hobson and McCarley, 1979; Jouvet, 1969; Ullman, 1973).

The location of the center of brain activity and a defined process of cognitive information processing places the issues of motivation and emotion out of the domain of 'scientific mysticism' (Kelly, 1955; Prentice, 1961; Simon, 1967; Taylor, 1960). As Biggs (1971, p. 32 - 33) stated so well:

motives - those like jealousy, anger, love and the like - are usually believed to be of an order of psychological reality quite other than that of cognitive or intellectual processes: they are emotions and follow different laws to cognitive events ... the distinction between motivation and cognition need not be made at all ... What is really meant when we accuse another of an 'emotional' argument is that reasoning is poorly carried out: the individual includes irrelevant data, or he omits relevant data, in order to achieve a goal that is not identical with his opponent's (1971, pp 32-33).

The Memory System

There is considerable evidence (Bousfield and Barclay, 1950; Freedman and Loftus, 1971; Goss and Nodine, 1965; Melton and Martin, 1972; Sternberg, 1969; Winzenz and Bower, 1970) indicating that human memory consists of three components: short term memory (STM), intermediate term memory (ITM) and long term memory (LTM).

Short Term Memory is an area of the mind used for storing input from sensory processors. Images are stored for a very short time (less than 1 or 2 seconds). In that time the mind decides whether it wishes to deal with the data (Hunter, 1964; Miller, 1966, 1956; Neisser, 1967; Postman, 1955; Treisman, 1966). Short term memory is located in the hippocampus region of the brain (Alton, 1983; Olton, Becker and Handelmann, 1980; O'Keefe and Nadel, 1978; Thompson, Berger and Madden, 1983; Thompson, Hicks and Shryrokov, 1980), located in the lower portion of the midsection of the central core of the brain (Hunt, 1976; Thompson, et al., 1983, 1980). Most people can store about 7 bits of data in STM which does not seem to be very much. Successive recoding of data lets us store a great deal of information in just 7 bits.

Intermediate Term Memory seems to also be located in the hippocampus as well (Goss and Nodine, 1965; Melton and Martin, 1972; Platt and MacWhimmey, 1983; Slobin, 1979). Information is stored in the intermediate area for a few minutes or whatever time it takes to make a decision concerning the data. Intermediate memory can be considered to be a temporary working storage area where data is identified, categorized and modified from sensory STM input and moved into the ITM (Sperling, 1960; Turvey, 1973).

Long Term Memory consists of memory traces which are retained for long periods of time. Long term memory resides in the temporal lobes and in the cerebral cortex (Bousfield, 1950; Freedman and Loftus, 1971; Harlow, 1959). When we first learn something synaptic connections are established between regions in the temporal lobes and areas in the cortex (Pellionisz and Linas, 1980, 1979; Squire, 1984, 1981). For, perhaps, several years the temporal and cortexual areas interact and the memory trace is conceptually integrated with other concepts by a reorganization of the neural circuits (the synaptic network), when complete, the temporal connections are no longer necessary and can be relegated to other tasks. The temporal area contains, primarily, procedural knowledge and the cortex contains the concepts related to experience, our understanding of our past experiences as well as a of familiarity with our environment. The cortex contains those neural structures which define the individual as a unique human being (Cohen and Squire, 1980; Tulvin, 1972).

The human mind is significantly different from the computer. The computer consists of hardwired circuits and software programs. Circuits are not modifiable and, to only a very limited extent, the software is modifiable by the computer. All of the synaptic connections and the complex network that humans form are simultaneously hardware and software. They are physical commodities and in this sense hardware. They can be modified based upon experience and in this sense software. Evidence of the modifiability of neural networks has been shown by Jackson (1958/1869). He demonstrated that if limited damage occurs to a part of the brain, that programming is moved to another part of the cortex.

The remainder of this chapter discusses how the different memory organizations interact with each other to produce reality. It will be helpful to use a concept taken from computer science: the **central processing unit** (CPU), a device which performs all computations and controls the flow of data.

Although it is useful to think of a single central processor controlling the actions of the brain, this is not the case. There is no evidence that a single area of the brain acts as the 'controller' of all thoughts and actions. There are many central processing units active at the same time acting on the same or different data. Action takes place when a group of processors controlling a group of functions and acting on the same data reach a decision. The **distributed information processing** model has found some utility in the study of human cognitive abilities (Collins and Loftus, 1975; Fahlman, 1979; Hunt, 1976, 1973; Hunt and Poltrack, 1974; Levin, 1976; McClelland, 1981; Mountcastle, 1975; Mountcastle and Edelman, 1978).

The Representation of Knowledge {learning}:

There seems to be two basic representations of knowledge: imagery and discursive language (Kosslyn, 1980; Neisser, 1967; Paivio, 1971; Tolaas, 1986) and is supported by unique representation systems. There is a body of research to support the belief that each knowledge representation (Benton, 1962; Bogen, 1960; Bogen and Mazzaniga, 1965; Colonna and Faglioni,

1966; Conners and Barata, 1967; De Rezi and Faglioni, 1965; Doehring and Reitan, 1962; Elner and Myers, 1962; Gazzaniza, 1967; Levy, 1969; Sperry, 1968, 1966). Discursive language is supported by a serial processing system and image data is supported by a parallel processing system (Kosslyn, 1980; Neisser, 1967; Paivio, 1971; Tolaas, 1986). Symbolic schemes are shifts from images (parallel) to verbal (serial) representations (Bruner, 1964; Bruner, Olver and Greenfield, 1966; Kosslyn, 1980; Grinder and Bandler, 1976; Piaget and Inhelder, 1977 Werner and Kaplan, 1963).

Tolaas (1986) has elequently presented the position of the transformation theorists as: "Presenting the experience of one representational system through language implies transformation. In the typical dreaming state, REM sleep, activity in the visual representational system is aroused internally so that all information drawn from memory, regardless of input channel during the waking state, tends to be given visual representation. Similarly, admitted external and proprioceptive input is generally transformed into visual imagery (Arkin, Artrobus and Ellman, 1978; Tolaas, 1980). What this means is that in reporting our dreams we impose one mode of being (waking consciousness) and one representational system (language) on another mode of being (dreaming) and another representational system (a sensory mode that is predominantly visual)." There is no need for controversy. The parallel distributive model provides for both serial and parallel processing of both verbal and image data.

Iconic Thinking

A study of concept formation and the evolution of thinking from childhood through adulthood yields insight into the developmental learning (DL) process.

The first DL stage is the formation of images of icons (Bruner, 1964). Icons are mental images. They exhibit form and structure. Once we disengage interpretive processes we have a pathway into the iconic world (Huxley, 1959). Depth and spatial organization disappears. The iconic world is a world of pure perception which retains extraordinary detail. At the iconic stage, people are able to remember extraodinary amounts of detail.

Thinking at the iconic stage is very rigid. New situations are compared with old situations on the basis of particulars (Piaget, 1932) and precise matches are required to imply equivalence. Developmental learning, at the iconic stage, does not distinguish between the reality or perception and is characterized by rule-bound behavior. Situations must be highly consistent with an individual's perception (Piaget, 1950; Vygotsky, 1962).

If information is not in concordance with past experience at the iconic stage, we often require more task-relevant information (feedback). There are two kinds of feedback: positive and negative feedback. Positive feedback occurs when new information is as, or more, discordant with the icon as the previous information. This results in more requests for information. Continuing positive feedback results in a state of high anxiety. *Anxiety is defined as the search for information in concordance with our world view.* Negative feedback decreases the level of anxiety. It occurs when we guide our search for knowledge using past knowledge, and new knowledge is sufficiently concordant with our reality constructs that anxiety is reduced (Miller, Galanter and Pribram, 1960).

The teacher needs to know that when he/she is introducing a new concept, it is being encoded at the iconic level. The concept must be presented at the conceptual level, soon followed with as much detail as possible. A new concept is followed by Recticular Activation System excitation and requests for new knowledge. New knowledge should be related to the concept being presented. When new knowledge is related to the defined concept and past knowledge, a state of negative feedback occurs and anxiety is reduced. When new knowledge is not related either to the major concept or past knowledge, positive feedback and anxiety results. Intense anxiety results from the presentation of uncoordinated information and information is stored in short term or intermediate term memory. If integration does not occur in a few minutes, information is lost and learning does not occur.

Information must be conceptually related, and *non-redundantly structured to data that came before.* Information should be logically structured to the information that precedes it. The information that exhibits a high degree of structural similarity is not processed unless it is somewhat different from what came before. Think about driving down a highway when there are no other cars on the road. Soon you will begin to daydream. The road seems to be a never ending stream of the same stimuli. The process of not attending to repetitive stimuli is called the *habituatory decrement.*

Habituatory decrement: If material is highly similar to what came before, a high degree of forgetting will take place (Graham, 1973; Groves and Thompson, 1973; Harris, 1943; Humphrey, 1933; Peeke and Herz, 1973; Sokolv, 1963; Syz, 1926; Underwood, 1966). **Conceptual repetition** (Anderson and Bower, 1973; Atkinson and Shiffrin, 1968; Biggs, 1969; Kintsch, Kozminsky, Strely, McKoon and Keenan, 1975; Wanner, 1974) will enhance memory but identical repetition will reduce retention.

Habituatory decrements and stimulation supplied by the 'partially known' (Biggs, 1971) is an effective instructional strategy. Successive presentation of the same or extremely similar stimuli results in a decrease in retention. The secret seems to be to: *diversify either the material or the method/means/mode of presentation sufficiently to make it seem novel and different,* and, *not to disguise the material so much that it seems unrelated to the topic of the lesson and/or past experience.*

The **art of developmental teaching** is to organize/sequence the presentation of material in such a way that it is related to what has come before, and is sufficiently different in either presentation mode or information content to excite the Recticular Activation System (i.e. stimulate the information gathering process).

Conceptual Generalizations

Iconic storage is very detailed. The search of iconic memory, detail for detail, is time consuming. 'Economy of storage' is reached through the generation of concepts, generalized forms of icons. Concepts are not as detail-rich as the icon itself. Memory integration is reached at the expense of many of the details.

Once something is learned and placed in the temporal region, dendrites emerge from that region extending into related areas of the cerebral cortex. Contexual sites are long columnar structures with thousands of nerve endings ending on a cortexual column. Thousands of nerves protrude from the cortexual column making their way into temporal areas and the cerebellum. As more information on a topic is accumulated, more neural pathways are 'grown.' Interrelationships between the temporal site and many areas of the cortex emerge. The "growth" process may span many years. At some magic point, when the learned relationship achieves "importance" the temporal site is "reconstructed" in the cortex-a concept is born.

A learned concept has lost much of the original detail of the icon, and the rigid concrete rule-bound behavior is absent. When a concept becomes highly differentiated, a person can identify "related" concepts and icons on the basis of "grayer," sparser and more flexible internalizations. Reality is a symbiosis of the network of neural pathways. The conceptual structure is abstract and represents "reality" to the individual.

The conceptual transformations and reorderings of information enhances recall at the expense of much of the detail (Lachman, Lachman and Butterfield, 1979). A bright student associates the word "algebra" with all of the algebraic manipulations at age 17. At age 47 that same bright student may associate the word "algebra" with a "branch of mathematics which deals with symbols and numbers which I knew very well (as defined by my teachers) at one time" and/or some basic formula solving skills. When asked how many bolts to buy at $0.35 each when he only has $176.42, the 47 year old former bright algebra student will solve the associated equation.

S/he may not write down the equation or follow all the steps presented in school but s/he will follow a proper process. A cortexual area is activated related subcortexual networks receive the signal and automatically process the data (Bartlet, 1932; Hamilton, 1859; Kintsch, 1972, 1975; Minsky, 1975; Selz, 1922; Winograd, 1975).

An implication of the memory consolidation process is that we must provide time for gestation. In the short term students can not be expected to understand the implications and ramifications of new information. If discovery learning is expected to result in concept formation, then a long time, perhaps years, must be provided for integration to occur. Time for intellectual gestation must be included in any instructional system.

As important as gestation time is the structure of the concepts presented. Remembering that iconic images are the first to form, lessons must be structured as so that elements of those icons are very similar to concepts and related to past events. Never assume that material recently presented have reached the concept stage. Recently presented materials are temporal with some neural pathways extending into the cerebral cortex. When presenting new information, it should be presented in such a way that it is reflective of relevant iconic elements of related concepts. Neural pathways will be established only with the cortex and also within the temporal area. A sufficient number of pathways established within the temporal area accelerates the transfer of information into concepts and relocation to sites in the cortex.

When presenting material which is related or dependent upon material taught in the distant past, remember that previously learned material has been conceptualized and many of the details have been forgotten. The relation between the new information and concepts previously learned may not be made by the developmental learner. The details of the prior icons must be reconstructed prior to introducing new information.

The process of concept formation may be why researchers have obtained results at variance with a linear curriculum design (Hashway, 1988). Classical linear progressions of topics have been invalidated and a cyclical model of learning optimization discovered. Advanced concepts related to topics, whose basic structure was learned at an early stage, should be introduced much later than classical curriculum designs would suggest. It is necessary to form conceptualizations related to the basic concepts prior to moving on to other more advanced topics in the same area. Other topics seemingly obliquely related to prior topics are presented in the interim. String of topics with cyclical reintroduction of advanced basic skills because topics must be temporally then cortextually and subsequently conceptually integrated.

It seems that the cyclical format postualated by Dienes (1967) and later expanded upon by Prendergast (1984) and Hashway (1988) is correct. Rather than a cycle, it seems that learning may take place in terms of intertwining helical pathways. The linear and/or two dimensional projection of those helical pathways of the mind would appear as optimal transfer of learning when different topics are studied in a non-linear ordering. Learning within a topical area may indeed be linear but given the element of time for concept formation and neural pathway development, that linear organization is best represented by a helix. Since different concepts mature at different rates dependent upon prior concept and iconic development, the helixes related to different concepts would overlap in time and instructional sequencing. What appears to be a hierarchical sequence is the ordering of conceptualization time.

CODING - Will reality please stand up!!

You may recall that the short term memory span contains approximately 7 'chunks' of information. A 'chunk' is defined as a memory element used to represent a single piece of information or a collection of information.

What is a memory element used to represent a single piece or collection of information? Consider the mathematical phrase "3+2". Each symbol of that phrase has relevance. The symbols 3 and 2 correspond to a number of concepts: what is a number, what is a unit, factorization of units under the operation of addition (i.e. $2 = 1 + 1$). The "+" symbol represents the concept/process of addition. Each symbol or "chunk" triggers other concepts in memory. Each chunk is insignificant in and of itself. The significance of a chunk is that it is the key to a pathway of the mind.

When presented with the phrase "3+2", most people will replace it in memory with "3+2=5" or merely the symbol "5." When this happens, people are interpreting the information. Think of chunks also as "codes." Codes or chunks can be considered to be links in what computer scientists call a "link list" data set (Harrison, 1973; Flores, 1970). Each piece of information contains an 'arrow' to the next piece of information. Examples of educational materials which make use of a technique of progressively higher coding levels fall into the category called "programmed instruction." (Fry, 1963; Green, 1962; Lysaught and Williams, 1963).

Information is received by the senses which process that information using relational data kept in long term memory. The senses transmit coded or chunked data to the short term memory. The chunks correspond to the icons or concepts associated by past experiences with each piece of information in the sensory data stream.

Given the example "3+2" we transmit sensory codes corresponding to the concepts underlying the symbols "3", "+" and "2."

The subtle, yet important, point is that words and numbers are nothing more than representations used for communication. Numbers and words are not representative of human thought processes. Humans do not process symbols. The fact that a student does not answer a question correctly not be indicative of understanding only that the student has not used a representational system for communication that the teacher is willing to accept.

Education is definable as the means by which society standardizes communication. Each person can be an excellent information processor. What discriminated man from animals was his ability to establish the "collective consciousness" - a corpus of knowledge common to all men. That collective consciousness is rooted in the symbolic representation of information in terms of language. Each person is not an animal unto him/herself nor immediate or "real time" processors. Our collective experience, transmitted through language, defines the core of humanity and a commonality of thought.

The sharing of information generates the concept of time which concept adds an additional dimension to the depth and breadth of information; time being defined as the concept of information processed by another person or not currently in our sensory input data stream.

Look at our example of "3+2". That character string can be considered to be made of three chunks: "3", "+" and "2". The chunks are replaced by areas in memory corresponding to where the underlying concepts associated with each chunk resides. Symbols correspond to concept locations. We have been conditioned (formed an associated neural network) to perform the operation of addition when we detect the "+" symbol in an environment consisting of numbers. Dependent upon the sophistication of our conditioning, we will replace the code "3+2" with either "=5", or just "5". In either case, the original problem situation has been replaced with an internal representation of the problem. What we have done is apply a "schema" or plan of attack which corresponds to stimulus symbols.

> A person may not apply the same schema if the stimuli are presented separately. Each stimulus activates a particular portion of the cortex. The combined effect of cortexual stimulations results in a particular plan of attack.

> So extra processes must be invoked to implement generalization in a localist scheme. One commonly used method is to allow activation to spread from a local unit to

other units that represent similar concepts (Collins and Loftus, 1975). Then when one concept unit is activated, it will partially activate its neighbors and so any knowledge stored in the connections emanating from these neighbors will be partially effective (Hinton, McClelland and Rumelhart, 1987).

Information about a complex concept is stored in memory and becomes available when the conept is activated. Furthermore, an element that is part of a knowledge frame is able to activate the whole frame. This process is one of pattern completioin: a partial stimulus pattern is matched with its representation in memory and activates the total knowledge unit, as when a visual stimulus activates the corresponding word concept in semantic memory ... . A schema is a representation of a situation or of an event; it is a prototype or norm and specifies the usual sequence of events that is to be expected. (Kintsch, 1978)

A person could say "so what" when presented with the sensory strand "3+2". Prior predisposition is the foundation through which our responses are generated.

The "so-what" response is an example of how attitudes are formed from the use of schema and pre-conditioned neural patterns. Attitudes are not mysterious metaphysical entities they are the direct result of neural networks.

The term schema was first introduced by Bartlett (1932). Schemas have been described as data structures which represent broad concepts, objects, events and actions (Rumelhart and Ortony, 1977), active organizations of past reactions (Bartlett, 1932), a set of propositions and images (Anderson, 1980), patterns of encoding (Johnson, 1978), higher level descriptions of chunks (Smolensky, 1987), a representation of a situation or event (Kintsch, 1978). Regardless of the definition used, it is commonly agreed that schema are filters. They serve as a means of internally organizing reality and filtering essential from non-essential information.

Consider our "3+2" example. We applied a schema and replaced the input with the single chunk "5". It became no longer necessary to remember the original stimuli; only the result was necessary.

When we are given materials to learn, reproductions in memory are different from the original materials (Bartlett, 1932; Hunter, 1964). Sensory and motor systems use different representation systems (Pellionisz and Llinas, 1980, 1979). Words are interpreted contextually and sequences of words are interpreted based upon experience (Anderson and Bower, 1973;

Filmore, 1968; Kintsch, 1978; Kintsch, Kozminsky, Strely, McKoon and Keenan, 1975). After reading, the internal representation of the text is retained and interpreted as reality (Bower and Winzenz, 1969; Johnson and Migdoll, 1971; Keeney, 1969; Mandler, 1967). Simple list recall tasks are dependent upon characteristics not included in the original list (Bousfield, 1953; Cohen, 1970; Schuell, 1968). Information received through different sensory channels are stored in terms of different memory maps (Grinder and Bandler, 1976; Tolaas, 1986).

Humans see the world through schema. The schema correspond to ganglic networks formed through experience via the temporal-cortexual assimilation process. Although there is a commonality of knowledge, if formal education was the only way of conveying knowledge, we would all be identical. By processing experiences, we modify our schematic structure. It is the diversity of experience and the resulting schemata that explain the rich diversity of human spirit.

The universe appears external to the observer (Beer, 1966) and is interpreted in terms of our neural network or accumulated knowledge. The details of existential reality are lost in our conceptions and cognitive mappings, and reality exists in each persons mind. Do not assume the existence of an existential reality separated from the observer (Norwich, 1983). A distinct reality exists in each consciousness. Consciousness involves the process of association, recollection and knowledge modification. The modification of knowledge occurs through recognition, and confirms or alters our concept of self and hence reality (Edelman and Mountcastle, 1978). What is perceived as reality is relative to our expectations.

The intent of any lesson is irrelevant. What is important is how the student perceives the lesson (Harvey, Hunt and Schroder, 1961). Teachers need to identify the reality constructs of the students. Learning can not occur until the learners can associate and interpret what is to be learned. Each student perceves different stimuli most effectively using different sensory modalities. Teachers must be aware of the preferable learning modes of their students and provide lessons using the greatest number of learning modes possible.

Students try to emulate accepted behavior patterns. Teachers must continuously provide structured feedback not only indicating that something incorrectly; but, constructive feedback informing the student when s/he is correct. In the event of an incorrect response, feedback must be framed in terms of what the correct response should be. Feedback to an incorrect response serves no useful purpose, does not contribute to growth and is a deterent to progress.

REFERENCES

Alton, D. L. (1983). Learning in a marine snail, *Scientific American*, 249, 70 - 84.

Anderson, A. L. (1951). The effects of laterality localization of local brain lesions on the Wechsler-Bellevue subtests, *Journal of clinical psychology*, 7, 149 - 153.

Anderson, J. R. (1980). *Cognitive psychology and its implications*. San Francisco: W. H. Freeman.

Anderson, J. R. and G. H. Bower (1973). *Human associative memory*. Washington, D.C.: Winston.

Archibald, Y. M., J. M. Wepman and L. V. Jones (1967). Performance on nonverbal cognitive tests following unilateral cortical injury to the right and left hemisphers, *The journal of nervous and mental disease*, 145, 1, 25 - 36.

Arkin, A. M., J. S. Artrobus and S. J. Ellman (1978). *The mind in sleep: Psychology and psychophysiology*. Hillsdale, NJ: Lawrence Erlbaum Associates.

Arrigoni, G. and E. De Renzi (1964). Constructional apraxia and hemispheric locus of lesion, *Cortex*, 1, 170 - 197.

Atkinson, R. C. and R. Shiffrin (1968). Human memory: a proposed system and its control processes, In: K. W. Spence and J. A. Spence, (Eds.), *The psychology of learning and motivation, Volume II*. New York: Academic Press.

Ausburn, F. B. (1975). *A comparison of multiple and linear image presentation of a comparative visual location task with visual and haptic college students*, ERIC Document Reproduction Service (ED 101 727).

Bartlet, F. C. (1932). *Remembering*. Cambridge, England: University Press.

Bennett, C. C. (1938). An inquiry into the genesis of poor reading. New York: Bureau of Publications, Teacher's College, Columbia University.

Beer, S. (1966) *Information and human learning*, Glenview, Illinois: Scott, Foresman and Company.

Benton, A. L. (1962). Clinical symptomotology in right and left hemisphere lesions. In: V. Mountcastle (ed.), *Interhemispheric relations and cerebral dominance*. Baltimore: John Hopkins Press.

Biggs, J. B. (1971). *Information and human learning*. Glenview, Ill.: Scott, Foresman and Company.

Biggs, J. B. (1969). Coding and cognitive processes, *British journal of psychology,* 60, 287 - 305.

Bitterman, M. E. (1967). Learning in animals. In: H. Helson and W. Bevan (eds.), *Contemporary approaches to psychology.* New York, New York: Van Nostrand.

Bitterman, M. E., W. F. Fedderson and D. W. Tyler (1953). Secondary reinforcement and the discrimination hypothesis, *American journal of psychology,* 66, 456 - 464.

Bloom, F. E., A. Lazerson and L. Hofstadter (1985). *Brain, Mind and Behavior.* New York: W. H. Freeman and Co., P. 110 - 132, 149 - 157, 164.

Blyth, J. W. (1960). Teaching machines and human beings. In: Lumsdaine, A. A. and Glaser, R. (ed.) *Teaching machines and programmed learning.* Washington, D.Cerimental Psychology, 40, 643 - 647.

Bogen, J. E. (1960). The other side of the brain. I: Dysgraphia and dyscopia following cerebral commissurotomy, *Bulletin of the Los Angeles neurological society,* 39, 73 - 105.

Bogen, J. E. (1965). Cerebral commissurotomy, *Journal of the American medical association,* December, 1328 - 1329.

Bogen, J. E. and M. S. Mazzaniga (1965). Cerebral commissurotomy in man. Minor hemisphere dominance for certain visuspatial functions, *Journal of neurosurgery,* 23, 391 - 399.

Bousfield, W. A. (1953). The occurrence of clustering in the recall of randomly arranged associates, *Journal of general psychology,* 49, 229 - 240.

Bousfield, W. A. and W. D. Barclay (1950). The relationship between order and frequency of occurence of restrictive associative responses, *Journal of experimental psychology,* 40, 643 - 647.

Bower, G. H. and D. Winzenz (1969). Group structure, coding, and memory for digit series, *Journal of experimental psychology monograph,* 80, 1 - 17.

Bruner, J. S. (1964). The course of cognitive growth, *American psychologist,* 19, 1 - 15.

Bruner, J. S. (1964). Some Theorems on Instruction. In: Hilgard, E. R. (ed.) *Theories of learning and instruction.* The sixty-third yearbook of the National Society for the Study of Education, Chicago: University of Chicago Press.

Bruner, J. S. (1957). On going beyond the information given. In: *Cognition: The Colorado Symposium*, Cambridge: Harvard University Press.

Bruner, J. S., R. R. Olver and P. M. Greenfield (1966). *Studies in cognitive growth.* New York: Wiley.

Cohen, B. H. (1970). Some or none characteristics of coding, *Journal of verbal learning and verbal behavior,* 9, 269 - 273.

Cohen, N. J. and L. R. Squire (1980). Preserved learning and retention of pattern analyzing skill in amnesia: Dissociation of knowing how and knowing that, *Science,* 210, 207 - 209.

Collins, A. M. and E. F. Loftus (1975). A spreading-activation theory of semantic processing, *Psychological review,* 82, 407 - 425.

Colonna, A. and P. Faglioni (1966). The performance of hemisphere-damaged patients on spatial intelligence tests, *Cortex,* 2, 293-307.

Conners, C. K. and F. Barata (1967). Transfer of information from touch to vision in brain-injured and emotionally disturbed children, *The journal of nervous and mental disease,* 145, 2, 139-141.

Coulson, J. E. and H. F. Silberman (1960). Results of an initial experiment in automated teaching. In: A. A. Lumsdaine and R. Glaser (eds.), *Teaching machines and programmed learning.* Washington, D.C.: National Education Association, Department of Audio-Visual Instruction, 452-468.

Critchley, M. D. (1961). Speech and speech-loss in relation to the duality of the brain. In: V. B. Mountcastle (ed.), *Interhemispheric Relations and Cerebral Dominance.* Baltimore: John Hopkins Press, 208 - 213.

Dearborn, W. F. (1933). Structual factors which condition special disabilities in reading, *Proceedings and Adresses, 57 th. annual session of the American Association on Mental Deficiency.*

Dearborn, W. F. (1931). Ocular and manual dominance in dyslexia, *Psychological bulletin,* 27, p. 704.

DeCecco, J. P. (1964). *Educational technology,* New York: Holt, Rinehart and Winston.

De Rezi, E. and P. Faglioni (1965). The comparative efficiency of intelligence and vigilance tests in detectinmission of tactual learning, *Journal of neurophysiology,* 25, 380 - 391.

Dienes, Z. P. (1967). Some basic processes involved in mathematics learning, *Journal of research in mathematics education,* 21-28.

Doehring, D. G. and R. M. Reitan (1962). Concept attainment of human adults with lateralized cerebral lesions, *Perceptual and motor skills*, 14, 27-33.

Edelman, G. and V. B. Mountcastle (1978). *The mindful brain*. Cambridge: Massachusetts Institute of Technology Press.

Edwards, R. (1963). Teaching machines and programmed instruction, *Canadian education and research digest*, 3, 4, 265.

Elner, F. F. and R. E. Myers (1962). Corpus callosum and the interhemispheric transmission of tactual learning, *Journal of neurophysiology*, 25, 380-391.

Fahlman, S. E. (1979). *NETL: A system for representing and using real-world knowledge*. Cambridge: Massachusetts Institute of Technology Press.

Filmore, C. J. (1968). The case for case. In: E. Bach and R. T. Harms (eds.), *Universals in linguistic theory*. New York: Holt, Rinehart and Winston, 1 - 90.

Fitzhugh, K. B., L. Fitzhugh and R. M. Reitan (1962). Wechsler-Bellevue comparisons in groups with "chronic" and "current" lateralized and diffuse brain lesions, *Journal of consulting psychology*, 26, 306 - 310.

Flores, I. (1970). *Data structure and management*. Englewood Cliffs, NJ: Prentice-Hall, Inc..

Freedman, J. L. and E. F. Loftus (1971). Retrieval of words from long-term memory. *Journal of Verbal Learning and Verbal Behavier*, 10, 2, 107-115.

Freud, S. (1922). *Beyond the pleasure principle*.   London, England: International Psychoanalytical Library.

Fry, E. B. (1963). *Teaching machines and programmed instruction: An introduction*. New York: McGraw-Hill.

Gazzaniza, M. S. (1967). The split brain in man, *Scientific American*, August, 24 - 29.

Gazzaniza, M. S., J. E. Bogen and R. W. Sperry (1967). Dyspraxia following division of the cerebral commissures, *Journal of nervous and mental disease*, 16, 606 - 612.

Geschwind, N. (1970). The organization of language and the brain, *Science*, 170, 940-944.

Goss, A. E. and C. F. Nodine (1965). *Paired-associates learning: The role of meaningfulness, similarity, and familiarization.* New York: Academic Press.

Graham, N. (1973). Spatial frequency channels in human vision: Detecting edges without edge detectors. In: C. S. Harris (Ed.), *Visual coding and adaptability.* Hillsdale, NJ: Academic Press, 163 - 218.

Green, E. J. (1962). *The learning process and programmed instruction.* New York: Holt, Rinehart and Winston.

Grinder, J. and R. Bandler (1976). *The structure of magic.* Palo Alto: Science and behavior books.

Groves, P. M. and R. F. Thompson (1973). A dual-process theory of habitation: Neural mechanisms. In: H. V. S. Peeke and M. J. Herz (Eds.), *Habitation.* New York: Academic Press, 175 - 205.

Hamilton, C. R. (1967). Effects of brain bisection on eye-hand coordination in monkeys wearing prisms, *Journal of comparative and physiological psychology,* 64, 434 - 443.

Hamilton, W. (1859). *Lectures on metaphysics and logic, Volume 1.* Boston: Gould and Lincoln.

Harlow, H. (1959). The formation of learning sets, *Psychological review,* 56, 51 - 56.

Harris, A. J. (1957). Lateral dominance, directional confusion and reading disability, *Journal of psychology,* 44, 283 - 294.

Harris, J. D. (1943). Habituatory response decrement in the intact organism, *Psychological bulletin,* 40, 385 - 422.

Harrison, M. C. (1973). *Data-structures and programming.* Glenview, Ill.: Scott, Foresman and Company.

Harvey, O., D. Hunt and H. Schroder (1961). *Conceptual systems and personality organization.* New York: Wiley.

Hashway, R. M. (1988). *Foundations of developmental education.* New York: Praeger Publishers.

Hebb, D. O. (1955). Drives and the C. N. S. (conceptual nervous system), *Psychological review,* 62, 243 - 254.

Hebb, D. O. (1946). On the nature of fear, *Psychological review,* 53 259 - 276.

Heron, W. (1966). The pathology of boredom. In: S. Coopersmith (ed.), *Frontiers of psychological research,* San Francisco: Freeman.

Hinton, G. E., J. L. McClelland and D. E. Rumelhart (1987). Distributed Representations. In: D. E. Rumelhart and J. L. Mclelland (Eds.), *Parallel distributed processing, Explorations in the microstructure of cognition, Volume 1: Foundations.* Cambridge: The Massachusetts Institute of Technology Press, 77 - 109.

Hobson, A. and R. McCarley (1979). The forms of dreams and the biology of sleep. In: B. Wolman (Ed.) *Handbook of dreams.* New York: Van Nostrand Reinhold.

Holland, J. (1959). A teaching machine program in psychology. In: Galanter, Eugene (ed.) *Automatic teaching: The state of the art.* New York: John Wiley, 69 - 82.

Hughes, J. E. (1962). *Programmed instruction for schools and industry.* Chicago: Science Research Associates.

Hull, C. L. (1952). *A behavior of Intelligence.* Hillsdale, NJ: Lawrence Erlbaum Associates, Publishers, 237 - 260.

Hull, C. L. (1943). *Principles of behavior.* New York: Appleton-Century-Crofts.

Hull, C. L. (1933). Differentiation habitation to internal stimuli in the albino rat, *Journal of comparative psychology,* 16, 255 - 273.

Hull, C. L. (1933). *Hypnosis and suggestibility: An experimental approach.* New York: Appleton-Century-Crofts.

Hull, C. L. (1931). Goal attraction and directing ideas conceived as habit phenomina, *Psychological review,* 38, 487 - 506.

Hull, C. L., C. I. Honland, R. T. Ross, M. Hall, D. T. Perkins and F. B. Fitch (1940). *Mathematico-deductive theory of rote learning.* New Haven: Yale University Press.

Humphrey, G. (1933). *The nature of learning.* New York: Harcourt.

Hunt, E. (1976). Varieties of cognitive power. In: L. B. Resnick (ed.), *The nature of intelligence.* Hillsdale, NJ: Lawrence Erlbaum Associates, 237 - 260.

Hunt, E. (1973). The memory we must have. In: R. Schark and K. Colby (eds.), *Computer models of thought and language.* San Francisco: Freeman.

Hunt, E. and S. Poltrock (1974). The mechanics of thought. In: B. Kantowitz (ed.), *Human information procesing: Tutorials in performance and cognition.* Hillsdale, NJ: Lawrence Erlbaum Assoicates.

Hunter, I. M. L. (1964). *Memory: facts and fallacies.* London, England: Penguin Books.

Huxley, A. (1959). *The doors of perception and Heaven and hell.* London, England: Penguin Books.

Jackson, J. H. (1958). On localization, In: J. H. Jackson (ed.), *Selected Readings , Vol. 2.* New York: Basic Books (Originally Published in 1869).

Johnson, N. F. (1978). Coding Processes in Memory. In. W. K. Estes (ed.), *Handbook of learning and cognitive processes, Volume 6: Linguistic functions in cognitive theory.* Hillsdale, NJ: John Wiley and Sons, 87 - 130.

Johnson, N. F. and D. M. Migdoll (1971). Transfer and retroaction under conditions of changed organization, *Cognitive psychology,* 2, 229 - 237.

Jouvet, M. (1969). Biogenic amines and the states of sleep, *Science,* 163, 32 - 41.

Kenney, T. J. (1969). Permutation transformations on phase structures in letter sequences, *Journal of experimental psychology,* 82, 28 - 33.

Kelly, G. A. (1955). *The psychology of personal constructs.* New York: Norton.

Kimura, D. (1961). Some effects of temporal lobe damage on auditory perception, *Canadian journal of psychology,* 15, 156 - 164.

Kimura, D. (1961). Cerebral dominance and perceptionof verbal stimuli, *Canadian journal of psychology,* 15, 165 - 171.

Kintsch, W. (1978). Comprehension and memory of text. In: W. K. Estes (ed.) *Handbook of learning and cognitive processes, Volume 6: Linguistic functions in cognitive theory.* Hillsdale, NJ: John Wiley and Sons, 57 - 86.

Kintsch, W. (1972). Notes on the structure of semantic memory. In: E. Tulving and W. Donaldson (Eds.) *Organization of memory.* New York: Academic Press, 249 - 308.

Kintsch, W., E. Kozminsky, W. J. Strely, G. McKoon and J. M. Keenan (1975). Comprehension and recall of text as a function of content variables, *Journal of Verbal learning and Verbal Behavior,* 14, 196 - 214.

Kintsch, W. and T. A. Van Dijk (1975). Comment on se repelle et on résume des histiores, *Languages,* 40, 98 - 116.

Kirk, S. A. (1934). A study of the relation of ocular and manual preference to mirror reading, *Journal of genetic psychology,* 44, 192 - 205.

Kosslyn, S. M. (1980). *Image and mind.* Cambridge: Harvard University Press.

Lachman, R., J. Lachman and E. C. Butterfield (1979). *Cognitive Psychology and Information processing.* Hillsdale, NJ: Lawrence Erlbaum.

Lansdell, H. (1969) Verbal and nonverbal factors in right-hemisphere speech: Relation to early neurological history, *Journal of comparitive and physiological psychology,* 69, 73t - 738.

Lashley, K. S. (1929). *Brain mechanisms and intelligence.* Chicago: The University of Chicago Press.

Levin, J. A. (1976). *Proteus: An activation framework for cognitive process models (Technical Report Number ISI/WP-2).* Marina del Rey: University of Southern California, Information Sciences Institute.

Levy, J., C. Trevarthen and R. W. Sperry (1972). Perception of bilateral chimeric figures following hemisphere deconnection, *Brain,* 95, 61 - 78.

Levy, J. (1969). Possible basis for the evolution of lateral specialization of the human brain, *Nature,* 224, 614 - 615.

Lysaught, J. . and C. M. Williams (1963). *A guide to programmed instruction.* New York: John Wiley.

McClelland, J. L. (1981). Retrieving general and specific information from stored knowledge of specifics, *Proceedings of the Third Annual Meeting of the Cognitive Science Society,* 170 - 172.

McClelland, D. C., J. W. Atkinson, R. A. Clark and E. L. Lowell (1953). *The Achievement motive.* New York: Appleton-Century-Crofts.

McDonald, F. J. (1964). The influence of learning theories on education (1900 - 1950). In: Hilgard, E. R. (ed.) *Theories of learning and instruction. The sixty-third yearbook of the National Society for the Study of Education.* Chicago: University of Chicago Press.

Mandler, G. (1967). Organization and memory. In: K. Spence and J. Spence (Eds.), *The psychology of learning and motivation, Volume I.* New York: Academic Press, 328 - 372.

Maslow, A. H. (1965). Some basic propositions of a growth and self-actualization psychology. In: G. Lindzey and C. Hall (Eds.) *Theories of personality: Primary sources and research.* New York: Wiley,307 - 316.

Maslow, A. H. (1962). *Toward a psychology of being.* Princeton, NJ: Van Nostrand.

Maslow, A. H. (1959). Psychological data and value theory. In: A. H. Maslow (Ed.), *New knowledge in human values,* New York: Harper.

Maslow, A. H. (1955). Deficiency motivation and growth motivation. In: M. R. Jones (Ed.) *Nebraska symposium on motivation.* Lincoln, Nebraska: University of Nebraska Press.

Maslow, A. H. (1954). *Motivation and personality,* New York: Harper.

Maslow, A. H. (1950). Selfactualizing principle: A study of psychological health. In: W. Wolf (ed.) *Personality symposium.* New York: Grune and Stratton.

Maslow, A. H. (1942). Self-esteem (dominance feeling) and sexuality in women, *Journal of social psychology,* 16, 259 - 294.

Maslow, A. H. and B. Mittelmann (1951). *Principles of abnormal psychology: The dynamics of psychic illness,* New York: Harper.

Melton, A. W. and Martin, E. (1972). *Coding processes in human memory.* Washington, D.C.: Winston.

Meyer, B. and H. G. Jones (1957). Patterns of cognitive test performance as functions of the lateral localization of cerebral abnormalities in the temporal lobe, *Journal of mental science,* 103, 758 - 772.

Miller, G. A. (1966). Information and memory. In: Coopersmith, S. (Ed.). *Frontiers of psychological research.* San Francisco: Freeman.

Miller, G. A. (1956). The magical number 7 + 2, *Psychological review,* 63, 81 - 97.

Miller, G. A., E. Galanter and K. Pribram (1960). *Plans and the structure of behavior.* New York: Holt.

Milner, B., C. Branch and T. Rasmussen (1966). Evidence for bilateral speech representation in some non-right-handers, *Transactions of the American Neurological Association,* 91, 306 - 308.

Milner, B. and L. Taylor (1971). Right hemisphere superiority in tactle pattern-recognition after cerebral ommissurotomy: Evidence of nonverbal memory, *Neuropsychologia,* 9, 1 - 15.

Minsky, M. (1975). A framework for representing knowledge. In: P. Winston (Ed.) *The psychology of computer vision.* New York: McGraw-Hill, 211 - 277.

Mountcastle, V. B. (1975). The view from within: Pathways to the study of perception, *John Hopkins medical journal,* 136, 109 - 131.

Mountcastle, V. B. and G. M. Edelman (1978). *The mindful brain: Cortical organizatin and the group-selective theory of higher brain function.* Cambridge: Massachusetts Institute of Technology Press.

Myers, R. E. (1961). Corpus callosum in visual goals. In: J. F. Delafresnaye (ed.), *Brain Mechanisms and Learning.* Oxford, England: Blackwell.

Myers, R. E. and R. W. Sperry (1953). Interocular transfer of a visual form discrimination habit in cats after section of the optic chiasma and corpus callosum, *Anatomical records,* 115, 351 - 352.

Nebes, R. D. (1971). *Investigation on lateralization of function in the disconnected hemispheres of man.* San Francisco: California Institute of Technology, unpublished doctoral dissertation.

Nebes, R. D. and R. W. Sperry (1971). Hemispheric deconnection with cerebral birth injury in the dominant arm area, *Neuropsychologia,* 9, 247 - 259.

Neisser, J. (1976). *Cognition and reality: Principles and implications of cognitive psychology.* San Francisco: W.H. Freeman.

Neisser, J. (1967) *Cognitive psychology.* New York: Appleton-Century-Crofts.

Newell, A., J. Shaw and A. Simon (1958). Elements of a theory of human problem solving, *Psychological review,* 65, 151 - 166.

Norman, D. A. (1970). I. Introduction: Models of human memory, In: D. A. Norman (Ed.), *Models of human memory.* New York: Academic Press, 1 - 15.

Norwich, K. E. (1983). To perceive is to doubt: the relativity of perception, *Journal of theoretical biology,* 102, 175 - 190.

Olton, D. S., J. T. Becker and G. H. Handelmann (1983). Hippocampal function: Working memory or cognitive mapping, *Physiological,* 70 - 84.

O'Keefe, J. and L. Nadel (1978). *The hippocampus as a cognitive map.* London, England: Oxford University Press.

Paivio, I. P. (1971). *Imagery and verbal processes.* New York: Holt, Rinehart and Winston.

Pavlov, I. P. (1927). *Conditioned reflexes: An investigation of the physiological activity of the cerebral cortex.* New York: Oxford University Press.

Peeke, H. V. and M. J. Herz (1973). *Habitation.* New York: Academic Press.

Pellionisz, A. and R. B. Llinas (1980). Tensorial representation of space-time in CNS: sensory-motor coordination via distributed cerebellar space-time metric, *Abstracts, Tenth Annual Meeting of the Society of Neuroscience,* p. 510.

Pellionisz, A. and R. B. Llinas (1979). Brain modeling by tensor network theory and computer simulation, *Neuroscience*, 4, 323 - 348.

Petit, T. L. (1987). The shape of intelligence, The cellular locus of learning is finally coming to light, *The sciences*, 27, 2, 58 - 61.

Piaget, J. (1950). *The psychology of intelligence.* London, England: Routledge & Kegan Paul.

Piaget, J. (1932). *The moral judgment of the child.* London, England: Routledge & Kegan Paul.

Piaget, J. and B. Inhelder (1977). *Mental imagery in the child.* New York: Basic Books.

Piercy, M. (1964). The effects of cerebral lesions on intellectual function, *British journal of psychiatry*, 110, 310 - 352.

Piercy, M. and V. O. Smyth (1962). Right hemisphere dominance for certain non-verbal intellectual tasks, *Brain*, 85, 775 - 790.

Platt, C. B. and B. MacWhimmey (1983). Error assimilation as a mechanism in language learning, *Journal of child language*, 10, 401 - 414.

Posner, M. I. and P. McLeod (1982). Information-processing models - In search of elementary operations, *Annual review of psychology*, 33, 477 - 514.

Postman, L. (1955). Short-term memory and incidental learning. In: Melton, A. (ed.) *Categories of human learning.* New York: Academic Press.

Prendergast, J. (1984). *A comparison of an a priori mathematics hierarchy with hierarchies generated from equivalent tests*, Unpublished Doctoral Dissertation, Boston University.

Prentice, W. C. H. (1961). Some cognitive aspects of motivation, American *Psychologist*, 16, 503 - 511.

Reitan, R. M. (1955). Certain differential effects of left and right cerebral lesions in human adults, *Journal of comparitive physiological psychology*, 48, 474 - 477.

Resnick, L. (1963). Programmed instruction and the teaching of complex intellectual skills, *The Harvard educational review*, 33, 4, 439 - 471.

Rogers, C. R. (1963). The actualizing tendency in relation to "motives" and to consciousness. In: M. R. Jones (Ed.), *Nebraska symposium on motivation.* Lincoln, Nebraska: University of Nebraska Press, 1 - 24.

Rogers, C. R. (1955). Persons or science? A philosophical question, *American psychologist*, 10, 267 - 278.

Rogers, C. R. (1947). Some observations on the organization of personality, *American psychologist,* 2, 358 - 368.M

Rogers, C. R., and R. F. Dymond (1954) Psychotherapy and personality change, *Co-ordinated studies in the client-centered approach.* Chicago: University of Chicago Press.

Rumelhart, D. E. and A. Ortony (1977). The representation of knowledge in memory. In: R. C. Anderson, R. J. Spiro and W. E. Montague (Eds.), *Schooling and the acquisition of knowledge.* Hillsdale, NJ: Lawrence Erlbaum, 99 - 136.

Scandura, J. M. (1977). Problem solving. New York: Academic Press.

Schuell, T. J. (1968). Retroactive inhibition in free-recall learning of categorized lists, *Journal of verbal learning and verbal behavior,* 7, 797 - 805.

Selz, O. (1922). *Zur psychologie des produktiven denkins und Intuns.* Bonn: Cohen.

Simon, H. A. (1979). Information processing models of cognition, Annual *review of psychology,* 30, 363 - 396.

Simon, H. A. (1967). Motivational and emotional controls of cognition, *Psychological review,* 74, 29 - 39.

Skinner, B. F. (1966). Teaching Machines (1961). In: Coopersmith, S. (ed.) *Frontiers of psychological research.* San Francisco: Freeman.

Skinner, B. F. (1964). The science of learning and the art of teaching, *Harvard educational review,* 116, 2, 86 - 97.

Skinner, B. F. (1955). Are theories of learning necessary, *Psychological review,* 57, 193 - 216.

Skinner, B. F. (1958). Teaching Machines, *Science,* 128, 969 - 977.

Skinner, B. F. (1949). *Walden Two,* New York: Macmillan.

Skinner, B. F., A. C. Solomon and O. R. Lindsley (1954). A new method for the experimental analysis of the behavior of psychotic patients, *Journal of nervous and mental disease,* 120, 403 - 406.

Slobin, D. I. (1979). *Psycholinguistics (2nd. ed.).* Glenview: Scott-Foresman.

Smith, A. (1966). Certain hypothesized hemispheric differences in language and visual function in human adults, *Cortex,* 2, 109 - 126.

Smith, K. U. (1951). Learning and the associative pathways of the human cerebral cortex, *Science,* 1141 117 - 120.

Smolensky, P. (1987). Information processing in dynamical systems: Foundations of Harmony Theory. In: D. E. Rumelhart and J. L. Mclelland (Eds.), *Parallel distributed processing, Explorations in the microstructure of cognition, Volume 1: Foundations.* Cambridge: The Massachusetts Institute of Technology Press, 194 - 281.

Sokolv, Ye. N. (1963). *Perception and the conditional reflex.* Oxford, England: Pergamon Press.

Solursh, L. P., A. I. Margulies, D. Psych, B. Ashem and E. A. Stasiah (1965). The relationships of agenesis of the corpus callosum to perception and learning, *The journal of nervous and mental disease,* 141, 2, 180 - 189.

Spence, K. W. (1958). A theory of emotionally based drive (D) and its relation to performance in simple learning situations, *American psychologist,* 13, 131 - 141.

Spence, K. W. (1956). *Behavior theory and conditioning,* New Haven, Conneticut: Yale University Press.

Spence, K. W. (1951). Theoretical interpretations of learning. In: S. S. Stevens (ed.), *Handbook of experimental psychology.* New York: Wiley.

Spence, K. W. (1944). The nature of theory construction in contemporary psychology, *Psychological review,* 51, 47 - 68.

Sperling, G. (1960). The information available in a brief visual presentation, *Psychological monographs,* 74, Whole Number 498.

Sperry, R. W. (1970). Perception in the absence of the neocortical commissures, *The Association for Research in Nerbous and Mental Dissease,* 48.

Sperry, R. W. (1968). Hemisphere deconnections and unity in conscious awareness, *American psychologist,* 23, 10, 1968, 723 - 733.

Sperry, R. W. (1967). Split-brain approach to learning problems. In: G. C. Quarton, T. Melnechuk and F. O. Schmidt (Eds.), *The Neurosciences: A study program.* New York: Rochefeller University Press.

Sperry, R. W. (1967). *Mental unity following surgical disconnection of the hemispheres,* The Harvey Lectures Series 62. New York: Academic Press.

Sperry, R. W. (1966). Brain bisection and mechanisms of consciousness. In: J. C. Eccles (eds.), *Brain and conscious experience.* New York: Springer - Verlag.

Sperry, R. W. (1964). The great cerebral commissure, *Scientific American,* January.

Spiegel, E. A. and H. T. Wycis (1968). Multiplicity of subcortical localization of various functions, *The journal of nervous and mental disease*, 147, 1, 45 - 48.

Squire, L. R. (1984). Memory and the brain. In: S. Friedman, et. al. (eds.), *Brain, Cognition and Education.* New York: Academic Press.

Squire, L. R. (1981). Two forms of human amnesia: An analysis of forgetting, *Journal of neuroscience*, 1, 635 - 640.

Sternberg, S. (1969). The discovery of processing stages: Extensions of Doners' method, *Acta psychologica*, 38, 276 - 315.

Stronberg, E. (1934). Monocular and binocular letter-position scores of defective readers in "range of attention" experiments, *Psychological bulletin*, 31, p. 589.

Suppes, P. (1964). Modern learning theory and the elementary school curriculum, *American educational research journal*, 4, 79 - 93.

Syz, H. C. (1926). Psycho-galvanic studies on sixty four medical students, *British journal of psychology*, 17, 54 - 69.

Taylor, D. W. (1960). Towards an information processing theory of motivation. In: Jones, M. R. (Ed.) *Nebraska symposium on motivation.* Lincoln, Nebraska: University of Nebraska Press.

Thompson, R. F., T. Berger and J. Madden (1983). Cellular processes of learning and memory in mammalian CNS, *Annual review of neuroscience*, 6, 447 - 491.

Thompson, R. F., L. H. Hicks and V. B. Shryrokov (1980). *Neural echanisms of goal-directed behavior and learning.* New York: Academic Press.

Thorndike, E. L. (1932). *The fundamentals of learning.* New York: Columbia University Press.

Thorndike, E. L. (1913). *Educational psychology Volume 2: The psychology of learning,* New York: Columbia University Press.

Tolaas, J. (1986). Transformatory Framework: Pictorial to Verbal. In: B. B. Wolman and M. Ullman, *Handbook of states of consciousness.* New York: Van Nostrand Reinhold Company, 31 - 67.

Tolaas, J. (1980). Dreams, dreaming and recent intrusive events. *Journal of altered states of consciousness*, 5, 3, 183 - 210.

Tolaas, J. (1980). The magic theater and the ordinary theater: A comparison, *Journal of mental imagery*, 4, 115 - 127.

Tolman, E. C. (1959). Principles of purposive behavior. In: S. Koch (ed.), *Psychology: A study of science, Volume 2.* New York: McGraw-Hill.

Tolman, E. C. (1948). Cognitive maps in rats and men, *Psychological review,* 55, 189 - 208.

Tolman, E. C. (1938). The determiners of behavior at a choice point, *Psychological review,* 45, 1 - 41.

Tolman, E. C. (1932). *Purposive behavior in animals and men.* New York: Appleton-Century-Crofts.

Tolman, E. C. and C. H. Honzik (1930). Degrees of hunger; reward and nonreward; and maze learning in rats, *University of California publications in psychology,* 4, 241 - 256.

Treisman, A. (1966). Human attention. In: Foss, B. M. (Ed.), *New horizons in psychology.* London, England: Pelican Original, A 775.

Tulvin, E. (1972). Episodic and semantic memory. In: E. Tulving and W. Donaldson (Eds.), *Organization of memory.* New York: Academic Press, 382 - 403.

Turvey, M. V. (1973). On peripheral and central processes in vision: Inferences from an information processing analysis of masking with pattern stimulii, *Psychological review,* 80, 1 - 52.

Ullman, M. (1973). A theory of vigilance and dreaming. In: V. Zigmind (Ed.), *The oculomotor system and brain function.* London, England: Butterworth, 455 - 465.

Underwood, B. (1966). Forgetting. In: S. Coopersmith (Ed.), *Frontiers of psychological research.* San Francisco: Freeman.

Vernon, M. D. (1957). *Backwardness in Reading: A study of its Nature and Origin.* Cambridge, England: Cambridge University Press.

Vygotsky, L. S. (1962). *Thought and language.* New York: Wiley.

Walker, H. A. and H. G. Buch (1970). Lateral preference and right - left awareness in schizophrenic children, *The journal of ervous and Mmntal disease,* 151, 5, 341 - 351.

Wanner, E. (1974). *On remembering, forgetting and understanding sentences.* The Hague: Mouton.

Washburne, C. W. (1922). Educational measurements as a key to individualizing instruction and promotion, *Journal of educational esearch,* 5, 195 - 206.

Watson, J. B. (1924). *Psychology from the standpoint of a behaviorist.* Philladelphia, Pennsylvania: Lippencott.

Watson, J. B. and R. Rayner (1920). Conditional emotional reactions, *journal of experimental psychology*, 3, 1 - 14.

Werner, H. and B. Kaplan (1963). *Symbol formation: An organismic developmental approacth to the psychology of language and the expression of thought.* New York: Wiley.

Winograd, T. (1975). Frame representation and the declarative-procedural controversy. In: D. G. Bobrow and A. Collins (Eds.), *Representation and understanding.* New York: Academic Press, 185 - 210.

Winzenz, D. and G. H. Bower (1970). Subject-imposed coding and memory for digit series, *Journal of experimental psychology*, 83, 52 - 56.

Witty, P. A. and D. Kopel (1936). Sinistral and mixed manual - ocular behavior in reading disabilities, *Journal of educational psychology*, 27, 119 - 134.

Woodworth, R. S. (1918). *Dynamic psychology.* New York: Columbia University Press.

Woodworth, R. S. and H. Scholsberg (1954). *Experimental psychology.* New York: Holt, Rinehart and Winston.

3

Cognition and Developmental Education

Kimberly Kinsler and Andrew Robinson

Increasingly, students enter college lacking assumed knowledge in reading, writing, science and mathematics, as well as the skills necessary to reason abstractly (Hashway, 1989; Holmes Group, 1986; Carnegie Forum, 1986; Bereiter and Scardamalia, 1987a). In response to these students, colleges have provided instructional supports which may range from peer tutoring to faculty led courses (Maxwell, 1981). All too often, however, the determination of who receives assistance and the methodologies used to provide these services remain anchored in age-old modes of diagnosis and instruction. That is, diagnostic testing for academically maladaptive cognitive styles, beliefs and operations is virtually nonexistent. Assignment to levels of remediation continues to be determined by absolute "cut-off" scores, rather than by the relative availability of needed cognitive skills and strategies. What is more, few teachers of developmental students are trained in the cognitive characteristics and needs of these learners or the methodological approaches needed to facilitate their academic competence at the college level. Thus, while techniques have been developed to analyze learners' problem-solving strategies and to instruct students in the use of appropriate reasoning processes, changes in developmental education have not kept pace with these innovations.

As the need for developmental education becomes increasingly more important, spurred by society's demand for logical reasoners and technological problem solvers, so too does the need for developmental educators who more fully understand the cognitive basis for poor academic performance and the methodological approaches needed to teach desired thinking skills. This knowledge is all the more important in light of current theory, which suggests that the higher-order reasoning skills necessary for adequate college-level performance may not spontaneously arise from simple exposure to scientific or theoretical materials, but instead, may have to be taught. For according to Vygotsky (1986), the origins of "scientific" thinking (i.e., abstract, higher-order reasoning) lie in verbal interactions and thus, direct instruction emerges not only as the principle source of "scientific" concepts but, as the basis for abstract reasoning as well.

If, as research suggests, explicit instruction in higher-order reasoning skills is rare and instruction in such skills might not only lead to greater proficiency in students' academic performance but help overcome persistent socio-economic and cultural differences in the outcomes of education as well (Bereiter and Scardamalia, 1987a; Chipman and Segal, 1985), the primary purpose of this chapter is to encourage developmental educators to shift their focus of instruction from an emphasis on factual content to one on the processes and strategies necessary for academic competence. Secondarily, this chapter is to provide instructors with basic information of the cognitive bases for poor academic performance and to introduce them to methodological approaches that stress thinking skills instruction. The chapter is organized in three sections: first the nature of academic competence is considered; second, the origins and functioning of factors that would qualify and/or inhibit its manifestation are discussed; and third, selected methodological approaches designed to facilitate the acquisition of the reasoning processes necessary for competent academic performance are briefly reviewed.

THE NATURE OF ACADEMIC COMPETENCE

Academic competence is a term associated with much consensus and disagreement. Most learning theorists would accept that it is the wherewithal to acquire and demonstrate the general processes and specific skills appropriate to one's instructional level. To acknowledge the possession of such competence, schools require that students exhibit classificatory knowledge and the use of formal symbol systems (e.g., mathematics and logic) and to variously apply these skills to a range of content areas and materials. Moreover, academic competence is hierarchical in nature. With ascending age and progress through the educational system, the knowledge and skills required for satisfactory performance become increasingly abstract. Highly controversial, however, are methods for its assessment, its general or specific nature and the extent to which it is innately determined.

Historically, academic competence has been both measured and characterized by "intelligence" (IQ) tests. These tests have their origin in an assessment scale commissioned by the Paris public school system to differentiate academically competent (successful) from academically incompetent (unsuccessful) students. Lewis Terman brought the scale to the United States as a test of intellectual ability. Terman reasoned that if all children in a particular school setting received identical instruction and, thus, had an equal opportunity to learn, then their differential achievement was due to differences in intellectual ability. IQ tests were subsequently used to measure "general intelligence" as well as to predict school success.

Controversy arose, not in their ability to predict school success, but in what tests of intelligence actually measure.

Early psychometric analyses of the skills and knowledges assessed by IQ tests revealed the operation of two separate factors. The first, a "general" factor (variously termed "g", fluid intelligence and Level 2 intelligence) was characterizedas the ability to engage in conceptual reasoning, general problem-solving and abstract thinking. This factor was said to be applicable across contexts and content areas and to be relatively unaffected by the environment. The other, a "specific" factor (termed "s", crystallized intelligence and Level 1 intelligence), was characterized as the ability to learn concrete content and domain specific information. While researchers postulated a varying number of specific factors, they concurred that its products were influenced by the environment. Emphasis was placed on "general" intelligence as the predominant determiner of IQ test performance and, by analogy, academic competence (Spearman, 1923; Cattell, 1971; Jensen, 1979; Weschler, 1958).

Subsequent thinking in the field shifted from a focus on factors of intelligence to an emphasis on cognitive operations and processes although controversy continued regarding the character of intellectual functioning. Consistent with earlier psychometric views, some (information processing) theorists asserted the predominance of general reasoning processes in relation to specific processes. General processes were characterized as "executive control strategies" which plan, monitor and evaluate problem solutions; specific processes were described as content-specific, procedural strategies, which are applied in the execution of particular problems. Thus, for example, in solving a mathematics word problem and in executing a large inner party, both problem-solving situations require procedures which utilize the general cognitive processes of planning, strategy monitoring and the evaluation of actions taken; however, the particular strategies used to execute the tasks are specific to each situation. General processes were believed to be universal, i.e., present in all individuals and applicable to a number of tasks and content domains while specific processes and strategies were believed applicable to particular content areas or problem situations (Sternberg, 1985).

Other psychologists contradicted the existence or predominance of general factors and processes of intelligence. They asserted that thinking cannot be separated from the contents of thought and that all reasoning is domain specific (Guilford, 1967; Gardner, 1983; LCHC, 1982, 1983). "General" intelligence as defined and measured by IQ tests, was said to be restricted to operations in the logico-mathematical domain (i.e., the academic environment). A range of evidence was gathered to support these assertions. Studies which found poor correlations between IQ test performance and "intelligent" behavior in everyday life revealeda substantial gap between the kinds of adaptations required for functioning outside of school and that required for performance in school and on IQ tests (Charlesworth, 1976; Sternberg, 1985). Cross cultural research comparing children on a range of logico-mathematical reasoning tasks, similar to those on intelligence tests, indicated that individuals who seemed to lack certain abilities (e.g., perspective taking, higher-order classificatory skills and verbal fluency) when tasks were administered in formal school or laboratory-like settings, were able to exhibit sophisticated use of these same skills in domains outside of the test situation (Labov, 1970; Cole, 1975; Rogoff, 1981). Indeed, even within the logico-mathematical domain, differences within individuals were found in their ability to apply particular cognitive processes (e.g., divergent or convergent thinking) and/or to utilize particular contents (e.g., numbers or words). What is more, IQ test items were found to be biased in favor of (i.e., specific to) members of particular socio-economic and ethnic groups (Ogbu, 1985; Gould, 1981). Many of these researchers concluded that (normal) individuals do not differ in their ability to think, but rather in the contexts to which they apply their cognitive processes. Those with experience in one context will be fluent in the application of skills to problems specific to that domain, but not necessarily to problems in other domains with which they are less familiar (Rogoff, 1981; LCHC, 1982,1983).

Closely related to this issue is the debate concerning the innate versus the learned character of intellectual functioning. General factors and processes of intelligence were often regarded as innately determined, while specific factors and processes were assumed to be the products of learning. Based on a series of studies comparing IQ test scores between identical twins reared together and those reared apart, Burt (1969) established the relative contribution of genetic factors to the determination of IQ at .80. These assertions were strongly challenged by researchers who denied a genetic link to conceptual skill and problem-solving ability (Ogbu, 1985). Later studies revised this statistic, asserting that when individuals are raised in similar environments, the extent to which intelligence is determined by genetic factors is .50 (Plomin, 1986) and when environmental situations differ between individuals the (heritability) rate is even smaller. Moreover, behaviors previously regarded as products of an innate cognitive ability and/or aptitude for learning were found upon closer inspection to be due to differences in the opportunity to acquire the knowledge and skills critical for success in school and test situations (Chipman and Segal, 1985; Sternberg, 1985). For example, cross cultural research indicated that children's ability to form conceptual or abstract groupings of diverse objects (e.g., "things that you cook with" and "things that give information") was directly related to exposure to Western forms of schooling (Greenfield, 1966) and that learning memory management strategies and knowledge specific to IQ test items significantly facilitated performance on these tests (Pellegrino and Glaser, 1982; Sternberg, 1986). While this research continued to indicate that genetic factors established an individual's reaction range to enviromental stimuli, it strongly suggested that in normal individuals (i.e., those unafflicted by genetic or organic abberations), competent academic and IQ test performance are largely the result of the type of academically oriented experiences to which individuals are exposed.

Summarizing the above, research indicates a dynamic interaction between (hypothesized) general and/or specific features of an individual's cognitive processes and the environment. This interaction determines the specific manifestation of intellectual capability by facilitating or inhibiting its demonstration. In the next section, the structures and processes associated with academic competence are more clearly explored as well as some of the factors which influence operational functioning. Emphasis is placed on variables that have an inhibitory, or moderating affect.

MODERATORS OF COMPETENCE

In cognitive theory, an important distinction is madebetween competence and performance. According to Flavell and Wohlwill (1969), competence is an abstraction, an idealized representation in terms of rule systems and central processing models of what the organism is capable of knowing and doing as a result of the pure, unimpeded functioning of hypothesized structures and processes. Performance, in contrast, is the actual functioning of these structures and processes reflected through environmental factors which moderate the manifestation of pure competence in a problem-solving situation. A subsequent reconceptualization of this distinction represented competence as the availability, within the individual, of certain problem-solving processes and performance as its actual utilization (Sternberg, 1985). This shift in the notion of competence, from an idealization in the head of the theorist to the availability of cognitive processes in the head of the individual (Neimark, 1985), allowed cognitive theorists to more realistically distinguish between factors believed to influence individual competence from those believed to influence performance. That is, competence could now be studied in terms of the existance within the individual of general cognitive processes but, more importantly, in terms of the possession of specific predicate (i.e., content) and procedural knowledge. This reinterpretation of the competence/performance distinction constitutes the organizing principle around which the concept of moderation is discussed below. Note, however, that this distinction is an arbitrary one, used primarily for purposes of discussion; in fact, it is nearly impossible to separate the two.

Competence Factors

Both biological and environmental factors may influence cognitive competence with effects that range from slight to profound. At the extreme, genetic abnormalities (e.g., Downs syndrome) and cumulative environmentally induced effects (e.g., prenatal radiation or drug ingestion) may inflict organic damage that results in limitations in intellectual development. In this chapter, however, discussion is confined to "normal" individuals, persons unimpaired by genetic and/or organic disorders. Biological moderators are discussed in terms of the maturation of the organism and associated systems; environment is considered in terms of the aggregate of surrounding things, conditions and influences - including people, objects, events and beliefs which would determine what predicate and procedural knowledge is possessed.

Maturation

Two major theorists who posit maturation as a significant influence in cognitive performance are Jean Piaget and Pascual-Leone. Piaget's stage theory is generally regarded as a competence model of cognitive development. Piaget represented each stage as a set of internal structures whose idealized functioning determined the form and complexity of the individual's cognitive performance across content domains. For Piaget, cognitive growth was always in the direction of increasing abstraction, differentiation and organization. Thus, in the first stage of development, the sensori-motor stage, the child's cognitive state is relatively global and undifferentiated and s/he knows the world only through his/her actions on the child defines his/her bottle by the vertical cupping of the hands and sucking movements of the mouth. In the second, preoperational, stage the child acquires the ability to represent the world through mental images, language, pictures and play. However, these representations and the reasoning which they reflect are egocentric and rigid e.g., the child might state: "That's not Mrs. Brown, that's Mommy!". By the third stage of development, the concrete operational stage, representational ability becomes more flexible and decentered (i.e., less tied to the self and superficial appearances). Problem solving, however, is still dependent on the child's previous experiences with the concrete referents of thought. For example, the child understands the concept of government, but only when it is related to elected officers in his/her class or school. With the final stage of development, the stage of formal operations, these last constraints are removed, such that individuals are able to represent objects with which they have had no direct experience and to perform very complex cognitive operations on these abstractions. For example, the child can calculate the composition of atomic rings in chemical bonding (Piaget, 1969).

It was further postulated that interactions between the organism and the environment supply the "aliments" (or experiences) needed to construct, exercise and advance stage movement. All natural environments were believed to provide interactions adequate to advance all normal individuals through the prescribed stages of development (Piaget, 1968). Thus, except in cases of extreme environmental deprivation or restriction, the time table for movement through the stages was reduced to maturational factors. Accordingly, sensori-motor development spanned the period of time from birth to approximately 18 months of age, preoperational development lasted until approximately age seven years, concrete operational development until approximately age 11 and formal operational reasoning was believed to be available by 15 or 20 years of age. Piaget initially maintained that all stages were universally constructed, although in a later work he suggested that formal operational competence might be domain specific in its manifestation (Piaget, 1972).

An information processing counterpart to Piaget's model is Pascual-Leone's theory of Constructive Operators. Seven "silent" operators (e.g., procedural knowledge and motivation) were believed to determine individual performance on cognitive tasks by influencing the interaction between one's available mental capacity (M-space), the mental strategies used to approach the task and the demand which these strategies put on mental capacity (M-demand). Of particular concern to the present discussion is M-space (the number of operations or concepts that may be simultaneously held in conscious (working) memory). M-space sets limitations on problem-solving ability and is developmental in nature. From an initial capacity in the three-year old of one concept/operation, it gradually increases until by age 16 individuals can simultaneously hold the maximum of approximately seven concept/operations. Maturation is the sole determinant of this developmental change. Moreover, with each increment in mental capacity the individual is capable of more advanced reasoning and complex problem-solving, with each advance directly paralleling movement through Piaget's stages of development. Consequently, by the age of 16 all normally functioning individuals possess the mental capacity to perform reasoning and problem-solving tasks indicative of formal operations. When age-appropriate adults are unable to evidence behaviors consistent with this pattern, the cause is attributed to an inappropriate or unjudicious use of available capacity. For example, in problem-solving, students may focus their attention on irrelevant facts or aspects of the task, diverting mental effort from consideration and pursuit of information needed for task solution.

Predicate and Procedural Knowledge

At any point in time, the particular facts and strategies known to an individual directly influence his/her problem-solving ability. Thus, an individual may have the ability to solve a problem, in terms of possessing the necessary mental capacity (M-space) and underlying structures, yet be unable to achieve solution due to the lack of needed facts and strategies. This illustrates the distinction between competence as an ability and an availability, for if the necessary knowledge is not owned by the individual and ,therefore, is unavailable for use in problem solution, s/he is rendered incapable of solving the task. This issue is brought out in the work of Sternberg (1985). He postulated a competence/performance model of intelligence, consisting of three broad components: metacomponents, which control the general executive processing of information by planning, monitoring and evaluating solutions to problem tasks; performance components, which execute the plans constructed bythe metacomponents; and knowledge-acquisition components, which selectively encode, combine and compare incoming data to previous knowledge to allow for new learning. According to Sternberg (1985), these three components are universal.

> Although individuals may differ in what material mechanisms
> they apply to a given task or situation, the potential set of
> mechanisms underlying intelligence is claimed to be the same
> across all individuals, social classes and cultural groups (p.
> 23-24).

While all individuals are believed to possess the basic components for intelligent cognitive functioning, they may differ in the specific strategies possessed and how these strategies are applied to specific tasks. The determination of what particular knowledges an individual owns is largely the result of specific learning and other environmental factors.

Cognitive development results from the accumulation and expansion of available component processes (e.g., new information processing strategies) and the increasing automatization of such processes. This development is heavily dependent upon specific learning and guided instruction. For example, the operation of the performance component (which contains many of the processes commonly measured by intelligence tests) may be enhanced by instruction in the use of strategies typically assessed by these tests (Sternberg, 1985). Cultures and societies which fail to instruct individuals in such strategies will result in their lowered intellectual performance, as measured by these tests.

Sternberg further asserted that an important inter- individual difference and an indicator of cognitive growth and intelligence, is the rate at which individuals transfer conscious mental processes to automatic procedures. However, this too may be the result of the amount and type of guided exposure individuals experience in a particular area. Environments which provide inadequate experiences with materials and operations in areas in which the automaticity of procedures is required for optimum cognitive performance will lead to decreased individual performance on tasks in that domain (LCHC, 1982, 1983). For example, essay writing is regarded as a higher-order reasoning skill, requiring the simultaneous consideration of a large number of factors (e.g., audience, genre, topic, organization, grammar, punctuation, etc.). By the time individuals reach college, the lower-order aspects of writing (e.g., grammar and punctuation), should be automatic or attention to them prioritized so as not to interfere with the higher-order reflective aspects. For many college students in need of remediation, these lower-order processes are neither automatic nor properly prioritized due to inadequate experience with these aspects of writing.

It, thus, appears that there are certain qualities of the individual and the environment that set constraints on competence. The availability of particular cognitive structures and mental capacities may be limited by the age of the individual and necessary predicate and procedural knowledge may be constrained by the opportunity to learn. Complicating this equation are individual and environmental variables which may affect the manifestation and utilization of available competence. It is to these performance factors that we now turn.

Performance Factors

Performance was characterized as the actual functioning of possessed structures and processes reflected through factors which intervene in the manifestation of pure competence. Such moderation may come from both the organism and from the environment. Organismic variables, in the form of dispositional factors, influence attitudinal states and cognitive inclinations. Of particular relevance to academic competence are those of motivation, maladaptive beliefs and cognitive style.

Motivation

Motivation is often conceptualized as the amount of personal energy applied to the task at hand. Much of the recent work in this field focuses on achievement motivation, defined by Atkinson and Raynor (1978) as the personal striving for excellence in a field. According to Atkinson, achievement motivation has its origins in the family and cultural group. That is, the specific domains valued by one's culture and parents are those in which children typically develop a corresponding drive to achieve. If one's culture and parents value and reinforce high academic performance, the individual is likely to be motivated to achieve in this area. As children mature, areas of achievementmotivation become increasingly influenced by peer group standards. If they support areas esteemed by parents and the larger culture, achievement motivation in those areas is enhanced; however, if peer group standards devalue these areas, achievement motivation is reduced (Hare, 1977).

Belief Systems

Closely related to achievement motivation are unconscious and conscious personal beliefs toward the self, the task and the problem-solving context. These perceptions include one's ability to perform the task, the difficulty or value of the task and the views of others toward the self as a result of task performance. As with psychologists, older children and adults hold differing views on the causality of academic competence and intelligence. These differences influence performance on cognitive tasks. Those who believe intelligence is an innately determined and stable ability regard efforts to improve their performance as futile. In contrast, those who consider it a malleable skill are more inclined to engage in cognitive activities designed to improve their performance (Dweck, 1983). Similarly, children may have beliefs concerning which subjects will and will not be of value to them in the future and as a consequence exert little effort in subjects regarded as of restricted future worth. It is further indicated that students in academic remediation harbor a number of maladaptive and counter productive beliefs which function to reduce motivation and severely limit academic performance (Brown, Palincsar and Purcell, 1986). For instance, many of these students believe that essays, once written, are relatively immutable and that the purpose of revision is to make text look neater and cleaner, rather than to reorganize, clarify and otherwise change it.

Cognitive Style

Traditionally viewed as the way in which one goes about solving a problem, cognitive style constitutes a dispositional variable reflecting a relative preference in the means by which an individual organizes, regulates and processes information. Researchers have identified a number of cognitive style variables. Of these, the most intensively studied in relation to academic performance are field dependence/field independence and reflectivity/impulsivity. Field dependence/field independence is currently conceptualized in terms of psychological differentiation i.e., the degree to which an individual is connected to or independent of referents external to the self. The field independent person is characterized as exhibiting a high degree of autonomy and self/non-self differentiation, in relation to the social and nonsocial world. In contrast, the field dependent person is described as exhibiting a high degree of dependence and limited self-non-self differentiation. While past research emphasized the greater adaptive value of field independence to academic performance (based on almost exclusive use of tasks within the logico-mathematical domain), more recent findings suggest that field dependence is also adaptive, albeit in the interpersonal domain. The cognitive style of impulsivity/reflectivity, also known as conceptual tempo, reflects the tendency to pause and ruminate upon alternative answers in problems involving a moderate to high response uncertainty (Kagan, Rosman, Day, Albert and Philips, 1964). Research has indicated the superior problem-solving performance of reflective individuals across a wide range of academic and affective tasks (Messer, 1976; Messer and Schacht, in press).

Variations in task performance should not be taken to indicate individual differences in competence, but more accurately to reflect differential access to competence. Those who adopt particular information-processing strategies as opposed to others are likely to have greater access to the full range of their capabilities and, therefore, are in a better position to use them. Thus, the superior performance of reflective over impulsive individuals in school related tasks does not, necessarily, indicate that the former are brighter than the latter, but rather that their more cautious and methodical response style may be more efficient at recognizing the need for and applying relevant knowledge and operations to the task at hand (Brodzinsky, 1985). Moreover, the utilization of particular cognitive styles is believed to be confined to tasks and situations characterized with the defining properties of the specific cognitive style in question.

In addition to dispositional factors, environmental factors may also significantly influence performance. In interaction with the organism, the environment may moderate the manifestation of competence through task effects, field effects and culture.

Task Effects

When the organism directly interacts with objects or problem situations are posed, features of the task/object and the cognitive state of the individual may combine to moderate performance. Crucial to the problem's outcome is the interaction between the task's contents and procedural demands and the individual's predicate and procedural knowledge. If both the task content and the strategy required for problem solution are unfamiliar, the task may be incomprehensible to the problem solver, for s/he has no schemes with which to make sense of the situation. If both the content and the strategy required are familiar, problem solution, while facilitated, may be rendered routine. However, if the materials are familiar but the strategies required are contrary to those routinely employed with the materials, problem solution is inhibited, as the previously utilized, but now inappropriate strategies may be elicited by the task materials. To solve the problem, the contradictory strategies must be dispelled and either the correct procedures elicited (provided they are within the individual's procedural repertoire or the appropriate strategies must be taught to the learner. If the contents are unfamiliar but the required strategies are familiar, the problem solver must recognize that the known strategy should be applied to the new content-this is the classic definition of cognitive transfer (i.e., the application of previously learned strategies to novel content). For maximum instructional effectiveness, instructors should assess the relationship between qualities of the task and states of the individual, particularly where the task contents and/or strategies are assumed to be familiar. For students who have previous associations which contradict task demands, cognitive performance may be inhibited.

Situational Effects

Many school-like and test situations not only involve a cognitive component, but a social component as well (Hundeide, 1988). Learning takes place in an environment of interactional exchanges in which what is learned is jointly constructed by the teacher and the student. In addition to conforming to the logical demands of an academic task, the learner is faced with the social presentation of the self. If the learning environment is perceived as hostile and unsupportive, students may become reluctant to risk exposing themselves to ridicule, shame and failure and react by losing interest and failing to cooperate. When a learner senses that aspects of the self (e.g., his/her discourse pattern and cultural background) are misunderstood or devalued in the school setting, academic performance often suffers (Gumperz, 1986; Labov, 1970; 1972). Such context-bound responses to the school situation may, to a large extent, be the cause of poor academic performance rather than lack of competence. This assertion is supported by ethnographic classroom studies. Michaels (1986), for example, describes a situation in which a first-grade speaker of non-standard English is asked to lead a sharing experience. Due to his "topic associated" style, with its seemingly unfocused progression of dialogue, the teacher inopportunely interrupts and prematurely terminates the exercise. On other occasions the teacher assumes control of such speakers' presentations by asking direct content-specific questions instead of allowing them to talk. Michaels concludes that such interactions likely result in the teacher's poor estimation of the children's ability, as well as the students' perception of the classroom as a hostile, intrusive place, in which one must not be emotionally invested.

Culture

Culture has been described as a collection of contexts or settings, each with characteristic tasks, props, casts of people and roles (Glick, 1985).

Through its artifacts, culture mediates interactions between the individual and the physical world, dictating from generation to generation ways of perceiving, thinking and acting upon the world that are deemed adaptive to and appropriate for the society. Although cultural mediation may be regarded as universal and, therefore, common to all individuals, the specific mediational forms vary between cultures and between subcultures. That is, cultures differ in the particular means used to perform life's activities. Thus, for example, while all cultures transmit their history and artifacts inter-generationally, not all develop the institution of formal schooling. Moreover, within a particular culture, the mediators provided members of various subcultures may vary in their adaptiveness to the larger culture.

Educational practices evolve in relation to their surrounding culture, particularly the subcultures from which both educators and those participating most fully in the school traditionally come (Chipman and Segal, 1985; Cook-Gumperz, 1986). Cross cultural research indicates that even among societies with formal school systems, there are significant differences in the specific concepts valued and the techniques used for learning material. In certain non-Western cultures, for example, the use of rote learning is stressed instead of the complex, taxonomic organizational strategies emphasized in Western-oriented schools (Scribner and Cole, 1981). In such societies, facile use of these techniques is considered intelligent, adaptive behavior. What is more, instructional procedures in Western schools emphasize specific reciprocation routines. In these instructional interactions, the teacher asks questions to which s/he already knows the answer; students are called upon to give responses that the teacher then evaluates (Dunkin and Biddle, 1974). Research indicates that these and other participant structures may be contrary to those typical to certain subcultures. Where such differences exist, students' academic performance may be depressed due to cognitive conflict or lack of experience with the desired patterns (Au, 1980).

What is more, educational practice is grounded in tacit assumptions about the skills and knowledge students bring to school and about the supplementary assistance and training provided at home (Chipman and Segal, 1985). There are large quantitative and qualitative differences between and within subcultures in the help provided on school work (Chall and Snow, 1982; Varenne, Hamid-Biglione, McDermott and Morison, 1982). SES and ethnic differences have been found on factors which directly influence academic performance, such as the explicitness of language (Labov, 1972) and parents' direction of children's behavior and problem-solving approaches (Wertsch, 1978; Richards and Siegler, 1981). Indeed, parents cannot transmit skills that they themselves have not had the occasion to develop nor to practice in their own occupational and social setting (Ogbu, 1978). Children who are members of subcultures which do not provide the mediational tools appropriate for academic competence are, thus, at a distinct disadvantage. Where such disparities exist between members of the different groups, they are best regarded as variations in cultural conventions, rather than as evidence of disjunction in mental development or cognitive ability (Street, 1984). Consequently, the omission by the schools of explicit training in thinking and learning skills may be one reason for the persistent class and cultural differences in school success (Chipman and Segal, 1985).

METHODOLOGICAL APPROACHES

A number of pedagogical techniques have recently been developed oriented toward the instruction of higher-order executive processes appropriate for school. Although procedures vary between the models, the methodological approaches selected for description herein all might be considered "cognitive apprenticeships" (Collins, Brown and Newman, in press). That is, based on analyses of the thinking and reasoning processes of experts in a field, these models instruct poor academic performers in the cognitive and metacognitive processes used by experts to handle complex problems and tasks.

Procedures are designed to externalize and socialize the desired metacognitive problem-solving processes, which then are internalized by poor or novice learners. Typically, the expert models and coaches the learner in the desired strategies, initially assuming primary responsibility for problem planning, monitoring and evaluation. The expert restructures the task by (re)conceptualizing it, planning strategies, dividing the problem into smaller, more manageable units, distributing and allocating subtasks and teaching appropriate procedures for problem solution. The expert then gradually removes this "scaffold", by transferring increasing responsibility to the learner, while simultaneously encouraging the development of self-correction and self-monitoring skills. The learner is assumed to gradually internalize the factual and procedural contents of the problem-solving zone such that s/he is able to perform similar tasks in the expert's absence. The process often requires the learner to alternate among different cognitive activities while carrying out tasks and frequently involves the development and externalization of a producer-critique dialogue that is then gradually internalized.

The methodologies described below differ in the domain specificity of their instructional objectives. Of the four methodologies reviewed, one is targeted toward general higher-order processes assumed applicable across a number of domains; the remaining three are targeted toward the acquisition of higher-order skills appropriate for particular subject areas. This distinction between general versus specific thinking and reasoning processes is also reflected in the materials used for instruction. Methodologies oriented toward general, non-domain specific skills are "content free" models (i.e.,the materials used for instruction range from abstract geometric figures to non-subject specific word problems). Methodologies oriented toward the acquisition of executive strategies appropriate for particular subject areas are "content-specific" models (i.e., the task contents and the strategies taught are particular to each of the subject areas).

Reviewed below are Feuerstein's Instrumental Enrichment program, which is a general process model and one content-specific model for each of the traditional areas of developmental instruction: Brown and Palincsar's Reciprocal Teaching approach to reading instruction; Bereiter and Scardamalia's Procedural Facilitation method for writing instruction; and Schoenfeld's approach to mathematics instruction. For each program, there isa brief summary of its underlying theory and goals, a description of procedures (and instruments where applicable), evaluative findings from previous implementation efforts and comments.

FEUERSTEIN'S INSTRUCTIONAL ENRICHMENT MODEL

Theory and Goals

According to Feuerstein, Jensen, Hoffman and Rand (1985), the most significant characteristic of low academic performers is their reduced level of modifiability. That is, when confronted with the need to acquire new information, new response modes, new content, or new thinking operations, these students show cognitive rigidity, perceptual deficits (e.g., blurred perception of details) and the passive experiencing of the world as a series of unrelated events (i.e., "an episodic grasp of reality"). This behavior, they assert, is due to a lack of quantitatively and qualitatively adequate mediated learning experiences (MLEs), in which an adult interposes him/herself between the learner and the external stimuli, altering both the learner's perception of and response to the stimuli. MLEs change random and accidental environmental stimuli to reflect the intentionality of the mediating adult. They also regulate the learner's response behavior to lead him/her to more focused and goal-oriented thought processes. According to Feuerstein, the mediator's modeling of planned problem-solving, even more than the interactional contents, produces in the learner the prerequisites of higher mental processes as well as intellectual modifiability and adaptation to the conditions of life. Based on the belief that, even as an adults, poor academic performers can develop and manifest cognitive modifiability if provided with MLEs in the logico-mathematical domain, the major goal of the Instrumental Enrichment program is to enhance the capacity of academically low functioning adolescents to benefit from direct exposure to environmental stimuli by provision of appropriate MLEs.

Procedures

There are two essential features to the Instructional Enrichment problem-solving tasks; (1) the generation and evaluation of appropriate problem definitions and strategies; and (2) the identification and illustration of general and specific problem-solving principles.

Instructional Enrichment lessons are divided into three phases: introduction; individual work; class discussion and summary. In the introductory phase, the teacher and students jointly define the task, its objectives and possible solution strategies. By identifying appropriate rules, relationships and strategies, the teacher prepares the students for the task by helping them acquire necessary concepts, vocabulary and operations. In phase two, students work on the task independently. While students work, the teacher interacts with them on a one to one basis, investigating cognitive processes, discussing strategies and interpreting the meaning of their approaches to the task and their effects. In the group discussion and summarization phase, the focus is on developing students' insight into those functions and strategies that were useful in mastering the task and on developing applications of these principles to a variety of school and non-school situations.

Essential to the success of the program is the teacher activity of Bridging. To facilitate students' ownership of the appropriate understandings and their recognition and application in other situations, during the second group discussion phase, they are prompted to draw on their experiences to provide examples of particular principles occuring both in and outside of school. This instantiation of higher-order cognitive processes in a variety of contexts encourages transfer. The burden of insight, however, is on the teacher who must foster the process of reflective abstraction by appropriate questioning and by exposing students to models of reasoning behavior.

Instruments

There are 20 instruments, each consisting of a number of pencil and paper exercises. Each instrument focuses intensively on one or more cognitive functions while simultaneously promoting others less intensively. For example, tasks are targeted toward the correction of students' episodic grasp of reality, their blurred, sweeping and global perceptions and the facilitation of analytic comparisons. Sophisticated content knowledge or reading ability is not presupposed, although deliberate attention is focused on problem definition and the use of strategies. Proper classroom implementation requires 3 to 5 hours per week for a period of 2 to 3 years.

Two of these task items are described below.

The procedure most often begins with one of the Organization of Dots tasks. In these tasks, students are presented with dots in an amorphous, irregular cloud from which they are to discern figures identical in form and size to those in a given model. The task becomes complicated by increasing the density of the dots, the overlapping of objects, the complexity of the figures and changes in their orientation. Successful completion demands the segregation and articulation of the field, the projection of relationships, form and size, as well as the discovery of strategies and the restraint of impulsivity. A task used to facilitate the relation of two or more sources of information, systematic exploratory behavior and the identification of essential versus irrelevant stimuli is Comparisons. Students are asked to look at a geometric figure. To the right of this figure are two frames, each containing four words which connote physical features or dimensions (e.g., form, number, shape, direction) one or more of which are encircled. In each of the frames the student is asked to make a drawing that is different from the sample only in those aspects indicated by the encircled words.

Feuerstein has also created a dynamic method of evaluating students' cognitive potential, the Learning Potential Assessment Device (LPAD). This instrument assesses specific mediational weaknesses in cognitive functioning by providing interactive learning experiences similar to those associated with scaffolding. Analysis of students' results produce strategy specific prescriptions.

Evaluative Data

The Instructional Enrichment program has been implemented in a number of countries including the United States, Israel, Canada and Venezuela. It has been used with students identified as educable mentally retarded, learning disabled, behavior disordered, as well as with average and gifted students. Students have ranged from 10 years of age to adults.

Of the four methodologies discussed in this section, Instructional Enrichment is probably the most extensively evaluated; space, however, does not permit a thorough discussion of the findings. The interested reader is referred to Bransford, Arbitman-Smith, Stein and Vye (1985) and Savell, Twohig and Rachford (1986) for extensive discussions. Overall evaluative results indicate that when students get a significant degree of exposure to the program (perhaps 80 hours or more in a year) and when used by teachers who are also teaching the students in another subject and are thus able to apply the relevant principles (bridge), Instructional Enrichment can enhance performance on standard nonverbal-IQ-type measures (Savell, Twohig and Rachford, 1986). On the down side, Bransford, Arbitman-Smith, Stein anf Vye (1985) concluded that there is no strong evidence that programs such as Feuerstein's, which attempt to develop general thinking skills, improve students' performance in tasks that are dissimilar to those targeted in the program. However, to the extent that these programs employ items that are similar to those contained in IQ tests and provide experience with these items, test performance is facilitated.

Currently there are three major programs which propose to teach general thinking and reasoning skills to adolescents and adults. In addition to Instructional Enrichment, there are the Problem and Comprehension program (Whimbey and Lochhead, 1986) and Intelligence Applied (Sternberg, 1986). Of these, Feuerstein's is the only one specifically targeted for a developmental population. Previous research by Hutchinson (1985), which used Whimbey and Lochhead's model with college students in remediation, found the materials a bit too advanced and subsequently had to adapt the items to their entering level. In the opinion of the current authors, the Sternberg model is the most advanced, targeted for "average" college students.

PALINCSAR AND BROWN'S RECIPROCAL TEACHING OF READING

Theory and Goals

Palincsar and Brown (1984, 1985) have been guided in their work by the belief that much of what is called reading, particularly in the upper grades, is actually critical thinking. Students are not only required to decode (i.e., translate written into spoken words, but also to understand text meaning critically evaluate the message, remember the content and apply this knowledge flexibly and creatively [Brown and Palincsar, in press]). Such behaviors, they assert, demand a split mental focus in which learners simultaneously concentrate on the material they are reading and on themselves as learners, checking to see if the mental activities engaged in are resulting in learning.

Based on the analysis of the reading processes engaged in by good and poor readers, Palincsar and Brown have identified particular comprehension fostering and monitoring strategies in which good readers engage, but which are characteristically absent in poor readers. Of these, four specific strategies, considered particulary vital to reading comprehension and adaptable to instruction, were selected for treatment: summarizing (self review of) the main content, formulating potential test questions, clarifying ambiguity and predicting future content. Their approach, Reciprocal Teaching, is designed to teach these four activities to improve students' reading comprehension and to induce self-monitoring in their reading comprehension.

Procedures

Based on the assumption that expert-led social interactions play a prominent role in learning and can provide a major impetus to cognitive growth, Reciprocal Teaching procedures emphasize four characteristic features: (1) the acquisition of desired reading strategies as a joint responsibility shared by the teacher and students; (2) the teacher's initial assumption of major responsibility for the instruction of these strategies by modeling their use in a very explicit fashion; (3) the discussion of these strategies in the context of a reading selection; where students take turns assuming the role of teacher and leading the discussion and (4) the conscious attempt to release control of dialogue to the students and to fade the leadership of the teacher (Palincsar, 1987).

Small group interactive dialogue is the primary instructional technique. The teacher first introduces and models each strategy and role. For example, s/he thinks aloud about how to generate a summary, what cues s/he uses to make predictions and how s/he uses rereading when unclear text is encountered. The students then follow the teacher's example by engaging in the same verbal activities when they assume the role of "teacher". The adult teacher also coaches, prompts and shapes the students' participation through the use of corrective verbal feedback. Instruction is typically done in groups of from 4 to 7, but larger groups may also be used.

Working with expository text, the teacher first asks the students to predict from the title what content might be included in the text. Students are encouraged to speculate, based of their own experiences, about information the author might discuss. After the group has read the first paragraph silently, the teacher models the four activities: first generating a question or several questions, then summarizing the text, predicting (if appropriate) and pointing out something potentially confusing in the text and how it could be clarified. The students answer the questions and are invited to elaborate on any point the teacher has made. After several paragraphs are completed in this fashion, the teacher assigns a student to assume the role of teacher for the next paragraph. The adult teacher prompts as necessary, shaping the student's response. When the student teacher has engaged in all four activities, s/he designates the next teacher. As instruction progresses, the adult teacher attempts to increasingly transfer responsibility for the activity to the students, but may continue to monitor their performance, providing specific feedback, as needed.

Evaluative Data

Reciprocal Teaching has been used with students with a range of reading abilities and grade levels. Students with severe to moderate reading deficits as well as students of average ability have utilized the program; grade levels have ranged from elementary school through junior college.

Palincsar and Brown (1984, 1985; Brown and Palincsar, in press, 1986) have extensively evaluated the effects of their program under varied conditions. Their evaluative research indicates that Reciprocal Teaching can dramatically improve students' reading comprehension test scores from a pre-intervention low of 15% accuracy to a post-intervention high of 85% accuracy. Successful results have been obtained in replications studies using teachers of non-Reading courses and with students who were relatively heterogeneous regarding both decoding and comprehension ability (Palincsar, 1987).

SCARDAMALIA AND BEREITER'S PROCEDURAL FACILITATION OF WRITING

Theory and Goals

According to Bereiter (1980), students go through a number of phases in the development of writing proficiency. The first and simplest phase, associative writing, or "knowledge telling" consists of writing down whatever comes to mind in the order in which it occurs. When the writer runs out of ideas, writing stops. Britton, Martin, McLoed and Rosen (1975) have identified a similar early phase in developmental college students, in which their writing is relatively unplanned, incognizant of audience reaction and, on the whole, closer to transcribed speech than it is to literate writing. The second phase, performative writing (which characterizes traditional school writing instruction), reflects an effort to shape students' associative writing into conformity with conventions of style and mechanics. Subsequent phases indicate an increasing awareness of audience (communicative writing) and an effort to integrate and unify associative, performative and communicative writing. Essential to competence in writing is the development of the ability to take the perspective of the reader and thus to "transform" written text so as to impart the intentions of the writer to the reader in a concise and fluid style (Bereiter and Scardamalia, 1987b).

Problems in writing arise from the sheer burden of having to maintain in working memory the host of variables needed in writing text (i.e., the lower-order demands of grammar, punctuation and content generation, as well as the higher-order demands of audience interpretation, textual organization, etc.). Because lower-order (associative and performative) demands are ordinarily preemptive, the higher-order, more reflective demands of writing are simply left out. The goal of Bereiter and Scardamalia's writing program, Procedural Facilitation, is to help novice writers handle the executive information processing burden to permit learners to make fuller use of the knowledge and skills they possess

(Bereiter and Scardamalia, 1982).

Procedures

Procedural Facilitation procedures are designed to have students conduct all of the central information processing tasks involved in essay writing under conditions that lessen the mental demands. The instructional principles which guide its methods and procedures are to: (1) use procedures that model mature executive processes in a simple way; (2) minimize the attention that must be paid to running executive schemes (i.e., procedures involved with planning, monitoring and evaluation of written text); (3) structure procedures to by pass immature and inappropriate tendencies; (4) foster metacognition (strategy awareness and control) by making overt, covert processes; and (5) use procedures that may be scaled up or down (Bereiter and Scardamalia, 1982).

There are several techniques used in Procedural Facilitation, although only two are discussed here (see Scardamalia and Bereiter, 1982 and 1987 for more detailed methodological descriptions). Probably, the most well known Procedural Facilitation activity uses a set of prompt cards, developed for both the text generation and revision phases of the writing process. Students take a card at points of "stuckness" in the writing process. In the text generation phase, for example, planning is broken down into five general processes or goals: (1) generating a new idea, (2) improving an idea, (3) elaborating an idea, (4) identifying goals and (5) putting ideas into a cohesive whole. For each process, a number of specific prompts have been developed, similar to suggestions that a teacher might make. The writer determines what kind of cue is needed, selects a card from the appropriate deck, inserts the phrase into the monologue or follows the suggested activity and continues as if that phrase had come to mind spontaneously. By suggesting specific lines of thinking for students to follow, the prompts serve to simplify the complex process of elaborating and reconsidering one's plans.

In introducing the technique, the teacher first models how to use the prompts in generating ideas about a topic. Students then try, individually, to plan an essay on a new topic using the cue cards. In this phase, students may assume both producer and critic roles (i.e., while each student practices individually) ["soloing"], the teacher as well as the other students evaluate the soloist's performance, monitoring, for example, discrepancies between the soloist's stated goals versus his/her proposed plans. Students also become involved in discussing how to resolve problems that the soloist could not solve. As students' skills improve, they increasingly assume more of the monitoring and problem-solving process from the teacher.

Co-investigation, another Procedural Facilitation technique, encourages students to reflect on both their existing strategies and the new one they are acquiring. The teacher proposes to the students that together they try to examine their own thinking as they carry out some task. Both, subsequently, engage in a process of thinking aloud as they execute the task. This procedure makes previously covert cognitive processes overt and motivates students to reflect upon their and the teacher's thinking.

Evaluative Data

Procedural Facilitation has also been used with a range of students, primarily in the elementary and junior high school grades. In a series of studies, the combined effects of procedural facilitation, co-investigation and modeling resulted in superior essay revisions for nearly every student (Bereiter and Scardamalia, 1987b).

While the Procedural Facilitation model was designed for younger children, it constitutes a respected model that may be adapted for college students in remediation or serve as a resource for the development of models oriented toward instruction of writing strategies. For example, in a study designed to improve the essay revision phase of developmental students' writing, the first author developed a model adapted from both the Procedural Facilitation and Reciprocal Instruction approaches. In this study, students were divided into groups of four, with each group member assuming one of four possible roles: writer/reader, unity/ main idea, thesis support or organization/coherence. Worksheets, one for each listener role, were distributed. As the writer read his/her essay to the group, members listened from the perspective of their assigned roles, guided by the worksheets. Notes were written on the worksheets to help listeners give appropriate role-specific feedback and to provide support for later group discussion of the essay. When listeners had given their feedback, roles changed and a new writer/reader presented his/her work. The study found students appeared to gradually internalize the listener roles and to write their essays in anticipation of the group interactions. The procedures also significantly improved the quality of their essays in each of the targeted areas (Kinsler, 1989).

SCHOENFELD'S APPROACH TO MATHEMATICS INSTRUCTION

Theory and Goals

Schoenfeld's (1985, 1987) analysis divides mathematical performance into four distinct components: (1) domain knowledge (i.e., an individual's repertoire of basic facts and procedures as well his/her misunderstandings concerning these knowledge); (2) heuristic strategies (i.e., "rules of thumb" or "tricks of the trade" for making one's way through complex tasks); (3)

executive control strategies (i.e., how an individual uses or fails to use known planning, monitoring, assessment and decision making information); and (4) beliefs (i.e., the set of not necessarily conscious determiners of problem solvers' behavior, such as perceptions of the self, mathematics, the topic, etc). According to Schoenfeld, teachers of mathematics must take into consideration and engage all these factors.

Schoenfeld (1987) further believes that mathematical facts and procedures are tools, which are only meaningful when they are used. The measure of an individual's mathematical understanding is, he asserts, the ability to correctly apply mathematical thinking in the appropriate situations, not the demonstration of rote techniques. Thus, the goal of Schoenfeld's approach is to create a "culture where mathematics becomes the medium of exchange," an environment where mathematics is talked about, explained and enjoyed, such that students come to experience mathematics in a way that makes sense.

Procedures

Schoenfeld employs a variety of activities designed to highlight different aspects of the cognitive processes and knowledge structures required for mathematical expertise. His procedures principally involve class demonstrations, collective problem-solving and small, collaborative group sessions. According to Collins, Brown and Newman (in press), his use of these techniques illustrates the essential elements of cognitive apprenticeship approaches: modeling, coaching, scaffolding and fading. In class demonstrations introducing heuristics, for example, Schoenfeld models their selection and use in solving relevant problems. In these demonstrations he thinks aloud, focusing students' attention on the use and management of specific heuristics, making overt the often covert thinking processes in mathematical problem-solving. At the beginning of class, Schoenfeld also offers to solve a difficult problem posed by students. In executing these challenges, Schoenfeld may produce less than errorless solutions. Such demonstration of errors and their correction models for students not only that strategies sometimes fail, but how experts deal with problems that they find difficult. Observing such behavior is believed critical to students' developing control strategies that prevent prolonged "goose chasing" and to a belief in their own capabilities.

In collective problem-solving sessions, Schoenfeld may give the class problems to solve that lend themselves to the use of the heuristics he has introduced. Acting as a moderator, he solicits heuristics and solution techniques from the students, consciously modeling the various control strategies for making judgments about how best to proceed. According to Collins, Brown and Newman, this division of labor, while turning over some of the problem-solving process to students-by having them generate alternative courses of action, also provides major support or scaffolding-by having the teacher manage such decisions as which suggestions to pursue or when to change course, etc.. Schoenfeld then fades support by modeling less and less of the entire expert problem-solving process, shifting students' observational focus during modeling from the application or use of specific heuristics to the application or use of control strategies in managing heuristics.

During small group sessions, students work in problem-solving pairs while Schoenfeld acts as a "consultant." In monitoring and coaching individual group performance, Schoenfeld poses three questions: What are you doing? why are you doing it? and how will success in what you are doing help you find a solution to the problem? He thus encouraging students to reflect on their activities. Gradually students, in anticipating Schoenfeld's questions, come to ask the questions of themselves, thereby gaining control over reflective and metacognitive processes in the problem-solving process. Students are forced to offer possible solutions to problems and to defend their choices to each other. This topic-specific articulation, discussion and argumentation are believed to encourage the development of metacognitive skills. In seeing other students' struggle with problems with which they are also having difficulty, some of students' insecurity is alleviated as they realize that difficulties in understanding are not unique to them, enhancing their self esteem relative to others (Collins, Brown and Newman, in press).

Evaluative Data

Mathematics instruction is only beginning to receive major attention in the field of cognitive science and, as a result, outside evaluation of Schoenfeld's model has been limited. He, personally, has gotten very good results from the approach and the model is well regarded in the field (Collins, Brown and Newman, in press).

As Schoenfeld's approach was initially designed for students taking regular college-level and subject-major mathematics courses, his procedures may have to be adapted to students in remediation. The present authors believe, however, that this approach represents a resource for a much needed reorganization in instructional approaches to mathematics for students in need of developmental education.

COMMENTS AND CONCLUSIONS

Developmental education has been the vehicle through which generations of adults have sought to achieve personal growth and access to society's rewards. However, the gap between the prepared and the underprepared has widened with progressive technological development. Closing this gap more and more depends upon the possession of the skills needed to manipulate and control technology. These skills demand that the average college student and worker own and utilize predicate and procedural knowledge characteristic of higher-order reasoning. Equipping individuals with this knowledge increasingly requires that developmental programs reinterpret the concept of "basic skills instruction." No longer can it mean the provision of deficit and/or prerequisite skills, narrowly defined as the essential techniques of reading, writing and mathematics; rather it now must stress the reasoning processes appropriate to mediate interactions in this rapidly changing society.

To facilitate the development of curricula designed to teach appropriate reasoning skills, the following recommendations are offered.

- Educators should capitalize on the learners' existing skills and knowledge. For many students, developmental education is a process of reculturalization. Having previously chosen to adapt to their more immediate culture, they now seek to acquire knowledge of the logico-mathematical domain. To faciliatate the acquisition of the necessary cognitive processess, instructors must consciously acknowledge and respect students' existing cultural mediators and actively seek to employ them in the current learning process.

- Higher-order reasoning skills must become the conscious objects of instruction. Being part of many educators' personal and educational socialization, these processes often consist of automatic and unconscious procedures, which are assumed to function "without saying." For individuals lacking this particular socialization, they constitute crucial elements in the learning process. By consciously modeling these strategies in the context of their use, instructors can demonstrate in a comprehensible and meaningful way, the cognitive processes appropriate for school and for work.

- Instructors need to socialize the learning process. Research increasingly indicates that individualistically oriented instructional techniques may be inconsistent with fostering abstract reasoning and inappropriate to the (cultural) learning patterns of many developmental students. Research further suggests that social interaction may be a necessary component in the transmission of higher-order reasoning. By encouraging the externalization, analysis and subsequent internalization by the learner of desired thinking skills, collaborative approaches offer a methodological means of transforming these findings into classroom practice.

- More thorough knowledge of the learner and of the instructional interaction is needed. Traditionally, developmental educators have restricted assessment to knowledge of students' entering facts and skills. Equally important, however, is knowledge of their cognitive styles and relevant beliefs. Only with a full understanding of where the student stands in relation to the classroom task and setting can beliefs and strategies that hinder the learning process be dispelled. However, therel earning process should not be at the expense of making the educational setting a personallydevaluing and threatening environment.

- Students should be encouraged to think broadly. By going beyond the immediate situation, instructors can bridge the gap between the logico-mathematical domain and the worlds of work and community. In specifically teaching for the transfer of information, instructors give power to classroom content by helping students recognize the relevance of the particular knowledge in the outside world.

- Research is needed to advise action and further knowledge in the field. To more expeditiously achieve its mission of providing access and personal growth, more objective and in depth information is needed to assist educators in this process. What is more, developmental education as a process of reculturalization is a new and unexplored field. New methodological approaches hold promise for success, but they require that these educators have a greater understanding of the cognitive processes and factors influencing learning and instruction. Research needs to be conducted to provide the necessary information to better understand these processes and better effect this redirection.

REFERENCES

Atkinson, J. and J. Raynor (1978). *Personality, motivation and achievement.* Washington, D.C.: Hemisphere.

Au, K.H. (1980). Participation structures in a reading lesson with Hawaiian children: Analysis of a culturally appropriate instructional event. *Anthropology and education quarterly.* 11, 91-115.

Bereiter, J. (1980). Development in writing. In L. Gregg and E. Steinberbg (eds.), *Cognitive processes in writing.* Hillsdale: N.J.: Lawrence Earlbaum Associates, 73-96.

Bereiter, J. and M. Scardamalia (1987a). An attainable version of high literacy. *Curriculum inquiry.* 17, 1, 9-30.

Bereiter, J. and M. Scardamalia (1987b). *The psychology of written composition.* Hillsdale, NJ: Lawrence Earlbaum

Bereiter, J. and M. Scardamalia (1982). From conversation to compositon: The role of instruction in developmental process. In R. Glaser (ed.), *Advances in instructional psychology.* Vol 2. Hillsdale, NJ: Lawrence Earlbaum Associates, 1-64.

Bransford, J., R. Arbitman-Smith, B. Stein and N. Vye (1985). Analysis-Improving thinking and learning skills: An analysis of three approaches. In J. Segal, S. Chipman and R. Glaser (eds.), *Thinking and learning skills.* Vol. 1. Hillsdale, NJ: Lawrence Earlbaum Associates, 133-208.

Britton, J., T. Burgess, N. Martin, A. McLoed and H. Rosen (1975). *The development of writing abilities.* London: Macmillan Education Ltd., 11-18.

Brodzinsky, D. (1985). On the relationship between cognitive styles and cognitive structures. In E. Neimark, R, DeLisi and J. Newman (eds.), *Moderators of competence.* New York: Lawrence Earlbaum Associates, 147-170.

Brown, A. and A. Palincsar (in press). Reciprocal teaching of comprehension strategies: A natural history of one program for enhancing learning. In Borkowski and Day (eds.), *Intelligence and cognition in special children: Comparative studies of giftedness, mental retardation and learning disabilities.* New York: Ablex.

Brown, A., A. Palincsar and L. Purcell (1986). Poor learners: Teach, don't label. In M. Neisser (ed.), *The school achievement of minority children.* Hillsdale, NJ: Lawrence Earlbaum Associates, 105-144.

Burt, C. (1969). The inheritance of general intelligence. *American psychologist,* 27, 175-190.

Carnegie Forum on Education and the Economy. (1986). *A nation at risk: Teachers for the 21st century.*

Cattell, R.B. (1971). *Abilities: Their structure, growth and action.* Boston: Houghton Mifflin.

Chall, J. and C. Snow (1982). *Families and literacy: The contribution of out of school experiences to children's acquisition of literacy.* Final report on NIE-G-80-0086. Harvard Graduate School, December.

Charlesworth, W. (1976). Human intelligence as adaptation: An ecological approach. In L. Resnick (ed.),, *The nature of intelligence.* Hillsdale, NJ: Lawrence Earlbaum Associates, 133-150.

Chipman, S. and J. Segal (1985). Higher cognitive goals for education: An introduction. In J. Segal, S. Chipman and R. Glaser (eds.), *Thinking and learning skills.* Vol. 1. Hillsdale, NJ:Lawrence Earlbaum Associates, 1-20.

Cole, M. (1975). An ethnographic psychology of cognition. In R. Brislin, S. Bochner and W. Lonner (eds.), *Cross-cultural perspectives in learning.* New York: Wiley and Sons.

Cole, M. and P. Griffin (1986). A sociohistorical approach to remediation. In S. de Castell, A. Luke and K. Egan (eds.), *Literacy, society and schooling.* Cambridge, Massachusetts: Cambridge University Press, 110-131.

Collins, A., J. Brown and S. Newman (in press) Cognitive apprenticeships: Teaching the craft of reading, writing and mathematics. In L. Resnick (ed.),, *Cognition and instruction: Issues and agenda.*

Cook-Gumperz. J. (1986). Introduction: The social constructionof literacy. In J. Cook-Gumperz (ed.), *The social construction of literacy.* Cambridge: Cambridge University Press, 16-44.

Dunkin, M. and B. Biddle (1974). *The study of teaching.* New York: Holt, Rinehart and Winston.

Dweck, C. S. (1983). Theories of intelligence and motivation. In S. Paris, G. Olson and H. Stevenson (eds.), *Learning and motivation in the classroom.* Hillsdale: NJ Earlbaum.

Feuerstein, R., M. Jensen, M. Hoffman and Y. Rand (1985). Instrumental Enrichment: An intervention Program for structural modifiability. In J. Segal, S. Chipman and R. Glaser (eds.), *Thinking and learning skills.* Vol. 1. Hillsdale, NJ: Lawrence Earlbaum Associates, 43-82.

Flavell, J. and J. Wohlwill (1969). Formal and functional aspects of cognitive development. In Elkind and Flavell (eds.), *Studies in cognitive development: Essays in honor of Jean Piaget.* New York: Oxford

University Press, 67-120

Gardner, H. (1983). *Frames of the mind: The theory of multiple intelligence.* New York: Basic Books.

Glick, J. (1985). Culture and cognition revisited. In E. Neimark, R. DeLisi and J. Newman, J. *Moderators of Competence.* Hillsdale, NJ: Lawrence Earlbaum Associates, 99-116.

Gould, S. (1981). *The mismeasure of man.* New York: Norton.

Greenfield, P. (1966). *On culture and conservation.* New York: Wiley and Sons, 225-256.

Guilford, J. P. (1967). *The nature of human intelligence.* New York: McGraw Hill.

Gumperz, J. (1986). Interactional sociolinguistics in the study of schooling. In J. Cook-Gumperz (ed.), *The social construction of literacy.* Cambridge: Cambridge University Press, 45-68.

Hare, B. (1977). Black and white children's self esteem in social situations. *Journal of negro education.* 46, 2, 145- 156.

Hashway, R. (1990). *Handbook of developmental education.* New York: Praeger Press.

Holmes Group (1986). *The report of the Holmes Group: Tomorrow's Teachers.* The Holmes Group Inc. Lansing, MI.

Hundeide, K. (1988). Metacontracts for situational definitionsfor presentation of cognitive skills. *Quarterly Newsletter of LCHC.* 10, 3, 85-91.

Hutchnson, R. (1985). Teaching problem-solving to developmental adults: A pilot project. In J. Segal, S. Chipman and R.Glaser (eds.), *Thinking and learning skills.* Vol. 1. Hillsdale, NJ: Lawrence Earlbaum. 499-513.

Jensen, A. (1979). *Bias in mental testing.* New York: Free Press.

Kagan, J., B. Rosman, D. Day, J. Albert and W. Phillips (1964) Information processing in the child. *Psychological monographs.* 78, 1 (Whole No. 578).

Kinsler, K. (1989). *The use of oral discourse and social activity to facilitate written composition in basic writing students.* Unpublished manuscript.

Laboratory of Comparative Human Cognition. (1982). Culture and cognitive development. In Kessen (ed.), *Mussen handbook of child development.* New York: Wiley and Sons. 1, 295-356.

Laboratory of Comparative Human Cognititon. (1983). Culture and intelligence. In R. Sternberg (ed.), *The development of human intelligence.* Cambridge Massachusetts: Cambridge Univ. Press, 642-719.

Labov, W. (1972). *Language in the inner city.* Philadelphia: University of Pennsylvania Press.

Labov, W. (1970). *The logic on non-standard English. In F. Williams (ed.), Language and poverty.* Chicago, Illinois: Markman, 153-189.

Maxwell, M. (1981). *Improving student learning skills: A comprehensive guide to successful practices and programs for increasing the performance of underprepared students.* San Francisco: Jossey Bass.

Messer, S. (1976). Reflection-impulsivity: A review. *Psychological bulletin,* 83, 1026-1052.

Messer, S. and T. Schacht (in press). A cognitive-dynamic theory of reflection-impulsivity. In J. Masling (ed.), *Empirical studies in psychoanalytic theory.* Hillsdale: Earlbaum.

Michaels, S. (1986). Narrative presentations: an oral preparation for literacy for first graders. In J. Cook-Gumperz (ed.), *The social construction of literacy.* Cambridge: Cambridge University Press, 94-116.

Neimark, E. (1985). Moderators of competence: Challenges to the universality of Piagetian theory. In E. Neimark, R. DeLisi and J. Newman (eds.), *Moderators of Competence.* Hillsdale, NJ: Lawrence Earlbaum Associates, 1-14.

Ogbu, J. (1985). The consequences of the American caste system. In U. Neisser (ed.), *The school achievement of minority children.* Hillsdale, NJ: Lawrence Earlbaum Associates, 19-56.

Obgu, J. (1978). *Minority education and caste: The American system in cross cultural perspective.* New York: Academic Press.

Palincsar, A. (1987). *Collaborating and collaborative learning of text comprehension.* Paper presented at the annual conference of the American Educational Research Association. Washington, D.C. April.

Palincsar, A. and A. Brown (1985). Reciprocal teaching: A means to a meaningful end. In Osborn, Wilson, Anderson (eds.), *Reading Education: Foundations for a literate America.* Lexington, MA: Lexington Books.

Palincsar, A. and A. Brown (1984). Reciprocal teaching of comprehension fostering and comprehension monitering activities. *Cognition and Instruction.* 1, (2), 117-175.

Pascual-Leone, J. (1970). A mathematical model for the transition rule in Piaget's developmental stages. *Acta psychologica.* 32, 301-345.

Pellegrino, J. W. and R. Glaser (1982). Analyzing aptitudes for learning: Inductive reasoning. In R. Glaser (ed.), *Advances in instructional psychology.* Vol. 2. Hillsdale, NJ: Lawrence Earlbaum Associates, 269-346.

Piaget, J. (1972). Intellectual Evolution from adolescence to adulthood. *Human development.* 15, 1-12.

Piaget, J. (1969). *The psychology of the child.* New York: Basic Books.

Piaget, J. (1968). *Structuralism.* New York: Harper Colphan.

Plomin, R. (1986). *Development, genetics and psychology.* Hillsdale, NJ: Lawrence Earlbaum Associates.

Richards, D. and R. Siegler (1981). Very young children's acquisition of systematic problem-solving strategies. *Child development,* 52, 1318-1321.

Rogoff, B. (1981). Schooling and the development of cognitive skills. In Triandis and Heron (eds.), *Handbook of cross cultural psychology. Developmental psychology.* Vol. 4. Boston: Allyn and Bacon. 233-294.

Savell, J., P. Twohig and D. Rachford (1986). Empirical status of Feuerstein's Instrumental Enrichment. *Review of educational research.* 56, 381-409.

Schoenfeld, A. (1987). What's all the fuss about metacognition. In Schoenfeld (ed.), *Cognitive science and mathematics education.* Hillsdale, NJ:Lawrence Earlbaum, 189-216.

Schoenfeld, A. (1985). *Mathematical problem-solving.* New York: Academic Press.

Scribner, S. and M. Cole (1981). *The psychology of literacy.* Cambridge: Harvard University Press.

Spearman, C. (1923). The nature of "intelligence" and the principles of cognition. London: Macmillan. Sternberg, R. (1986). *Intelligence applied.* New York: Harcourt, Brace, Jovanovich Publishers.

Sternberg, R. (1985). *Beyond I.Q.: A triarchic theory of human intelligence.* Cambridge: Cambridge University Press.

Street, B. (1984). *Literacy in theory and practice.* Cambridge: Cambridge University Press.

Varenne, Hamid-Biglione, R. McDermott and A. Morison (1982). *The acquisition of literacy for learning in working class families.* Final report NIE G-400-79-0046. Teachers College, Columbia University.

Vygotsky, L. (1986). *Thought and language.* Cambridge: MITPress.

Wertsch, J. (1978). Adult-child interactionand the roots of metacognition. *Quarterly Newsletter of the Institute of Comparative Human Cognition.* 1, 15-18.

Weschler, D. (1958). *The measurement and appraisal of adult intelligence.* Baltimore: Williams and Wilkey.

Whimbey, A. and J. Lochhead (1986). *Problem solving and comprehension.* Hillsdale, NJ: Lawrence Earlbaum.

4

Fostering Student Learning and Development through Effective Teaching

Charles S. Claxton

One of the hallmark traits of the effective teacher is the ability to see "good" students as individuals but to see each student as a unique individual. Inspite of that, there is a strong tendency for faculty to view poor students as a monolithic group. In fact developmental education students are as diverse as any other group of learners. If we are serious about designing learning in ways that contribute to the growth of the student, then it is important that we keep this diversity in mind.

That caveat aside, however, there are some generalizations about developmental education students that can be useful to faculty. Several years ago, Cross (1971) analyzed an extensive body of research and described what she called higher education's "new students." The data indicated these students were typically (a) the first ones in their family to attend college, (b) more concrete and passive in their orientation to learning with few skills in abstract thinking, and (c) very pragmatic, with little interest in learning for its own sake.

These descriptors would probably hold today for many developmental education students. But instead of calling them "new students," it may be more useful to think of them as "strangers" in higher education. That is an appropriate term for, even though developmental education is not new, it is safe to say that it has not found a home here and that the environment of the academy is generally not a welcoming one.

Palmer (1986) draws on history and literature to remind us that the stranger who comes to our door is not necessarily someone to be feared or rejected. Rather, strangers are people for whom we should be the gracious host and to whom we should extend the greatest hospitality. For they often are very special people who bring important and unexpected gifts.

Instead of seeing the presence of developmental students on our campuses as leading inexorably to a lowering of standards, it may be more accurate to view them as strangers in the sense that Palmer describes: persons who can bring us important new insights as we work with them.

Many developmental students bring learning orientations to the academy which it is not used to but which are, nevertheless, legitimate. As just one example, their concreteness forces us to design learning activities which are heavily laced with direct experience. But traditional higher education is oriented so much towoard abstraction and cognitive thought that serious observers have concluded that the teaching of all students would be enhanced if we found ways to link concreteness with abstraction (Astin, 1985; Mentkowski, 1988; Meyers, 1986). Thus crafting ways to teach more effectively in developmental education is vital--not only because of the needs of these students but also because it can point the way to more effective teaching in colleges and universities generally.

But an affirming stance alone is not enough. Faculty need to have in hand specific tools for teaching in ways that help developmental education students learn. Fortunately, theorists and researchers are building a base to guide ways of teaching that honor not only the learning orientations which many developmental education students bring but also use the more theoretical approaches of traditional higher education. The purpose of this chapter is to describe some of these helpful streams of thought and fashion them into a rationale that is academically sound and responsive to the needs of developmental students.

The focus of the discussion which follows is not primarily on "teaching technique" because there are substantial limitations to such an approach. As Kegan has phrased it in another context, a "technique can only stop being a technique when it is embodied by a person with a specific set of ideas and hopes which he is himself trying to bring to life through the medium of the 'technique'." (Kegan, 1982, p. 278). It is at this level of "ideas and hopes" which this chapter seeks to function in the belief that only at this core, foundational level of educational inquiry will we find our way to more effective teaching.

KNOWLEDGE AS SOCIAL CONSTRUCTION

In a recent conversation with a friend who teaches developmental writing in a two-year technical college, I asked what she had found that works with her students. Immediately she responded "Collaborative learning." She said that when she skillfully structures small group-work and has it augmented by lecture, reading and other activities, invariably her students learn better.

Her endorsement of collaborative learning is consistent with anecdotal evidence from developmental education faculty throughout the country. It also is consistent with an emerging body of research and commentary growing out of the examination by philosophers, sociologists, linguists and others on what is perhaps the most fundamental question of all: what is knowledge?

Some very helpful work has been done in this area by Bruffee (1984). He notes that the guiding metaphor of knowledge since the time of Descartes is the "mirror nature of reality." The mind has two working elements a mirror and an inner eye. The mirror reflects reality; the inner eye contemplates that reflection.

The resulting model for teaching is quite familiar. As teachers, we contemplate the reflection in the mirror of our mind and share that with students who see it with their own mirror and inner eye. Good teachers present reality as accurately as possible. Good students are those who have the most polished reflection of reality and the most discerning inner eyes to comprehend that reflection.

In contrast, the social construction view proceeds from very different assumptions. Knowledge is created as persons engage in an ongoing conversation. Oakeshott argues that what distinguishes human beings from other animals is that we participate in an unending conversation:

> As civilized human beings, we are the inheritors, neither of an inquiry about ourselves and the world, nor of an accumulating body of information, but of a conversation, begun in the primeval forests and extended and made more articulate in the course of centuries. ...Education, properly speaking, is an initiation into the skill and partnership of this conversation ... (cited in Bruffee, 1982, p. 638)

Bruffee believes that conversation and thought are related. This view assumes not that thought is an essential attribute of the human mind but that it is instead an artifact created by social interaction:

> We can think because we can talk and we think in ways we have learned to talk. To think well as individuals we must learn to think well collectively-that is, we must learn to converse well. The first steps to learning to think better, therefore, are learning to converse better and learning to establish and maintain the sorts of social context, the sorts of community life, that foster the sorts of conversation members of the community value (1984, p. 640).

In developmental education the "sorts of conversation" which faculty want to foster are the ideas and information found in their subject areas that is, writing, mathematics, reading and study skills. The social construction view of knowledge helps us understand that collaborative learning is not so much a technique. Rather, it is at the core of what education is all about for it requires students to participate in "conversation." That is, they must learn to engage in an active way with the material to be learned and learn to think for themselves.

The social construction view of knowledge seems clearly akin to the constructivist view of learning and human development proposed by Perry (1986) and Kegan (1982). This perspective suggests that "we constitute reality, rather than somehow happen upon it." (Kegan, p. 9). Citing Huxley's statement that, "Experience is not what happens to you, it's what you do with what happens to you," Kegan (p. 11) invites us to think in terms of "that most human of 'regions' between an event and a reaction to it-the place where it actually becomes an event for that person" (p. 2).

This perspective is a familiar one to educators through the work of Piaget and others. It makes the point that "that which is given must be taken" (Sayers, 1985, p. 114), that knowledge is not something that the teacher "has" and that he or she is to "give" to the student. Rather, students must be involved in "appropriating" (Meyers, 1986, p. 48) the information for themselves and thereby making it their own. As Blais notes, constructivism "does not say that knowledge is something that the learner ought to construct for and by himself. Rather, it says knowledge is something that the learner must construct for and by himself." (1988, p. 3). He adds, "There is no alternative."

Yet that which is familiar is not necessarily widely practiced. Most of the teaching practices in higher education ignore this constructivist view and rely primarily on conveying information to relatively passive students. Even in elementary and secondary schools, where teachers have been specifically trained in teaching methodology, most of the time is spent with the teacher talking (Goodlad, 1984). While many professionals insist this is not the case, our language gives us away. Faculty members routinely talk about "exposing" students to content and "communicating" to them what they need to know.

Wigginton's admonition pushes us in a different direction when he says a fundamental question should be carved in stone over every school entrance: "Who processes the information ...?" (1985, p. 206). He believes that in too many instances teachers overlook the corollary to that question: "The extent to which the learner processes the information to be acquired is the extent to which it is acquired." (pp. 206-207). Thus the primary task of the teacher is not simply (or even primarily) to convey information. It is instead to design learning situations where students can engage in "conversation," an activity in which they make meaning for themselves of the information and experiences we provide them.

STUDENT LEARNING STYLES

The second stream of research, learning styles, has been a central interest of developmental education faculty for many years. Some of the most important work in this area has been done by Cohen (1969), who in the 1960's studied children and schooling in inner city Pittsburg as part of an investigation into cultural bias in standardized testing. She noted that in earlier research on "cognitive styles," Kagan, Moss and Siegel (1963) had classified learners as either "splitters" (i.e., they see attributes of a particular stimulus as having significance in themselves), or as "lumpers," (i.e., they think such attributes have significance only as seen in their total context).

Cohen observes that achievement in schools requires skills in the analytic, splitter approach to learning and that children "with inadequate development of these skills and those who develop a different cognitive style could be expected not only to be poor achievers early in their school experience but also to grow worse, comparatively, as they move to higher grade levels" (p. 829). This occurs even though the "literature indicates that cognitive styles are independent of native ability" (p. 829). Students who learn in ways other than the dominant, analytical style are seen as deviant and are often labelled as failures.

Cohen notes that an analytic mode of abstracting information is reflected in the total school environment, not just in teaching practices. She observes that schools are somewhat impersonal and outer-centered, students are required to sit for increasingly long periods of time, activities are arranged by strict time allotment schedules and students are asked to concentrate alone on impersonal learning stimuli.

In her own investigation and in her examination of earlier research, Cohen identified another style which she called "relational" and which seems to be similar to the "lumper" category identified by Kagan, Moss and Siegel. A descriptive rather than analytic, mode of abstracting information, it is oriented more to the self and the global characteristics of a stimulus rather than to the parts specific centered orientation used by analytic learners. She concluded that this style was generally correlated with lower income environments where family organization tended to be characterized by "shared functions." Tasks such as leadership, child care and discretionary use of time were periodically performed or shared by all members of the group. In contrast, the analytical mode of abstracting information was associated with middle-income families who were characterized by a more formal organization with tasks being carried out according to status or role.

Cohen's framework of analytical-relational styles bears resemblance to the well-known work of Herman Witkin (1976) on field independence-field dependence. According to this model, learners with the first style generally gravitated to majors such as science and math and performed better on tasks calling for analytical skills. Learners with the second style often preferred fields which called for stronger social skills, such as sales and counseling and performed better on tasks calling for intuitive, interpersonal skills. Persons in the first group tended to judge things independent of context, while those in the second group tended to judge things in their own context.

The majority of students in developmental education programs are white, although a disproportionate number are from minority groups. Therefore a question that hßs been the focus of considerable interest in recent years is whether minority students have learning styles that are different from students of the dominant culture.

In 1987 the New York Board of Regents issued a report entitled, "Increasing High School Completion Rates: A Framework for State and Local Action," which was carried out to help educators address the high dropout rate among African-American and Latino American students in the public schools in the state. Part of the report dealt with learning styles of students from minority groups and reported research which said that many such students had learning styles different from those of white students.

This part of the report engendered intense, sometimes bitter, debate, so much so that the board subsequently established a panel of scholars and practitioners, to examine in greater detail the research on this issue. In the panel's report, Edmund W. Gordon of the Yale University Institution for Social and Policy Studies, observes that the notion that students have different learning styles is generally accepted by educators. But "controversy arises when such stylistic preferences are used to characterize groups of people, especially groups identified along ethnic or cultural lines" (p. 6). This is because "... So much has been directed at developing support for the notion that all people are equal and entitled to equal access and treatment that any focus on possible differences is likely to be interpreted as an argument for inequality."

The panel reviewed papers from leading researchers on learning styles and concluded that the research base to date does not demonstrate "definitive evidence to link learning style with specific cultural, ethnic or sex groups" (p. 6). The panel also found that most of the literature was inconclusive with respect to cultural styles as well.

The panel noted the danger and inappropriateness of using language about the learning styles of some students which is then generalized to entire populations without recognition of the diversity in all groups. But it went on to say that "learning style and behavioral tendency do exist and that students from particular socialization and cultural experiences often possess approaches to knowledge which are highly functional in the indigenous home environment and can be capitalized upon to facilitate performance in academic settings." (p. 3). In effect, the panel was urging educators to think of learning styles information as useful tools in enhancing their efforts at individualizing the learning process. As we adapt instruction to the "typical learning behaviors of learners, whether called learning style, cultural style, behavioral style, or something else, we are honoring one of the best traditions in education and may also succeed in reducing school failure" (p. 8).

Such a perspective is a very helpful one developmental education faculty, since individualization is so important. While it is interesting to ask whether the learning styles of particular groups of students differ from others, the more important question to be discerned from research on learning styles is what information do we have about particular students which can help inform our efforts at enhancing their educational experience?

Further, the research which focuses on the learning styles of minority students invariably points the way not only to more effective education for these learners but for all learners. In the words of Pemberton, "...recognizing the need to teach minority students well ... must also involve teaching white students more effectively" (p. 3).

The research of several writers who are concerned with the learning styles of minority students is extremely useful in this area, among them Hale-Benson, Ramirez, Anderson and Cooper. Hale-Benson (1982) argues that Blacks in this country have a distinct cultural heritage and that learning styles are linked with culture. She believes that as a result of their cultural heritage, Blacks are more relational, affective and intuitive in their orientation to learning, in contrast to white students, who are more cognitive, analytical and rational.

Ramirez (1973) has studied the education of Mexican-American children. He reports research which shows, for example, that Anglo children perform better in competitive situations but Chicano and Mexican-American children do better when members of the family would benefit from their performance (p. 897). Further, he reports that, "While the middle class Anglo is typically encouraged to establish an identity independent of the family, the Chicano from a traditional community is encouraged to always view himself as an integral part of the family. He is reared in an atmosphere which emphasizes the importance of interpersonal relationships. Consequently, he develops greater sensitivity to social cues and to the human environment in general" (p. 902).

Reporting on research carried out by numerous scholars in several disciplines which describes the influence of the African culture, Anderson (1988) notes that Blacks' psychological orientation is more affective than that of Caucasians and that "The most characteristic feature of the African philosophical system is its focus on unity and connection" (p. 5), a clearly different world view than that of Anglo-Europeans.

Cooper (1987) takes a similar position in her discussion of linguistics: "Black language is anchored in an aesthetic and a world view that are different from those of the Western tradition ... (It) reflects a holistic cognitive style and a right-brain hemispheric dominance that is in diametric opposition to the Western ideal of analytic style and left hemispheric dominance" (p. 61).

Matthews (cited in Cooper, p. 62) elaborates: "The Black mind sees a thing as a connected whole, as against the view of the things as a build of isolated particulars ... The wholeness approach is a habit of seeing things whole before they are seen as broken apart. Instead of seeing 10 things as 10 separate units, the Black perspective tends to see 10 things as 10 parts of a single whole ... one wants to envision the ecology rather than the cell because the cell behaves one way outside of the ecology and in a totally different way when put back into the ecology."

One of the problems in the research on learning styles done to date is that there is much ambiguity about the term with substantial overlap between different models. However, Kirby (1979) has made an observation that may begin to help untangle some of the ambiguity in terminology and research focus. She has said that the many different conceptions of style may be "only correlates of a few basic styles [that] fall under splitter and lumper types" (p. 36), a distinction [that] overlaps 'left-brain' and 'right-brain' activity" (p. 4).

Kirby's comment suggests that the various frameworks developed by several different authors (Kagan, Moss and Siegel; Cohen; Witkin; Hale-Benson; Anderson; and Cooper) while not the same, certainly have echoes of each other and may at least have common antecedents. Further, it may be more accurate to call these issues of epistemology, rather than models of learning style. Epistemology is a more inclusive term and points to a deeper level of inquiry, one which may be more helpful in the long run in helping us find more effective ways of teaching.

ALTERNATIVE WAYS OF KNOWING

The research on the learning preferences of minority students has echoes of recent research on women's development and relates to the concerns expressed by the New York panel (more effective individualization of the learning process) and by Pemberton [1988] (improved learning for all students, whether from minority or majority groups). In *Women's Ways of Knowing* (1986) Belenky, Clinchy, Goldberger and Tarule identified two fundamental epistemologies or "ways of knowing." The first epistemology, called *Separate Knowing*, emphasizes *knowledge* (Belenky et al., p. 101). It entails a separation between the object of study and the knower and it is oriented towards impersonal, rational rules by which data or an issue is evaluated.

The second epistemology, *Connected Knowing*, focuses on *understanding* in the sense of the French word connaitre, which implies a personal acquaintance with the thing or person being studied. It "emerges not out a need to conform to the demands of external authorities but out of a need to understand the opinions of other people" (Belinky, et al, 1986, p. 101). It requires the learner to see the other person in his or her own context.

Separate Knowing and **Connected Knowing** are not gender specific. However, the authors say there are probably more men oriented to the former and more women oriented to the latter. The two ways of knowing are akin to the concepts described by Gilligan (1982) and Lyons (1983) who describe two "different conceptions or experiences of the self, ... essentially autonomous (separate from others) or ... essentially in relationship (connected to others)" (op. cit., p. 102).

In **Separate Knowing** truth is sought through impersonal procedures and an objective perspective. Separate knowers adopt methods of making meaning which are impersonal and do so because they understand the critical value of "disinterested reason" (op cit., p. 110).

In **Connected Knowing** "truth emerges through care." (op. cit., p. 102). Connected knowers "develop procedures for gaining access to other people's knowledge. At the heart of these procedures is the capacity for empathy ... (They see the other person) not in their own terms but in the other's terms." (op. cit., p.113). This way of knowing assumes that "the most trustworthy knowledge comes from personal experience rather than the pronouncements of authorities" (op. cit., pp. 112-113).

Belenky and others suggest that education could be enhanced significantly for all students if faculty helped learners develop skills in both Separate and Connected Knowing. Teachers should "try to discern the truth inside the students." However, it is essential that the search be disinterested." (op. cit., p. 223). "Teaching can be simultaneously objective and personal. There is no inherent contradiction, so long as objectivity is not defined as self-extrication" (op. cit., p. 224).

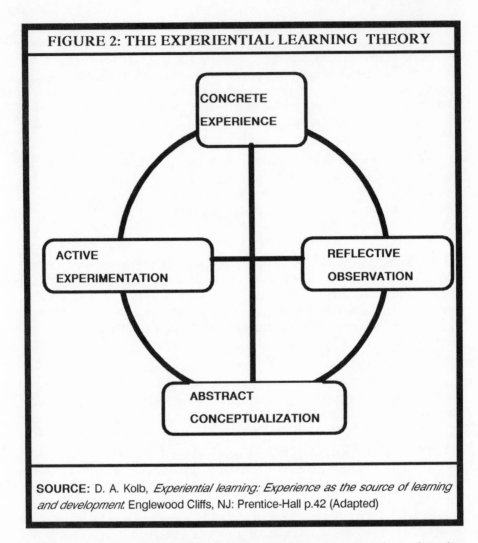

FIGURE 2: THE EXPERIENTIAL LEARNING THEORY

CONCRETE EXPERIENCE

ACTIVE EXPERIMENTATION

REFLECTIVE OBSERVATION

ABSTRACT CONCEPTUALIZATION

SOURCE: D. A. Kolb, *Experiential learning: Experience as the source of learning and development.* Englewood Cliffs, NJ: Prentice-Hall p.42 (Adapted)

As we can see from the foregoing discussion of research on learning styles of minority students and on women's development, there seem to be two dominant ways of knowing: one more analytical, objective and cognitive, the other more relational, subjective and affective. Yet schools and colleges are clearly oriented to the first, thereby working to the detriment of students who are more oriented to the second.

Further, the issue of epistemology is not inconsequential. Palmer (1987) argues that how one knows becomes a way of being. He believes that "objectivism" separates the knower from that which is to be known and, in effect, separates the knower from the world. When we do not employ other ways of knowing that serve as a counterweight to objectivism, we foster qualities of separateness. As a result, our students are never "invited to intersect their autobiographies with the life story of the world." (p.22).

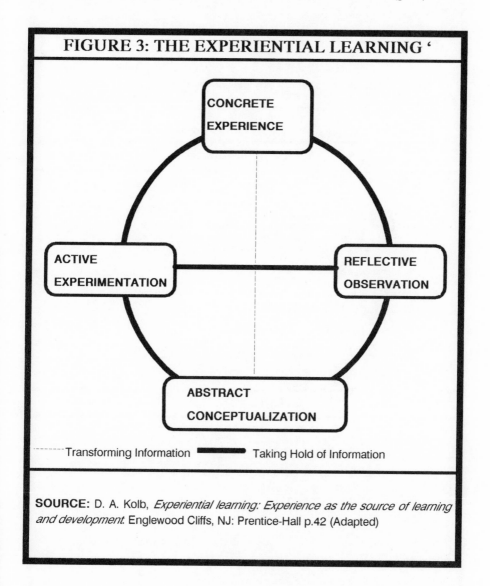

FIGURE 3: THE EXPERIENTIAL LEARNING '

CONCRETE EXPERIENCE

ACTIVE EXPERIMENTATION

REFLECTIVE OBSERVATION

ABSTRACT CONCEPTUALIZATION

-------- Transforming Information ▬▬▬▬ Taking Hold of Information

SOURCE: D. A. Kolb, *Experiential learning: Experience as the source of learning and development.* Englewood Cliffs, NJ: Prentice-Hall p.42 (Adapted)

Table 2: LEARNING STYLES

Divergers

Prefer concrete experience and reflective observation

Greatest strength is in imaginative ability

Able to see situations from many perspectives

Intersted in people; tend to be emotional

Broad cultural interests; often specialize in the arts, humanities

Feeling oriented, high awareness of meaning and value

Often work in counseling, personnel management, organization development

Assimilators

Primarily use abstract conceptualization and reflective observation

Greatest strength is in ability to create theoretical models

Excel in inductive reasoning and integrating disparate observations

Concerned with abstract concepts, not with practical use of theories

Place great value on soundness and precision of theory

Where plan does not fie "fact," is likely to disregard them and keep working with plan or theory or re-examine the facts

Characteristic of persons in basic sciences and mathematics

Less focused on people and more concerned with ideas

Frequently work in research and planning

Convergers

Primarily use abstract conceptualization and concrete experience

Greatest strength is in practical application of ideas

Perform best at tests with single correct answer or solutin to a problem

Relatively unemotional, like to deal with things

Often have strong technical interests

Frequently work in the physical sciences, engineering, nursing and computer science

Good at problem solving and decisioin-making

Good at deductive reasoning

Prefer dealing with technical problems rather thansocial issues

Table 2: LEARNING STYLES

[CONTINUED]

Accommodators

Primarily use concrete experience and active experimentation

Greatest strength is in doing things, carying out plans

Action-oriented

Tend to be risk takers

In situations where the theory or plan does not fit the "facts," will likely discard the plan and try another approach

Tend to solve problems in intuitive trial and error manner

Rely on other people for information, not on own analytic ability

At ease with people, but under pressure are sometimes seen as impatient or "pushy"

Frequently work in business, marketing, sales

Adapted from D. A. Kolb (1984). *Experiential learning: Experience as the source of learning and development.* Englewood Cliffs, New Jersey: Prentice Hall.

TEACHING MODELS

These streams of inquiry kowledge as social construction, learning styles and alternative epistemologies) lead to several conclusions useful in practical applications in developmental education:

- knowledge is primarily a social artifact and thus "learning as conversation" should be the guiding metaphor for the design of developmental education courses;

- learning activities should be heavily collaborative and designed in so that students are able to make meaning of their experience for themselves;

FIGURE 4: THE EXPERIENTIAL LEARNING THEORY OF GROWTH AND DEVELOPMENT

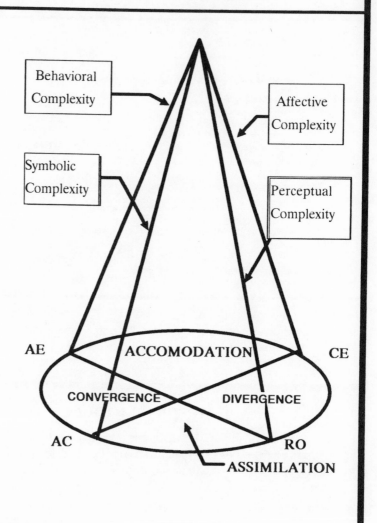

Table 3: TEACHING STRATEGIES FOR KOLB'S EXPERIENTIAL LEARNING CYCLE

Concrete Experience

Activities which involve the learner in the experience either physically or emotionally. Hands-on, uses the senses, engages the learner affectively. May have to be vicarious experience. "Here and now" data.

Field Experience	Interviews	Simulation/Case Study/ Games
Role Play	Debates	
Guest Speakers	Films	Observations
Demonstrations	Fantasizing	Modeling
Slide Presentations		Recalling past experience

Reflective Observations

Activities which require the learner to step back and look at experience, get perspectives of others, make connections to other experiences.

Structured Small Group Discussions	Reflective papers
Journals	Copying class notes
Asking learners how they felt about a lesson	
Asking learners to make connections to other learning	
Asking learners to discuss class sessions with other people	

Abstract Conceptualalization

Information from autoritative sources. Use of symbols. Using research and methods of the discipline to develop hypotheses and principles. "There and then" data.

Print	Programmed instruction	Computer assisted instruction
Lectures	Films	

Active Experimentation

Opportunities for the learners to try out principles or theories in problem solving.

Application; Internship/field placement; Individual and group projects; Laboratory

Independent study

- the almost exclusive reliance on analytic, parts-specific, cognitive practices and values of schools and colleges is inappropriate and places a particularly heavy burden on developmental education students, many of whom have orientations to learning that are more relational, holistic, concrete and affective; and,

- neither of these two ways of knowing is adequate when used alone.

Thus ways need to be found which honor both epistemologies and use them in tandem.

There are two teaching models which seem particularly useful for developmental educators: the Connected Teaching model developed by Belenky and others as well as the experiential learning model developed by Kolb (1984). They both call for an integration of the two alternative ways of knowing discussed here, are heavily collaborative and interactive in nature and can be used flexibly so that teachers can tilt them more to concreteness and affect or to abstraction and cognition, depending on the needs of a particular group of students and the demands of particular content.

The Connected Teaching Model

This model of teaching contrasts sharply with traditional teaching in postsecondary education but reflects well the kind of student centered teaching that often goes on in effective developmental education classes. Further, it seems to be responsive to the concerns mentioned by Hale-Benson, Ramirez, Anderson and Cooper, particularly in regard to building in activities which tap affective, intuitive ways of knowing.

The model has five important characteristics. *First, its central metaphor is "teacher as midwife," rather than "teacher as banker"* (p. 217). According to the authors, "Midwife-teachers are the opposite of banker-teachers. While the bankers deposit knowledge in the learner's head, the midwives draw it out. They assist the students in giving birth to their own ideas, in making their own tacit knowledge explicit and elaborating it" (ibid.). Such a perspective is extremely important for many developmental education students whose main problem may not be so much that they do not possess certain cognitive skills but that they do not have the self-confidence needed to learn the skills that are required. Creating learning situations in which the students draw on what they already know as a vehicle for learning new skills and concepts is critical if students are to develop the confidence they need to be successful in college.

Second, the emphasis in Connected Teaching is on problem posings rather than on imparting knowledge. While traditional teaching practices focus almost exclusively on disseminating information, usually through lecture or print, in *Connected Teaching* learners are engaged in working on problems of direct relevance in their lives. An intuitive insight that many experienced developmental teachers report is that if they involve students quickly in working on such issues, the energy and motivation engendered pave the way to success in the classroom.

Third, the emphasis is on dialogue rather than one-way communication. The model suggests that knowledge is not so much located in the mind of an individual (the teacher), waiting to be communicated to the students. Rather, knowledge "is an emergent feature of the social interaction among people" (Whipple, 1987, p. 5). In developmental education classes students often find support by working in small groups, thus encouraging them to ask the teacher about points they do not understand or to receive affirmation from fellow students in areas that they have grasped. This more interactive orientation to learning is thus not only more helpful to many students but is also one strongly supported in the rapidly developing professional literature on knowledge as social construction and collaborative learning.

Fourth, "disciplined subjectivity" replaces traditional teaching's heavy emphasis on objectivity. In traditional teaching the major focus is the discipline and the specialized body of knowledge it has developed. Here students are encouraged to consider the materials through the eyes of the teacher (Belenky, Clinchy, Goldberger and Tarule, 1986, p. 224). In Connected Teaching there is objectivity, but here it "means seeing the other, the student, in the student's own terms." (op. cit., p. 224). It is the clear linking of *Separate Knowing* and *Connected Knowing* that is needed to meet both the cognitive and affective needs of developmental education students. Such a stance does not mean that tests are any less rigorous or that exit standards are lowered. It simply suggests that helping students develop the expected competencies comes about through seeing them in their own context and helping them identify and use the abilities, often nascent, which they bring to the classroom learning situations.

Fifth, the environment fosters a sense of collaboration and community, rather than one of competition and individualism. Many developmental education students come from schools where they have typically done poorly in terms of grades and success and therefore they are in particular need of learning environments which are highly supportive. Since learning is seen as a process of collaboration and discussion among students and teacher, the emphasis moves from having students compete with each other for grades or teacher approbation to encourageing them to help each other learn what they need to know.

An example from Pirig (1974) suggests how *Connected Teaching* can function in a typical classroom. He was discouraged with the passivity of students in his freshman English class as he tried to teach them the rules of composition. One day instead of lecturing he gave them a collection of essays written by students in earlier semesters, some of which were quite good, some of which were very poor.

He told them, "Read each essay and judge it as 'good' or 'poor'." After the students completed the task, the professor responded by saying that their judgements were essentially those he himself had made. He then began to ask students to explain why they considered certain essays as good and others as poor. Their responses included such comments as, "This one was clear and I understood what the person was trying to say;" and, "This one seemed to have a beginning, a middle and an ending."

He then helped them see that the reasons they gave were essentially the principles he wished to share with them from the discipline of composition. He helped them sharpen and formalize somewhat their understanding of the principles. Most of all, he helped them see that good writing was not so foreign to them. They knew more than they had realized.

This small example highlights (1) the importance of drawing on the students' personal experiences in the learning process, (2) the wisdom of the teacher working to help students "birth" their emerging and sometimes nascent understandings and (3) the collaborative and dialogic nature of the search for understanding. All of these aspects reflect the notion of *Connected Teaching*.

The *Connected Teaching* model is highly congruent with the social construction view of knowledge discussed earlier. It capitalizes on the experience learners bring to the learning event and it creates a place for both the "hard" aspects of lecture, abstractions and principles (Separate Knowing) and the "soft" traits of intuition and relationship (Connected Knowing), both essential aspects of collaborative learning. Through the creative tension caused by the employment of both epistemologies, learners have opportunities not only to master content but also to enhance their skills in analysis and problem solving.

The model's clear call for dialogue is not to discount the value of lecture and other methods of teaching in which information is conveyed. It simply places them in a different perspective, one which says that learning activities must be structured so as to allow students to discuss and work with the information they have received. The emphasis shifts from "the teacher conveying" to "the student constructing knowledge." Teaching methods which encourage dialogue between teacher and student and student and student are thus essential.

The experiential learning model

The second of the two models of teaching has been developed by David

Kolb (1984). It not only gives a comprehensive view of how effective learning occurs but also links learning to development of the person. Further, developmental education faculty who use it are able to move easily from the theory to selecting specific teaching methods to employ in the classroom.

Kolb's experiential learning theory suggests that effective learning requires an integration of cognitive and affective activities and is thus consistent with the implied need of the *Connected Teaching* model to integrate analytic and relational ways of knowing. Kolb began his work not by asking what are people's different learning styles but, rather, how does learning occur? In answering that question, he suggests it is a four-step process (see Figure 2). Learners have an immediate *concrete experience*, involving themselves fully in the experience and then reflecting on it from different perspectives. After these *reflective observations* ("what was that like?" "have I ever had an experience like that before?"), they engage in *abstract conceptualization.* Here they develop larger generalizations or principles that help them integrate their observations into sound theories or conceptual frameworks.

Finally, learners use these generalizations as guides to further action, or *active experimentation* and apply what they have learned in new, more complex situations. Erik Erikson once said that "truth is found in action," and this part of the Kolb cycle is a higher order task, where theory and practice come together. Learners then have another concrete experience and the cycle begins again, but this time the learner operates at a more complex level. Thus, the experiential learning cycle is a circle, but it is best thought of as a helix, as learners move to increasing levels of complexity in their learning and in their development as persons.

Another way to look at the cycle is to distinguish between what Kolb saw as the two dimensions of learning: *prehending*, or grasping information or experience and then processing (or, more accurately, *transforming*) it (Figure 3). The grasping dimension of learning (the vertical line) is made up of two adaptive modes (i.e., ways of adapting to the world) that are dialectical in nature: concrete experience, in which learners grasp the experience through direct contact and abstract conceptualization, in which learners grasp the experience through conceptual interpretation and symbolic representation.

Similarly, the transformational dimension (the horizontal line) is made up of two dialectical adaptive modes: reflective observation, in which learners transform the information through internal reflection and active experimentation, in which they transform the information by testing it in action.

To determine people's learning preferences, or styles, Kolb developed the Learning Style Inventory (1976 and 1985) which can be used to help people identify their learning style. The four styles envisioned in the model are described in Table 2. Essentially they make the distinction between four ways of thinking: divergence (where experience or information is prehended through concrete experience and transformed through reflective observation) is concerned with the integration and synthesis of knowledge; assimilation (abstract conceptualization and reflective observation) involves the analysis of information to derive larger principles; convergence (abstract conceptualization and active experimentation) is concerned with determining how to apply knowledge; and accommodation (concrete experience and active experimentation) involves putting knowledge into practice in our day-to-day lives.

The relationship among the learning styles and human development is most clearly seen in the "cone" (see Figure 4), a visual representation of the relationship between the four modes of the experiential learning cycle and adult development. Here the four modes reflect fundamental aspects of the self: affect (concrete experience); perception (reflective observation); symbolism (abstract conceptualization); and action (active experimentation). We develop greater sophistication and differentiation in each of the four parts of the self as e have experience in each mode of the cycle and develop greater skill and sophistication in each. We thus are increasingly able to move away from simplistic, dualistic thinking and have greater comfort with the ambiguities, polarities and conflicts that are part of mature adulthood.

There are at least two ways the Kolb model can be used by developmental education teachers. First, the teacher may wish to administer to students the Kolb Learning Style Inventory (or other similar inventories, some of which have a vocabulary which is more appropriate for poorly prepared students). This may be done either in class or in orientation or study skills courses. In this way the students are helped to understand something of how learning occurs and that people learn differently. But, more importantly, they can see that they bring particular skills to the learning event.

This is important since what many developmental education students most need is something very basic: to begin to realize that they have competence. The successful teacher will help them to identify their competence, which is probably bound up with their preferred style of learning. Finding out what we do well and then engaging in learning experiences which are both reflective of those strengths and sensitive to our areas of weaknesses are critical ingredients in being successful.

The most successful learning experiences are those in which learners engage with the information to be learned in each of the four modes of the experiential learning cyle: concrete experience, reflective observation, abstract conceptualization and active experimentation. Thus another way developmental educators can use the model is to design learning activities in which they systematically involve their students in each of the four modes.

For example, in a traditional math class the teacher might begin by explaining a concept (abstract conceptualization) and working a problem on the board and then having the students work similar problems themselves (active experimentation). That is essentially a convergent approach, helpful to students of that orientation and often unhelpful to others. To engage the students in each of the four modes instead, a teacher could have students try to work several problems in small groups and help each other as they do so (concrete experience); lead a discussion in the groups concerning how they worked the problems, why they believe they are correct and where they had difficulty (reflective observation); a presentation by the teacher in which he or she explains the principles involved and works sample problems on the board (abstract conceptualization); and, finally, having the students work similar problems individually or in groups where they try to apply the principles presented in the lecture (active experimentation).

Using the experiental learning cycle as a guide to the design of learning has been found to be extremely useful by developmental education faculty in various subject areas. Table 3 contains a number of the teaching strategies which can be used in each of the modes.

This example demonstrates how teachers can not only help students master content but also develop critical thinking skills. According to Meyers (1986), the development of critical thinking requires the ability to derive larger principles or abstractions from the specific concrete experience. When the teacher uses the experiential learning cycle as a guide, the learning activity begins with having students work on a problem. Later, the teacher helps them understand larger, abstract principles which are grounded in their experience in working on the problem. In some instances the teacher has to provide those abstractions but over time he or she can help students develop greater skill in deducing the principles for themselves.

Next, our ability to relate larger principles or abstractions to the concrete instance requires continuous transforming of our experience through reflection and action. When the students discuss in small groups the problems they worked on and, later, when they work on problems using the larger principles given to them by the teacher, they are gaining skill in transforming their experience through reflection and action, respectively.

Third, the linkage Kolb makes between the experiential learning cycle and adult development (see the "cone" in Figure 4), suggests that engaging in concrete experience, reflection, abstraction and action enables persons not only to become more competent as students but also to become more whole as persons. Having students systematically engage in all four modes of the cycle is a way of helping them "develop" in the sense that Perry (1981) and others describe.

There is much similarity and overlap between the two teaching models presented here. When a teacher designs learning activities "around the Kolb circle," he or she is involved in "connected teaching." In the example given above, there is a clear emphasis on the teacher as midwife rather than as banker and the learning activities are heavily collaborative. Further, there is a strong reasonance between Separate Knowing and Abstract Conceptualization (symbolism) and between Connected Knowing and Concrete Experience (affect).

It is here we find the insight that developmental education students, the "strangers" in higher education, present to us. Traditional higher education, with its orientation to abstraction and symbolism, fosters partialness because it focuses almost exclusively on an analytical way of knowing. Developmental education, in order to be successful, has to involve students in more active, more affective experiences and build on these to lead students to mastery of principles, logic and abstract thinking. In the words of Hale-Benson, "We should build on the students' natural learning styles so that we may then help them develop strengths in novel ways of learning." (1982, p. 5).

Thus the presence of developmental education students is forcing faculty in colleges and universities to think more deeply about what effective education is. By teaching in ways that help students develop skills in Connected Knowing as well as Separate Knowing, developmental education teachers are fostering not partialness, but wholeness. Such an experience helps students develop not only the qualities of symbolism and detachment but the qualities of affect and relatedness as well.

Hence the experiential learning cycle and the Connected Teaching model are guides for developmental education teachers who wish to design learning in ways that help students master content. More importantly, it enables them to do so in ways that contribute to the student's development as well.

These teaching models are useful, then, in the sense that Perry (1986) talks about teaching. Teaching, he says, is "derivative ... It has no rules of its own but only those that are derived from the process it seeks to serve." (p. 187). That process is development and in our vocation as teachers in developmental education we are privileged to be instrumental in helping our students develop and thereby become more competent adults.

REFERENCES

Anderson, J.A. (1988). Cognitive styles and multicultural populations. *Journal of teacher education*, 39, 2-9.

Astin, A.W. (1985). Involvement: The cornerstone of excellence. *Change*, 35-39.

Belenky, M.F., B. M. Clinchy, N. R. Goldberger and J. M. Tarule (1986). *Women's ways of knowing: The development of self, voice and mind.* New York: Basic Books.

Blais, D. M. (1988). Constructivism: A theoretical revolution in teaching. *Journal of developmental education*, 11, 2-7.

Bruffee, K. S. (1982). Liberal education and the social justification of belief, *College English*, 68, 95 - 114.

Bruffee, K. S. (1984). Collaborative learning and the 'conversation of mankind'. *College English*, 46, 635-652.

Cohen, R. A. (1969). Conceptual styles, culture conflict and nonverbal tests of intelligence. *American anthropologist*, 71, 838-856.

Cooper, G. C. (1987). Right hemispheric dominance, holistic cognitive style and Black language. In J.A. Anderson (Ed.), *The emerging Black scholar.* Indiana, PA.: Benjamin E. Mays Monograph Series, 61-86.

Cross, K.P. 1971. *Beyond the open door.* San Francisco: Jossey-Bass.

Gilligan, C. (1982). *In a different voice.* Cambridge, MA: Harvard University Press.

Goodlad, J. I. (1984). *A place called school: Prospects for the future.* New York: McGraw-Hill.

Gordon, E. W. (n.d.). *New York State Board of Regents' Panel on Learning Styles.*

Hale-Benson, J. (1982). *Black children: Their roots, culture and learning styles.* Baltimore: The Johns Hopkins University Press.

Kagan, J., H. A. Moss and I. E. Siegel (1963). Psychological significance of styles conceptualization. In *Basic cognitive process in children.* Society for Research in Child Development monograph 86. Chicago: University of Chicago Press.

Kegan, R. (1982). *The evolving self: Problem and process in human development.* Cambridge, MA: Harvard University Press.

Kirby, P. (1979). *Cognitive style, learning style and transfer skill acquisition.* Information Series No. 195. Columbus: Ohio State University, National

Center for Research in Vocational Education.

Kolb, D.A. (1976). *Learning style inventory.* Boston: McBer and Co.

Kolb, D.A. (1985). *Learning style inventory.* Boston: McBer and Co.

Kolb, D.A. (1984). *Experiential learning: Experience as the source of learning and development.* New York: Prentice-Hall.

Lyons, N.P. (1983). Two perspectives: On self, relationships and morality. *Harvard educational review,* 53, 1-10.

Mentkowski, M. (1988). Paths to integrity: Educating for personal and professional performance. In S. Srivastva and Associates, *Executive integrity: The search for high human values in organizational life.* San Francisco: Jossey-Bass, 89-121.

Meyers, C. (1986). *Teaching students to think critically: A guide for faculty in all disciplines.* San Francisco: Jossey-Bass. Palmer, P.J. (1985). The company of strangers. New York: Cross.

Palmer, P. J. (1987). Community, conflict and ways of knowing: Ways to deeper our educational agenda. *Change,* 19, 20, 22, 24-25.

Perry, W. G. (1981). Cognitive and ethical development: The making of meaning. In A.W. Chickering (ed.), *The modern American college.* San Francisco: Jossey-Bass.

Perry, W. G. (1986). Review of The Experience of Learning [edited by Ference Marton, Dai Hounsell and Noel Entwistle]. *Harvard educational review,* 56, 187-94.

Pemberton, G. (1988). *On teaching the minority student: Problems and strategies.* Brunswick, MA.: Bowdoin College.

Ramirez, M. (1973). Cognitive styles and cultural democracy in education. *Social science quarterly,* 53, 895-904.

Sayers, S. (1985). *Reality and reason: Dialectic and the theory of knowledge.* New York: Basil Blackwell.

Whipple, W. R. (1987). Collaborative learning: Recognizing it when we see it. *AAHE Bulletin,* 3-7.

Wigginton, E. (1985). *Sometimes a shining moment: The Foxfire experience.* Garden City, NY: Anchor Press, Doubleday.

Witkin, H. A. (1976). Cognitive style in academic performance and in teacher-student relations. In S. Messick (Ed.), *Individuality in learning.* San Francisco, California: Jossey-Bass.

5

Program and Course
Design Guidelines

Robert M. Hashway

The Advanced Concepts Learning Center was born in 1983 as an advanced educational technology center. Its purpose was to bring the best of what we know about learning to meet the training needs of industry and the general public. To justify its existence we needed to immediately come to grips with the problem of delivering training with consistent quality in a number of different locations and to the broadest possible client base. It was to this objective that this course design scenario was developed.

A Microware program of studies is a set of specific activities designed to maximize the knowledge and skills acquired in a minimum amount of time. Each program is a managed instructional sequence where intended for delivery by different individuals at different locations with the same high degree of quality and all elements of the learning experience are controlled. The Microware plan insures each trainee a highly productive experience. Each Microware training course is part of a sequence of courses called a Microware learning program and a part of the Microware training system. The Microware Family Of Educational Systems is a dynamic and growing set of systems designed to meet educational, industrial, business and personal needs with the highest quality of instruction.

To produce a Microware program, a rigid production format is followed. That format defines the characteristics of each part of the learning process. What a trainee sees, hears, is to think and work with is defined in terms of training outcomes. How the trainee spends his/her time and will be evaluated, the outcome of each learning activity is defined and the level of acceptable performance is defined. A Microware program is developed in terms of a system which specifies the learning complete experience, insuring total system compatiblity.

A course or program designed in the Microware mold is compatible with other courses or programs in the Microware family, can be managed regardless of the number of trainers presenting the material and designed to insure learner productivity. There are two goals of this chapter. After studying the material, the experienced curriculum designer can format courses in the Microware style. The instructional design manager will then be able to determine whether a course is compatible with the Microware family of instructional services. Each System in the Microware family, each program in a System, and each aspect of a program must conform to a general structure. The details of that structure is described in terms of three components: the Microware philosophy, system structure and program structure. Each area will be described in a separate section.

PHILOSOPHY AND DEVELOPMENT PROCESS

Training has different meanings to different people. No two educators can agree on a definition of training or the training process. The Microware family of training systems is a dynamic training program designed to grow with the needs of the society. To insure continuity between programs in a system and systems in the family, it is necessary to define an educational philosophy. Microware's educational philosophy is defined in this section. Programmatic details which result from the implimentation of this philosophy are described in the remaining sections.

The Microware philosophy incorporates an overall view of the training process and starts by defining the role of the trainee as an internalizor of events in his/her environment, interpreting events which occur in the environment and integrates those events into a world view. That world view determines how the trainee will interpret and react to events yet to occur in the environment. How the trainee reacts to new environmental events is the outcome of the training.

The training environment is defined in terms of three types of environmental events.

1. **Auditory Events**: What is heard from the instructor, media and/or other trainees.

2. **Visual Events**: What is seen in manuals and other course materials.

3. **Activities**: What is experienced from individual and group laboratory experiences.

The outcomes of training are defined in terms of three event classes: Cognitive, Affective and Psychomotor. *Cognitive outcomes* are the set of all rules which must be applied and the processes required to determine which rules are required in particular situations. *Affective outcomes* are the attitudes required for ordered creative thinking, problem solving, teamwork and leadership. *Psychomotor outcomes* are the skills required to properly operate equipment and respond to software or process cues. The environment and outcome events are precisely defined in any Microware course.

Training Outcomes

There are two types of cognitive outcomes: rules and processes. Consider any event, a trainee is 'trained' when he/she exhibits a particular response to that event. A *rule* is the association of a particular event with a particular accepted response. The set of all rules (stimulus-response pairs) defined for a particular course is the *KNOWLEDGE BASE* of the course. In most practical situations, knowledge is not enough. The ability to determine which rules apply to a different situation is required. A *process* is the skill of determining which class of rules apply to a particular problem situation. The set of all processes compose the *APPLICATION BASE* of a course. Cognitive outcomes are defined in terms of two sets of skills: the knowledge base and the application base.

Microware courses are not only concerned with skill training. In the work place, depending upon the role of the worker, each worker is called upon to perform creative and analytical tasks as well as working in a team and exercising a leadership role. Each of those skills require that the worker have certain attitudes toward work and working which constitute the affective experience.

Microware defines affective experiences in terms of three classes: structured creativity, ordered thinking and team building.

Young people often start their careers 'trying to set the world on fire,' believing that they will be able to develop new ideas or products which no one ever thought of before. As they become experienced, they realize that progress occurs in small steps and most new ideas are either reorganizations of existing knowledge or an extension of what is known. . Microware defines the process of extending knowledge in small steps and the process of reorganizing knowledge as *Structured Creativity.* Each program contains structured creativity outcomes.

Solutions to problems often require an orderly process where parameters are identified, characteristics of the solution defined, knowledge about the parameters and the solution identified. This information organized into a solution process. The process of solving problems and defining procedures in this way is called *Ordered Thinking* requiring an orderly attitude toward work and problem solving and included as a part of the expected outcomes.

Problems are often so complex that individuals with different skills, talents and temperments are required. Individuals often play different roles in a work team. At certain times a person may be a team member. At other times he/she may be called upon to be a team leader. Microware programs define teamwork and leadership skills as expected outcomes.

The information revolution is extending the definition of operation beyond switch fliping. An operator needs to be able to respond to prompts and call up certain prompts as needed dependent upon the situation and software package used (i.e., process control procedures, word processors, spreadsheets, etc.). The ability to react to 'bells and whistles' and to call upon prompts on demand form the *Psychomotor* outcomes. Microware programs include all of the necessary psychomotor outcomes.

The first step in the design of a Microware course/program is to define the outcomes. Those outcomes are organized in terms of three classes. The class of *Cognitive Outcomes* are classified in terms of a *Knowledge Base* and a *Process Base.* Knowledge is composed of rules. Processes are the abilities to identify which rules apply to particular situations. The class of *Affective Outcomes* consist of *structured creativity, ordered thinking, teamwork* and *leadership* attitudes. *Psychomotor Outcomes* are the abilities required to operate machinary and software in a situation adaptive fashion. Each Microware program includes cognitive, affective and psychomotor outcomes.

Environmental Activities

Once the outcomes are defined, it is necessary to identify the experiences which will lead the trainee toward achieving those outcomes. The environment is defined in terms of three classes of events: auditory, visual and activities. The *auditory,* and *visual* events are trainer delivered and assume that the trainee is a passive participant in the process. The trainee hears and observes what the trainer says and displays. The trainee assimilates the trainer delivered information. *Activities* are individual and group exercises where the trainee interacts with machinery, other individuals and problem solving situations to elaborate and integrate the knowledge and process base, develop psychomotor skills as well as affective attributes.

The auditory environment is defined in terms of trainer presentations and taped lectures. Each of these presentations modes are designed so that they are uniform from trainer to trainer.

The visual environment is controlled in terms of standard Microware prepared slides and manuals.

The activities environment is composed of two types of exercises: individual and team. The individual exercises are designed to develop psychomotor and cognitive outcomes. The team exercises are designed to realize affective outcomes. Each aspect of the environment and each facet of each aspect is keyed to specific training outcomes. Each are designed with the basic Microware philosophy in mind: **for each outcome an activity and for each activity an outcome.**

Time Allocation

Microware programs are designed to be delivered in segments over a period of time. Trainees experience individual and group interaction. The time between training sessions gives the trainee the opportunity to review

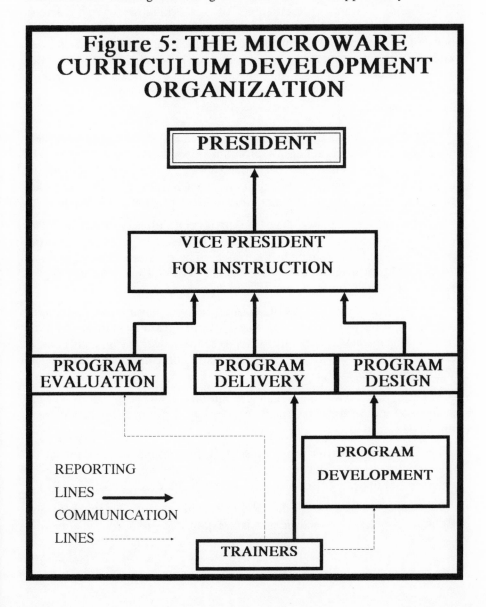

Figure 5: THE MICROWARE CURRICULUM DEVELOPMENT ORGANIZATION

materials and 'think about' or 'digest' what has been experienced.

Because training is provided in short time blocks, it is provided in small segments. The small segments make learning comfortable. However, the Microware program designer must pay attention to time on task. The proper allocation of time to activities is very important. If too much time is provided, non-goal directed behavior results. If enough time is not allocated, proper information transfer does not occur.

In general, each Microware training session should be segmented into three partitions: formal activities, experiential activities and synthesis. Trainer and/or trainee presentations of new cognitive or psychomotor activities are delivered in the **formal activities** time partition. Hands-on, team building and problem-solving activities are presented in the **experiential activities** time partition. The sessions' activities are integrated with past knowledge and activities in the last or, **synthesis** time partition. Each time partition must be present in each training session.

Staff Roles

We have discussed the role of the trainee. However, the development and delivery of a comprehensive program depends on many people. The Microware organization is partitioned into three areas: corporate, development and delivery. The function of each area and the individuals involved in the training development and delivery process are defined below.

At the delivery end we have the **program delivery manager**. This person is responsible for the scheduling of courses, material and facilities coordination, and the training or the trainer. The program delivery manager is responsible for insuring that programs are provided with the high degree of quality that Microware demands.

The **program development manager** is responsible for defining a program in terms of expected outcomes. The **program development staff** report to this manager. The staff role is to refine outcome statements and to develop activities which will achieve those outcomes as well as all student/trainer materials.

The program development manager interacts with the program delivery manager to insure that programs are practical from the standpoint of training deliverability.

The **program evaluation manager** is responsible for developing all evaluation protocols. This manager will evaluate all materials, delivery processes and the extent to which outcomes are achieved.

All managers report to the **Vice President for Training** at the corporate level. This individual is responsible for coordinating all development and delivery activities. This person reports to the corporate **President**. The president is directly responsible for fiscal services, advertising and physical plant operations.

The point of training delivery is the most important point in the process. At that point we have four elements: trainee, materials, activities and the trainer. The roles of the trainee, materials and activities have been previously defined. What remains is to define the role of the trainer.

The role of the trainer is somewhat different from the classical educational model. Classically, the trainer develops, delivers, evaluates and refines training. Microware believes that this is the best way to provide instruction and in the specialization of tasks and roles in people who have task specific expertise. Development and evaluation is performed by specialists in those fields. Therefore, the trainer role needs to be defined in terms of delivery skills. The trainer is the manager of the instructional process. He/she manages the process by which trainees interact with their environment. He/she must be knowledgeable with the materials and methods so that he/she can modify and match experiences as the needs demand.

More importantly, the trainer must have a high degree of interpersonal interaction skills. The Microware philosophy is that the trainer and the trainees form a part of the Microware team. The mission of that team is to share the Microware experience and achieve the desired outcomes. The trainer is the team leader.

An accepted training philosophy does not exist in the education literature. To develop a system which grows with society' needs, the program development and delivery process must be well defined. Otherwise, program compatiblity will not be achieved. The Microware development and delivery process has been designed to insure quality program delivery and program compatiblity with the Microware family of training systems. In general, that philosophy is:

- for each activity there is a well defined training outcome that is to be achieved;

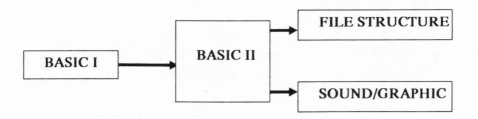

- for each training outcome there is an activity by which the outcome will be achieved;
- for each training outcome there is a way to evaluate attainment;
- for each activity there is a way to evaluate effectiveness;
- for each task in the development/delivery process there is an individual with primary responsibility;
- for each individual there is a well defined role and reporting responsibility; and,
- items 1 to 6 interact dynamically for program revision and growth.

The purpose of this chapter is to describe the guidelines for the program developer and a means by which the development manager can determine whether or not a program is compatible with other training Programs. To accomplish that, four elements are necessary: a philosophy, a development process, a program and a course structure. The philosophy and development process have been described above. The program structure will be described in the next section.

THE STRUCTURE OF TRAINING

The Microware family of educational programs consists of many individual programs. Each program is designed to be 'relocatible.' Each program and each course in each program can be presented by many trainers at many different sites. The key to the transportability of courses and programs is their design. Each program is designed to conform to a specific and well defined structure. The purpose of this section is to describe the structure of a program and a course.

The Microware Program

A Microware program is a set of courses designed to achieve a particular training goal. That goal may be somewhat general. In the case of a general programatic goal, the program will, most likely, contain many courses. The programatic goal may be specific and correspond to only a few courses.

The first program design element is the name of the program followed by a statement of the goal. The goal statement incorporates a beginning phrase, "The trainee will". It is followed by a list of general training goals. i.e., **PROGRAM 22: BASIC COMPUTER PROGRAMMING**. The trainee will learn the elements of a computer and how to operate them; the elements of a good computer program; the BASIC command set and how to build a program using it; basic problem-solving skills; and how to work in a problem-solving team. The program statement should be sufficiently specific as to be directly related to each course description.

The second element of a program definition is a set of specific program goals. For example,

> 1.0.0 The trainee will operate the main computer and peripherals.
> 1.1.0 The trainee will know how to use input, screen output, arithmetic, printer output, for-next, goto, gosub and data-read commands in a BASIC program.

Each course within a program may address one or more program goals. To reinforce prior learning, a single program goal may be addressed by more than one course goal.

Program Outcome Matrix: There is a need to establish which courses address which goals. To do this, each goal is organized in terms of the outcome categories of Cognitive, Affective and Psychomotor. These categories have been previously described. The association between courses and outcomes are contained in the Program Outcome Matrix. That is a matrix where the program outcomes are listed horizontally and the course numbers are listed vertically. If a particular outcome is to be derived from a particular course, an X appears in the corresponding row and column.

Program Sequencing Matrix: In addition to defining the outcomes for the courses, it is necessary to define the sequencing of courses. Certain courses may be required before others. Other courses may not be required before certain others. The sequencing is defined in terms of the program sequencing matrix. The program sequencing matrix is a matrix with course titles forming the horizontal and vertical axes. If the second course is prerequisite to the third course, an X appears in the second row and third column. If a course is not prerequisite to another course, the corresponding row and column is left blank.

Consider the previous prerequisite relationship between courses in a BASIC programming program.

The program sequencing matrix for this program is:

	BASIC I	BASIC II	FILE STRUCTURES	SOUND/GRAPHICS
BASIC I		X	X	X
BASIC II			X	X

In this case, BASIC I is an entry level course. FILE STRUCTURES and SOUND & GRAPHICS are **terminal program courses**. BASIC II is called an **intermediary course**.

Many organizational sequences are possible. There may be many entry level, intermediary and terminal courses in a particular program. The sequencing of a program is generally related to the complexity of the expected outcomes. The more complex the course, the more elaborated the structure.

Programs are defined in terms of four structures: definitions, goals and outcome/sequencing matrices. The definition of a program is a general statement of outcomes. The **goals** are more specific statements of outcomes and are directly related to specific courses via the **program outcome matrix**. The final element of a program is the **program sequencing matrix**. The program sequencing matrix indicates the prerequisite relationships between courses in a program. The sequencing results in a trilevel ordering of courses: entry, intermediate and terminal.

The Course Development Document

Each course is considered a self-contained unit of instruction. The course is designed to train a trainee in a particular set of skills. The structure of a course consists of training modules, behavior expectations, training resources, evaluation scenarios, trainer materials and trainee materials. Course development starts by preparing the course development document. From the course development document all training materials evolve. The purpose of **The Course Development Document** is to specify the structure of a course. The document defines the outcomes to be derived from each module, the resources to be used to achieve each expected outcome and how those outcomes are to be evaluated.

ELEMENTS OF A STIMULUS DEFINITION

- **STIMULUS** A phrase which defines the physical characteristics of the stimulus.
- **OBJECT** i .e. memo, letter, agenda, etc.. A phrase which further specifies the content of the stimulus.
- **STIMULUS** i.e. vocabulary, length, affective character
- **QUALIFIER** such as assertive, docile, etc..

Training Modules: A course is a sequence of activities designed to achieve a set of program goals. Those goals are defined in the Program

Outcome Matrix. In the same way that a program is composed of courses which are designed to address a limited number of program outcomes, a course is composed of training modules. A training module is designed to achieve a limited goal.

Course Goal Statement: The first element of the Course Development Document is a list of the program goals addressed by the course. That list is the set of all program goals which are to be addressed by the training activities. That list derives directly from the Program Outcome Matrix.

Module Outcome Matrix: A course is composed of finer units of training called modules. Each module is designed to address a limited number of program goals. To assure that each module is well defined and that the program goals are achieved by the course, it is necessary to prepare a matrix which identifies which program goals are associated with each training module. The module outcome matrix, the second element of the Course Development Document, is a matrix with program goals listed horizontally and module names listed vertically. If an X appears in a particular row and column, the corresponding goal will be addressed by the appropriate training module. Otherwise, it will not. A training module may address more than one program goal. To reinforce learning, a program goal may be addressed by more than one training module.

Module Documentation

The third element of the Course Development Document is the Module Documentation. That element specifically defines each training module. The Course Development Document contains a separate section for each module in the course. The documentation of a training module is the most important part of the Course Development Document. It is most often the most difficult and time consuming part to prepare.

The Expectation Scenario

Each training module is designed to address one or more program goals. Each goal is a broad statement of an outcome. A training goal is not achieved by some mystical process. It is achieved through a process of acquiring specific well-defined skills using a well-defined training experience. The purpose of the expectation scenario is to document those small steps, how they will be achieved and how evaluation will be performed. Each program goal associated with a training module is also tied to a number of expectation scenarios. Each of those scenarios define a small step by which the training outcome will be achieved. **The module documentation is a statement of each associated program goal followed by expectation scenarios**.

Structure of an expectation scenario. The purpose of an expectation scenario is to define each step by which a program goal will be achieved. Each scenario consists of a precise behavioral statement of the training outcome as well as the methods and techniques that will be used to provide the training and evaluate the extent to which the training has been successful.

Performance Objectives. In the training literature a training outcome is called a performance objective. *The outcomes of a training experience must reflect an observable behavior change.* Programs, modules and outcomes are designed to have some impact on the lives of the trainees, therefore, performance objectives must be stated in behavioral terms. A performance objective is defined as: **the specification of the expected impact of a program goal on the lives of trainees in precise behavioral terms**.

Humans do not arbitrarily exhibit particular behavior patterns. Behaviors manifest themselves as a response to particular stimulii such as directives and the psychological environment in effect when the stimulus is encountered. Practical human response is never merely good or bad. Humans are proficient in the execution of any task or the manifestation of any particular behavior to some extent. The specification of a performance objective must take the human condition in to account.

There are four components to a performance specification: **environment, stimulus, expectation** and **performance level**. The environment is the physical and psychological state in effect when the desired behavior is expected to be manifest. The stimulus is the behavioral catalyst to which the desired behavior is a reaction. The expectation is a statement of the desired behavior. The performance level is the expected level of proficiency that trainees are expected to manifest. Performance objectives which specify behaviors to be manifested at any time in the work day, for example, usually do not need environmental components. Examples of statements not requiring an environment statement are:

- Given a directive to prepare an agenda for a staff planning meeting, an administrative assistant will prepare a well structured agenda in 90 percent of all instances.
- Given a letter containing common vocabulary and no more than 100 words, a secretary will always prepare error-free copy in five minutes or less.

Performance objective 2 is a poor objective. The time required to prepare an error-free copy depends upon the work environment. Two elements need to be added to objective 2 in order to insure that it is realistic. The statement "under distraction-free conditions" can be added to the objective. However, in most cases the environment is not controllable. Therefore, to strictly specify "distraction-free conditions" is not realistic. The time line (performance component) can be adjusted to account for environmental conditions by extending the time to 30 minutes or one hour. If the program is intended to train secretaries in environmental management techniques, the statement "under normal office conditions" should be inserted.

The stimulus definition of objective 2 is: "Given a letter containing common vocabulary and no more than 100 words." That definition contains tow basic elements: "Given a letter" and "containing common vocabulary with no more than 100 words." The first element is a **stimulus object**. The second element is a **stimulus qualifier**. Good stimulus definitions contain both object and condition or qualifier phrases.

The four elements of a performance statement fit within a common structure or format: "*Given [stimulus object, stimulus qualifier] the trainee will [expectation] at a level of [performance level] when [conditions].*" When the format is understood by all parties involved in the program design process, a clear perception of program expectations will result. Additionally, the basis for the selection of performance indicators, evaluation of materials, methods and procedures are both clear and commonly understood.

For example, consider the following performance objective.

Given a large report (over 50 pages) which requires many editing cycles, the office manager will always direct his/her employees to use the word processor in all instances.

In this case, the stimulus object is "a large report" and the qualifiers are that the report is over 50 pages in length and requires many editing cycles. The expectation is that the manager will direct clerical hires to use the word processor. The performance level is "always" or 100% of the instances of the occurrence of the stimulus. The condition statement has been omitted. The assumption being that the stimulus-condition reaction will occur under all circumstances.

Consider the following objective.

Given a time of fiscal constraint, where many layoffs are contemplated, the manager will implement procedures which reduce anxiety by 50 percent.

In this case the stimulus is "a time of fiscal constraint" qualified by "many layoffs are contemplated." This is an instance of when the stimulus and condition are one and the same. The expectation is that the manager will implement anxiety reduction techniques. It is anticipated that the techniques will be 50% effective (the performance level).

Training Process Section: Each performance objective documents some small behavior change which will lead to the achievement of the program goal. The next step in the expectation scenario is to define the experiences which will lead to the actualization of that behavior change. The process may involve a small lecture, some reading material, a visual or audio tape, a controlled group or individual problem solving task, working with a particular machine or some combination of all of these. Whatever the training process, it must be well defined. This section will often consist of a large amount of text which define how each performance expectation will be achieved (the training experience).

Evaluation Section: This is the last part of the **expectation scenario**. It contains precise directions as to how the evaluation of trainee performance will be assessed. If controlled exercises or tests are to be used, examples of the exercises or test questions are presented. If a product is to result from an activity, the evaluation check list is included. The checklist includes a statement of what is expected and one or more examples of appropriate and inappropriate behaviors. Many outcomes in the affective category do not yield themselves to clearly definable product, in most cases concern attitudes which are reflected in trainee behavior and a checklist or other type of observational protocol is provided with instructions in terms of how the checklist or protocol will be used. The checklist, protocol and instructions are included in **The Expectation Scenario.**

Course Evaluation

The elements of the **Program Development Document** and **The Course Development Document** have been described. Those documents are the plan by which training materials are developed. Those training materials are intended for the trainee or the trainer. The general nature of the materials provided the trainer and the trainee remain to be outlined. Those materials will be described below.

The Trainer Package

The trainer package consists of six types of materials:

- Trainer Manual
- Slides
- Audio Tapes
- Hardware & Manuals
- Activities Manual
- Software & Manuals

Software, hardware and their respective manuals are generally manufacturer prepared. Each piece of hardware and software, however, are part of the training process. They are associated with an outcome through some training activity or activities defined in the Course Documentation Document. Their relation to course content is also defined in the trainer and trainee manuals.

Trainer Manual: The trainer manual is a comprehensive guide to the course. It contains the definitions of each goal, training models and objective. The trainer is provided with detailed instructions concerning what he/she is expected to do and what the trainees are expected to do to achieve each expectation. The evaluation protocols are located directly following each training expectation. In general, this manual is the **primary reference by which the trainer directs the course**. It is also **the primary training document for training the trainer**. It is the main source of criteria for the performance evaluation of the trainer.

Activities Manual: The trainer is provided with an Activities Manual. This can be a document distinct from the Trainer Manual, or a section of that manual. It describes in detail the problem sets, group/individual projects, assignments and activity evaluation instruments for a course. Each problem set, project and/or assignment is specifically associated with a training expectation. That expectation as defined in the Course Documentation Document is printed next to the activity in this manual. Instructions concerning how each activity is to be used and deviations which are allowable are described.

Audio and Visual Material: Each slide or audio tape is keyed to a particular training expectation. Tapes and slides describe single concepts. They are developed to introduce, enhance or elaborate training. Their structure and purpose are described in the Course Documentation Document. The purpose and procedures for using each audio visual device is described in the Trainer Manual.

The Trainee Package

The trainee is presented with three types of materials: Trainee Manual, Activities Manual and necessary hardware/software. The hardware and software complement the training program and are provided by the trainer.

Trainee Manual: The trainee manual contains the course expectations contained in the Course Documentation Document. Along with each expectation, the necessary written material and instructions by which the trainee will acquire the desired behavior is presented.

Trainee Activity Manual: This manual contains all of the exercises the trainee will be asked to participate. Each activity is associated with an expectation contained in the Course Documentation Document. Prior to each activity, the trainee is advised of the purpose of the activity (expectation) and how performance will be evaluated. This manual may be a separate document or contained in the Trainee Manual.

SUMMARY

Microware training programs are designed to fit into a mold which provides a consistent program of training for all trainees regardless of who the trainer is or where the training is taking place. The purpose of this chapter is to describe the format by which Microware programs are designed and developed. All Microware courses and programs contain, as a minimum, the elements described. Courses that do not contain these elements are not Microware products. They do not insure consistency and a high quality of training. Four topics have been addressed: the Microware training philosophy, training development process, program structure and course structure.

The philosophy incorporates an overall view of the training process. The training philosophy starts by defining the role of the trainee as an internalizor of events in his/her environment and integrates those events into a world view. That world view determines how the trainee will interpret and react to events yet to occur in the environment. How the trainee reacts to new environmental events is the outcome of training.

The training environment is defined in terms of three types of environmental events: auditory and visual events as well as activities. The outcomes of training are defined in terms of three event classes: cognitive, affective and psychomotor. Cognitive outcomes are the set of all rules which must be applied and the processes required to determine which rules are required in particular situations. Affective outcomes are the attitudes required to become a creative and systematic problem solver, a team member as well as a team leader. Psychomotor outcomes are the skills required to properly operate equipment and respond to software or process cues. The environment and outcome events are precisely defined in a Microware course.

The role of the trainer is somewhat different from the classical educational model where the trainer attends to all aspects of the course development, delivery and evaluation processes. Microware believes that this is the best way to provide training. Microware believes in the specialization of tasks and roles in people who have task specific expertise.

The trainer role is defined as a facilitator in the instructional delivery process and the manager of the instructional process. He/she manages the process by which trainees interact with their environment. He/she must be knowledgeable with the materials and methods as so that he/she can modify and match experiences as needs demand. The trainer must have a high degree of interpersonal interaction skills. The Microware philosophy is that the trainer and the trainees form a part of the Microware team. The mission of that team is to share the Microware experience and achieve the desired learning outcomes. The trainer is the team leader.

A development process was defined. That process involves individuals with particular administrative, evaluative, development and delivery roles to insure quality assurance at each step.

Each Microware program is structured in terms of outcomes and courses. A program is typified by a course - program structure matrix. That matrix indicates the particular goals addressed by each course. The structure of each course is defined by the Course Documentation Document which defines the outcomes to be derived from each training module, the resources to be used to achieve each expected outcome and how those outcomes are to be evaluated. Finally, the structure of the trainer and trainee materials are developed. Those materials and their development follow directly from the information contained in the Course Documentation Document. In general, each aspect of training definition, documentation and delivery reflect the general Microware philosophy: **for each outcome an activity and for each activity an outcome with a means of evaluating performance at each step in the process.**

6

The Learning Center from 1829 to the Year 2000 and Beyond

L. Scott Lissner

The primary focus of this chapter is the description of the next evolutionary stage in learning centers. Through a brief historical review and survey of current practices the role learning centers have to play in higher education will be discussed. Based on this role a conceptual model for the development of learning centers will be presented.

The conceptual model describes learning centers as proactive, integrated with the curriculum and sensitive to student needs. The next evolutionary phase for learning centers will create programs that assist students in maximizing their academic performance and learning efficiency, assist institutions in maintaining and improving academic standards, provide faculty with the opportunity for curriculum development, research on learning and instructional methodology. The model itself is a compromise between the concrete and the abstract. The current level of abstraction should provide the flexibility needed to apply it to a wide range of institutional contexts. References to aspects of existing programs should provide the concrete detail necessary for the model to be meaningful and practical.

The body of this chapter can be divided into three sections. The first section will define the role and goals of learning centers based on their history and current practices. The second section will use these goals to build the components of the conceptual model. This model will then be placed within the institutional context. The third section will establish a hierarchy for the delivery of services within each component. Before beginning the chapter, it is important to establish the perspective from which it was written. The four following assumptions were made in the historical review, the survey of current practices and the building of the conceptual model. In a broader sense, these four assumptions represent the common thread that runs throughout the history of learning assistance programs and binds the incredible diversity of professionals and programs in developmental education.

First this chapter uses a definition of developmental education rooted in the definition of development. According to *Webster's Ninth New Collegiate Dictionary*, Development can be defined as the process of working out the possibilities, making resources available, moving from an original position to one providing more opportunity or a gradual unfolding (Mish, 1987). Developmental education in this context, is an educational process aimed at moving the student towards the above goals. This definition of developmental education is the ideal definition for all education. While common usage has made developmental nearly synonymous with remedial, it is truly a move back to the traditional emphasis of education. It is only during this past century that the pace and delivery of education have been standardized for group presentation.

A second underlying perspective to this chapter is a holistic view. This view extends to both individual and program development. Individual development cannot be examined or encouraged from any one dimension in isolation. For the individual, intellectual growth is inexorably bound to social and emotional growth. The holistic perspective views people in their environmental context, but remains essentially person centered. Programs do not exist in isolation either. The structure and direction of a program must be integrated into the institution if it is to be effective.

The third influence on this chapter is the perspective that the essence of an educational institution is best defined by its curriculum, while the forms and methods used within an institution are best derived from the needs of its students. Developmental education in general and learning centers in particular, must be fully connected to the institution's curriculum and to the diverse needs of its students. The final perspective that shaped this chapter is that development is uneven in nearly all individuals. The best students have their weak areas and the weakest students have their strengths. To effectively aid in the development of all students, programs must have the flexibility to address a wide range of individual circumstances. This assumption relates to the need for developmental services at the best schools in two ways. The first is obvious: all students can benefit from a process that builds on their strengths and strengthens their weaknesses. On the other hand, the higher the caliber of the average student, the higher the academic standards and challenges should be. This means there will always some portion of students who are on the margin of success; such students at any level can benefit from services. A case in point is Harvard's Bureau of Study Council, established over forty years ago.

LEARNING CENTERS: PAST AND PRESENT

Learning centers originated as one of a long series of responses to two trends: the perception that entering students are less prepared for collegiate work than the previous generation and the increasing accessibility to higher education. Space constraints do not allow a detailed history here; a brief synopsis will be presented (with an emphasis on the past 20 years). Those interested in a more detailed history are referred to *Improving Student Learning Skills* by Martha Maxwell and *Bridging The Academic Preparation Gap: An Historical View* by Ellen Brier. Ellen Brier (1984) traces the presence of underprepared students on American college campuses back to at least 1828 when the "Yale Report" called for an end to the acceptance of students with defective preparation. In 1852 Henry P. Tappan was inaugurated as President of the University of Michigan. In his inaugural address he stated that American colleges were too involved in teaching rudimentary courses that belonged in secondary or even primary schools (Maxwell, 1979). These statements could have been included in any number of recent reports on higher education. These and later, calls for increased standards were countered by an expanding national philosophy of educational egalitarianism. This movement was largely responsible for the Morrill Acts of 1862 and 1890 which created land grant colleges. These colleges made higher education a financial reality for a large proportion of the population for the first time (Cremin, 1982).

With the increased number and diversity of students participating in higher education, institutions began to address student needs in more structured ways. One response was the emergence of the modern degree format; with its prescribed major and core course (Cremin, 1982). Other responses tended to target the "new non-traditional" students. In 1849 the University of Wisconsin established a "preparatory department" and in 1869 Cornell University admitted students on condition. Conditions included tutoring and special class sessions (Brier, 1984). In 1874 Harvard instituted a writing course (now called freshman English) to address the faculty dissatisfaction with the writing skills of entering students (Maxwell, 1979).

The level of concern over the academic preparation provided by high schools, combined with the establishment of institutionally generated entrance examinations increased during the late nineteenth century. Tutoring schools were another response to these concerns. Tutoring schools were private enterprises that offered tutoring in college courses, preparation for college entrance examinations and tutoring in college preparatory subjects. These schools were the Princeton Reviews and Stanley Kaplans of their day (Brier, 1984). This period culminated in the creation of the College Entrance Examination Board in 1890. The Board was an attempt to make college admissions requirements uniform (Maxwell, 1979).

The nineteenth century is the pre-history of learning centers. However, during this period a foundation was laid for individual tutoring (a mainstay of todays learning centers), identification of entry level skills and supplemental instruction. The basic goals of these services were to assist students in mastering the curriculum. Entry standards were established and exceptions promptly made. The primary role of these various programs was to compensate for the exceptions in admissions standards. Primarily this role was fulfilled through services tailored to the individual.

By 1915, 350 colleges reported having college preparatory departments. In 1936 New York University's Reading Laboratory was established and the following year Harvard and the University of Minnesota began remedial reading courses (Maxwell, 1979). Harvard's course (Reading and Study Skills), is still in existence today (after many transformations). This course formed the seed for Harvard's Bureau of Study Council formally established by combining several support programs in 1947.

World War II had two major impacts on the development of learning centers. During the war, colleges reduced the amount of time required to complete degrees by shortening courses and adding intensive summer sessions. This was done to increase the pool of college educated officers. Study skills programs were created in order to assist servicemen in completing these accelerated courses. Frank Robinson's SQ3R system of text reading was one result of these efforts (Maxwell, 1979). With programs such as SQ3R, not only were services being developed to address students' needs in the face of a demanding curriculum, but the services were directed toward students from both strong and weak preparatory background. Additionally, services began to both build on existing research and contribute to the learning theory literature.

After World War II, the G.I. Bill sent millions of former servicemen to college. Government funding established veterans' programs to assist them. These programs included counseling services, reading and study skills programs, tutoring services, among others. This funding allowed these programs to become established and to prove their worth. As the pool of veterans declined over the years, many of these programs were institutionalized and made available to all students (Maxwell, 1979).

These programs were developmental in nature, but were not remedial nor were they focused on "high risk" students. They also addressed the adjustment to college (an obvious necessity for returning veterans) and included a counseling dimension. This added new and important dimensions to the foundations of future learning centers. A more holistic approach, a wider population to be served and an emphasis on integrating services into the curriculum (in place of segmented programs) were three of the most important new dimensions.

A final contribution of this period was an increased emphasis on research and student outcomes. As the pool of veterans and the funds supporting them declined programs faced increasing competition for government and institutional funding. This competition encouraged the tracking of student outcomes, research into effective delivery systems and teaching methods, among other things. The demand to justify the existence of such programs has ebbed and flowed but is still present. The positive impact of these demands is increasingly coherent, well-researched programs.

The decrease in funding and a concomitant decrease in focus on underprepared students peaked in the 1950s. The spirit of the times was moved by Sputnik. Funding and efforts focused on math and science. Programs tended to focus on the upper 10 percent of the students (Maxwell, 1979). While there was a decrease in efforts (or at least funding) for underprepared students, there was much research on teaching methodology, curriculum design and instructional delivery. Supplemental and enrichment programs were established, self-paced and discovery learning systems were experimented with and research on study skills was undertaken (Woolfolk, 1987). The focus of the 1950s brought a broader range of professionals to the field and provided an incubation period for existing programs. Learning assistance programs emerged from the 1950s with a more cohesive and overt philosophy. The basic tenets of this philosophy were diagnosis, individualization, integration, developmental (as opposed to compensatory or remedial) and a student-centered (as opposed to content centered) approach. These tenants supported a goal of services tailored to individual needs and focused on assisting all students in achieving maximum learning efficiency (Enright, 1975). During the 1960s open admissions policies were established. These policies were the Morrill Acts of this century. Once again there was a sudden increase in both the number and diversity of students participating in higher education. With this influx of the new "non-traditional" student came an increase in available funds and a growth in developmental and remedial programs.

Some of this growth was in existing programs. These programs tended to focus on tutoring, study skills and students who were not fully isolated from the college curriculum. Newly conceived programs tended to establish a layer of remedial courses, more isolated programs (of the preparatory department type seen in the 1800s) and the use of tutoring and study skills as a supplement and a bridge to the curriculum (Decker, Jody and Brings, 1976). The results of the initial efforts at basic skills remediation was found wanting in a number of ways and programs with a more holistic approach began to spring up (Enright, 1975)

One response was the rebirth of "How to Study" courses for freshmen. These courses were expanded to include a heavy counseling component. This counseling orientation tended to focus on three primary areas: the general adjustment to the institution's social environment, self-management and academic achievement motivation and career development and academic planning (Decker, Jody and Brings, 1976).

Another direction taken was to increase individualization. This took a number of forms including programmed instruction, mastery learning and peer tutoring. These new approaches, the increasing availability of sophisticated technology and the increased funding combined to form a branching point in the development of learning centers. One direction was the center that used technology as its prime delivery system. The other branch utilized paraprofessionals as a prime delivery system (Enright, 1975).

Another product for this period resulted from staff shortages. There were not many learning assistance professionals available in the 1960s. Gwyn Enright commented in 1975 that 57 percent of the learning centers in the country were begun since 1970 (although many components of their programs are considerably older) and that a learning assistance center director is considered a mature practitioner after only four years (Enright, 1975). This necessitated the recruitment of and interaction with the full college faculty at a much higher level than previously. This interaction laid the foundations for the learning center as a faculty consultant. This trend was augmented by the advent of self-paced instruction. Learning centers had the technology and the expertise to use it. Faculty had courses, materials and a desire to experiment with this very attractive new technology.

The late 1960s and early 1970s brought tremendous growth to developmental education. This growth was reflected in the size, increasing number and diversity of programs. One aspect of this growth was the **learning center movement**. The title learning center became popular. At many institutions previously separate support programs (tutorial, self-paced learning labs, study skills courses, etc.) combined into learning centers. The concepts, philosophies and methods from the history of learning assistance were melded into a formal concept of the learning center (Enright, 1975).

This process was aided by a repetition of many of the factors that influenced the post World War II period. The influx of funding that followed the open admissions movement began to dry up. Programs were again in a position where they had to justify their existence. Many of the new programs were institutionalized and made available to the entire student population as grant funding decreased.

Initially, attempts were made to categorize support services. In 1970 four categories were proposed: (1) Instructional Materials Center, (2) Reading

Laboratory, (3) Study Skills Center and (4) Audio-Tutorial Center (Enright, 1975). In 1975 a new classification schema was proposed. This system included Library/Non-Print Centers, Reading and Writing Laboratories and Learning Centers (Enright, 1975). The use of such classification systems was an effort to deal with the diversity of center names, origins and functions which had developed in partial or total isolation in reaction to local crisis situations (Enright, 1975).

Throughout this period, conference papers and presentations on learning assistance centers, their methods, technology and philosophies began to appear. In 1978, Long Island University began the annual National Conference on College Learning Centers.

Learning centers emerged from this period with a formal concept as a coherent set of services organized into an integrated center and aimed at assisting all students in achieving maximum efficiency in learning (Christ, 1977). The common philosophical framework for learning centers was seen as holistic, student centered and developmental (in the original intent of the term). Professionals involved in the movement considered their role as providing support and feedback to the learning process within their institution through the provision of services to students, faculty and staff. Enright characterized learning centers as combining the principles of humanism and the potential of technology, as embodying most of the educational philosophies theorized since 1900 while working actively towards futuristic education (Enright, 1975).

By 1980, learning centers were being described as the most frequently employed campus wide system of assisting students in their academic success. Assistance that may have the underprepared freshman as a particular goal but is aimed at the full spectrum of students and the institutions core curriculum (Beal, 1980; Newton, 1983; Baker and Pointer, 1983).

In 1984 the conservative estimate of the number of learning centers in the United States reached 1,400 (Collins, 1984). These programs were described as being at the crucial crossroads of the new emphasis on student development and the traditional focus on cognitive development. They were further described as being in a unique position from which to maintain and improve academic standards in the face of the demographic outlook for college enrollment (Collins, 1984).

In 1986, the Council for the Advancement of Standards for Student Services/Development Programs [CAS] released its preliminary Standards and Guidelines for Learning Assistance Programs. These standards were revised in 1987. While these standards can apply to any developmental education program, they are particularly appropriate to the learning center

SERVICES	FOUR YEAR — PUBLIC (N=101)	FOUR YEAR — PRIVATE (N=144)	TWO YEAR — PUBLIC (N=144)	TWO YEAR — PRIVATE (N=36)
INDIVIDUAL CONTENT TUTORING	98	97	96	100
GROUP CONTENT TUTORING	71	82	66	41
INDIVIDUAL STUDY SKILLS TRAINING	88	87	79	61
	63	68	59	33
GROUP STUDY SKILLS TRAINING	27	21	34	19
INDIVIDUAL ASSESSMENT TESTING	24	20	30	14
GROUP ASSESSMENT TESTING	23	17	27	25
DEVELOPMENTAL/REMEDIAL COURSES	21	18	34	28
SELF PACED INSTRUCTION	18	11	21	19
ACADEMIC ADVISEMENT	55	69	47	28
ACADEMIC/PERSONAL COUNSELING	63	66	59	72
	19	24	12	11
SERVICES FOR LEARNING DISABLED	38	30	41	22
FACULTY/STAFF DEVELOPMENT	19	9	25	8
	8	3	12	0
FACULTY/STAFFCONSULTATION				

TABLE 4: SERVICES OFFERED BY INSTITUTION TYPE[1]

[1.] Expressed in percents of institution type.

organization.

These standards set the common mission of learning assistance programs as providing instruction and services that, "A) Support students in the development of skills necessary for their effective performance in and positive adjustment to the learning environment and B) support faculty and staff in the improvement of classroom teaching and other instructional activities." (Council for the Advancement of Standards, 1987). This mission is clearly related to the goals that have evolved for learning centers. The CAS standards provide five sub-goals to accomplish this mission:

- Provide remedial and other programs designed to teach skills which maximize the learning potential, academic performance and adjustment of students.
- Provide services in a context that promotes the transfer of skills to the required curriculum.

TABLE 5: MEAN FIRST YEAR ATTRITION RATES BY INSTITUTION TYPE [1,2]

FOUR YEAR				TWO YEAR			
PUBLIC		PRIVATE		PUBLIC		PRIVATE	
SAMPLE	NATIONAL	SAMPLE	NATIONAL	SAMPLE	NATIONAL	SAMPLE	NATIONAL
(N=98)	(N=513)	(N=132)	(N=1,248)	(N=104)	(N=539)	(N=22)	(N=225)
24.9%	29.5%	18.7%	21.8%	43.3%	47.8%	26.7%	28.9%

[1.] Based on survey responses, figures for the 1987 - 1988 academic year.

[2.] Based on the annual institutional survey performed by the American College Testing Program, figures for the 1986 - 1987 academic year.

TABLE 6: OPERATIONAL BUDGET BY INSTITUTION TYPE
(*In Dollars Per Year*)

	FOUR YEAR		TWO YEAR	
	PUBLIC	PRIVATE	PUBLIC	PRIVATE
	(N=84)	(N=123)	(N=126)	(N=29)
MEAN	63,372	23,979	83,129	15,653
MEDIAN	59,500	21,800	52,000	16,500
RANGE	200-250,000	500-198,000	2,000-950,000	500-45,000
MEAN ANNUAL DOLLARS/	11.74	21.82	27.34	28.60

1. Operational budgets exclude salary and wages.

2. Calculated as a weighted mean based on each institutions enrollment and budget.

- Provide faculty with services and resources for improving teaching and supplementing classroom instruction.
- Provide for individualized and self-paced programs.
- Provide services within a framework that develops positive attitudes and confidence about their learning ability in students.

The standard go on to list four critical assumptions that should be made in developing services to accomplish these goals:

- Learners are the central focus of programs and services.
- Learners include all students as well as faculty and staff.
- Learning assistance programs should assist their parent institutions in maintaining standards of academic excellence.
- Learning assistance programs should be based on a holistic philosophy that considers the influences of the cognitive, affective and psychomotor domains.

The above set of assumptions and goals comprise an almost complete picture of the mission of the model learning center. The missing components are repeatedly implied by the standards but never receive overt attention. These two missing components belong respectively to the mission and assumptions for learning centers.

The mission statement of a learning center should include the provision of services that are fully integrated with the mission, curriculum and programs of the parent institution. A learning center that operates in isolation from the curriculum and the faculty of its institution will at best become a service for dealing with students who have been (at least temporarily) rejected or ejected from the mainstream of the institution. Such conditions foster negative stereotypes, lowered self-esteem and movement towards the bottom of the institution's priorities for staffing, funding and space.

The assumptions underlying the ideal learning center should include the perspective that learning takes place within an environmental context. Services and programs should be designed with an awareness of this environment and its impact on the holistic development of students.

In a national survey of college learning assistance programs, 66 percent of responding institutions reported that they were aware of the CAS standards. Of those reporting awareness, 42 percent were using the standards for program evaluation, 38 percent were using them for program planning, 11 percent were using them to build their professional image on campus and 9 percent did not specify how the standards were being used (Lissner, 1989a). The above numbers indicate a reasonably wide spread acceptance of the CAS standards. They also indicate that programs and professionals are less isolated than in the recent past.

Another result from the same survey provides a picture of the services offered by today's learning center. As you can see from Table 4. learning centers offer a range of services including tutoring, counseling, remediation, self-paced courses as well as faculty development and curriculum development (Lissner, 1989).

Tables 5 and 6 give some indication of the resources devoted towards today's learning centers and their impact. It is not being suggested that learning centers are the only relevant variable. Sample institutions from the national survey of learning centers have significantly lower first year attritioin rates than the general population (Lissner, 1989b). Table 6 indicates the operational funding of learning centers. The average institution with a learning center spends $22.38 per student per year for services; calculations for this figure excluded professional salaries and wages (Lissner, 1989a). When the retention and expenditure information are viewed as a whole, a picture of a high-impact, cost-efficient service-delivery system emerges.

THE LEARNING CENTER CONCEIVED

The history of learning centers as a delivery system for academic support provides the working parameters for the conceptual model. These parameters must reflect a holistic-learner centered philosophy in the provision of services across the spectrum of individual students, groups of students, faculty and staff. While these services are developed with the earner's needs, abilities and perspectives in mind; they must also account for the goals and demands of the curriculum. The role or mission set by these parameters is to provide support and feed-back to the learning process. This mission has two superordinate goals. The goals are assisting students in becoming confident independent learners and in maximizing their learning efficiency.

The first goal of assisting students in becoming independent learners extends to all students. While learning centers may have as a special priority the underprepared student their services are typically part of a broad program of assistance available to the full spectrum of students (Collins, 1984). The second goal of maximizing learning efficiency serves, in part, to reinforce the focus on all students. Everyone has areas in which they are less efficient and could benefit from learning new approaches. Our best students tend to overcommit themselves, suffer unnecessary stress and too often fail to meet their own (overly high) expectations.

The parameters also call for the recognition that each learner is unique, that individualized services are the ideal and the paradoxical reality that

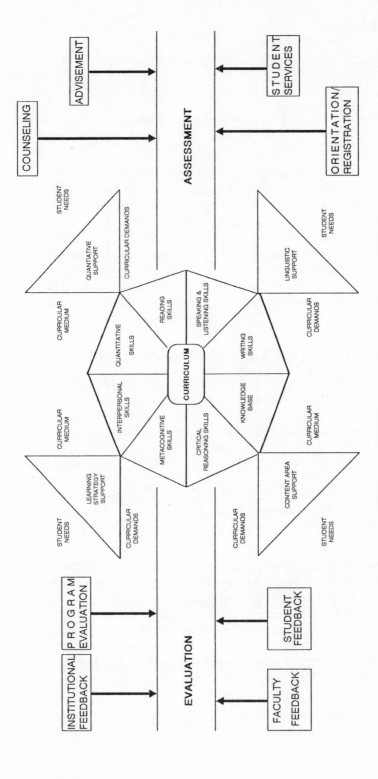

Figure 6: **AN INTEGRATED PROGRAM MODEL**

group interventions are a pragmatic necessity. The solution to this paradox is that individualized services do not require individual services. With the use of assessments, services can be developed that meet common needs. The conceptual model must provide for both learning center assessment procedures and a connection to campus-wide assessments.

The mission and philosophy of learning centers make them uniquely suited to addressing the issues raised in the recent reform movement in higher education. Since the publication of *A Nation At Risk* in 1983 there have been overriding trends in the efforts to reform higher education. One emphasis has been on basic skills (National Commission on Excellence in Education, 1983; Collins, 1984). Bridging the gap between pre-college preparation and the demands of the college curriculum is one of the traditional roles of learning centers. This role serves to maintain institutional standards in an educational system that supports full and equal access. In both current and previous times the definition of "underprepared" has varied with the institution's internal standards. It is certain that students participating in Harvard's Reading and Study Skills course would not be defined as underprepared at Bunker Hill Community College across the river. Programs focusing on these goals must be sensitive to the institution's standards both in the present and as they change over time. The second emphasis of today's reform movement is "critical thinking" or "analytical reasoning". I put these terms in quotation marks because there are almost as many definitions for these term as there are authors discussing them. What is being called for in the reform movement is a movement away from the accumulation of knowledge in student's memories and toward an emphasis on the application of knowledge in a problem solving context. Given the rapid pace of change in modern society, the reform movement considers reasoning skill the "fourth R" of basic skills and the ability to integrate new and constantly changing information (independent learning skills) as an important goal of higher education (National Commission on Excellence in Education, 1983; Collins, 1984). The ability of learning centers to individualize instruction, to provide for extensive modeling and to be integrated with the curriculum as supplemental services seems custom tailored to addressing this issue.

The elements for the model learning center developed below are an extrapolation of the history and current practices of learning centers. There is no single learning center that possess all of its characteristics at this time. Despite a long history, learning centers as organized professional services are relatively young. The average learning center today is only a little over 13 years old (Lissner, 1989a). However, examples of each element in the model will be drawn from the pool of today's centers. After the model is described, a hierarchy of services levels will be explored. The final discussion will focus on the staffing and implementation of a comprehensive learning center.

The model is presented diagrammatically in Figure 6. Before exploring the specific elements of the model, examine its over all configuration and flow. Central to the institution is its curriculum. The curriculum is composed of the disciplinary knowledge bases and seven primary skills. The four supporting triangles represent areas of interaction between the curriculum and learning centers. Each area is addresses a set of curricular demands, based on student needs and using elements of the curriculum as a medium within which to teach the targeted skills.

The flow of the diagram can be read from two perspectives: the student's and the institution's. First, from an institutional perspective, input from student assessments, academic advisors, counseling and student services as well as freshmen orientation/general registration provide the needs analysis necessary for designing or adjusting learning center programs. Learning center programs, once established, become part of this needs analysis through internal program evaluations and research. This information then becomes feedback for the learning center as well as faculty and the institution at large. From the student's perspective much of this needs analysis information can be utilized for advising, counseling and course selection, or as a foundation for curricular, instructional or program development that is sensitive to recent student experience.

Every abstraction overlooks some aspects of the full reality. The major shortcoming of Figure 6 is its failure to show the interconnections between the four major support areas. If this were a three dimensional model you might imagine the four triangles as pyramids whose vertices shared a common point under the center of a sphere representing the curriculum. In reality, learning center services are connected by common staff, resources and philosophy.

Early in this chapter the assumption was made that the curriculum best defined the essence of an institution. This logically points to the curriculum as a starting place for developing a service aimed at supporting institutional goals and standards. The curriculum can be viewed and defined in many ways.

The perspective used here is rooted in the information processing approach to cognitive psychology and can best be described as a cognitive process instruction approach (Lochhead, 1979). From this perspective the curriculum is seen as a cohesive set of interrelated skills and knowledge. Some of these skills are domain specific and are applicable to relatively restricted sets of knowledge. Other skills are transferable across domains and therefore are useful (or necessary) in manipulating large sets of knowledge (Lochhead, 1979). The seven skills listed in Figure 6 are not an exhaustive list. However, as higher order or generic skills, they are pervasive throughout the curriculum. Additionally, most domain- or discipline-specific skills can be thought of as hybrid combinations of these seven skills as applied to specific sets of knowledge. Some of these skills may be the overt goals of the curriculum or specific courses, others are implicit in the curriculum design, instructional method or instructional materials (Arons, 1979). The descriptions of the skills embodied in the curriculum will be presented at an abstract level. These skills will be referred to and presented with concrete examples as the support mechanisms and services are described.

Knowledge Base

The knowledge base of the curriculum is drawn from the various disciplines represented in it. Some of this base comprises the core knowledge (required of all students through general education or core requirements). A fuller base of knowledge within a student's major discipline represents the rest of the knowledge base. The knowledge base is the language (definitions), facts, assumptions and postulates of each discipline. If knowledge were the sole goal of the curriculum, rote memorization would be the only skill required. Each discipline's knowledge base has included in its postulates and assumptions an organizational hierarchy that is often implicit in the course materials and instructional methods.

Writing Skills

Writing skills are such a major focus of developmental education and the most frequent target of interdisciplinary or "across the curriculum" efforts that they hardly need formal definition. Writing skills include the reasonable application of the mechanics of grammar, spelling and punctuation, the appropriate use of general and discipline specific vocabularies, and the cohesive representation of one's thoughts for the purpose of description, persuasion or entertainment. Beyond this, writing skills represent the tools of inquiry and the end product of several disciplines (English, philosophy, etc.). Additionally, writing can be a major tool in independent learning. As a primary method for the communication and preservation of knowledge, writing is inarguably a skills that is pervasive throughout the curriculum.

Reading Skills

Reading skills are the counterpart to writing skills and have also been a long-standing focus of developmental education. Since texts, research articles and theoretical essays are a primary mode of instructional delivery, reading skills are pervasive throughout the curriculum. From the cognitive processing instruction perspective, reading skills go beyond those typically measured on a standardized test. Most reading instructors will freely admit that the timed reading tasks, multiple choice questions and vocabulary assessed by standardized tests are a pale reflection of the demands made in the classroom. Reading skills should include recognizing the organizational patterns, the patterns of discourse, the inferences and biases of the authors.

Speaking And Listening Skills

With the exceptions of a few courses (public speaking, interviewing skills, counseling skills, etc.) these skills have little overt emphasis in the curriculum, yet lecture and group discussion are the primary modes of classroom instruction. These skills are perhaps two of the most important tools to the learner. On all of the essential dimensions, speaking and listening skills mirror writing and reading skills.

The four skills mentioned above can be grouped as generative and receptive language skills. These skills not only comprise the medium by which knowledge is transferred but also the medium of most academic thought. (Visual art and music might be excluded, however, as they can easily be defined as other forms of symbolic communication; i.e. language.) Since most thought takes place in language, language skills are the pre-requisite of most thought.

Quantitative Skills

Quantitative skills include not only computational skills but proportional logic as well as graph and table interpretation, among others. These skills are central to mathematics and disciplines in the sciences that use mathematics as a method of analysis. Yet quantitative skills are present in almost every discipline. Statistics and mathematical models are frequent in the behavioral and social sciences, mathematical perspective and proportions are taught in every visual arts program and statistically presented information and the mathematics of budgeting are realities in almost every profession.

Critical Reasoning Skills

Rather than sift through the myriad of definitions in the literature, the following two definitions of critical thinking are offered. First is the manipulation of internal dialogue to isolate a causal factor, predict outcomes (and/or assign probabilities), to evaluate information for reliability and validity, or to achieve a specified goal state. Second is the mental processes of pattern recognition, synthesis, abstraction, elaboration and translation applied to information in order to achieve a specified goal and expand the initial information or its areas of application (Lissner, 1988). The one term in the above definition that is used in an atypical way is **translation**. The process of translation is meant to include linguistic translation, the translation for word problems to algebraic statements, diagrammatic translations such as Figure 6 among others.

Critical thinking is clearly an overt goal of the curriculum, yet it is rarely explicitly taught. It is assumed that students will intuit the process when exposed to enough breadth and depth of knowledge. This may have been true in previous times when the boundaries of knowledge defined a distance that could be traversed within a lifetime. These skills can be explicitly taught, within a discipline, through instructional techniques such as modeling, graded examples and counter examples and discovery learning (Nickerson, Perkins and Smith, 1985).

Interpersonal Skills

This category of skills is meant to apply to the skills relevant to affective and social development. This includes motivation, goal setting, recognizing and social context and selecting appropriate social behaviors. These skills are crucial to the communication of knowledge, the independent pursuit of learning and the renewal/continuation of academia in general as well as specific disciplines as subcultures to our society. The useful pursuit of knowledge is a social endeavor and professions are social organizations whose goals are the maintenance and transmission of knowledge and skills (Delworth, Hanson and Associates, 1981).

Metacognitive Skills

Metacognitive has been a very popular term in the literature for the past ten years. The term is used here from an information processing approach and is meant to cover those skills involved in the conscious or preconscious monitoring of cognitive, affective and social behavior for the purposes of adapting current behavior, selecting future behaviors or developing a strategy to achieve some goal (Halpern, 1984; Nickerson, Perkins and Smith, 1985). These skills might be referred to as the executive controls of the learning process. Students, particularly freshmen, apply a very limited subset of these strategies across contexts and disciplines. Metacognitive skills require a base of the six skills mentioned above upon which to operate. By the definitions presented, metacognitive skills and critical thinking skills are closely related.

How can a program address the eight areas above across both the curriculum and student population? In the next section, four categories of services will be described. Remember, these categories are artificial and in reality these service areas are interwoven. The distinctions in the categories are made in terms of primary goals. As these descriptions are presented, references to existing programs will be made.

Before examining each of the four support areas let us place them in the context of their commonalties. Each support area is represented by a triangle. The three sides of the triangle represent the demands of the curriculum, the student needs and strengths and the curricular medium (structure, content and methods). Each of these three areas is of little use if viewed in isolation. It is at the intersection of these realities that learning and development takes place (Vygotsky, 1978). In designing each support area, it is important to start with a definition of success. This definition flows from the demands, expectations and goals of the curriculum. Often such definitions are built up by induction based on particular course demands. Inductively designed services run a serious risk of developing in a reactive and disorganized fashion. In order to develop a cohesive and integrated service that addresses both the interdisciplinary and intradiciplinary demands of the curriculum, a deductive approach is suggested. Begin with the highest-order goals of the curriculum, define the demands this places on students' skills and then move down to the next level of detail; the result is a ranked hierarchy of subordinate and superordinate goals. This hierarchy allows for various levels of outcomes to be defined for program development, research and program evaluation. Additionally, a deductivley generated goals hierarchy provides a long range plan for services that are directly linked to the curriculum. Based on the changing needs of students, services can be adjusted along this hierarchy.

The curricular goals remain relatively constant as compared to student needs. This next design consideration must be sensitive to changes in the general student population as well as individual needs. The curriculum demands identification of the skills and knowledge that students' are to acquire at different points in the curriculum. Through formal and informal assessment, the skills and knowledge currently possessed by those students can be evaluated. Based on this evaluation, a service package can be tailored addressing the needs of individual students or targeted populations. Formal evaluations are typically cyclical and may be based on placement testing and post-testing, analysis of course grades, among other activities. Informal evaluations may be based on learning center intake interviews, student use surveys, anecdotal data from advisors and faculty, initial tutoring sessions, and more. The evaluations, in conjunction with the curricular demands, narrow the choice of services.

Support services are further narrowed when you take into account the curricular medium. The goal of support services is to assist students in developing skills that can be readily transferred to the curriculum. Teaching for such transfer is what is meant by the curricular medium of a support service. In order to clarify the concept of the curricular medium, review the following example. There is a set of very clear and useful remedial mathematics book. Which provides fairly typical explanations and teaching examples in the text of each chapter. What is unique about these books is the answer keys to the practice problems. The answer keys show hand written full solutions that include every step. These solutions are incredibly powerful learning tools and help students through the self-paced materials quickly. The catch is that when students take a mathematics course in the curriculum, the design of the book is radically different. This causes a great deal of stress and failure to transfer their new found mathematics (and learning skills). Such a failure is due to mismatch in the media of the remedial and mainstream curriculum.

Linguistic Support

As Figure 6 illustrates, linguistic skills are composed of reading, writing, listening and speaking skills. These four skills form the medium within which most learning takes place, therefore they are truly basic skills. Services provided by learning centers in this area range from developmental and remedial courses to individual tutoring to writing labs.

Support services that fit with the model being proposed can be found at a number of institutions. An exemplary program was developed by John Chaffee at Laguardia Community College in New York (Chaffee, 1983). The program begins with the assessment and placement of students into a set of courses that includes reading, writing and critical thinking. These courses are supported by a writing lab and tutoring. In addition to this high level of integration, a key element in the success of these courses is the follow-up. Work from any one course in the freshman semester is likely to be related to assignments in another. Additionally, materials from courses further along in the curriculum were drawn on when the syllabi and assignments we made. The capstone to the program is that the skills taught are reinforced explicitly in advanced courses. As a result of his experience with this program, John Chaffee (1985) has written a book *Thinking Critically.* I recommend the book as interesting reading full of practical suggestions; unfortunately it was written as a course text and does not convey the unique features of Lagurdia's program.

Another program that follows the conceptual model is the Freshman Studies Program at New York Institute of Technology's New York City campus. This program was built on three elements: (1) an integrated developmental reading and writing course (2) a freshmen orientation course focusing on problem solving and analytical reasoning and (3) tutoring and computer-assisted instruction (CAI) laboratories. Students were placed in the program based on placement tests. They were registered for a five-credit equivalent combined developmental reading and writing course, the two-credit freshmen orientation course, a mathematics course based on skills

FIGURE 7

SUPPORT AREA:	LINGUISTIC QUANTITATIVE CONTENT AREA LEARNING STRATEGY EVALUATION
INTERVENTION LEVEL	
REMEDIAL COURSES	
INDIVIDUAL INTERVENTION	
COURSE RELATED SERVICES	
COMPREHENSIVE SYSTEM	
FEEDBACK	

level, a three-credit speech course and one additional course of their own choosing.

The developmental language course met in the traditional classroom two days a week. The tutoring course meet in the CAI lab as a group two days a week and scheduled for two hours a week of independent use of the CAI lab. Attendance was taken for these two hours and students utilized software for word processing, reading and vocabulary development among other skills. The instructor utilized these two hours for individual conferences. This process was supported by peer tutors who were assigned at either the students' or the instructors' request. Additionally the course utilized peer review of papers and group study sessions on the readings. Readings from this course were also utilized by the freshmen orientation course for analytical reasoning exercises (Lissner, 1985).

An example from the other end of the spectrum is the Harvard Reading and Study Skills course. Material for this course is drawn from student exams in such courses as Western Civilization. Student essays covering the range of grades are presented to students to read and evaluate. Later, actual instructors' comments and grades are revealed and discussed (Perry, 1978). This use of modeling as an instructional method is compatible with cognitive process instruction and typical of developmentally based courses.

Quantitative Support

As mentioned above, quantitative support involves both computational and quantitative reasoning skills. Here again services run the gamut from remedial course work to advanced self-paced instruction. The Learning Resource Center at California State University, Northridge provides supplemental self-paced instruction across this spectrum. This self-paced instruction is supported by tutoring, and materials are developed by full-time faculty from the mathematics department on release time. This insures a level of integration with the departments goals while providing customized resources in a cost-efficient fashion. Another program rooted in the combination of self-paced instruction, tutoring and faculty developed materials is the Center for Individualized Instruction at Jacksonville State University in Alabama. This program has two unique aspects. The mastery learning criteria for self-paced courses include a fluency measure. Students' must not only demonstrate mastery of the material, but the testing is done under tight time requirements. Therefore, students must not only accumulate knowledge and skills but they must be highly familiar with them and have easy access to them in memory.

The second aspect of this program is that the center offers several split courses. The knowledge base is taught in a self-paced format. Upon completion of the knowledge base, students register for a more traditionally structured course that explores applications.

A third format is supplemental instruction. Based on student performance in introductory economics courses at Longwood College, the following program was developed. The four introductory economics instructors and the Learning Center staff worked together to develop a diagnostic test for basic skills in mathematics, graph construction and interpretation and table interpretation. This assessment was administered to all introductory economics students during the first week of classes. The assessment is self-scoring and the scoring system refers students to tutoring and a set of supplemental instruction workshops. These workshops meet one hour a week for five weeks and focus on the assessed skills, course- and text-specific study skills and the structure of information in economics. Materials for the workshop are the current chapters and lectures presented in the introductory economics course. The workshops are lead by a Learning Center professional with the assistance of a peer tutor. Throughout the workshop, informal assessment is carried out and students are referred to tutoring and/or self-paced materials. At the end of the five week workshops the students are offered the opportunity to continue to work as a study group with the aid of a peer tutor.

Content Area Support

The above service areas and programs obviously support content from the curriculum but their main focus is on quantitative or linguistic skills. As mentioned above, these categories are interrelated and cannot be fully separated. Supplemental instruction, the development of course-specific self-paced materials and tutoring are major modes of content support. Content area support as a category must be linked to specific courses and relate to both the knowledge base and skill goals of the course. The examples above provide a basic framework, for a more detailed discussion see Rosemary Wolfe's "The Supplemental Instruction Program" in *Issues In College Learning* Centers Vol. 5 (1987).

Learning Strategies

Learning strategies support consists of services designed to the attitudes, perspectives, techniques and organization of learning. Such services include study-skills courses and training, motivational counseling as well as stress and time management etc. Many study skills and learning strategy programs exist in isolation from the main curriculum. The model and philosophy being followed calls for programs that are integrated with the curriculum.

Cornell University's learning center is an example of a program that emphasizes learning strategies in an integrated fashion. The organization of Cornell's center mirrors the organization of the university. Each department of the center is associated with one of Cornell's schools (eg., engineering or natural and life sciences) The center began with tutoring, expanded to include workshops and tutoring group and currently offers partially self-paced versions of introductory courses. Introduction to biology is a good example. The center offers a self-paced version of the course that is supplemented by weekly sessions that review materials. These review session cover course content through teaching learning strategies. In the biology course, there is a particular focus on note taking and cognitive mapping. Over the past decades there has been a great deal published on learning strategy programs. *Thinking and Learning Skills* provides an excellent overview of current programs and research (Segal, Chipman and Glasser, 1985) There are a number of common elements in the diverse programs referred to under the four support areas. All of the programs referred to above provide services that are overtly connected to the curriculum and to student needs. These programs were all initially designed for each institution's "high risk" students and later expanded to provide services to the full student population and faculty. All of these programs utilize faculty to supplement their staff (either through release time, as paid instructional staff, or through funded materials development). Finally, while the provision of direct services is their primary function, these programs have sponsored research on learning, curriculum design and/or instructional methods.

The previous section categorized services by the skills they support. A second dimension in categorizing services is the level of intervention. Level of intervention is defined by the amount of integration with the institution's curriculum (Keimig, 1983). In reviewing the history and current practices, there are four landmarks on this dimension. As programs move to higher levels of intervention it is assumed that they will typically maintain (in a modified state) lowerlevel programs.

The four levels of intervention are Remedial Courses, Individual Interventions, Course Related Services and Comprehensive Systems. These four categories will be used to catalog the repertoire of learning center services. This listing is meant to convey the breadth of services, but is by no means exhaustive.

Remedial Courses

Learning centers provide remedial courses in writing, reading, mathematics and study skills, although they are most likely to be involved in reading and study skills courses (Lissner, 1989). Remedial courses tend to isolate the student from the curriculum based on two basic assumptions. The first is a basic skills deficit interferes with college-level work; overcome that deficit and the student will succeed. The second is that skills such as critical thinking, reading and quantitative reasoning are generic and can be developed in special courses. Neither of these assumptions are well-supported in the literature (Keimig, 1983). This is not to say that remediation is not valuable, just that it is insufficient.

Individual Interventions

Individual interventions add a considerable amount of flexibility. At this level a more holistic approach is common because tutoring and mastery learning materials are its typical delivery systems. These methods provide role models, address motivation and esteem issues. This level is more likely to provide counseling, account for atypical student difficulties and meet some of the needs of the wider student population. (One does not refer an honor's student to a remedial course; however, counseling and tutoring are reasonable referrals.) At this level the learning center begins to act as a consultant to faculty.

Course Related Services

Course-related services have their beginnings in individual tutoring. Later self-paced materials, targeted workshops and supplemental instruction were used in the delivery of services. The highest level of course-related services is the integration of developmental objectives and methods into specific course assignments (Keimig, 1983). At this level the learning center not only acts as a faculty consultant, but begins to participate in faculty and curriculum development.

COMPREHENSIVE SYSTEMS

Services reach the level of a comprehensive system when the scope of course-related services expands to all major areas of the curriculum. At this level services not only focus on alternate presentations of skills and content for review and reinforcement, but enrichment materials for more advanced students.

By adding evaluation to the four support areas and feedback to the four service levels a five by five matrix in Figure 7 is created. This matrix can be used in program development and evaluation or in the categorization of learning centers.

The final subject to be considered is staff configurations for our model learning center. In order to provide the range of services depicted in the model, learning centers must have large flexible staffs, or unrealistically skilled and flexible staffs. Flexible staffing is the most realistic method. A flexible staff configuration can be divided into four staff categories. The learning center will need clerical and secretarial staff. The size of this staff will vary with the size of the center. This staff may be augmented by student aids but should not be solely dependent on them. The skills and continuity provided by a good secretary are important to the center's functioning and atmosphere.

Paraprofessional staff such as peer tutors, peer counselors and peer advisors are a valuable resource. The use of paraprofessionals provides an involved atmosphere built in outreach to other students and role models. Additionally, it provides a legitimate educational experience for the paraprofessionals and attracts brings the best students into the center. Available graduate interns and graduate assistants can augment the professional staff of the center.

Full-time professional staff must include a director and, depending on the size and format of the center, an appropriate number of other professionals. There is no simple student/staff ratio to define an appropriate size for the professional staff. However, two rules of thumb are offered. On an average week the professional staff should spend about 20 percent of their time on professional and program development activities such as research, reviewing the literature and case conferences. During the times of the semester that student demand is the heaviest, students should have access to the professional staff within one week of requesting an appointment.

Professional staff should have competencies in learning theory, educational (or psychological) research, human relations and learning disabilities. Depending on the exact composition of the center the professional staff should possess skills in assessment and diagnosis. Some centers may "contract" some of these skills from faculty, institutional research staff or a counseling staff.

Professional internal consultants are used to provide flexibility and to connect the learning center to the faculty. Most of the learning centers used as examples in this discussion utilize faculty release time and/or overload pay to augment learning center staff. There are three basic formats for the use of faculty: under research or development grants; for program development or evaluation; and, as coordinators for services related to specific disciplinary expertise.

As research and development consultants, faculty work with learning center professional and paraprofessional staff to conduct research, program development or curriculum development. These projects may be generated by the learning center staff or by the faculty. Faculty consultants bring a wide range of skills to the learning center. The learning center provides expertise in learning theory, instructional methodology and student development as well as a focus on developmental goals for the project. Such appointments are made for time spans appropriate to the project, so it is a relatively simple matter to adjust the center's pool of expertise. Additionally, if faculty-generated projects are supported, faculty are likely to take an active and supportive interest in the center. Program development and program evaluation works the same way, but with internal funding. Program evaluation does not have to be limited to current services. Included in this category are projects that provide an analysis of student needs and difficulties. Faculty can be recruited to conduct a student needs analysis as it relates to their discipline.

Many learning centers use faculty coordinators for services related to a discipline or disciplinary expertise. For instance, a mathematics faculty member might be given release time over an academic year to coordinate a mathematics laboratory. This appointment might rotate from year to year. Utilizing faculty in this manner insures the relevance of the learning center's services to the curriculum and provides faculty with an opportunity for professional development.

The learning center model that has been developed depicts a cohesive set of services integrated with the institution, a program that has the sensitivity to student needs and the flexibility necessary to act as an internal consultant or problem solving task force. Based on this model, an ever-growing program can easily be envisioned. Such growth is neither a goal or proper to the model.

The insurance against such growth is the model's view of the highest level of services: integrated systems. The learning center is seen as and ideal environment for developing and nurturing new services and instructional methods. Based on the institutional goals and philosophies. Many of the services would cease to be "learning center services"once they were developed and validated. They would become integral components of courses, departments and faculty skills. Both the model and the challenges facing higher education call for continuous change, not continuous growth.

REFERENCES

Arons, A.B. (1979). "Some Thoughts on Reasoning Capacities Implicitly Expected of College Students". In J. Lochhead and J. Clement (eds.) *Cognitive process instruction*. Philadelphia, Pa.: The Franklin Institute Press.

Baker, G.A. and Pointer, P.L. (1983). "The Learning Center: A Study in Effectiveness". In J.E. Rouche (ed.) *A new look at successful programs*. New Directions for College Learning Assistance, No 11. San Francisco: Jossey-Bass.

Beal, P. E. (1980). "Learning Centers and Retention". In O.T. Lenning and D.L. Wayman (eds.) "New Roles for Learning Assistance". *New Directions for College Learning Assistance*, No. 2. Sanfrancisco: Jossey-Bass.

Brier, E. (1984). "Bridging the Academic Preparation Gap: An Historical View". *Journal of developmental education*, 8, 2-5.

Chaffee, J. (1985). *Thinking critically*. Boston, Ma.: Houghton Mifflin Company.

Chaffee, J. (1983). "Teaching and Integrating Critical Thought Skills into the Academic Curriculum. *Issues in college learning centers*, 1, 18-39.

Christ, F. L. (1977). Management of a Learning Assistance Sector. In G. Enright (ed.) *Personalizing learning systems: ecologies and strategies*. Proceedings of the Tenth Annual Conference of the Western College Reading Association.

Collins, W. (1984). College Learning Centers and Excellence. *Issues in college learning centers*, 2, 1-11.

Council for the Advancement of Standards and Guidelines for Student Services/Development (1986). *Standards and guidelines for learning assistance programs*.

Cremin, L. A. (1982). *American education: The national experience 1783-1876*. New York: Harper and Row.

Decker, A. F., Jody, R. and Brings, F. (1976). *A handbook on open admissions*. Boulder, Co.: Westview Press.

Delworth, U., Hanson, H.R. and Associates (1981). *Student services*. Sanfrancisco: Jossey-Bass.

Enright, G. (1975). College Learning Skills: Frontierland Origins of the Learning Assisstance Center. In R. Sugimoto (ed.) *College learning skills Today and Tommorowland*. Eighth Annual Proceedings of the Western

College Reading Association.

Halpern, D. F. (1984). *Thought and knowledge: An introduction to critical thinking.* Hillsdale, N.J.: Lawrence Erlbaum Associates.

Keimig, R.T. (1983). *Raising academic standards: A guide to learning improvement.* ASHE-ERIC Higher Education Research Reports, No. 4. (ED2233668 HE016607).

Lissner, L.S. (1989). College Learning Assistance Programs: The Results of a National Survey. *Issues in college learning centers,* 9, In press.

Lissner, L. S. (1989). *Supplemental instruction as a faculty consulting ervice.* Unpublished manuscript, Longwood College Academic Support Cente, Farmville, Va.

Lissner, L. S. (1988, April). *Teaching critical thinking.* Paper presented at the annual meeting of the New York Metropolitan Association of Developmental Education, New York.

Lissner, L. S. (1985, May). *An integrated approach to developmental language instruction.* Paper presenta at Critical Issues in Tutoring, Bronx Community College, New York.

Lochhead, J. (1979). "An Introduction to Cognitive Process Instruction". In J. Lochhead and J. Clement (eds.) *Cognitive process instruction.* Philadelphia, Pa.: The Franklin Institute Press.

Maxwell, M. (1979). *Improving student learning.* San Francisco: Jossey-Bass.

Mish, F.C. (ed.) (1987). *Webster's ninth new collegiate dictionary.* Springfield, Ma.: Merriam-Webster Inc.

McDade, C.E. (1984). Computer Assisted Instruction Within the Center for Individualized Instruction. *Issues in college learning centers,* 2, 23-30.

National Commission on Excellence in Education (1983). *A nation at risk* (A report to the Secretary of Education). Washington, D.C.

Newton, E. S. (1983). *The case for improved college teaching: instructing High-risk college students.* New York: Vantage Press.

Nickerson,R.S., Perkins, D.N. and Smith, E.E. (1985). *The teaching of thinking.* Hillsdale, N.J.: Lawrence Erlbaum Associates.

Perry, W. G. (1978). *Annual report of the fureau of study counsel (1977-1978),* Harvard University, Cambridge Ma.

Segal, J. W., Chipman, S.F. and Glasser, R. (eds.) *Thinking and learning skills,* Vol. 1 and Vol. 2. Hillsdale, N.J.: Lawrence Erlbaum Press.

Vygotsky, L.S. (1978). *Mind in society: The development of higher mental processes.* Cambridge, Ma.: Harvard University Press.

Wolfe, R.F. (1987). The Supplemental Instruction Program: Developing Learning and Thinking Skills Across the Curriculum. *Issues in college learning centers,* 5, 5-12.

Woolfolk, A. E. (1987). *Educational psychology,* Third Edition. Englewood Cliffs, N.J.: Prentice-Hall Inc.

7

College Learning Assistance Centers: Places for Learning

William G. White, Jr.,
and Mary Lee Schnuth

While formal learning assistance efforts in American colleges can be traced back for more than one-half century (Enright and Kersteins, 1980), college learning assistance centers as known today originated less than twenty years ago. In this chapter the authors briefly trace the evolution of learning assistance centers, define tem and describe services and activities which characterize assistance programs. The chapter concludes with comments about the types of services learning assistance centers of the future should offer.

EVOLUTION OF LEARNING ASSISTANCE CENTERS

Formal learning assistance programs are a fairly recent phenomenon in American higher education. They emerged, in part, out of the individualized instruction movement of the 1960s and were necessitated by the emergence of new, more diverse student populations in American colleges and universities in the 1970s, an era of open admissions (Baker and Painter, 1983). Open admissions also resulted in large scale attrition of students unprepared for college work (Sullivan, 1979).

The 1970s and 1980s were characterized by efforts to accomodate the changing student clientele (Baker and Painter, 1983). With both fiscal and altruistic motives, many institutions searched for better ways to address the learning needs and achievement levels of students and to seek means by which these new students could learn to participate successfully in the core curriculum and in their choosen fields of study. Many institutions decided they needed special units, programs and/or facilities specifically designed to assist students in developing and improving learning skills. From this impetus the learning center movement came into existence (Sullivan, 1979, 1980). "Today, the whole nation is involved in the effort to respond to learners who need to develop or refine the learning skills that are requisite for academic success" (Burnham, 1983, p. 33).

Emerging learning assistance centers were typically designed to assist capable but underprepared students to acquire learning skills necessary for success in college. While varying greatly, centers usually sought to increase retention, enhance learning skills, minimize academic failure and improve academic performance of students through the use of a variety of supportive instructional components and a wide variety of educational materials and instructional technologies (Sullivan, 1979). By 1974 when Devirian, Enright and Smith (1975) surveyed more than 2600 accredited two- and four-year institutions, 759 reported having learning skills units already in place; another 115 had plans to begin centers within two years. By 1976, 80 percent of the nation's community colleges had learning assistance centers (Roueche and Snow, 1977). As it gained momentum, the learning center movement promised to exert a significant impact on future practices in higher education (Sullivan, 1980).

By 1978, slightly more than one-half of 2700 U.S. institutions surveyed by Sullivan (1979) had one or more learning center programs. He identified an additional 200 programs between 1978 and 1980 (Sullivan, 1980). Learning assistance centers had become so pervasive in community colleges that Rounds (1984, p. 9) said, "It would be difficult to find, in the 1980's, a community college that does not have some kind of learning assistance center." In two-year institutions they are frequently part of comprehensive learning resources programs (College and Research Libraries, 1982).

Learning assistance programs range from comprehensive developmental education programs to drop-in learning centers characterized by an emphasis on individualized instruction (Baker and Painter, 1983). Types of programs, in terms of both comprehensiveness and centralization, vary greatly based on the type and size of institution (Sullivan, 1980). While community colleges are the first to come to mind as needing comprehensive learning assistance programs because of their special mission (Garner, 1980), programs are found in all types of institutions. No one type of institution is unique in seeking to improve student skills; public and private as well as two-year and four-year institutions are involved (Burnham, 1983). "Today, learning centers represent the most frequently employed campus-wide program to assist students to be successful in academic endeavors" (Baker and Painter, 1983, p.74).

Definition

In 1971 Frank Christ formulated the concept of the learning assistance center as a "place concerned with the learning environment within and without, functioning primarily to enable students to learn more in less time with greater ease and confidence; offering tutorial help, study aids in the content areas, and referrals to other helping agencies; and serving as a testing ground for innovative machines, materials, and programs" (Christ, 1971, p. 35). He further explained that a learning assistance center is "a facility where students (learners) come to effect change in their learning assistance skills and attitudes" and is "any place where learners, learning data, and learning facilitators are interwoven in a sequential, cybernetic, individualized, people-oriented system to service all students (learners) and faculty (learning facilitators) of any institution for whom learning by its students is important" (Christ, 1971, p. 35).

Peterson (1975) stated simply that a learning center was a place for nontraditional learning. The Committee on Learning Skills Centers (1976) defined a center as a place where students receive special instruction not usually received in a regular college classroom.

The names by which learning assistance centers are known do not provide a great deal of help in defining their role. Various surveys have noted at least fifteen different titles for such centers (Enright, 1975).

That both the names and functions of learning assistance centers vary greatly among institutions reflects the fact that they are designed to meet the needs of specific institutions and specific student populations (Enright and Kersteins, 1980). Centers do, however, share some common goals including the creation of a learning environment that is individualized, personal and supportive of students regardless of the institutional approaches utilized (Materniak, 1980). Frank Christ (1980) identified a common mission as assisting learners to learn by providing accessible environments for a dynamic interface with equipment, materials and learning facilities. Sullivan (1980) summarized common aims as limiting unnecessary dropouts, enhancing learning skills, minimizing the trauma of academic failure and improving academic performance.

A common element that seems to pervade all discussions of learning assistance centers is their "comprehensive" nature: comprehensive by offering a full range of services including remedial and/or developmental courses, individualized learning opportunities, tutorial assistance, counseling and other services (Burnham, 1983) comprehensive in its mission, target populations and resources (Fuller, 1985). Programs should be broadly conceived and offer assistance to every student with a discernable need (Garner, 1980).

Functions

The overall purpose of the learning assistance center is to act as an extension of the classroom instructor (Roueche and Snow, 1977). This protraction is accomplished through a basic cycle of activities involving interview, assessment/diagnosis, prescription, instruction and evaluation (Henry and Omvig, 1981). Peterson (1975), Sullivan (1979) and Enright and Kersteins (1980) agree that the concept of teacher extension is consumated as learning assistance centers become an amalgamation of four services: library, audio-visual, nontraditional learning activities in nontraditional learning spaces and instructional development.

Maxwell (1981) views the purpose of the learning assistance center as meeting specific goals or outcomes. She recommends inclusion of the following goals for developing a successful learning assistance program: *provide academic support for underprepared college students

- increase student retention and academic performance
- assist students in developing their self-concepts, self-confidence and reducing fear of failure
- help students develop positive human relations
- give individual assistance
- help students develop study skills
- provide support services related to specific coursework
- diagnose learning problems

Based on the definitions, functions and wide-spread acceptance of learning assistance centers, it is obvious that they are a necessary and integral component of most institutions of higher education. In the present age of large, impersonal institutions, learning assistance centers frequently take the lead in developing services to meet the special requirements of all students (Lauridsen, 1980).

COMPREHENSIVE COMPONENTS

While much has been written about successful learning assistance programs, two primary factors appear to be related to their success: institutional commitment and comprehensiveness (Boylan, 1983; Keimig, 1983; Roueche, 1983). The Center for Developmental Education (1983) characterizes successful learning assistance programs as those that provide services designed to diagnosis student needs, improve student mastery in the basic skill areas, promote students' personal development and academic adjustment, promote the development of reasoning and critical thinking and provide on-going program evaluation. Roueche (1983) identified eleven elements that characterize successful developmental programs:

- strong administrative support
- mandatory counseling and placement
- structured courses
- award of credit
- flexible competition strategies
- multiple learning systems
- volunteer instructors
- use of peer tutors
- monitoring of behaviors
- interfacing with subsequent courses
- program evaluation

common goal of assisting students to become more efficient and effective by providing tutorial assistance, learning skill development, instructional resources and instructional development for faculty and staff. To view more definitively the components of a successful learning assistance program it is necessary to examine Keimig's Hierarchy of Learning Improvement Programs.

Keimig (1983), who reports that successful developmental education programs increase student grade point averages and retention, developed the Hierarchy of Learning Improvement Programs to describe how students are best served by emphasizing program components that have the greatest impact in those two areas. Level I of the hierarchy is defined as remedial courses. "Separate remedial, basic skills courses are at the lowest level of the hierarchy because they are the least likely to effect long-term academic achievement and persistence" (Keimig, 1983, p. 21). Though at the lowest level, remedial courses act as a foundation on which to build and expand programs.

Level II of the model finds learning assistance for individual students as increasing the likelihood of improved learning. The advantage of programs offering such services is that they allow students to receive individual help with academics in informal situations that provide on-going social and psychological support as well as instruction. Tutorial assistance based on voluntary participation is one of the services recommended at this program level.

Level III incorporates course related learning services. This level is characterized by systematic coordination of developmental objectives and activities with emphasis on mastery learning. Adjunct learning experiences play an important role in Level III programs, and close interaction of faculty and tutors is necessary. The feature that most distinguishes Level III is the link of services to specific academic courses.

The fourth level of the hierarchy is designated as a comprehensive learning system. Programs achieving this level provide for the total learning needs of students through more sophisticated and complex methods. Individual student needs and attitudes are addressed. In such a program the student's overall development is important, and educational experiences in courses are systematically designed according to the principles of learning theory. Level IV programs are comprehensive and, therefore, the most likely to effect change. Comprehensive systems evolve from the lower level programs. It is evident that the learning assistance center is instrumental in helping programs reach the point of comprehensiveness which characterizes Level IV status.

It is virtually impossible to separate learning assistance centers from developmental education programs because they have become subsidiary to one another and are both involved in responding to institutional needs. Learning centers integrate educational media, learning skills, instructional development and instructional resources (Flamm, 1984) in an effort to provide "intensive remedial training and support services for those students most in need of remediation through a highly concentrated approach that combines innovative, multi-disciplinary instruction with individualized and prescriptive learning techniques" (Yamba, 1982, p. 31). While Roueche and Snow (1977) find learning centers to be integral parts of developmental education programs, others like Wong (1982) feel that learning assistance centers should really house developmental programs. Learning assistance centers can be correctly viewed as the facilities which house some or all of the components of comprehensive developmental education programs.

The relationship between developmental education programs and learning assistance centers is confirmed by Burnham (1983, p. 33) who said, "Practitioners and other experts involved in developmental education generally agree that learning centers should help to remediate the academic deficiencies of learners so that they can participate in the core curriculum and that centers should provide continuing support to learners who are taking core curriculum courses. Thus, centers represent a blend of instructional resources, instructional media, learning skills development, and tutoring and instructional development."

LEARNING ASSISTANCE CENTER SERVICES

There is concensus that services offered through learning assistance centers should be based on the needs of the population being served. Services can be categorized into two broad components: academic and support.

Academic Component

Developmental education advocates view the academic component as a critical part of any program and a firm foundation on which to build a successful system (Burnham, 1983; Christ, 1980; Deming and Valeri-Gold, 1986; Donovan, 1975; Flamm, 1984; Garner, 1980; Keimig, 1983; Lauridsen, 1980; Peterson, 1975; Walker, 1980; Whyte, 1980). Although specific developmental and remedial courses offered are dependent on the institution and its population, there are some remedial courses which are almost universally accepted. They include: English, English as a second language, mathematics, reading, study skills and writing (Clark, 1980; Dempsey and Tomlinson, 1980; Gray and Slaughter, 1981; Hecht and Akst, 1981; Kunz, 1981; Maxwell, 1981; Pearse, Agrella and Powers, 1982; Walker, 1980; Waters, 1981; Wong, 1982; Yamba, 1982).

Though not as common, other courses are frequently included in developmental programs. They include oral communication, science, chemistry, statistics, critical thinking, psychology, personal development and critical reading. Some academic areas that are treated as independent courses at one institution may be included in other courses at other institutions. For example, not all institutions find it necessary to offer a course in critical reading but instead teach such skills as part of their general reading classes. Such institutional decisions should be based on student needs determined by a needs assessment.

Instructional practices. Since learning assistance centers are concerned with underprepared, developmental and nontraditional students in need of academic help, they must be willing to break the traditional mold of instruction. Since such students have been unable to acquire the necessary knowledge and skills for success through traditional classroom techniques, there is general agreement that their successful accomodation requires individualized approaches. Students are frequently provided with self-paced and competency based instruction. There is an increased emphasis on student-centered rather than teacher-centered instruction and on specialized instruction for individual learners (Baker and Painter, 1983; Cross, 1976; Dempsey and Tomlinson, 1980; Garner, 1980; Materniak, 1980; Obler, 1983; Peterson, 1975; Roueche and Kirk, 1973).

Such programs require flexibility (variable time and credit), continuous monitoring and tracking of student progress (Garner, 1980). Materniak (1980) suggests that variable group size, lecture discussion sessions and experiential programs are important. This is supported by Karwin (1973) who feels that direct learning experiences in the form of field studies and work participation are necessary for the creation of a viable program. The utilization of a competency based system is advocated because achievement of specific learning outcomes should determine student success and improve evaluative methods (Baker and Painter, 1983). Many high-risk, nontraditional students are not verbal learners. They need to be actively involved, and it is advantageous for course content to be divided into small, manageable tasks. Though much of the course content and materials students receive is identical to that in the regular classroom, a distinguishing feature of learning assistance center instructional methods that aids student learning is the emphasis on individualized, self-paced and continuously monitored learning activities (Roueche and Kirk, 1973).

Support Component

Support services offered through learning assistance centers are as varied as institutions and students. Though numerous and diverse, the literature reveals two services commonly provided by learning assistance centers:

counseling and tutorial services. Diagnostic and placement services and resource/material centers are almost as common. Other services, not as popular but increasingly offered, include consultation, orientation, transportation, child care, programs for the disabled and professional development.

Counseling services. Counseling services have a home in learning assistance centers. The result of incorporating counseling services into programs has been so successful that many view them as a priority support service on the university campus (Chausow and Barshis, 1983). The benefits of counseling for developmental students has made it a rapidly growing field and a component of every successful learning assistance program. "Counselors address the needs of the non-traditional student through a preventive model of developmental counseling which emphasizes college adjustment and realistic educational planning. Their primary task is to help the student develop personal and academic competencies which will enhance self-concept" (Flamm, 1984, p. 21). It is generally agreed that counseling services should include both individual and group therapies and be comprehensive and aggressive (Baker and Painter, 1983). When properly developed, organized and administered, counseling services can provide a broad spectrum of activities.

Personal guidance is strongly supported for developmental students (Boylan, 1981; Burnham, 1983; Christ, 1980; Clark, 1980; DeBernardis, 1984; Donovan, 1975; Glennen, 1983; Keimig, 1983; Maxwell, 1981; Obler, 1983; Walker, 1980; Whyte, 1980). Personal counseling is related to self-awareness, problem solving strategies, goal-setting, values clarification, decision-making, coping techniques, interpersonal skills and social interaction (Flamm, 1984). "Counseling is likely to be most effective and best regarded by students when the perceived purpose of such activity is personhood development" (Roueche and Kirk, 1973, p. 74).

Another type of counseling advocated by developmental educators is career counseling (Davenport, 1972; Garner, 1980; Peterson, 1975; Whyte, 1980; Yamba, 1982). Career counseling includes interests, vocational strengths, personality traits and job-seeking and employment skills (Flamm, 1984).

Academic counseling includes academic advisement, basic skills strengths and deficits, efficient course selection and study techniques (Flamm, 1984). Proponents of academic counseling believe it to be an integral part not only of the learning assistance center's counseling service but also of the overall college system (Clark, 1980; Walker, 1980).

Peer counseling is the most recent and fastest growing counseling component. With weakened economic conditions and decreasing student enrollment, colleges are relying more heavily on student help (Roueche and Snow, 1977). Peer counseling maximizes student utilization, and supporters report that such programs are of benefit not only to the counselee but also to the peer counselor (Walker, 1980).

Intercultural counseling is slowly finding its way into higher education (Kunz, 1981). Such programs are dependent on the cultural composition of their sponsoring institutions. Another newly created area is financial counseling (Walker, 1980). Given the economic condition of the nation and the changing student population on its campuses, this component may become increasingly important.

Tutorial services. Tutorial services have evolved as one of the two most visible support services in learning assistance centers (Boylan, 1981; Christ, 1980; Clark, 1980; Glennen, 1983; Keimig, 1983; Lauridsen, 1980; Maxwell, 1981; Walker, 1980; Yamba, 1982). Chausow and Barshis (1983) feel tutoring is the top priority in the learning assistance center; others, like Cross (1976), believe it is viable only if other support measures are present. As a single service it does not address the real weaknesses in knowledge and skills.

Since 1970 there has been a transformation in the area of tutorial services. The number of colleges and universities offering tutorial services has expanded; tutors have changed from predominantly faculty, para-professionals and graduate students to peers; services are no longer only for academically deficient students; and services are free in most institutions (Rouche and Snow, 1977).

Roueche and Kirk (1973) report that tutoring has three primary functions: supportive teaching (intervention which occurs immediately after a mistake is made), crisis teaching (intervention when student anxiety over failure to learn reaches a high peak) and diagnostic teaching (tutorial services which are provided when a student is in great difficulty and showing no progress).

The means by which tutoring services are provided are institutionally dependent. The universally accepted concept that programs must be flexible (Maxwell, 1981) stands out as the most important factor in determining the success of a tutoring component. Just as individual and group therapies were recommended for counseling services they are also for tutorial services (Flamm, 1984; Maxwell, 1981; Peterson, 1975). There is also considerable support for peer tutoring services, for student choice of tutors and for tutoring services available for weekends, evenings and other high demand times (Deming and Valeri-Grold, 1986; Maxwell, 1981; Obler, 1983; Roueche, 1980; Walker, 1983).

Many institutions find it beneficial to operate drop-in tutorial services (DeBernardis, 1984; Flamm, 1984; Maxwell, 1981). Drop-in services provide one-on-one help in various subjects, and students have the option of using study aids on their own (DeBernardis, 1984). Drop-in service also alleviates problems associated with students making, cancelling or not arriving for appointments. It also eliminates the need for a student to anticipate when he might expect problems with certain subjects or assignments.

As institutions expand their services to meet the needs of non-traditional students there will be increased demand for tutorial assistance. Increased demand occurs, according to Maxwell (1981), when students are underprepared for college level work, classes are taught using the lecture method, course skills required are higher than students possess, students have fewer skills than the institution's typical student and when there is a lack of faculty-student interaction.

Diagnosis and placement. Diagnosis and placement services are considered essential functions of learning assistance centers (Boylan, 1981; Clark, 1980; Flamm, 1984; Garner, 1980; Maxwell, 1988; Pearse, Agrella and Powers, 1982; Peterson, 1975; Roueche and Snow, 1977; Wong, 1982). It permits proper and complete identification of student problems, abilities and needs (Whyte, 1980) and permits follow-up of students as they progress through a program as well as providing a means by which to assess their achievement upon completion of a prescribed plan of study (Yamba, 1982). The most commonly used method of diagnosing and placing students is standardized testing (Roueche and Snow, 1977).

Resource/materials center. The resource/materials center has proven a significant part of the learning assistance center and essential to successful developmental education programs (Garner, 1980; Langhoff, 1980; Lauridsen, 1980; Maxwell, 1981; Minkoff, 1974). Technological advances have greatly influenced educational institutions and the impact has been felt through the increasing importance placed on resource centers and self-learning systems. No longer is it necessary to have professional or other personnel available at all times for learning to take place. This has been advantageous since most institutions have felt the effects of decreased budgets. It is more cost effective to purchase the necessary equipment for students to self-learn than to employ persons to teach. The resource/ materials center serves not only students but also faculty, tutors and counselors.

A resource/materials center normally contains a computer laboratory with programmed materials (Chausow and Barshis, 1983; Materniak, 1980; Wong, 1982) as well as workbooks, texts, lecture notes, handouts/packets, film strips, audio cassettes, video cassettes, slides, overheads, learning programs and equipment for use of all audio-visual materials (Materniak, 1980; Maxwell, 1966, 1981; Walker, 1980). In addition to housing materials for in-house use, the resource/materials center should serve as a dispensary for equipment and materials (Christ, 1980; Karwin, 1973). The capacity of the center to loan materials increases students' further learning. If the concept of self-paced learning is beneficial to learner outcomes, then students should have access to the necessary resources even at times when the facility is inaccessible.

Other services. Child care is a more recent service found to benefit non-traditional students (DeBernardis, 1984; Roueche and Snow, 1977). With increasing numbers of adults (especially single parents0 returning to college campuses, child care has become a necessity. As a relatively new service of colleges, child care has been primarily nursery care. As such services increase and become more highly organized it would be profitable to alter their mission and transform them into child development programs (Roueche and Snow, 1977).

As well as providing services to assist developmental learners, learning assistance centers should be especially concerned about the disabled population. As with other nontraditional groups, increasing numbers of handicapped persons are attending college. Educational institutions have an obligation to create accessible environments for these students (DeBernardis, 1984; Deming and Valeri-Gold, 1986; Garner, 1980; Walker, 1980). Services for the handicapped could include registration assistance, interpreters for the deaf, writers, readers, counselors, ramps, elevators, designated parking and special entrances (DeBernardis, 1984). Walker (1980) suggests that disabled liasons with volunteer resources be utilized. Altering facilities to meet the needs of handicapped students is an area that must be addressed by facility and program planners.

Few colleges assist students with transportation, but it is a service which might be considered if a needs assessment indicates that it would be beneficial (Roueche and Snow, 1977). Larger institutions have led the way by operating bus services, arranging car pools and providing allowances for public transportation.

As colleges and universities expand programs for increasing numbers of nontraditional students, learning assistance centers must change and amplify their role. To meet institutional needs many centers have done that and have assumed some responsibility for training professionals. This is a rapidly growing function and is becoming one of the primary responsibilities of the learning assistance center (Christ, 1980; Deming and Valeri-Gold, 1986; Lauridsen, 1980; Maxwell, 1981; McPheeters, 1980). In meeting this challenge learning assistance centers are providing programs such as in-service, continuing education for faculty and administrators, counselor training, alumni self-development, standardized test preparation, staff development, personal learning skills for faculty and staff and teacher training. As higher education systems, student populations and societal demands continue to change, the learning assistance center will have to maintain a position of flexibility, allowing itself to reorganize, expand or eliminate program components as the need arises. It is not enough to wait until individual needs become apparent; learning assistance center planners must project future needs and make allowances for inevitable changes.

Staffing

Learning assistance center staffing is dependent upon the scope of services and programs offered. However, adequate staffing, including clerical personnel, is essential to a successful center (Whyte, 1980). Needs assessments assist administrators in determining the total number of staff needed to operate centers efficiently and effectively. Whyte (1980) has developed guidelines through an integrated help model that can assist in determining staff needs of learning assistance centers. He suggests the following student:faculty ratios as guidelines:
- 50:1 for students requiring mainly motivational assistance, career guidance, speed reading and other similar types of services
- 25:1 for students requiring general basic skills and counseling
- 10:1 for students needing intensive basic skills remediation, counseling and diagnostic work
- 5:1 for students with learning disabilities or handicaps such as blindness or deafness

In addition to adequate numbers, centers need personnel dedicated to and understanding of developmental students. Specially trained faculty and staff who are committed, honest, open, concerned about students and able to maintain a positive attitude are essential for learning assistance programs (Roueche and Kirk, 1973). A learning assistance center which lacks adequate numbers and quality of staff is a center that will fail in its mission to improve learning outcomes.

COLLEGE LEARNING ASSISTANCE CENTERS OF THE FUTURE

While it is impossible to forsee all the types of services that will be offered by learning assistance centers of the future (Peterson, 1975), several authorities have speculated about what learning assistance centers will be doing as higher education enters the twenty-first century. In addition, current literature in the field offers a number of implications for future practice.

Champaign (1980) believes that the center of the future will be one where students can go to learn anything they feel a need to learn. He sees centers becoming both educational brokers and providers. As brokers, centers will serve as intermediaries in linking learners to individuals, institutions and agencies that can help them. As providers, centers will help students to formulate educational plans and contracts, assess learners' competencies, provide appropriate institutional vehicles and assist in evaluating instructional outcomes.

In their brokerage role, learning assistance centers will link increasingly diverse types of learners to helping people, agencies and institutions. Most authorities agree that the clientele of the learning assistance center of the future will not be limited to underprepared or skill-deficient students (Garner, 1980; Maxwell, 1981). It will provide services for all students on campus who desire them including increasing numbers of foreign students, the physically handicapped and the learning disabled (Christ, 1980; Dempsey and Tomlinson, 1980). Services provided to all students may expand to include some presently offered elsewhere on campus, such as academic/scheduling advisement, assistance with registration and orientation services (Glennen, 1983).

In fact, the concept of who is a learner will be expanded beyond the campus to include many nonmatriculating individuals, such as alumni, veterans, distant learners and community residents ranging from professionals and displaced workers to illiterates (Christ, 1980; Emery, 1986; Maxwell, 1981; McPheeters, 1980, Sullins, 1987; Vegso, 1982) who take advantage of services, such as preparation for a variety of standardized examinations; basic literacy programs; programs teaching special skills like speed reading, resumé writing and job hunting (Champaign, 1980); and personal improvement through training in behavior modification, biofeedback and desensitization services (Christ, 1980) and anxiety reduction (Dempsey and Tomlinson, 1980).

Many of the new clientele in the expanded community may never or seldom need to come to campus to utilize learning assistance center services. Centers will use new and developing technologies to deliver learning opportunities to sites off campus, such as homes, remote areas, businesses, industry, governmental agencies and elementary or secondary schools. This will also be accomplished as the resource/materials collections housed in learning assistance centers are loaned for use at other on- and off-campus sites (Drea and Armistead, 1988; Emery, 1986; Karwin, 1973, McNeil, 1980, Sullins, 1987). Colleges and universities have offered off-campus courses for many years. Learning assistance programs should become increasingly involved in offering a much wider range of courses as well as support services to students in nontraditional settings such as shopping malls, borrowed and rented facilities, homes, community education centers, alternative learning centers and storefront schools (Charles and Parkins, 1978; Decker, 1980; Dovalina, 1981; Duerden, 1980; Eliott, 1983; Field, 1978; Harlocher and Hencey, 1977; Luskin and Smith, 1980a, 1980b; Potter, 1980; Schoolland, 1984; Smith, 1977). Some off-campus centers may be well equipped learning centers, but to "many colleges the satellite or extended center is nothing more than a large storefront or classroom for brokering educational programs" (Charles and Parkins, 1978, p. 2).

A few words about learning assistance programs outside higher education may be in order. While traditionally focusing on training employees for specific job skills, educational endeavors in business, industry, health care and governmental agencies, to mention only a few have expanded their role to include more general educational activities (Craig, 1985; Keating, 1982; Scarborough, 1985).

Corporate education and training programs have become a major focus of business and industry in the United States. Between $40 and $100 billion are spent each year for education and training of employees, and 60 to 80 percent of this is accomplished within the corporate environment (Eurich, 1985). While predominantly in-house education is provided, learning experiences are also offered through cooperative agreements with colleges and universities. The need for compensatory education of employees has been spurred by increased employment of minorities, immigrants, school dropouts and those with inadequate educational backgrounds. Regretably, employers are finding that remedial reading, writing and math classes must be provided to employees for adequate functioning in the workplace. Stating the obvious, Eurich (1985, p. 124) said, "Corporate classrooms should not be so busy teaching the three R's of reading writing, and arithmetic."

Corporate education has, however, gone far beyond teaching basic skills. Many major corporations have established well-funded, sophisticated educational programs with the best personnel, facilities and equipment that money can buy; several have established degree-granting "universities." Most corporate education programs, like many of those in government, military and health care, include fully equipped and staffed learning assistance centers providing specific types of services needed by sponsoring organizations. Among corporations which operate noteworthy educational programs are AT&T, Control Data, Digital Equipment Corporation, IBM and Xerox (Eurich, 1985).

Corporate educational programs are posing an unintended challenge to higher education. With declining college enrollments and economically difficult times in higher education, one would wonder why institutions have been slow in creating profitable partnerships with business and industry.

College learning assistance centers could provide a hub for learning activities, especially in the basic skills areas, with little alteration in existing programs. Because of the breadth and depth of skills development available through learning assistance centers, colleges could provide more efficient and effective learning experiences than business or industry (Bray, 1984). Many of the learning activities deemed necessary by employers are available through college centers; simple alterations in scheduling could open the doors to corporate utilization. Speech communication, writing skills, problem solving, decision making, basic English grammar, effective listening, reading development and general arithmetic are just a few of the topics being stressed in corporate education that overlap learning assistance programs in colleges (Eurich, 1985; Feuer, 1985; Miller, 1984; Pinsker, 1983). In addition to providing courses for corporate employees, college learning assistance centers could be instrumental in coordinating and intensifying contacts with business, conducting needs assessments, increasing placement services and improving communication throughout the community (Mahoney, 1982).

There has long been a cooperative relationship between higher education and the world of business and industry. For decades higher education educated those who invested in and managed America's industrial and financial complex, engaged in research and development activities for the benefit of business and industry and educated a relatively affluent and literate class to consume the goods and services produced. Today, many corporate education, training and learning assistance programs are not only better funded and more technologically sophisticated but also more outcome-oriented than those in higher education. However, both college learning assistance centers and their counterparts in non-traditional settings have much to offer each other. College learning assistance centers have the ability to reach out to business and industry to form those partnerships that would prove mutually beneficial (Keating, 1982). Existing and emerging technologies make such cooperation more likley and especially exciting.

In their provider role, learning assistance centers will also undoubtedly develop and utilize more sophisticated diagnostic, assessment, placement, prescription and evaluation techniques for students. Those improved techniques will provide for greater learner control over the learning experience including goal setting, teaching methodology and evaluation. Increased learner control will result in greater individualization of programs in terms of instructional style, level of desired proficiency, time frames for learning and student learning styles; in the use of multiple learning systems; and in the decreased significance of grades (Champaign, 1980; Roueche, 1983).

While there may be few new courses provided, learning assistance centers will provide help for students in any course through peer tutoring, volunteer tutors, faculty assisgned to and housed in the center and the use of computer aided instruction and a variety of media (Champaign, 1980). While the role of peer tutors and counselors will greatly expand and their importance increase in the years ahead (Maxwell, 1981; Roueche, 1983), the diversity of services offered will still require a professional staff including instructional specialists, computer programmers, instructional designers, media specialists and counselors (Champaign, 1980).

The future will find learning assistance centers more involved in providing assistance to faculty in all academic areas. Most college faculty have no pedagogical training; learning centers are expected to provide professional development for teachers in the art and science of teaching their respective disciplines (Maxwell, 1988). Professional personnel across the campus will be developed through the use of seminars, workshops, teleconferences and the use of a variety of media and technology (Clark, 1980; McPheeters, 1980). To improve teaching and learning, centers will provide assessment of faculty teaching styles and student learning styles (Champaign, 1980) and perhaps facilitate the matching of teachers and students with compatible styles. Preservice training of professional personnel will be accomplished by using centers as sites for internships for graduate students interested in the broad field of learning assistance (Christ, 1980).

The expanded clientele and services of learning centers of the future will be both the impetus for and the result of continuous experimentation and of creative innovation (Peterson, 1975). While it may never really be all things to all people, Fuller (1985, p. 516) realistically brings the future into focus when he says, "Broader in scope and nearly all-inclusive in potential services to students, the new college learning assistance center may truly be deserving of the title 'comprehensive.'"

REFERENCES

Baker, G.A. III and P.L. Painter. (1983). The learning center: A study of effectiveness. In J.E. Roueche (ed.), *A new look at successful programs.* San Francisco: Jossey-Bass, 73 - 88.

Boylan, H.R. (1981). Program evaluation: Issues, needs, and realities. In C.C. Walvekar (ed.), *Assessment of learning assistance services.* San Francisco: Jossey-Bass, 3 - 16.

Boylan, H.R. (1983). *Is developmental education working?* (Research Report No. 2). Boone, North Carolina: The National Association for Remedial/Developmental Studies in Post-Secondary Education.

Bray, D. (1984). *The evaluation of remedial programs in the community colleges.* Sacramento: Sacramento City Colleges.

Burnham, L. B. (1983). Profiles of success among Texas programs for low-achieving students. In J.E. Roueche (ed.), *A new look at successful programs.* San Francisco: Jossey-Bass, 31 - 42.

Center for Developmental Education. (1983). *Successful programs: Recent research efforts.* Boone, North Carolina: Center for Developmental Education.

Champaign, J.R. (1980). *2001: Future directions of learning assistance centers.* Paper presented at the meeting of the American College Personnel Association, Boston. (ERIC Document Reproduction Service No. ED 205 413)

Charles, R. F. and M. Parkins (1978). *The development of an alternative to Proposition 13 losses in student services for non-traditional students: The DIAL program for students at the Sunnyvale center.* Unpublished paper, Cupertino: De Anya College (ERIC Document Reproduction Service Number ED 160 142).

Chausow, H. M. and D. Barshis. (1983). *A developmental education program: An experiment and revised guidelines for academic year 1983 developmental education program.* Chicago: Chicago City Colleges, Center for the Improvement of Teaching and Learning.

Christ, F. L. (1971). Systems for learning assistance: Learners, learning facilitators, and learning centers. In F.L.Christ (ed.), *Interdisciplinary aspects of reading instruction.* Proceedings of the fourth annual conference of the Western College Reading Association.

Christ, F. L. (1980). Learning assistance at a state university: A cybernetic model. In K.V. Lauridsen (ed.), *Examining the scope of learning centers.* San Francisco: Jossey-Bass 45 - 56.

Clark, E. A. (1980). The learning center in the urban university. In K.V. Lauridsen (ed.), *Examining the scope of learning centers.* San Francisco: Jossey-Bass, 9 - 17.

College and Research Libraries, Board of Directors (1982). *Guidelines for two-year college learning resources programs,* revised June 30, 1981. *C & RL News,* January/February 1982.

Committee on Learning Skills Centers. (1976). *Learning skills centers: A CCCC report.* Urbana, Illinois: ERIC Clearinghouse on Reading and Communication Skills and Conference on College Composition and Communication.

Craig, R. (1985). Industry training efforts in adult education. In C. H. Shulman (ed.), *Adults and the changing workplace: 1985 yearbook of the American Vocational Association.* Arlington, Virginia: American Vocational Association, 107 - 110.

Cross, K.P. (1976). *Accent on learning: Improving instruction and reshaping the curriculum.* San Francisco: Jossey-Bass.

Davenport, L.F. (1972). *Mandamus for change in student services.* Paper presented at the meeting of the Congress of Black Professionals in Higher Education, Austin, Texas.

De Bernardis, A. (1984). Excellent facilities yield excellence in education. *Community and junior college journal,* 35-36.

Decker, E. H. (1980). Utilizing part-time faculty for community-based education. *New directions for community colleges,* 8, 2, 61 - 65.

Delworth, U. and G. R. Hanson (1980). *Student services: A handbook for the profession.* San Francisco: Jossey-Bass.

Deming, M.P. and M. Valeri-Gold (1986). *The writing center: A leader in change and service.* Paper presented at the annual meeting of the Southeastern Writing Center Association Conference, Mobile, AL. (ERIC Document Reproduction Service No. ED 275 001)

Dempsey, J. and B. Tomlinson (1980). Learning centers and instructional/ curricular reform. In O.T. Lenning and R.T. Nayman (eds.), *New roles for learning assistance.* San Francisco: Jossey-Bass, 41 - 58.

Devirian, M.C., G. Enright and G. D. Smith. (1975). Survey of learning programs in higher education. In *Twenty-fourth yearbook of the National Reading Conference.* Clemson, South Carolina: National Reading Conference.

Donovan, R. A. (1975). *National project II: Alternatives to the revolving door.* New York: Bronx Community College.

Dovalina, R. H. (1981). *Administering adult education - A community based approach.* Paper presented to the College Board Southwestern Regional Workshop, San Antonio, Texas (ERIC Document Reproduction Service No. ED 202 557).

Drea, J. T. and L. P. Armistead (1988). *Serving distant learners through instructional technologies.* Unpublished paper, Quincy, Illinois: John Wood Community College (ERIC Document Reproduction Service Number 289 575).

Duerden, N. H. (1980). Down with walls, up with malls: Taking classes to the shopping centers, *CASE currents,* 6, 11, 30 - 31.

Eliott, I. H. (1983). *The challenge of faculty development for part-timers in noncampus community colleges.* Paper presented at the Conference on Quality in Off-Campus Credit Programs Challenges, Choices and Concerns. Atlanta, Georgia: Division of Continuing Education, Kansas State University (ERIC Document Reproduction Service Number 289 575).

Emery, M. (1986). *Some potentials and limitatios of technology in serving rural postsecondary learners.* Paper presented at the National Invitational Conference on Rural Adult Postsecondary Education, Arlie, Virginia. (ERIC Document Reproduction Service Number ED 296 854).

Enright, G. (1975). College learning skills: Frontier land origins of the learning assistance center. In R. Sugimoto, (ed.) *College learning skills: Today and tomorrow land.* Proceedings of the Eighth Annual Conference of the Western College Reading Association. Anaheim: The Western College Reading Association.

Enright, G. and G. Kersteins (1980). The learning center: Toward an expanded role. In O.T. Lenning and R.L. Nayman (eds.), *New roles for learning assistance.* San Francisco: Jossey-Bass, 1 - 24.

Eurich, R. (1985). *Corporate classrooms.* A Carnegie Foundation Special Report. Lawrenceville, NJ: Princeton University Press.

Feuer, D. (1985). Where the dollars go, *Training,* 22, 10, 45 - 53.

Field, H. F. (1978). Delivery systems: Meeting the multiple needs of diversified clientele. *New directions for community colleges,* 6, 1, 27 - 33.

Flamm, A.L. (1984). *Reading Area Community College basic skills program review.* Reading, Pennsylvania: Reading Area Community College.

Fuller, J. (1985). Beyond comprehensive learning assistance centers. *Library Trends,* 33, 513-521.

Gardner, J. N. and A. J. Jewler (1985). *College is only the beginning.* Belmont: Wadsworth.

Garner, A. (1980). A comprehensive community college model for learning assistance centers. In K.V. Lauridsen (ed.), *Examining the scope of learning centers.* San Francisco: Jossey-Bass, 19-31.

Glennen, R.E. (1983). Effective outcome measures of intrusive advising programs. In J.E. Roueche (ed.), *A new look at successful programs.* San Francisco: Jossey-Bass, 59 - 72.

Gray, B.Q. and V. B. Slaughter (1981). Writing. In A.S. Trillin and Assoc. (eds.), *Teaching basic skills in college.* San Francisco: Jossey-Bass, 12 - 90.

Harlocher, E. L. and R. E. Hencey (1977). Renewal: The new learning process. *Community and junior college journal,* 48, 1, 9 - 12.

Hecht, M. and G. Akst (1981). Mathematics. In A.S. Trillin and Assoc. (eds.), *Teaching basic skills in college.* San Francisco: Jossey-Bass, 208 - 260.

Henry, S. and C. P. Omvig (1981). *Learning center handbook.* Kentucky University, Division of Vocational Education. (ERIC Document Reproduction Service No. ED 215 106)

Hosford, R. E. and T. A. Ryan (1970) Systems design in the development of counseling and guidance programs. *Personnel and guidance journal,* 49, 3, 221-230.

Karwin, T.J. (1973). *Flying a learning center: Design and costs of an off-campus space for learning.* Berkeley: The Carnegie Commission on Higher Education.

Keating, W. G. (1982). General Electric's education outreach. In *Business-industry-education: Toward a working partnership.* Conference proceedings, Northeast Regional Exchange, Chlemsford, Massachusetts, 41 - 47.

Keimig, R. T. (1983). *Raising academic standards: A guide to learning improvement* (ASHE-ERIC/Higher Education Research Report No. 4). Washington, D.C.: Association for the Study of Higher Education.

Kunz, L.A. (1981). English as a second language. In A.S. Trillin and Assoc. (eds.), *Teaching basic skills in college.* San Francisco: Jossey-Bass, 145 - 207.

Langhoff, H. F. (1980). Learning resource centers: Organizational components and structural models. In K. Mikan (ed.), *Learning resources center conference: Proceedings and evaluation.* Birmingham,

Alabama (ERIC Document Reproduction Service No. ED 222 180), 6 - 16.

Luskin, B. J. and J. Small (1980a). *Coastline community college: An idea beyond tradition.* Paper presented at the Conference of the American Association for Higher Education, Washington, D. C. (ERIC Document Reproduction Service Number 184 610).

Luskin, B. J. and J. Small (1980b). The need to change and the need to stay the same. *Community and junior college journal,* 5, 4, 24 - 28.

Lauridsen, K.V. (1980). *Examining the scope of learning centers.* San Francisco: Jossey-Bass.

Mahoney, J. R. (1982). *Community college centers for contracted programs: A sequel to shoulders to the wheel.* Washington, D.C.: American Association of Community and Junior Colleges.

Materniak, G. (1980). *Developing a learning center from A to Z: Guidelines for designing a comprehensive developmental education program in a post-secondary educational setting.* Unpublished paper. Pittsburg: University of Pittsburg.

Maxwell, M.J. (1966). An individualized college learning laboratory. *Reading improvement,* 4, 5-6.

Maxwell, M.J. (1981). *Improving student learning skills.* San Francisco: Jossey-Bass.

Maxwell, M. J. (1988). Personal communication with Mary Lee Schnuth. McNeil, D. R. (1980). Progress of an experiment. *New directions in continuing education,* 5, 47 - 53.

McPheeters, V. W. (1980). Learning resources centers -- past, present, and future. In K. Mikan (ed.), *Learning resources center conference: Proceedings and evaluation,* 1 - 5. Birmingham, Alabama. (ERIC Document Reproduction Service No. ED 222 180).

Miller, M. B. (1984). Developmental education and speech communication in the community colleges, *Communication education,* 33, 4 - 8.

Minkoff, H. (1974). A reading resource center: Why and how. *College management,* 9, 3, 17-18.

Obler, S. S. (1983). Programs for the underprepared student: Areas of concern. In J.E. Roueche (ed.), *A new look at successful programs.* San Francisco: Jossey-Bass, 21 - 30.

Pearse, C.A., R. F. Agrella and S. Powers (1982). *Identification and placement of college students in developmentaleducation programs.*

Paper presented at the annual meeting of the California Educational Research Association, Sacramento, California. (ERIC Document Reproduction Service No. ED 231 415)

Peterson, G.T. (1975). *The learning center: A sphere for nontraditional approaches to education.* Hamden, Connecticut: The Shoe String Press.

Pinsker, S. (1983). Business and communicating, *Business,* 33, 4, 47 - 48.

Potter, V. (1980). Breaking the barriers of isolation. *Community and junior college journal,* 50, 7, 35 - 37.

Roueche, J.E. and R. W. Kirk (1973). *Catching up: Remedial education.* San Francisco: Jossey-Bass.

Roueche, J. E. and J. J. Snow (1977). *Overcoming learning problems.* San Francisco: Jossey-Bass.

Roueche, S.D. (1983). Elements of program success: Report of a national study. In J.E. Roueche (ed.), *A new look at successful programs.* San Francisco: Jossey-Bass, 3 - 10.

Rounds, J.C. (1984). *Attrition and retention of community college students: Problems and promising practices.* Marysville: Yuba College.

Scarborough, R. E. (1985). Collaborative efforts with industry, government and education. In C. H. Shulman (ed.), *Adults and the changing workplace: 1985 yearbook of the American Vocational Association.* Arlington, Virginia: American Vocational Association, 249 - 256.

Schoolland, L. B. (1984). *College in paradise! (Paradise Valley Shopping Mall).* Paper presented to the Paradise Valley Mall Advisory Committee, Phoenix, Arizona (ERIC Document Reproduction Service Number 250 750).

Smith, P. P. (1977). *Case study No. 1: The "without walls" type: Community College of Vermont.* Paper presented at the Seminar for State Leaders in Postsecondary Education, Orlando, Florida. (ERIC Document Reproduction Service Number ED 202 297).

Sullins, W. R. (1987). Increasing access to postsecondary education for adults in rural Appalachia, *Community college review,* 15, 1, 46 - 53.

Sullivan, L. L. (1979). *Sullivan's guide to learning centers in higher education.* Portsmouth, New Hampshire: Entelek/Ward-Whidden House.

Sullivan, L. L. (1980). Growth and influence of the learning center movement. In K.V. Lauridsen (ed.), *Examining the scope of learning centers.* San Francisco: Jossey-Bass 1-7.

Vegso, K. A. (1982). *The adult resource center: A community educational brokerage service.* National Council on Community Services and Continuing Education Working Paper Series (No. 3). Cleveland, Ohio: National Council on Community Services and Continuing Education. (ERIC Document Reproduction Service Number ED 224 507).

Walker, C. (1980). The learning assistance center in a selective institution. In K.V. Lauridsen (ed.), *Examining the scope of learning centers.* San Francisco: Jossey-Bass, 57 - 68.

Waters, M.M. (1981). Reading. In A.S. Trillin and Assoc. (eds.), *Teaching basic skills in college.* San Francisco: Jossey-Bass, 91 - 144.

Whyte, C.B. (1980). An integrated counseling and learning center for a liberal arts college. In K.V. Lauridsen (ed.), *Examining the scope of learning centers.* San Francisco: Jossey-Bass, 33 - 43.

Wong, E. C. (1982). *A master plan for developmental education: A proposal* (Rep. No. 82-06). Los Angeles: Los Angeles Trade-Technical College, Office of Instruction. (ERIC Document Reproduction Service No. ED 248 913)

Yamba, A. Z. (1982). The rescue of Essex County College. *The College Board review,* 123, 9-10, 31-32.

8

College Learning Assistance Centers: Spaces for Learning

William G. White, Jr., Barney Kyzar and Kenneth E. Lane

Educational facilities, from the one-room school of the colonial period with its limited space, sparse furnishings, lack of interior sanitary facilities and poor ventilation, heating and lighting to the present special purpose facilities designed for study and research and containing the latest in technological innovations share a common element. Each represented a human response to a need for educational space. The form of the schoolhouse reflected the perceived function of education.

In this chapter the two elements of college and university facility planning, process and people, are examined. College learning assistance centers are highly specialized spaces which attempt to meet specific educational needs. To help learning assistance specialists participate more effectively in the planning process, the authors address a number of general and specific facility considerations for planning college learning assistance centers.

COLLEGE AND UNIVERSITY PLANNING

College and university planning in most states is now governed by legislation or regulations in the case of public institutions and by economic realities and good business practices in the private sector. Institutions are now required or elect to involve the users in the development of written educational specifications or program requirements to guide the architects and engineers as they develop architectural plans. This kind of planning requires two basic components: people and a well-defined planning process. Such a system provides the best facilities today and the flexibility to continually adapt to future change (Jenkins, 1985; *Campus Planning*, 1983; Engelhardt, 1970; Giljahn and Matheny, 1981; *Guidelines for developing*, 1985; *Space planning guidelines*, 1985).

Process

The successful planning of higher education facilities is a five-step process that includes: (1) analysis, (2) goal setting, (3) plan development, (4) plan implementation and (5) evaluation. Each component is vital to the realization of facilities that will make possible maximum teaching and learning.

Analysis

A careful inventory and analysis of existing conditions is the starting point for future development. Analysis of needs for a specific facility requires the consideration of a number of variables, some facility-specific and others campus-wide; the relative importance of some vary depending on whether the need is for a new facility or expansion or renovation of an existing one. Variables include: (1) environmental features such as topography, soil, hydrology, vegetation and land forms; (2) the number, functionality and condition of existing facilities; (3) land use, circulation systems, parking and utilities; and (4) regulatory factors, including campus master plan, regional and local master plans, zoning, state and local building, fire and safety codes and buildings.

Goal Setting

Institutional and program goals must be specific and measurable if they are to be statements around which facility planning can occur. In addition to campus-wide goals and enrollment projections, planning for a specific facility must include goals of the program(s) to be housed, enrollment projections, curricular organization, academic and support activities and staffing patterns to name a few.

Plan Development

The plan development phase results in recommendations that should be examined in light of goals and other considerations described above. Specific programs and enrollments will determine building requirements in terms of square footage and student stations. These in turn will affect such campus-wide concerns as parking, street locations, pedestrian circulation patterns and service requirements. Plan development also involves consideration of aesthetic and ecological environments and the realities of financial resources. The plan document, known as program requirements or educational specifications, should be complete and include lucid descriptions, drawings necessary to explain and illustrate and a rationale underlying major decisions in narrative form. The completed document serves as a proposed guideline for space planners and as a public relations tool.

Plan Implementation

A realistic process for implementing a facility plan must include considerations about the use of portions of buildings that are constructed in phases over a long period of time, the consequence of construction on the campus as a whole and the displacement of people and programs in renovation projects. Plan implementation must be well coordinated.

Evaluation

The evaluation phase permits facility planners and users to determine whether or not the facility successfully fits into the campus master plan and meets the goals and objectives set forth in the plan development phase of the planning process. In reality, evaluation of the facility also involves an evaluation of the planning process. The evaluation phase requires the participation of campus planners, architects, administrators and the users of the facility including, administrators, faculty, support staff and students.

People

Successful planning for higher education facilities requires the involvement of many people in a participatory planning process. The institution's professional planning staff is responsible for coordination and production of the planning document. They are assisted by the institutional planning committee, consultants and users of the faclity.

Professional Planning Staff

The in-house staff can range from one campus planner to as many as fifty or sixty people at a large university. A consistent planning process and ideas generated by a variety of people working together are more critical for good results than staff size. The in-house staff usually undertakes the following duties:

- **intelligence function** (evaluating exisitng activities and facilities; predicting the effects of physical changes on curricula, programs, goals and enrollments)
- **community relations function** (studies, communications, meetings and other measures necessary to coordinate institutional campus planning and other long-range objectives)
- **programming function** (identifying development problems, posing alternative solutions, preparing documents to ensure that project designs reflect long-range plans and development policy)
- **physical plant development** (preparing capital improvement budgets and preliminary and final project plans, supervising construction)
- **secretarial function** (keeping records, documents and other materials necessary to carry out planning, programming and physical plant development)

Institutional Planning Committee

The institutional planning committee is the common channel for input into the planning process. It normally includes executive officers, academic deans and/or department heads, maintenance and operations personnel, faculty, support staff and students. The size of the group should permit operational efficiency. The committee must have access to the chief executive officer of the institution.

The role of the committee is to review, propose and advise. Specific activities include the review of existing facilities, assessment and verification of needs and development of priorities for the number and quality of facilities and related services. The group advises the administration of its priorities and communicates with the larger campus community.

Consultants

Consultants can be of significant assistance in campus and facility planning. They can include campus planning specialists, architects, engineers of all types, designers and academic and support services specialists.

Facility Users

The involvement of the users in facility planning is perhaps the most critical element in the entire process. These people possess the professional expertise that will guide instruction and must adapt practices to the constraints of the facility. These persons must be actively involved and be given the opportunity and encouragement to articulate the philosophy, goals, activities and future of their specialty.

It is from this systematic process that planning the learning assistance center must eminate. The following sections address specifics.

PLANNING THE LEARNING ASSISTANCE CENTER

The goal-setting and plan-development phases described above involve detailed specification of the characteristics and needs of learners to be served, the content of the instructional programs to be provided to those students, the instructional techniques to be employed (appropriate consideration of the students' needs, curriculum requirements, recent advances in instructional techniques) and resources available to the program (Karwin, 1973). Even the most carefully planned facility cannot ensure the success of the program(s) it houses. The important point is what goes on in a structure. Is the atmosphere informal? Is it conducive to learning? Does it meet students' needs? Do students want to come back? (Bailey, Qazilbash and Deichart, 1972).

Learning always occurs within an environment which consists of components that bring learners into contact with learning experiences. Depending on characteristics of the learning experiences and the learners, environments need to provide (1) conditions appropriate for practice and performance, (2) conditions suitable for optimal interactivity and (3) privacy as needed (Cobun, 1981).

General Planning Considerations

In planning a learning assistance center, it is imperative that definite guidelines be followed throughout the process to ensure that an environment conducive to learning is attained. By themselves, facilities do not generate learning. The instructional media and methods used in facilities generate learning, negatively or positively. "Facilities of an appropriate nature expedite learning to the extent that they implement the duplication of characteristics of experience. Facilities are the manifestation of an interacting team" (Cobun, 1981, p. 177). The components of the "interacting facilities team" are:

- **experiences** - selected by a professional manager of individualized learning experiences
- **personnel** - to design, manage, procure, produce and validate media as necessary 3. environment - for specific and individual practice and performance, interactively as valuableand privacy as useful to expediate learning
- **hardware** - portable, fixed and remotely controllable as required by characteristics of the learning experiences
- **media** - to carry the message content of the experience in appropriate ways (Cobun, 1981).

The learning assistance center is a support facility for the learning program. Its design should spring from the center's clearly determined purposes and from the nature of the instructional program the facility is intended to support, rather than from a series of speculations, however carefully made (Currey, 1980; Karwin, 1973). The emphasis of a center often reflects the expertise or enthusiasm of the center director and staff, the intramural environment for instructional change, the political temperament and the architectural flexibility of the entire campus (Enright and Kersteins, 1980). A design based upon the personnel in the center, even if the director is enthusiastic and knowledgable, may be inappropriate when people with different perspectives are employed. A design based upon the instructional program is not subject to this type of frivolous change. Renovation of design based upon instructional change, not personnel change, is acceptable.

Individualized, prescription-based programs which characterize learning assistance centers require a facility with an open design (Garner, 1980). The facility must be flexible in its ability to be easily arranged to meet changing instructional requirements and the needs of the users (McPheeters, 1980). Interior flexibility is the capacity for continual change and expansion accomplished conveniently and routinely (Peterson, 1975). The facility must be adaptable to the individual, not the individual to the facility. This flexibility includes the design of spaces which allow for individual, small-group and large-group use. A facility which is designed without considering its adaptabilty to people is destined to fail in its instructional purpose (College and Research Libraries, 1982).

The facility should be attractive, comfortable and designed to encourage student use (Briley, 1976; Crettol, 1975; Garner, 1980; Henderson, 1972; Sharpe, 1978). Minkoff (1974, p.17) claims that the physical appearance of the learning assistance center is an important tool to "hook them [developmental students], to get them into the center." The use of appropriate color, carpeting and wall covering will enhance the design to create a better learning environment. As Robert Mager (Sharpe, 1978, p. 138) vividly states, "Things that are surrounded by unpleasantness are seldom surrounded by people."

The planning of the facility should include the director, support staff, student users and needed consultants. With this team approach, the facility can be designed to provide appropriate space to meet institutional and instructional objectives. It should also be sufficient to accommodate present operations and reflect long-range planning to provide for anticipated expansion and changes in educational mission, program and technologies (College and Research Libraries, 1982; McPheeters, 1980; Sharpe, 1978).

When estimating the facility's capacity, an important consideration is the types of students who will be using the learning assistance center. In most cases, students "drop-in" at their convenience. Optimum availability is likely to prove most attractive to these and part-time students (Karwin, 1973). With these guidelines in operation, the facility will have the flexibility to change both instructional design and physical design best to meet the needs of users. Additionally, the facility will meet the needs of users by providing them with the skills needed to function successfully in the world today and tommorrow.

Specific Planning Considerations

The specifications presented here are intended to provide parameters for the design of a learning assistance center tailored to the needs of the institution, students and instructional programs. It should be clearly understood that these are guidelines, not inflexible standards. It is important in developing the specifications for the center that the design reflect the institution's philosophy and be within the institution's budget constraints both for building and maintaining the facility.

Location on Campus

Because learning assistance center activities are closely related, each service is strengthened by proximity to the others. Learners benefit by collaboration and consultation among staff members. Administrative time is reduced and staff are utilized more efficiently when learning assistance programs are centralized rather than functioning separately in multiple sites on campus (Currey, 1980; Walker, 1980).

The name of the learning assistance center and its location on campus are important; more students, especially drop-ins, use the center when its name is "inclusive" and when they know where it is (Walker, 1980). For years learning assistance centers, reading and writing labs and math tutorials have been housed in basements and trailers far from the center of campus (Christ, 1980). A central, prominent location helps students avoid any stigma associated with either going to or being referred to the center (Briley, 1976).

Spaces

In discussing space requirements and other planning considerations, it is important to remember and adhere to the standards for facilities of the Council for the Advancement of Standards for Student Services/ Development Programs which state that each functional area must be provided adequate facilities to fulfill its mission. As applicable, facilites for each functional area must include, or the function must have access to, the following: private offices or private spaces for counseling, interviewing or other meetings of a confidential matter; office, reception and storage space sufficient to accommodate assigned staff, supplies, equipment, library resources and machinery; and conference room or meeting space. All facilities must be accessible to disabled persons and must be in compliance with relevant federal, state and local health and safety requirements (Council for the Advancement of Standards, 1986).

While adhering to these standards, the learning assistance center should provide a variety of adequate spaces and equipment for a wide range of teaching, learning and study situations pursuant to the academic programs supported by the center (Karwin, 1973; Sharpe, 1978). A variety of spaces are required to bring students, learning facilitators and media together in varying configurations (McPheeters, 1980). The following discussion focuses on space allocation requirements, spatial relationships, technological concerns, furnishings, equipment and other design considerations for the various areas of the learning assistance center.

Learning/media lab. [35 asf (assignable square feet) per student station (*Space planning*, 1985; Dahnke, Jones, Mason and Romney, 1971)]. The open-space learning/media lab (Peterson, 1975) should be centrally located and constitute the largest single space in the center. It should be comfortable and quiet. Basic furnishings should include study carrels (Crettol 1975; Karwin, 1973), tables and chairs (Briley, 1976). Dry (nonelectrified) carrels are for independent study; wet (electirified), possibly networked, carrels are for the use of a variety of media including video cassette players, sound filmstrip projectors, computer terminals, microcomputers and compact devices such as tape recorders and calculators. Lounge chairs should be provided for reading (Henderson, 1972; Sharpe, 1978).

The room should be irregularly shaped to provide some "private" areas (Karwin, 1973). It should be flexible, i.e. easily rearranged to meet the needs of various size groups and be adaptable for different types of group activities (Sharpe, 1978; Whyte, 1980).

Resource/learning materials center. The resource/learning materials center should be located next to the learning/media lab. In a sense, it is the library that serves the learning/media lab. As such, it should have a library-style circulation center where students and staff check out certain types of instructional equipment and materials for use in or out of the learning assistance center (Henderson, 1972; Peterson, 1975). The area should accommodate the storage and retrieval of a variety of media and materials - print, nonprint and electronic. Storage units range from traditional library shelving to special units for audio and video cassettes to file cabinets. Open shelving is preferable for as many items as possible (Karwin, 1973). The collection will surely grow; therefore, it is essential to plan adequate space and storage units for years of growth (Hansen, 1972).

Technical services/support space. The technical services/support area provides space for ordering, receiving and cataloging print and nonprint media. Print media will be mended, bound and laminated here. Electronic/instructional equipment and hardware will be maintained and serviced and some items stored in this area. The space should facilitate the production of media, such as video and audio casettes (Langhoff, 1980; McPheeters, 1980)and may house photocopying equipment/services for the learning assistance center (Henderson, 1972; Peterson, 1975). The area may also be used to store supplies, as a mailroom, for shipping and receiving (Karwin, 1973) and as a general instructional work space (Whyte, 1980).

Seminar rooms. [20 asf per student (*Space planning*, 1985)]. Seminar rooms should accommodate a maximum of 20 students (400 asf) in informal surroundings. They will be used for seminars, informal gatherings of students, student and tutor meetings and staff meetings (Karwin, 1973). They should provide opportunities for individuals or groups to interact with media (Langhoff, 1980; Sharpe, 1978; Whyte, 1980). Flexible walls will permit reconfiguration and multiple use of these spaces (Henderson, 1972).

Tutorial rooms. [240 asf, 6 student maximum capacity]. Tutorial rooms should be adjacent to the learning/media lab and are used for meetings of tutors with 1-5 students, testing, individual assistance and guidance of independent study (Karwin, 1973). Rooms should be furnished with multi-person carrels, small tables and chairs (Henderson, 1972).

Classrooms. [16 asf per student (*Space planning*, 1985)]. Since many learning assistance programs encompass courses in developmental English, reading, math, study skills, etc., the learning assistance center may need classroom spaces (McPheeters, 1980). If enrollments are kept small enough and there are enough seminar rooms, they could double for this purpose. Like seminar rooms, classrooms should have flexible or movable walls that permit easy reconfiguration to meet the needs of various types of classroom activities (Henderson, 1972; Sharpe, 1978).

If classrooms are needed they should be designed with audio-visual media and projection equipment in mind (Henderson, 1972). Room size and shape relate to projection screen size and placement. Ideally, two classrooms could be separated by a small room used for rear screen projection; or, a square of four classrooms could all share a common rear screen projection room in the center of the square. Classroom spaces should be designed for easy control of lighting, projection and audio from the instructor's desk or lectern (Sharpe, 1978).

Counseling offices. [120 asf each]. Private offices (Briley, 1976) permit counselors to work with students in personal and career counseling, in defining learning goals and in academic advisement (Karwin, 1973; Whyte, 1980). The counseling suite should have a career library (200-300 asf is probably adequate) (Peterson, 1975). A room (400 asf) furnished with tables and chairs for various types of individual and small group testing, diagnosis and assessment is desirable. A seminar room could double for this function if necessary (Henry and Omvig, 1981; McPheeters, 1980).

Administration and staff offices. Administrators' offices [140-160 asf each (*Space planning guidelines*, 1985)] must be large enough to allow for the direction of the learning center. They should have room for administrative records, communications equipment, computer hardware (Karwin, 1973). Furnishings should be comfortable, attractive and functional and set an appropriate "executive tone."

If there are multiple administrators or coordinators housed in the same suite, a shared conference room is desirable. Size will depend on the number of persons normally involved in meetings; 20-25 asf per person is usually adequate. If there is only one administrator, the office could be enlarged to accommodate a small conference table and chairs for small committees and work groups.

Faculty and staff offices should have 110-150 asf and be appropriately furnished. Administrative, faculty and staff offices should be clustered in groups of four or five around secretarial/reception areas. Graduate assistant offices should have 40-70 asf (*Space planning guidelines*, 1985).

Receptionist/clerk station. [120 asf per person]. The receptionist/clerk station should be located near the main entrance of the center. It should contain necessary office and communication equipment (Karwin, 1973). If this station serves the entire learning assistance center it should be large enough to provide comfortable seating for individuals waiting to see a staff member. Other secretarial/reception areas should be located to serve suites of administrative, faculty and staff offices.

Typing/word processing stations. [60 asf each]. Typing/word processing stations can be designed as part of receptionist/clerk/secretarial stations, or they may be desinged for student use and strategically located in the center. In either case, stations should be acoustically treated to deaden excess noise. Student stations can also be used for individual study when not being used for typing or word processing (Karwin, 1973). Word processing could take place in the learning/media lab at carrels with the actual printing of documents taking place at a word processing station.

Storage space. The center will need adequate storage spaces. Ample centralized storage is needed for instructional and clerical equipment and supplies. Many areas, such as tutorial services, counseling and the resource/learning materials center, will need storage space for special materials and equipment. Of course, the center will also need adequate mechanical/custodial/utility spaces (Briley, 1976; Karwin, 1973).

Commons. [5-10 asf per person, maximum occupancy (*Space planning*, 1985)]. A commons area and/or lounge spaces should be provided for the convenience and comfort of students and staff (Karwin, 1973). Such areas should be furnished with comfortable but durable tables and chairs. Food and drink vending machines could be located here. An outdoor commons area, perhaps an attractively landscaped courtyard with seating would be a nice addition (Henderson, 1972).

Child care center. A child care center should house a supervised playroom opening onto a small play yard for students with children. It should be visually and acoustically isolated from the rest of the facility, yet physically close (Karwin, 1973). Space in this area depends upon the number of children to be served, their size and the activities in which they are to be engaged. A typical kindergarten classroom, for example, allocates 75 sf per child including storage and rest rooms (Castaldi, 1987).

Rest rooms. Rest room size depends upon the estimated full capacity of the center and local, state and federal laws and regulations concerning the handicapped. As in other rest room facilities on campus, commercial-grade fixtures, wall- and floor-coverings are essential.

Other spaces. While learning assistance centers have supplanted writing centers, math and reading labs and study skills centers on most campuses, some learning assistance centers may still need to include such identifiable spaces (Christ, 1980). As far as space requirements, 20-35 asf per student should be a generally acceptable standard (*Space planning guidelines*, 1985). Exact space requirements, furnishings, equipment and other design considerations for such spaces must emerge from the participatory planning process described earlier.

Microcomputer Considerations

Understand this if nothing else regarding microcomputers: they should be selected to meet the software needed for the center, not vice versa. There should be at least one printer for every four microcomputers. Surge protectors and radio frequency protectors should be installed on microcomputers. Power conditioners for circuit breaker boxes or portable isolation voltage regulators should also be installed.

The temperature should be maintained at 60 to 90 degrees when the system is on and at 50 to 110 degrees when the system is off. Humidity should be maintained at 8 percent to 80 percent at all times (Lane and Lane, 1988).

Furnishings and Office Equipment

Furniture should be attractive and comfortable, yet durable, functional and easily maintained. A wide range of colors, fabrics and styles permit a decor that enhances the aesthetics and appeal of the center. Furniture should also be considered as to its use, whether it be for lounging or studying at tables or carrels (Cobun, 1981). All furnishings should be adult-sized (Henry and Omvig, 1981) and designed for use by handicapped individuals.

Flexible, movable furniture is essential for innovative and mediated instructionand there must be adequate storage space for items not in use (Sharpe, 1978). Seating for individualized instruction requires comfort, durability, beauty, ease of unit movement and ease of movement of the user.

"Research has shown that seated learners tend to generate discomfort with the passage of time. Expressed in broad humor, the activity of the cerebrum tends to vary inversely by the square of the compaction of the gluteus maximus" (Coburn, 1981, p. 182). If persons are going to remain seated for more than an hour, upholstered chairs with 3 inch padding and contour backs are desirable.

The following furnishings and equipment are usually found in learning assistance centers: student combination desks; student chairs; office desks, credenzas and chairs; tables (round, square and rectangular); file cabinets (2-drawer, 4-drawer and lateral); book cases; communications and photocopy equipment (Materniak, 1980); circulation control desk, shelving and electronic media storage units; dry and wet individual study carrels; and wet group carrels (Henderson, 1972).

Thermal Environment

Adequate heating, cooling and ventilation are necessary in all areas, especially in those housing microcomputers and group meeting rooms. Separate zoned heating/cooling controls should be accessible by staff for the different areas of the center. Fresh-air intake and air-exchange rates are important (Briley, 1976; Crettol, 1975; Henderson, 1972). This part of the planning process requires careful attention as research "indicates that students learn best when the conditions of the air and surrounding surfaces are most conducive to physical and mental well being. Although it is possible for the human organism to adjust itself to a wide variety of environmental conditions, it is done with a considerable expenditure of energy which distracts the student from learning . . ." (Evans & Neagley, 1973, p. 208). Factors to be considered in this regard include air temperatures, radiant temperatures, relative humidity, air movement, odors, dust, dirt and atmosphere contaminants. Prohibiting smoking throughout the center will improve air quality (Henry and Omvig, 1981).

Lighting

Lighting, whether natural or artificial, should be controllable in each area of the center because various instructional activities require varying levels of illumination (Sharpe, 1978). Windows should be equipped with miniblinds or shades to control natural lighting when using projection equipment. The installation of light switches to allow only a portion of the lights in a fixture to be turned on would provide flexibility. Generally, 30 footcandles of llumination should be adequate for any activity in the center (Briley, 1976; Jenkins, 1985).

Natural light is important, but large expanses of glass can cause problems. Unprotected southern exposures can result in heat gainand western exposures pose glare control problems. Skylights, while highly desirable in some areas of the learning assistance center, make the use of electronic visual media more difficult (Sharpe, 1978).

Electrical

Extensive use of electronic media and microcomputers makes adequate electrical planning essential. Every wall should contain outlets for proper usage of educational and maintenance equipment. Floor outlets should be provided liberally. Light controls should be installed by each exit door in a room. Light controls in hallways and other similiar "public" spaces should be key rather than switch controlled. Extra conduit, circuits, wiring and outlets should provide for present and future technological needs (Peterson, 1975; Sharpe, 1978).

Acoustics

Acoustic control is important in the learning assistance center, especially in large open spaces and in tutorial and seminar rooms (Briley, 1976; Crettol, 1975; Henderson, 1972). The use of various types of electronic media and a variety of instructional activities requires appropriate acoustic treatment (Sharpe, 1978). Acoustic control does not require making all spaces sound proof or so acoustically dead that users work in complete silence. In fact, the complete absence of noise is unnatural and is actually distracting and the presence of ambient sound is desirable (Peterson, 1975). The real concerns should be the control of noise within given spaces and sound transmission from one space to another (Castaldi, 1987). Acoustical engineering and treatment, therefore, include not only individual spaces but also entire buildings to control noise transmission (Sharpe, 1978).

Special attention will need to be given to floor coverings, wall and ceiling surfaces, window coverings and flexible wall systems. It will be necessary to reduce or control mechanical and other noise makers. For example, hydraulic closers should be used on most doors. Quiet models of chair swivels and rollers, file drawer slides, pencil sharpeners and typewriters should be selected. Conversation areas should be located away from study areas (Henry and Omvig, 1981; Sharpe, 1978).

Floor Coverings

A special word about floor coverings is in order. Carpeting should be a serious consideration due to its acoustical qualities and its ability to create a "warm" atmosphere. Due to recent technology, carpet is more economical in the long run than tile flooring. Colors and styles available provide immense flexibility. Floor covering is an important aspect of providing appropriate acoustic treatment for the center (Briley, 1976; Henry and Omvig, 1981; Sharpe, 1978).

Instructional Equipment

Facilities, in a large measure, determine the degree to which instructional media will be used effectively and innovatively. Instructional media should be housed conveniently for use by professional staff in classrooms or other formal settings and by students individually. Adequate storage is a necessity since all of the equipment needed for specific programs housed in the learning assistance center must be provided there. An electronic security system will be required because of the tremendous value of instructional equipment in the center (College and Research Libraries, 1982; Sharpe, 1978).

If new equipment is needed in the center, three principles should guide selection: (1) flexibility to ensure maximum utilization, (2) compatibility and (3) standardization (Langhoff, 1980). The following are equipment items typically housed in learning assistance centers: tape recorders/players, video recorders/players, slide projectors, overhead projectors, projection screens, film strip projectors, chalkboards, White boards, color television monitors, microcomputer systems and modems for microcomputers (Materniak, 1980).

CONCLUSION

Planning for a new facility or for renovation of an existing facility for a college learning assistance center is both a serious challenge and a unique opportunity. Facility planning is a challenge because careful, participatory planning is time-consuming, hard work. However, the opportunity of planning a space that can positively contribute to the performance of both staff and students is one to be cherished. Most educators have their work shaped by the spaces in which it is performed. When the opportunity arises to plan for spaces that are shaped by the needs of the learning assistance program, that planning must be done wisely. The planning process, principles and considerations presented here will help the learning assistance professional make the most of that opportunity.

REFERENCES

Bailey, C. Jr., H. Qazilbash, K. Deichart, K. (1972). *The adult learning center.* No. 6. Morehead, Kentucky: Appalachian Adult Education Center, Bureau for Research and Development, Morehead State University. (ERIC Document Reproduction Service No. ED 086 894)

Briley, P. (1976). *Planning and implementing learning skills centers in the state of Kansas.* Paper presented at the annual meeting of the International Reading Association, Anaheim, California. (ERIC Document Reproduction Service No. ED 123 603)

Campus Planning: Redesign - Redevelopment - Rethinking. (1983). Proceedings of a professional development symposium at Baylor University, Waco, Texas. Myrick, Newman, Dahlberg and Partners, Inc.

Castaldi, B. (1987). *Educational facilities: Planning, modernizationand management.* Boston: Allyn and Bacon.

Christ, F.L. (1980). Learning assistance at a state university: A cybernetic model. In K.V. Lauridsen (ed.), *Examining the scope of learning centers.* San Francisco: Jossey-Bass, 45 - 56.

Cobun, T.C. (1981). Facilities technology for individualized instruction. In P.J. Sleeman and D.M. Rockwell (eds.), *Designing learning environments.* New York: Longman, 174 - 188.

College and Research Libraries, Board of Directors. (1982). Guidelines for two-year college learning resources programs, revised June 30, 1981. *C & RL News,* January/February 1982.

Council for the Advancement of Standards for Student Services/ Development Programs, Consortium of Student Affairs Professional Organizations. (1986). *CAS standards and guidelines for student services/development programs.*

Crettol, M. (1975). *Libraries and instructional materials centers.* (ERIC Document Reproduction Service No. ED 109 802)

Currey, J. W. (1980). Creating functional learning resource centers. In K. Mikan (ed.), *Learning resources center conference: Proceedings and evaluation.* Birmingham, Alabama. (ERIC Document Reproduction Service No. ED 222 180), 17 - 24.

Dahnke, H. L., D. P. Jones, I.R., Mason, T. R Romney, & L. C. Romney (1971). *Classroom and class laboratory facilities* (Higher Education Facilities Planning and Management Manual No. 2). Boulder, CO: Western Interstate Commission for Higher Education.

Engelhardt, N.L. (1970). *Complete guide for planning schools.* West Nyack, NY: Parker.

Enright, G. and G. Kersteins (1980). The learning center: Toward an expanded role. In O.T. Lenning and R.L. Nayman (eds.), *New roles for learning assistance.* San Francisco: Jossey-Bass, 1 - 24.

Evans, N. D.and R. L. Neagley (1973). *Planning and developing innovative community colleges.* Englewood Cliffs, NJ: Prentice Hall.

Garner, A. (1980). A comprehensive community college model for learning assistance centers. In K.V. Lauridsen (ed.), *Examining the scope of learning centers.* San Francisco: Joeesy-Bass, 19 - 31.

Giljahn, J.W. and T. R. Matheny (1981). *A guide for the adaptive use of surplus schools.* Columbus, Ohio: Columbus Landmarks Foundation.

Guidelines for developing a program of requirements. (1985). Columbus, OH: Council of Educational Facility Planners, International.

Hansen, D. E. (1972, August). Systematic approach to learning resource center design. *Educational technology,* 63-64.

Henderson, D.D. (1972). *Report on alternatives and considerations for the design of a learning resource center (LRC) at Georgetown University.* (ERIC Document Reproduction Service No. ED 124 121)

Henry, S. and C. P. Omvig (1981). *Learning center handbook.* Kentucky University, Division of Vocational Education. (ERIC Document Reproduction Service No. ED 215 106)

Jenkins, J. (ed.) (1985). *Guide for planning educational facilities.* Columbus, Ohio: Council of Educational Facility Planners, International.

Karwin, T.J. (1973). *Flying a learning center: Design and costs of an off-campus space for learning.* Berkeley: The Carnegie Commission on Higher Education.

Lane, M. and K. Lane (1988). Design considerations for microcomputer laboratories. *CEFP Journal,* 26(1), pp. 10-11.

Langhoff, H. F. (1980). Learning resource centers: Organizational components and structural models. In K. Mikan (ed.), *Learning resources center conference: Proceedings and evaluation.* Birmingham, Alabama. (ERIC Document Reproduction Service No. ED 222 180), 6 - 16.

Materniak, G. (1980). *Developing a learning center from A to Z: Guidelines for designing a comprehensive developmental education program in a post-secondary educational setting.* Unpublished paper. Pittsburg:

University of Pittsburg.

McPheeters, V. W. (1980). Learning resources centers -- past, presentand future. In K. Mikan (ed.), *Learning resources center conference: Proceedings and valuation.* Birmingham, Alabama. (ERIC Document Reproduction Service No. ED 222 180), 1 - 5.

Minkoff, H. (1974). A reading resource center: Why and how. *College management,* 9(3), 17-18.

Peterson, G.T. (1975). *The learning center: A sphere for nontraditional approaches to education.* Hamden, Connecticut: The Shoe String Press.

Sharpe, A. D. (1978). Essentials for an effective learning environment. In J.D. Terry and R.W. Hotes (eds.), *The administration of learning resources centers.* Washington, D.C.: University Press of America, 128 - 139.

Space planning guidelines for institutions of higher education (1985). Columbus, Ohio: Council of Educational Facility Planners, International.

Walker, C. (1980). The leraning assistance center in a selective institution. In K. V. Lauridsen (ed.), *Examining the scope of learning centers.* San Francisco: Jossey-Bass, 57 -68.

Whyte, C.S. (1980). An integrated counseling and learning center for a liberal arts college. In K.V. Lauridsen (ed.), *Examining the scope of learning centers.* San Francisco: Jossey-Bass, 33 - 43.

9

Stress and the Developmental Student

George H. Roberts

Academic skills are not the only problems developmental students must face in college. They must also make personal and social adjustments just like the 'typical' college student. Developmental students often realize that they have an inadequate educational background and fear failure; that fear affects other areas of their lives. However, when students are able to overcome learning problems, they gain confidence in their ability and themselves. This confidence helps them to cope more effectively with other problems.

This chapter focuses on the problems developmental education students have in adjusting to the academic demands of university life, the nature of those problems, their causes, and suggested strategies for their mediation.

Developmental students are defined as those whose skills, knowledge, and academic abilities are significantly below those of the 'typical' students in the college in which they are enrolled (Maxwell, 1981). Entrance standards, faculty expectations, and the characteristics of the average student vary between universities. Underpreparedness is relative to the institution at which a student seeks admission. However, the problems of developmental students affect every institution.

There are many causes for the increase in developmental students in institutions of higher education (Cross, 1971). Some of the reasons for the increase in developmental students are:

- the post-war baby boom
- the permissive environment of today's high schools
- lowered high school standards
- increased absence rates
- grade inflation
- deemphasis of traditional college preparation
- the open-door admissions policies.

The need for basic skills services has been documented since the beginning of American higher education (Brubacher and Rudy, 1974). Public and private institutions have always admitted underprepared students. Failure has always been an inherent part of academic life, even prior to open admissions. Many students failed or dropped out and left higher education never to return. Colleges have become revolving doors through which the same students continue to enter and exit. Today, there seems to be a greater concern about retaining students in college since a declining birthrate indicates a period of economic hardship for institutions of higher education as they compete for the declining number of high school graduates. That phenomenon is causing a great diversity in the student population which is to continue; the problems of developmental students will be with us for many years. With this in mind, it is evident that institutions of higher education must continue to offer comprehensive and intensive academic support services to their students if those students are to succeed in higher education.

CLASSIFICATION OF DEVELOPMENTAL STUDENTS

Institutions, faculty, and student service workers must realize that developmental students are not a homogeneous group of students. They must be recognized as members of the larger total population of students within a group with similar and unique needs.

Williams (1978) states that it should be an accepted practice to test developmental students and to tailor instruction to their individual learning needs. However, a systematic study of individual personalities and personal circumstances to determine why each student needs developmental education and what kinds of instruction will achieve the best results has not been performed.

When students begin college, individual personalities begin to emerge. Students begin to engage in various patterns of behavior. Ultimately, the instructor should be able to analyze and classify the problems these students have brought with them to the classroom.

Williams (1978) suggests eleven categories for classifying developmental students according to personality and circumstance. Some students may be classified into more than one of these categories. These categories are as follows:

- relearners
- disadvantaged
- new learners
- individualists
- slow learners

- entertainers
- poor performers
- disturbed
- role players
- distracted
- incompetents

The greatest value of this type of classification of developmental students is the recognition that they are people with problems and obstacles. They become encouraged when instructors and counselors take a personal interest and intervene on an individual basis.

WHAT IS STRESS?

Although there are many different definitions of stress, the most often cited is "a nonspecific response of the body to any demand made upon it" (Greenberg, 1977). Bennington (1984) defines stress as a stimulus having sufficient magnitude to produce the breakdown of the normal, relatively constant conditions in the body's environment. Swogger (1981) defines a stressor as any stimulus, internal or external, which activates physiological and psychological coping mechanisms and allows individuals to avoid or control the stimulus.

Stress is an individual matter and is not necessarily harmful. The way an individual perceives and labels the world around oneself and one's own internal thoughts and feelings, serves to define events as potentially dangerous or relatively harmless. Each individual has a unique way of defining events as challenging or threatening and of responding to a given event (Lagreca, 1985; Ramsey, 1986).

The Stress Response

The major work on the stress response is credited to Hans Selye (1956), who noticed a commonality of certain symptoms in illnesses of all types. His observation of a nonspecific reaction of the body to various types of stressors has been the focus of much of his work on stress.

Selye (1956) exposed laboratory animals to numerous stress-provoking stimuli and observed the physiological responses of the animals. Regardless of the type of stressor, the response was the same. This nonspecific response led Selye to formulate a theory of stress response which he called the general adaptation syndrome (GAS). The physiological response of the body to any stressful stimulus is always the same and is characterized by three major stages: alarm, resistance and exhaustion stages.

Each stage is characterized by biological, hormonal, and nervous system changes.

During the alarm stage, the presence of the stressor causes an increase in the metabolic rate of the individual. This change helps the individual eliminate the stressor and regain equilibrium (Girdano and Everly, 1979; Greenberg, 1977; Selye, 1956).

The stress response is channeled into the specific organ system best able to handle it during the resistance stage. The body struggles to counterbalance the physiological changes that developed during the alarm stage.

The exhaustion stage follows the resistance stage when the stressful event does not subside. As the body responds to stress, it depletes its storehouse of adaptation energy. Energy reserves are completely utilized, and the body begins to malfunction. When the body is exposed to additional stressful events, chronic illness can result (Macek, 1982; Ostfield and D'Atri, 1975; Rapley-Evans, 1983; Riley, 1981).

Selye (1956) concluded that the body possesses a predetermined amount of adaptation energy at birth and that the store of energy cannot be replenished. When the store house is depleted, the body falls prey to one of many diseases. It is impossible to elude all the stressors in an individual's life. Therefore, Selye recommends that individuals learn to become aware of stressors, remove those that are avoidable, and learn to adjust to those which cannot be removed or avoided.

Stress and Learning

The topic of student stress generates a variety of responses from complete indifference to the desire to minimize or eliminate all stress faced by students. Student personnel service workers want to minimize stress since they believe that stress has a negative effect on learning. However, stress can exhibit both positive and negative effects. Stress can help students achieve their goals but also can become a destructive force with negative consequences. Therefore, it is extremely important for faculty, administrators, and student personnel service workers to be aware of the results of stress when they evaluate and develop academic and administrative policies and procedures.

A critical issue regarding stress among students is the effect that stress has on learning. Yerkes and Dodson (1908) experimented with animals and formulated the Yerkes-Dodson law: animals under low or high stress learn least while those under moderate stress learn the most. This relationship has also been used to describe human learning behavior (Hockey, 1979; Mandler, 1982).

Bossing and Ruoff (1982) report the demonstration of the Yerkes-Dodson law in a study of school children. Students were divided into three classrooms with teachers who were instructed to be demanding and highly authoritarian (a high level of stress), nondirective or laissez-faire in another (a low level of stress), and democratic in another (optimum level of stress). In the authoritarian classroom, students were initially most productive, but over several weeks their resulting aggressive behavior began to reduce their high level of productivity. The laissez-faire teaching style resulted in the lowest levels of productivity and produced levels of aggressive behavior that were almost as high as the high stress group. The democratic style in which the teacher regularly involved the students in discussion about what was best to study and what was best at motivating students, resulted in the highest level of productivity and reduction of frustrations. Silver (1968) demonstrated those effects in law students.

Being a student means experiencing stress. However, stress is a very necessary and positive aspect of learning if that stress is experienced as a challenge. As a result of the challenge, the student should exhibit an increased capacity to learn. However, many students experience distress and feel threatened and helpless, and exhibit a lowered ability to learn. Whitman, Spendlove, and Clark (1984) assert that the education program in which many students find themselves can add to stress levels. Stress may originate from what the student perceives as excessive demands, too little feedback from the teacher, inappropriate feedback, promotion of feelings of not belonging in the academic environment, and lack of a personal relationship with those in authority.

An additional source of stress is the developmental stage that students experience. Erikson (1950, 1963, 1980) explains that life is marked by stages during which individuals must meet and resolve certain basic life tasks. Some of the stressors that individuals deal with are related to some stage in life, work, and the contrast between expectations and realities. In the young adult years, the stressors are associated with graduating from high school and completing college, finding employment, and proving competence by establishing an identity of self. The resolution of these goals necessitates the often stressful task of meshing educational goals, sex roles and work roles.

Chickering (1969) identified seven developmental vectors that operate in the university student's life:

- achieving competency
- managing emotions
- becoming autonomous
- establishing an identity
- clarifying purposes
- freeing interpersonal relationships
- developing integrity

Those developmental vectors have both direction and magnitude and affect attitudes, interests, values, aspirations, and intellectual abilities more frequently for students than non-students of the same age group.

Stress that is experienced as a threat is harmful to performance. Characteristic cognitive reactions to distress are documented in the literature on human performance.

Janis (1982) states that hypervigilance, similar to Selye's alarm reaction, "is an excessive alertness to all signs of potential threat which adversely affects cognitive functioning." Students feel panicked and become overwhelmed by the vast multitude of material, become cognitively inefficient, and are not able to focus on the important issues and perform poorly on examinations.

Janis (1982) goes on to point out that another consequence of stress in decision making is quickly choosing a solution to end a stressful situation (premature closure). Individuals rush through a test and choose inappropriate answers without studying all of the alternative solutions presented. Thus poor grades may not reflect underpreparedness but premature closure due to the high degree of stress students feel.

Prolonged exposure to environmental stressors (classroom factors) and/or information overload can result in cognitive fatigue. Overload may result in an inadequate attention reserve to allow the performance of cognitive tasks (Cohen, 1980). The negative effects of performance are magnified when the individual does not feel in control of the particular stressor.

Stress may also result in some social effects including an insensitivity to others, decreased willingness to help others, disregard of individual differences, and increased aggressive behaviors (Cohen, 1980). Those social effects will diminish student performance to the extent that an adequate support system helps mediate the stress (Cobb, 1976).

With an understanding of the research on stress and coping, faculty, administrators, and student personnel service workers can better evaluate the student's environmental setting, identify the sources of stress, and make informed judgements on changes needed so that the optimal level of stress necessary for learning to occur will not be exceeded (Whitman, Spendlove, and Clark, 1984).

Stress and Coping

Lazarus, Averill, and Opton (1974) define coping as "problem-solving efforts made by an individual when the demands he faces are highly relevant to his welfare (i.e., a situation of considerable jeopardy or promise) and when these demands tax his adaptive resources." Those problem solving efforts may be indirect or direct. Indirect methods for coping may include exercising, going to a movie, drinking excessively, and/or giving oneself a pep talk (Whitman et al., 1984). Indirect methods do little to enhance cognitive actions since they provide no useful feedback. Direct coping methods include talking to the instructor or counselor regarding effective study methods, reviewing the test and its contents, and withdrawing from the class. Any of those actions should result in the provision of feedback which will benefit the student.

Many different demographic variables as well as personal characteristics will influence how an individual determines the stressfulness of a situation and copes with that situation. There are three specific demographic variables that influence students: race, sex, and marital status (Whitman, etal., 1984). Other variables may exert an influence. Stress and coping strategies are individual matters.

Indicators of Stress

The three major indicators of stress in the educational environment, suicide rate, use of campus counseling services, and the drop-out rate.

The total number of teenagers who commit suicide has increased 300 percent in the last 30 years (Garfinkel, 1988). Suicide attempts have increased between 350 percent and 700 percent. Those individuals who commit suicide or attempt to do so are experiencing significant distress in their lives which may include failing grades, difficulties with peers, and trouble at home. The stressors responsible for that action are not unique to that group of individuals. Apparently it is an accumulation of various stresses that overwhelms students and cause them to believe that suicide is the only solution.

An increasing number of college students seek psychiatric and counseling help as the result of distress each year (Ellis, 1969; McWilliams and Gerber, 1978; Whitman, Spendlove and Clark, 1984). The reasons given for seeking help portray a picture of stress and include depression, inability to do school work, nervousness, and anxiety.

A third measure of stress is the high school and college dropout rate (Clayton, 1985; Ekstrom, Goertz, Pollack, and Rock, 1986; Larsen and Shertzer, 1987; Sherraden, 1986). Reported dropout rates vary from 8% to 60%. Those numbers represent individuals who choose to change neither themselves nor the environment but to increase the distance between themselves and their source of stress, the educational environment. That action represents a mismatch between the student and the educational environment.

Stress and Health

A comprehensive research project conducted by Holmes and Rahe (1967) studied the effects of rapid and multiple change on health. This research indicates that unusual stress caused by life changes can be a great risk to an individual's health. Stress-related reactions and diseases are intimately related to individual styles of coping with stress.

The effects of stress on health is a focus of much current research. The most commonly recognized detrimental results of stress are peptic ulcers, heart disease, hypertension, muscle tension, backaches, cancer, and other chronic illnesses (Chobanian, 1982). Heart disease alone is the leading cause of death in the United States today. The precise mechanism underlying many of those conditions is unknown at present. However, many diseases possess a stress component. The stress component of coronary heart disease appears to be the result of chronic elicitation of the fight-or-flight mechanism (alarm reaction). Research into the role of the stress response in chronic and infectious diseases has recently focused on the effects of stress on the immune system. Though precise mechanisms are unknown, the evidence tends to indicate that stress has a detrimental effect on health.

Sources of Student Stress

Girdano and Everly (1979), Melingo (1977), and Wallace (1978) state that stress originates from three sources: conditions in the immediate environment, characteristics of the individual's personal life, and situations within the task or job itself. Everyone is exposed to a certain amount of stress during normal contact with other individuals. Johnson (1981) asserts that much of the stress in a person's life has its origin in change of values, society, environment, and of self. He suggests that all change leads to psychological loss which leads to anger, and anger changes to depression.

Stress is conceptualized as a need to adapt to life event changes. College students experience a great deal of stress. Greenberg (1981) studied a college population to determine the changes experienced by the students upon entering college. Those changes experienced by over 50 percent of the students included:

- entering college;
- holding a job while attending school;
- changing sleeping habits;
- revising personal habits;
- changing eating habits;
- achieving outstanding personal goals;
- changing residence or living conditions;
- changing type or amount of recreation;
- changing social activities;

- changing the amount of independence
- taking a trip or vacation; and, or responsibility;
- changing schools.

Greenberg's research indicates that the stress produced by those changes is related to illness and disease in the college student population.

A common source of stress in young adolescents that has not been fully investigated is the school experience of the unsuccessful student (Stevens, 1980). Prolonged failure has been determined to depress subsequent performance and failure-expectant students use less effective problem-solving skills. Students with a poor school history differ from their classmates not only in the level of academic skills that they bring to the college environment but also in the expectation of future success.

The results of Stevens' study indicated significant differences between 'typical' students and a group of students whose history included less success and more failure. Therefore, school failure, and even the threat of that failure, appears to have a detrimental effect on subsequent school performance.

Numerous researchers have studied stress in various college populations utilizing a variety of sampling techniques and statistical procedures (Archer and Lamnin, 1985; Beard, Elmore, and Lange, 1982; Dintman and Greenberg, 1986; Johnson, 1981; Mayes and Mc Conatha, 1982; Mullinex, Fadden, Broch, and Gould, 1980; Sagaria, Higginson, and White, 1980). Those studies exhibit some commonality in the types of stressors listed as most important and include:

ACADEMIC STRESSORS:

- Test and finals - performance anxiety
- Grades and competition
- Too many demands, not enough time, deadlines
- Professors and class environment
- Career and future success
- Procrastination, getting behind, being underprepared
- Studying
- Finances - problems with financial aid
- Papers and essay exams
- Registration procedures
- Speaking in class
- Size of classes

PERSONAL STRESSORS:

- Intimate relationships
- Parental conflicts and expectations
- Finances
- Interpersonal conflicts with friends and others
- Peer pressure, judgement and acceptance by peers
- Personal achievement - goal setting
- Roommate conflicts
- Approaching and meeting other students
- Future and career plans and success identity
- Not enough free time
- General adjustment to unexpected change
- Personal appearance
- Living conditions
- Current job

Roberts (1989) reported the academic and personal stressors reported by a group of developmental education students. The most important academic stressors in descending order of importance were:

- Career and future goals
- Studying
- Tests and finals
- Problems with financial aid
- Procrastination

The most important personal stressors in descending order of importance were:

- Living conditions
- Personal appearance
- Not enough free time
- Roommate conflicts
- Approaching and meeting others
- Parental conflicts and expectations
- Intimate relationships

THE ACADEMIC DIMENSION OF STRESS

The ordering of academic stressors somewhat matches the common perception and indicates that developmental education students are concerned about their career and future goals. That fact may be because the student is wondering "if I'll ever be successful in life." Students appear to be concerned with their ability to find employment in their chosen field and about what courses will best prepare them for employment in today's labor market. That problem may also be germaine to students who do not know what they really want out of life.

A large percentage of the students in Roberts' (1989) study listed majors in fields considered to be the most difficult by traditional students with no academic deficiencies. Those students feel frustrated, and the feelings of frustration may be compounded by teachers in these and related fields. Students may be told that they have no hope of attaining their educational objectives and that they should reorder their lives to include majors with less strict academic standards or discontinue the pursuit of a college education.

Studying was the second most important stressor for developmental education students. That may reflect a poor quality of instruction the students have received, the ability of many students to complete high school graduation requirements without learning how to study, social promotion, the inability to see the need for developing effective study habits, the increased amount of study required for college success, fear of failure in college or a combination of any or all factors. Additional sources of stress are tests and finals. That suggests that developmental education students are competitive and grade conscious. It is possible that part of the problem is related to the way examinations are scheduled and weighted. Problems may also arise from the large amounts of material covered on the examination, the lack of knowledge of how to study, procrastination, work and family responsibilities, and the possibility of several examinations on the same day or within the same week. The study, work, and family requirements all combine to frustrate students and to compound their other problems. When students are unable to mesh their goals and roles, they may feel defeated and withdraw from the university to meet the more basic needs of present-day life.

College costs are rising, there is increasing unemployment, and government and private grants as well as loans are difficult to obtain. Problems with financial aid is a major stressor for students. The reduced ability to obtain financial aid places additional pressures on the already stressed developmental student. Students must take on employment in addition to their academic work to support themselves and pay college expenses. To be able to work, students may have to take reduced course loads which necessitates a longer time to complete graduation requirements which causes additional frustration and stress.

Another facet of these financial problems may be the students' disdain of the apparent large amount of paperwork, waiting lines, and answering personal questions that impinge upon little free time they have.

A major stressor for those students was procrastination indicating that they have not matured sufficiently to be able to set goals for themselves and to stick to the requirements to achieve those goals. Students are constantly being drawn into other activities which interfere with studying and tests and finals.

THE PERSONAL DIMENSION OF STRESS

The most important personal stressor was living conditions. That fact reflects dissatisfaction with the living arrangements on campuses. Many dormitories are thermally uncomfortable which adversely affects student health and well-being. During some semesters three individuals are housed in rooms designed for two. There are also problems with roommates, suitemates, the house director, the resident assistant, and other individuals. Students have little or no privacy. Many of the campus dwellers do not have transportation and are unable to travel freely about town for socialization.

The second most important stressor was that of personal appearance. This is in apparent conflict with the listing of peer pressure as one of the least important stressors. Peer pressure is assumed to be one of the primary determinants of personal appearance. The trend is to wear namebrand clothes, use the best beauty aids, join a health club, and look, dress, and act just like everyone else.

The listing of not enough free time as a major stressor probably indicates a true overload for many of the students, an inability to manage time and priorities, and a probable conflict between school, work, family, and socialization.

Living conditions as a major stressor relates very closely to the problems expressed as roommate conflicts, intimate relationships, and parental conflicts and expectations. Entrance into college involves transitions in personal development, separation from family and friends, development of new interpersonal relationships, examination of values, and acceptance of new responsibilities. Loneliness is a problem for college students, particularly freshmen. The family has been considered the primary unit of social support throughout a person's life and is a moderator of stress. Transition to college seems to be one life transition in which family support is most important.

These students may also encounter problems associated with their own perception of the university in terms of physical size and total number of students. There may also be pressures associated with changing finances, religion and morals, worry about future success, and sheer laziness or procrastination and worrying.

Many problems may be associated with intimate relationships and parental conflicts and expectations. Those problems may include stresses related to ongoing relationships or to the absence of a steady relationship.

Another problem for students is approaching and meeting other students. Students perceive men as having the sex role responsibility of beginning relationships. Men may have problems because they are afraid of being rejected. Females may have problems because they feel that it is a man's perogative to initiate a relationship.

STRESS AND THE HEALTH OF DEVELOPMENTAL STUDENTS

The transition to the university environment, although a step toward independence and development, may consititute a period of new and intense academic, interpersonal, and personal pressures. These heightened demands and life changes may be mostly positive, but even positive life events may increase stress and vulnerability to mental and physical ill-health. Roberts (1989) used the Health Index Survey (HIS; Marx, Garrity, and Bowers, 1975) to determine the health status of developmental students. Those students reported having at least one of the problems listed in the Health Index Survey between three and four times during the previous 45 days.

There was no apparent relationship between any of the HIS categories and personal stressor scores. There was a weakly negative relationship between academic stressor scores and some of the HIS categories, indicating that as academic stressor scores increase injuries and accidents, bacterial and viral infections, and respiratory infections decrease.

Comparison of those results with those reported for a population of 'typical' college students indicates that the 'typical' students reported significantly more injuries and accidents, respiratory infections, and gastrointestinal infections than can, perhaps, be explained by differences in climate, atmosphere, diet, and academic atmosphere of the two populations studies.

Demographic Differences and Health Problems

Employed students reported a greater occurrence of bacterial and viral infections than did unemployed students. Significantly more females reported neurological/emotional problems than males. More black individuals reported neurological/emotional problems than white individuals. Only 4 percent of the students with ACT composite scores of 16 or greater reported neurological/emotional problems while 50 percent of those with ACT scores under 16 reported problems of this type.

Four times as many females reported problems of the 'other' types as did their male counterparts. Twice as many blacks reported problems in this 'other' area than did whites. No student with ACT composite scores of 16 or above reported problems in this area while approximately one-third of all students with scores below 16 reported problems.

IMPLICATIONS FOR STUDENT PERSONNEL SERVICES

What constitutes a stressor and one's reaction to it often differ from individual to individual. The differences observed are the result of the students having varying emotional, social, and cognitive resources to cope with stress. There must be intensive and comprehensive student personnel services available to these students if they are to progress to the point where they can succeed in typical college curricula. A significant challenge for institutions of higher education is that of determining what efforts can be undertaken to lessen the likelihood of college-related stress for students. The key to reducing stress is providing students with a feeling of control over their education, informing them about what to expect, offering feedback concerning what can be done to improve performance, and offering programs to help students cope with their stressors.

Because of the academic, personal, interpersonal, and health-related problems expressed by developmental education students, student personnel administrators should consider expanding counseling services. One possible action could be the provision of more highly trained and experienced counselors which would undoubtedly cost more. That action should increase funding since expanded counseling services should be expected to increase the retention of students and decrease the withdrawal rate. Counselors should direct their attention toward the areas indicated as being most important to their student population including study skills, career counseling, peer-support groups, test-taking skills, time management, relationships, and stress management. Those programs should be directed toward the ever increasing population of developmental education students who are entering college without effective skills for coping with the academic and personal stresses they encounter. Counselors could help students develop effective and appropriate coping skills.

Counseling programs should not be limited to developmental students. Those counseling programs should be open to all student who are either directed to them or who feel a personal need to participate. Other students will adopt their own particular and personal coping mechanisms.

A number of other approaches are possible to help students become successful:familiarize students with service activities within the university and local community;

- develop an orientation program for parents, spouses, and significant others involved with the student
- develop a peer 'buddy' system to help students understand academic pressures and requirements, which classes to take, what instructor to take, and how to do well in a particular course
- develop a peer counseling system
- develop a drop-in student counseling center open at hours when students need help
- have faculty members present seminars on how to succeed in their particular courses
- provide alternative ways to demonstrate mastery than the conventional paper and pencil test or examination
- use teachers whom students evaluate positively to teach introductory level courses
- provide seminars and workshops for faculty members to help them improve the effectiveness of their teaching
- institute remedial-tutorial programs using adult volunteers, peer tutors, or student teachers
- provide services at a time when it is beneficial to the student rather than during 'typical' working hours
- offer stress reduction/management courses and seminars and
- design a system for counselors to keep in touch with students once they complete developmental courses and enter the 'regular' college curricula

What is needed is a sizable long-term commitment to the creation of effective programs for at-risk students. Several groups of researchers and developers should be funded to follow a rational sequence of development and pilot-testing including comprehensive formative and summative evaluation systems. We must focus the best minds in educational research, evaluation and development in the pursuit of a well-defined objective of enormous importance: the prevention and remediation of learning problems among students at risk of academic failure.

REFERENCES

Archer, J. and A. Lamnin (1985). An investigation of personal and academic stressors on college campuses. *Journal of college student prsonnel,* 26, 210 - 215.

Beard, S., R. Elmore and S. Lange (1982). Assessment of student needs: Areas of stress in the campus environment. *Journal of college student personnel,* 23, 348 - 350.

Bennington, J. L. (1984). *Saunders dictionary and encyclopedia of laboratory medicine and technology.* Philadelphia, Pennsylvania: W. B. Saunders Company.

Bossing, L. and N. Rouff (1982). *A review of the effects of stress on the teaching-learning process.* Alexandria, Virginia: ERIC Clearinghouse on Higher Education Publishers. (ERIC Document Reproduction Service Number ED 219 363).

Brubacher, J. and S. Rudy (1974). *Higher education in transition.* New York: Harper and Row Publishers.

Chickering, A. (1969). *Education and identity.* San Francisco: Jossey-Bass.

Chobanian, A. (1982). *Heart risk book.* New York: Bantam Books.

Clayton, M. (1985). Operation rescue: Targets nation's lost youth. *NEA Today,* 4, p. 3.

Cobb, S. (1976). Social support as a moderator of life stress. *Psychomatic medicine,* 38, 300 - 314.

Cohen, S. (1980). Aftereffects of stress on human performance and social behavior: A review of research and theory. *Psychological bulletin,* 88, 82 - 108.

Cross, K. (1971). *Beyond the open door: New students to higher education.* San Francisco: Jossey-Bass.

Dintman, G. and J. Greenberg (1986). *Health through discovery.* New York: Random House.

Ekstrom, R., M. Goertz, J. Pollack, and D. Rock (1986). Who drops out of high school and why? Findings from a national study. *Teachers College Record,* 87, 356 - 373.

Ellis, V. (1969). Students who seek psychiatric help. In: *No time for youth,* J. Katz (ed.). San Francisco: Jossey-Bass, 41 - 49.

Erikson, E. (1950). *Childhood and society.* New York: Norton.

Erikson, E. (1963). *Childhood and society.* New York: Norton.

Erikson, E. (1980). *Identity and the life cycle: A reissue.* New York: W. W. Norton.

Garfinkel, B. (1988). Understanding and preventing teen suicide. *Phi delta kappan,* 70, 290 - 293.

Girdano, D. and G. Everly (1979). *Controlling stress and tension.* Engelwood Cliffs, New Jersey: Prentice Hall.

Greenberg, J. (1977). Stress, relaxation, and the health educator. *The journal of school health,* 47, 522 - 525.

Greenberg, J. (1981). A study of stressors in the college student population. *Health education,* 12, 8 - 12.

Hockey, J. (1979). Stress and the cognitive components of skilled performance. In V. Hamilton and D. Warbutin (eds.). *Human stress and cognition.* New York: John Wiley and Sons, 121 - 132.

Holmes, T. and R. Rahe (1967). The social readjustment rating scale. *Journal of psychosomatic research,* 11, 213 - 218.

Janis, I. (1982). Decision making under stress. In L. Goldberger and S. Bregnitz (eds.). *Handbook of stress: Theoretical and clinical aspects.* New York: Free Press, 201 - 219.

Johnson, E. (1979). *Student-identified stresses that relate to college life, Report Number CG 013 410.* Washington, DC: ERIC Clearinghouse on Teacher Education (ERIC Document Reproduction Service Number ED 170 630).

Johnson, J. (1981). More about stress and some management techniques. *Journal of school health,* 51, 36 - 42.

Legreca, G. (1985). The stress you make. *Personnel journal,* 64, 42 - 47.

Larsen, P. and B. Shertzer (1987). The high school dropout: Everybody's problem? *The school counselor,* 34, 163 - 169.

Lazarus, R., J. Averill and E. Opton (1974). *The psychology of coping: Issues of research and assessment, Coping and adaptation.* New York: Basic Books.

Macek, C. (1982). Of mind and morbidity: Can stress and grief depress immunity. *Journal of the American medical association,* 248, 405 - 407.

Mandler, G. (1982). Stress and thought processes. In L. Goldberger and S. Bregnitz (eds.). *Handbook of stress: Theoretical and clinical aspects.* New York: Free Press.

Marx, M., T. Garrity and F. Bowers (1975). The influence of recent life experience on the health of college freshman. *Journal of psychosomatic research,* 19, 87 - 98.

Maxwell, M. (1981). *Improving student learning skills.* San Francisco: Jossey-Bass.

Mayes, A. and J. Mcconata (1982). Surveying student needs: A means of evaluating student services. *Journal of college student services,* 6, 473 - 476.

McWilliams, S. and K. Gerber (1978). A mental health epidemiology survey of a university population. *Journal of college student personnel,* 2, 128 - 131.

Melingo, B. (1977). Stress and performance: Are they always incompatible? *Supervisory management,* 22, 3 - 12.

Mischell, W. (1976). *Introduction to personality.* New York: Holt, Rinehart and Winston.

Mullinex, S., T. Fadden, M. Broch and B. Gould (1980). A brief survey technique for environmental assessment. *Journal of college student personnel,* 21, 468 - 469.

Ostfield, A. and D. D'Atri (1975). Psychophysiological responses to the urban environment. *International journal of psychiatry in medicine,* 6, 15 - 28.

Ramsey, M. K. (1986). A comparative study of the effectiveness of the relaxation response and personalized relaxation tapes in medical technology students. *Health education,* 17, 22 - 25.

Rapley-Evans, S. (1983). The signs of stress. *Corporate fitness and recreation,* 2, 9 - 24.

Riley, V. (1981). Psychoneuroendocrine influences on immunocompetence and neoplasia. *Science,* 212, 1100 - 1109.

Roberts, G. (1989). *Personal and academic stressors affecting developmental students.* Doctoral dissertation, Grambling State University, Grambling, Louisiana.

Sagaria, M., L. Higginson and E. White (1980). Perceived needs of entering freshman: The primacy of academic issues. *Journal of college student personnel,* 21, 243 - 247.

Selye, H. (1956). *The stress of life.* New York: McGraw Hill Book Company.

Sherraden, M. (1986). School dropouts in perspective. *Educational forum,*
51, 15 - 31.

Silver, L. (1968). Anxiety and the first semester of law school. *Wisconsin law
review,* 4, 1201 - 1218.

Stevens, R. (1980). *At risk for school failure. A comparison of the
competence and the performance undo stress of at-risk and normal
seventh graders.* Paper presented at the annual meeting of the American
Psychological Association in Montreal, Quebec, Canada.

Swogger, G. (1981). Toward understanding stress: A map of the territory.
The journal of school health, 51, 29 - 33.

Wallace, J. (1978). Living with stress. *Nursing times,* 74, 457 - 458.

Whitman, N., D. Spendlove and C. Clark (1984). *Student stress: Effects and
solutions.* Washington, DC: Association for the Study of Higher
Education.

Williams, W. (1978). Recognizing individual differences among
developmental students. *Community college frontiers,* 6, 42 - 44.

Yerkes, R. and J. Dodson (1908). The relation of strength of stimulus to
rapidity of habit formation. *Journal of comparative and neurological
psychology,* 18, 459 - 482.

10

Developmental Mathematics

Joan M. Dodway

Historically, changes in the mathematics curriculum occurred in response to crisis. In the first half of the twentieth century the curriculum evolved with little aim or direction as to meeting the needs of special groups such as the gifted or the "slow-learner." Society's and accordingly the individual's needs were met with the college-bound program or the non-college bound program in most high schools.

This changed with the launching of Sputnik in 1957. American children were behind in mathematics and science! Many curriculum reform projects were started to upgrade programs such as The University of Maryland Mathematics Project, The School Mathematics Study Group and The University of Illinois Committee on School Mathematics. The focus was on creating a new program for the college-bound that would better prepare the student for a more rigorous mathematics course at college. The race was on and the United States wanted to come up from behind. The slow learner was largely ignored. Money and attention were directed to the more able learner who was considered the nation's technological hope for the future. The slow learner was thought only to need more time and a less-formal approach. The same materials could be used for both the slow and rapid learner. Later research as well as classroom educators would refute this notion (Osborne and Crosswhite, 1970).

By the early 1960s, it was apparent that the reform movement was not a success due in part to the leaders lack of concern for individual differences. The nation was in crisis again with protests, racism and riots erupting throughout the country. The schools had to respond again. New programs needed to be created in response to the outcry and unrest in the nation. Part of the money from President Johnson's war on poverty found its way into schools. The student that had been an after-thought in the earlier reform movement now became the focus of attention. The low achiever and ways to assist him/her to overcome academic problems became a major concern.

In 1964 The National Council of Teachers of Mathematics and the U.S. Office of Education sponsored a conference on "The Low Achiever in Mathematics." Phillips (1965) introduced the conference report with the acknowledgement that the potential school dropout (the future unemployable portion of society) exhibited a pattern of low achievement in mathematics. No longer could this portion of the school system be allowed to flounder along in school to succeed as best it could or to drop out. The labor market had changed. There was no longer a high need for unskilled labor. This type of student found few opportunities available and frequently became a drain on society causing many of the problems our nation was facing. Some exceptional school districts such as Baltimore, Maryland and Fort Worth, Texas had begun intensive mathematics programs for the low achiever(Gerardi, 1965; Bezdek, 1965).

Muller-Willis (1965) called for better teachers to help the low achiever in mathematics. To her, better teachers meant those teachers better prepared psychologically - exposed to the ideas of Piaget and active teaching. The student was to be an active learner, manipulating objects and cooperating with other students. According to Piaget, this was how someone learned with hands-on activity and from their peers. The role of the educator was to provide the learner with the necessary materials and to structure the situation so that the student could spontaneously construct the generalization on his/her own. According to Piaget, this tendency to learn and understand the world is natural to a human being. The educator need only structure the situation and then let the individual progress at a pace suited for his/her intellectual capacity. The student will naturally put the emphasis where he/she is having the most difficulty. The learner needs to verify and decide what is right and wrong. The educator should provide the means to check without doing the actual checking for the student. All the answers that a learner generates, wright or wrong are important. The educator should seek to discover the processes underlying the wrong answers as well as the right ones. The materials used should be as interesting as possible; games could be beneficial. Classrooms of mixed ages where students can learn from each other might help. Low achievers need more concrete manipulations than others. If the classroom is of mixed ability, provide materials so that the advanced students would be able to work at their intellectual level while the low achiever is encouraged to actively manipulate concrete objects to discover the concepts he/she needs.

Rosenbloom (1965) called for tasks to be broken down into small items so that all students would have a high likelihood of success. He belived that frequent fresh starts in a non-repetitive manner would be better than allowing failure and discouragement to become accumulated. Brain (1965) noted that slow learners have a short retention span. Yet, he believed that sound, practical mathematics was within their grasp, defining "practical" mathematics as skills which would qualify a person for a job and the ability to manage personal affairs.

The first articles to appear in professional journals after the 1964 conference described what various schools were attempting. The articles lacked any research data or evidence to support their findings. Greenholtz's (1967) article is typical of this era in mathematics education. She reviewed a number of school district's programs and developed guidelines as well as specific suggestions for teaching. To her, a low-achiever was a student with sufficient ability to be in a regular classroom, but with an achievement record below the thirtieth percentile. Her guidelines were that a student:

- should experience some success each day;
- discover new relationships by working with concrete problems;
- be involved in meaningful experiences; and, most important of all,
- have a sympathetic teacher.

Williams (1970) suggested, without any supporting data, a solution of merely providing the low achiever with more time (e.g., teach a course in mathematics in three semesters instead of the usual two semesters). He also felt that the teacher should work on changing the attitude of the low achiever by using a variety of motivating and stimulating activities such as team competitions. He advocated that students take part in classroom planning activities as a way to enhance relevancy.

Homan (1970) synopsized the nature of and examined steps for diagnosing arithmetic disabilities. This represented a break from the generic notion of underachievement and a move toward methodological approaches.

According to Homan (1970), an arithmetical learning disability stems from either a cerebral dysfunction or an emotional disturbance; not from mental retardation, sensory deprivation, cultural nor instructional factors. Dyscalculia to a neurologist is a disability in learning number relationships; to an educator it is an arithmetical learning disability. Homan (1970) credited Bateman as the originator of the following steps in the diagnostic-remedial process.

- Determine if a learning problem exists.
- Perform a behavioral analysis and develop a description of the disability by examining samples from a particular problem area.
- Study the relevant correlates of the disability.
- Administer tests such as intelligence tests to determine the learning capacity of the individual and compare those results with classroom achievement.
- Complete medical and neurological examinations are necessary to rule out

organic causes.
- A psychological examination is necessary to rule out emotional causes.
- Formulate a clear, concise and accurate hypothesis concerning the disability.

The disability should be confirmed by at least two objective tests and be evident in everyday behavior. There should be a pattern of internal consistency to the behavior. Educational recommendations must be a joint decision of everyone concerned and focus on learning new skills as well as strengthening old.

Homan (1970) credited Frierson and Barbe for describing the symptoms associated with an arithmetical learning disability. A student could have a *perceptual skill* problem Causing him/her to experience difficulties with spatial and size relationships. That is,

- size relationships (big, small, long and short);
- perception of sequences (first, next and last);
- left-right discrimination;
- inversion-reversal tendencies;
- difficulty reading and writing number symbols; and,
- inability to understand relative directions and distances (up, down, over, under, top, bottom, high, low, near, far, front and back).

The student may also experience a *motor disinhibition* and be unable to coordinate sight, hearing and motor activity as evidenced by being able to identify but not use numbers. A student may experience a *perserveration* dysfunction (difficulty in shifting between learning tasks such as between addition and subtraction). A student may not be able to either adapt to the special language and symbols of mathematics or may experience reasoning difficulties.

Empirical research was being conducted at this time. However, the methodologies were frequently questionable. For example, Jones (1968) claimed success for modified programmed lectures (which he did not define) and mathematical games with slow learners and underachievers. No control group was used. It is impossible to conclude that the results were not due to maturation. Perhaps any type of instruction using small groups with individualized instruction reviewing material previously discussed in another situation would have similar results.

Cohn (1971) reported the results of a longitudinal study of individuals diagnosed as arithmetically learning disabled from childhood through adolescence. Although Cohn (1971) did not make any recommendations, he did establish a comprehensive longitudinal database. He found that it was unusual to observe an arithmetical learning disability without also observing disabilities in other areas. He reported that it was commonly believed that arithmetical disabilities could be corrected by repeated drill exercises. The argument being that, since an individual can use a calculator or hire an accountant or tax expert, arithmetical disabilities were not great handicaps.

In the thirty-fifth yearbook of The National Council of Teachers of Mathematics, dedicated to the slow learner, Pikaart and Wilson (1972) reviewed over 170 research studies in the area and found them lacking for many reasons. There are many variables associated with the learning situation such as previous learning experiences, environmental influences, personality characteristics and aptitudes that make the learning situation very complicated to study. Research results were frequently generalizable only to small populations. It may be that researchers had not studied the appropriate variables. Conceptual models had not grown from the research. Pikaart and Wilson (1972) believed that research should focus on discovering specific aptitudes of the slow learner and adapt instruction to capitalize upon those aptitudes.

The 1972 yearbook contained many specific suggestions for teaching the slow learner.

- create a favorable learning environment
- adjust teaching styles
- use different aids and activities
- use a mathematics laboratory
- use of diagnostic-prescriptive teaching

That Yearbook is a good resource tool for the teacher of slow learners desiring specific activities and approaches. A variety of possible activities is always useful since slow learners are not similar. An activity which works for one may not work for another.

Schulz (1972) points out that it is difficult to classify slow learners with any degree of precision. While have much in common, they each have their own set of strengths and weaknesses. He did describe various characteristics frequently found in slow learners. The slow learner tends to:

- have a *poor self-image,*
- be *deficient in cognitive ability,*
- have a learning style that *requires manipulatives,*
- come from a *disadvantaged environment,*
- *question the value of schooling,*
- *need immediate reinforcement,*
- *lack* the *skills schools require* (listening and persistence);

- *lack social skills,*
- *lack meaningful adult relationships,* and,
- have *different response styles* based on sex differences.

Just as there is no universal slow learner, there can be no single prescription or treatment plan. Schulz (1972) pointed out a few principles to remember when working with slow learners: build a sense of trust; have a pleasant classroom environment; use concrete manipulatives; use a variety of alternatives; use sequences and pacing appropriate to the level of development; use meaningful materials; and use peer tutoring and create a success-oriented environment utilizing immediate informative feedback. In the early 1970s the educator was sent mixed messages. When reading the literature of that period, one wonders if he/she is reading about the same type of learner. A "scientific" research-oriented approach was beginning to emerge in that period. The National Council of Teachers of Mathematics (NCTM), the leading professional teacher organization, ignores the research-oriented approach in favor of a casual approach! NCTM appears to have been describing an underprivileged student leftover from the riots of the sixties.

Kosc (1974) documented extensive details of testing procedures for and specific case studies of developmental dyscalculia. He felt that since society did not view the disability as disabling as the inability to read or write, the condition was relatively unknown. He felt that the cause of developmental dyscalculia was that a portion of the brain was either defective from birth or became impaired during the course of development. Kosc (1974) felt that no amount of intensive systematic training would enable a developmental dyscalcic to acquire certain skills! The dyscalcic was perceived as having a disorder in mathematical ability maturation. According to Kosc, dyscalculia is not caused by poor instruction, neurosis, objective illness or fatigue.

Symptoms of developmental dyscalculia may occur individually or in combination and include:

- **Verbal dyscalculia:** The inability to designate verbally mathematical terms and relations.
- **Practognostic dyscalculia:** The inability to manipulate real or pictured objects mathematically.
- **Dexical dyscalculia:** The inability to read mathematical symbols.
- **Graphical dyscalculia:** The inability to manipulate mathematical symbols in writing.
- **Ideognostical dyscalculia:** The inability to understand mathematical ideas and relations in order to perform mental calculations.
- **Operational dyscalculia:** The inability to carry out mathematical operations.

An individual suffering from this type of problem requires a very different mathematical program. The very definition of success must be adapted to the particular person. This disorder requires thorough and careful professional diagnosis to be accurately identified and classified.

By 1975, educators still paid little attention to mathematical learning problems. Time and effort were directed toward having the student be "literate" and success in mathematics was defined as rote manipulation of calculations with little understanding of principles. Few programs, tests, methods and/or materials were available. There was little research in the area of developmental activities (Bartel, 1975).

According to Bartel (1975), developmental mathematics learning problems occurred because instruction did not match the developmental level of the student. An individual needed to be ready to learn. Readiness was characterized by the student having specific abilities: classification; conservation; one-to-one correspondence; flexibility; reversibility;seriation ordering; and, understanding of space and spatial representation

A strong Piagetian influence is evident. Bartel would not have the teacher just wait for readiness to occur spontaneously, he preferred that activities be structured. He believed that inappropriate instruction was the major cause of developmental dyscalculia and that few formal or informal assessment procedures were available for teachers to use.

By 1976, the presence of the mathematically disadvantaged student was acknowledged at all levels of education from the elementary school on through the university. Colleges were struggling to develop modes of instruction suitable for developmentally weak mathematics students. The traditional lecture-recitation mode of instruction was being challenged. Small-group laboratory settings with a variety of visual and audio enhancements could be more easily adapted to developmental differences. Studies comparing the effectiveness of instructional methods were initiated (Williams and Mick, 1976). Also, teacher training programs began to address the special needs of the slow learner by including instructional methods thought particularly suitable for work with the slow learner, such as individualized instruction (Fennel and Trueblood, 1977).

Flinter (1979) identified and elaborated on each of the symptoms set forth by Kosc while accompanying each with specific suggestions for remediation. No data was offered to judge the worthiness of his suggestions. The overriding goal was to help the individual achieve independence in society. The program should be kept practical, and concepts as opposed to rote learning be emphasized. The learning situation should use manipulatives with direct hands-on experiences. The instruction must be carefully organized to use compensational mechanisms to their fullest.

The NCTM addressed the issue of a developmental mathematics education again in 1981. The approach was radically different from that which came before. Even the title was changed. Gone were the words "slow learner." Instead, the phrase "exceptional children and youth" appeared. Chapters in the 1981 NCTM yearbook were devoted to identifying and creating mathematics programs for individuals with special needs such as those with perceptual and cognitive processing deficits, social and emotional impairments, slow-learners, the mentally retarded, the visually impaired, the deaf and hard of hearing, those with physical and health impairments and the gifted and talented! Dyscalculia along with other disabilities were discussed. Many of the different problems a student could experience while having difficulty with mathematics were dealt with separately. The developmental learner was now regarded as an individual whose rate of development was slower than "normal." That student was no longer confused with one whose problems stem elsewhere. The developmental student needs frequent repetition of material in a variety of contexts and at different conceptual levels before mastery can be achieved. They can not be expected to cover a full year's worth of work in a year's time. Their behavior is characterized by hyperactivity, inattention, lack of motivation, a lag in social-emotional development and conduct disorders. They may have a language problem which will manifest itself when the student attempts word problems. The student learns from manipulating concrete objects and has trouble transferring knowledge from one situation to another (Spickler and Mcleskey, 1981). In order to best serve the student, the curriculum and manner of instruction both might need to be adapted to the specific form of disability. Consideration needs to be given to such questions as "Is the individual intrinsically or extrinsically motivated?", "Does the student perform best with telling or guided discovery?" and "Does the student require hands-on materials?" (Glennon, 1981).

Austin (1982), in a review of related literature, found that the research on remedial and developmental arithmetic deficiencies in learning disabled individuals did not concentrate on the structure of arithmetic or on the student's stages of development. If IQ was held constant, little difference could be found between learning disabled individuals and "normal" individuals on certain Piagetian tasks. The major type of instruction strategy had for many years been diagnostic-prescriptive, however the success of that system had not been documented (Austin, 1982). He found specific recommendations concerning how to teach developmental students inconsistent. Perhaps, Austin (1982) was not taking into account the individual differences within the group of developmental learner! He found suggestions of drill and practice, concrete discovery, task analysis, explicit instructions, well organized board work and worksheets which allow for different methods of feedback useful for the whole population of learners, not just the developmentally disabled. According to Austin (1982), little research can be found on the effectiveness of these suggestions. Research as of that time provided little guidance for the teacher of the developmental mathematics student. That may be due to the fact that the population of developmentally disabled individuals is too diverse to make recommendations.

The student who has problems with mathematics has become the focus for a relatively new journal *Focus on Learning Problems in Mathematics.* There, the topic is treated for the most part with a more "scientific" research orientation and in greater depth. Frequently whole issues are devoted to one viewpoint or explanation. Nason and Redden (1983) use an information processing approach to explain how academic problems in mathematics might be thought to exist and be remediated. Basically they explained the information processing approach of learning to teachers. In that way, teachers had a better perspective on how their students' learned and could better use compensating methods of instruction to overcome a weakness with a strength. Although Nason and Redden (1983) claimed a high degree of success, they provided no data to support their claim. It is hard to judge their claim without comparative groups or any data of any sort except the fact that the authors liked their field observations! Since a conceptual model was presented, the article is an improvement over past papers. The concept of using a student's strengths is not new. However, having a theoretical base from which developmental mathematics educators can draw upon is an improvement over the previous state of affairs.

Another guide to developmental mathematics education was provided by Stein, Jenkins and Arter (1983). They claim that their suggestions were based upon research results. However, they offered no data to support their claims! In their review of the literature, they claim that the highest rate of academic achievement was found in classrooms taught by direct instruction conducted in a business-like fashion with all students engaged in similar activities. Although their results came from studies on traditional classroom settings, they found no problem with applying the results to the developmental student! If the developmental dyscalcic learner was capable of learning using this instructional organization why would he/she be developmental? *If a developmental intervention is necessary, why should more of the same methodology be applied when it was not successful in the first place?* The recommendations of Stein, Jenkins and Arter (1983) included the writing of specific behavioral objectives recognizing that the developmental dyscalcic would not be expected to master as many behavioral objectives as others, a cognitive routine designed and the associated strategies identified and taught separately as well as the construction of a specific teaching format. They prescribe a system which would allow for frequent practice of a skill so that it would not be forgotten since a short memory span, they claim, is characteristic of a developmental dyscalcic.

Many educators have favored using games and manipulatives with developmental dyscalcics. Larson and Slaughter (1984) investigated the use of manipulatives and games in elementary classrooms. The data is coming in as to whether or not this type of instruction is successful with developmental mathematics students. They found that developmental students had difficulty transferring from the concrete to the abstract and that peer games had management problems. They attributed those difficulties to a lack of individualized instruction. They felt that the problems could be overcome by grouping of mathematical skill levels. Although the authors found games and manipulatives being used by developmental students, they questioned whether they were an appropriate match to the developmental need of the child. *The news is not good.* It may be true that developmental learners learn best with manipulatives, but the teacher must be trained in the selection of appropriate manipulatives and how to teach for transfer. Transfer does not just happen with developmental students. If it is to occur, it must be by design.

In an attempt to enrich the work reported earlier on dyscalculia, research has been conducted in the area of brain physiology, developmental mathematics and learning disorders. Cawley (1984) summarizes the results of an in-depth literature review. He concluded that the research was at too early a stage of development to establish functional deficits as either acquired or developmental stages. Again, a lack of attention to mathematics and brain deficiencies was attributed to the educators' over concern for reading and language skills. He felt that mathematical difficulties were not being investigated as they should be. People at this time can only theorize about the relationships among the brain, learning disabilities and mathematics. Those people who try to stipulate interactions in terms of treatment or educational planning are only guessing. "As far as education is concerned, there is no basis whatsoever to recommend anything other than research." (Cawley, 1984, p. 31). Webster (1984) in a similar review of the literature found it difficult to link dyscalculia with a particular localized area of the brain. He reasoned that higher order mathematics required many cognitive skills which could easily be located in various parts of the brain.

Fletcher and Loveland (1986) reported that the educational component of arithmetic disabilities had not been thoroughly addressed. Specifically, they felt that there was a need for research on school related performance and remedial methods. They concluded that a cognitive deficit was present in arithmetic-disabled individuals, but that the nature of that deficit was unknown at the present time. Fletcher and Loveland (1986) offered principles and guidelines to follow when remediating the arithmetic disabled student. They contended that the principles came from their anecdotal clinical experiences and had not been validated. Here, again, was another case where validation was lacking for developmental mathematics methodology.

Reisman (1983) offered another checklist of specific learning disabilities in mathematics and instructional strategies for remediation. No data was offered to validate the suggestions other than the statement that they have been found to be "particularly effective." He developed a theoretical framework for his suggestions. General characteristics of learning were applied to developmental mathematics learning and translated into influences upon the learning of mathematics. Research on developmental mathematics has conceptually progressed, but the data is not here yet; however, learning theories are being applied.

An interesting article germinated from a private mathematics learning clinic in Switzerland (Gubler, 1983). Their theory base appeared to be family systems. The clinic, which called its form of remediation "therapy", actively involved parents in the diagnostic and therapy processes. They used topics that are only indirectly related to mathematics. For example, if they found that the student had few responsibilities at home or seldom had to think for him/herself the clinic insisted on changes. It was their belief that the family system had to change if the students' mathematical development was to improve. They use only a few selected materials with each student. After finding that students became overwhelmed by an abundance of learning resources. Their view was that students having trouble learning mathematics were having trouble with common learning methods and this was what their therapy was designed to correct. Again, no data was available to validate their recommendations, but they were theory-based.

A recent book, *Mathematical Learning Difficulties in Secondary School* (Larcombe, 1985), appears to be a Piagetian update. Again, no data is presented to validate the recommendations. Larcombe's (1985) major thrust was that mathematical materials and teaching styles used with a student should be based upon the mathematical stage of development the student is in instead of the person's chronological age. The mathematical development of a person is highly individual. Do not assume that there are common patterns of understanding progressing at a fixed rate over everyone. Look at the student to determine materials, not at a preplanned syllabus. The student needs an individualized approach where close monitoring must be sustained in order to maintain the match of material to the student. What works today may not work tomorrow as the student will not be learning at a constant rate. When grading, the student should be compared to his/her own previous performance rather than compared to other members of the class.

In order for the student to build mathematical concepts, opportunities to have fundamental mathematical experiences must be available. Have the student handle concrete materials and focus the attention of the student to what is there to be seen and experienced.

According to Larcombe (1985), the least effective way to handle a student deficient in concept learning is by giving him/her a worked out example followed by practice. In order to learn, the individual needs active involvement with the learning materials (Larcombe, 1985). The teacher needs to shift from being an expositor of mathematics to a director and tutor of students. There should be a change from teaching mathematics to promoting mathematics learning. Larcombe (1985) appears to have taken the individualization of Skinner and the discovery approach using concrete models of Piaget and blended them.

These ideas and other suggestions coming from research and learning theories on ways to teach the developmental mathematics student appear throughout journals dedicated to the teaching of mathematics. Moyer and Moyer (1985) reported the hazards of using too much drill and practice with the developmental student. They felt that too much drill might result in rigid thinking (perserveration) or the reinforcement of errors. They advocated smaller assignments of mixed-problem sets where the students first identify when the new concept is appropriate and then work on only one substep of the concept until mastery is achieved before putting all the substeps together into a single process. Thorton and Wilmont (1986) presented ways to use manipulatives with the developmental learner. Learning theorists might suggest using them. Whereas, these mathematics educators have developed general procedures/guidelines to follow.

The only safe conclusion this researcher is able to make regarding what research has to offer about ways to assist individuals overcome difficulties in mathematics is that the topic requires more research! The developmental learning problem is much more complex than originally believed. Although mathematics educators have been trying to help developmental students for many years, informally and formally in remediation programs, little actual conclusive research has been done. Suggestions abound, including: individualization, guided discovery and concrete manipulatives to mention a few. Those ideas are not new. They appear in the literature thoughout the years with various twists and rationales. Unfortunately, little research data is available to help the teacher to decide which technique is best at what time to use with what type of developmental mathematics student.

There are many sub-categories within the broad classification of development which need to be investigated. It is too simplistic to think that one method can help all students or even that one method can help an individual student at all times. There are many different variables to be considered when doing research of this type. This makes the research effort a slow process.

On the promising side, the work of the 1980s is an improvement over earlier work and there is no reason not to expect the future to be an improvement on the present. Many advances are being made in understanding how an individual learns and how the brain operates. All this along with improved research methods and technology make the future bright. Perhaps all that is needed to answer the question of appropriate strategies for the developmental mathematics student is time and dedicated researchers.

REFERENCES

Austin, J. D. (1982). Children with a learning disability and mathematics. *School science and mathematics*, 82, 3, 201 - 208.

Bartel, N. (1975). Problems in arithmetic achievement. In D. Hammill and N. Bartel (ed.). *Teaching children with learning and behavior problems*. Boston: Allyn and Bacon, 61 - 88.

Bezdek, J. (1965). The mathematics program for the low achiever in the Fort Worth public schools. In L. Woodby (ed.), *The low achiever in mathematics*. Washington, D.C.: U.S. Department of Health, Education and Welfare, 54 - 57.

Brain, G. (1965). Mathematics for low achievers: Responsibilities of school administrators. In L. Woodby (ed.), *The low achiever in mathematics*. Washington, D.C.: U. S. Department of Health, Education and Welfare, 33 - 37.

Cawley, J. (1984). Brain, mathematics and learning disability. *Focus on learning problems in mathematics*, 6, 4, 13 - 39.

Cohn, R. (1971). Arithmetic and learning disabilities. In H. R. Myklebust (ed.), *Progress in learning disabilities, Volume II*. New York: Grune and Stratton, 322 - 389.

Fennell, F. and C. Trueblood (1977). The elementary school as a training laboratory and its effect on low-achieving sixth graders, *The journal for research in mathematics education*, 8, 2, 97 - 106.

Fletcher, J. and K. Loveland (1986). Neuropsychology of arithmetic disabilities in children, *Focus on learning problems in mathematics*, 8, 2, 23 - 39.

Flinter, P. (1979). Educational implications of dyscalculia, *Arithmetic teacher*, 26, 7, 42 - 46.

Gerardi, W. (1965). Baltimore's basic program in secondary mathematics. In L. Woodby (ed.), *The low achiever in mathematics*. Washington, D.C.: U.S. Department of Health, Education and Welfare, 49 - 53.

Glennon, V. (1981). Variables in a theory of mathematics instruction for children and youth. In V. J. Glennon (ed.), *The mathematical education of exceptional children and youth*. Reston, Virginia: National Council of Teachers of Mathematics, 23 - 49.

Greenholz, S. (1967). Successful practices in teaching mathematics to low achievers in senior high school, *The mathematics teacher*, 60, 4, 329 - 335.

Gubler, R. (1983). Helping students with learning problems in mathematics, *Focus on learning problems in mathematics*, 5, 2, 5 - 17.

Homan, D. (1970). The child with a learning disability in arithmetic, *The arithmetic teacher*, 17, 3, 199 - 203.

Jones, T. (1968). The effect of modified programmed lectures and mathematical games upon achievement and attitude of ninth-grade low achievers in mathematics, *The mathematics teacher*, 61, 6, 603 - 607.

Kosc, L. (1974). Developmental dyscalculia, *Journal of learning disabilities*, 7, 3, 164 - 177.

Larcombe, T. (1985). *Mathematical learning difficulties in the secondary school*. Philadelphia: Open University Press.

Larson, C. and H. Slaughter (1984). The use of manipulatives and games in selected elementary school classrooms, from an ethnographic study, *Focus on learning problems in mathematics*, 6, 4, 31 - 49.

Moyer, M. and J. Moyer (1985). Ensuring that practice makes perfect: Implications for children with learning disabilities, *Arithmetic teacher*, 33, 1, 40 - 42.

Muller-Willis, L. (1965). Stages in the child's intellectual development: Piaget's view. In L. Woodby (ed.), *The low achiever in mathematics*. Washington, D.C.: U. S. Department of Health, Education and Welfare, 17 - 22.

Nason, R. and M. Redden (1983). Mathematical learning disabilities: An information-processing view, *Focus on learning problems in mathematics*, 5, 2, 57 - 77.

Osborne, A. and F. J. Crosswhite (1970). Reform, revolution and reaction. In A History of mathematics education in the United States and Canada. Washington, D.C.: National Council of Teachers of Mathematics, 235 - 300.

Phillips, H. (1965). Why we are concerned about low achievers in mathematics. In L. Woodby (ed.), *The low achiever in mathematics*. Washington, D.C.: U. S. Department of Health, Education and Welfare, 1 - 6.

Pikaart, L. and J. Wilson (1972). The research literature. In W. C. Lowry (ed.), *The slow learner in mathematics*. Washington, D.C.: National Council of Teachers of Mathematics, 26 - 51.

Reisman, F. (1983). Synthesizing specific learning disabilities, instructional strategies and mathematics learning tasks, *Focus on learning problems in mathematics*, 5, 2, 43 - 55.

Rosenbloom, P. (1965). Implications of psychological research. In L. Woodby (ed.), *The low achiever in mathematics.* Washington, D.C.: U. S. Department of Health, Education and Welfare, 23 - 32.

Schultz, R. (1972). Characteristics and needs of the slow learner. In W. C. Lowry (ed.), *The slow learner in mathematics.* Reston, Virginia: National Council of Teachers of Mathematics, 1 - 25.

Spickler, H. and J. McLeskey (1981). Exceptional children in changing times. In V. J. Glennon (ed.), *The mathematical education of exceptional children and youth.* Reston, Virginia: National Council of Teachers of Mathematics, 1 - 22.

Stein, M., J. Jenkins and J. Arter (1983). Designing successful mathematics instruction for low-performing students, *Focus on learning problems in mathematics,* 5, 2, 79 - 99.

Thornton, C. and Wilmont, B. (1986). Special learners, *Arithmetic Teacher,* 33, 6, 38 - 41.

Webster, R. (1984). Mathematical disabilities: Their symptoms and suggested neurological bases, *Focus on learning problems in mathematics,* 6, 4, 41 - 58.

Williams, E. and H. Mick (1976). Measuring the effectiveness of using slide-tape lessons in teaching basic algebra to mathematically disadvantages students, *Journal for research in mathematics education,* 7, 3, 183 - 192.

Williams, L. (1970). Motivating low-achievers in ninth-year mathematics, *New York State Mathematics Teachers' Journal,* 20, 1, 4 - 7.

11

Reading as "Big Business" to Developmental Education

Gwendolyn Trotter

Reading is big business, whether elementary school, junior high, secondary, college or in the business environment. As big business, reading as a field of study and instruction becomes as complex as some of the United State's major business and industrial corporations. Investments in a literate academic or work force can make or break our schools, communities and companies, in terms of economics. Investing in the reading needs of students or workers is an investment in human capital or resources. Reading must be viewed with all of its complexities if we are to move developmental learners along the reading continuum as the reading continuum interfaces with their academic and career objective. Not only are we concerned with the developmental learner, but also with reading as a developmental process. The evolving reader goes through several stages to become competent. However, there is lack of agreement as to the "real client" to be served by reading instruction in the developmental education context. There is agreement that in the year 2000, a knowledge base on this reading process will be critical to our work force as technology and the information age continues to place extraordinary demands on the reader and worker. This chapter will explore reading in the developmental context of remedial college courses, re-entering older students (non-traditional) as well as business/industrial and community literacy agencies (literacy/illiteracy). By clarifying definitions, issues, directions and state of the art programs, an agenda in reading for the twenty-first century will be established. Figure 8 provides the graphic organizer for this chapter.

Developmental Reading-Macrostructures

Those working in developmental education must begin to organize the reading knowledge base beyond the traditional basic skill areas of word attack, comprehension and study skills. Developmental reading programming can build upon the traditional approach to reading instruction but must go beyond. The traditional approach starts with learning to read in the kindergarten and continues through the elementary grade. Reading to learn, also a part of elementary reading, cuts across the content areas. The

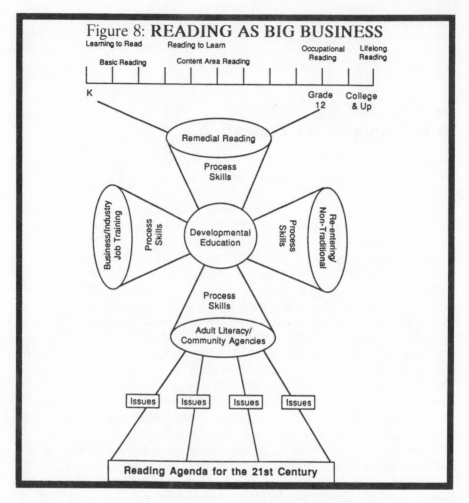

Figure 8: **READING AS BIG BUSINESS**

middle school or junior high grades continue with reading to learn. High school reading moves towards "occupational reading" and lifelong reading. Unlike traditional reading instruction, reading instruction for the developmental client is big business. The developmental client is either a part of the working world or only a few years away. Reading instruction is a major foundation skill for the success or failure of the developmental client. The developmental client, whether remedial, re-entering/non-traditional, in the business/industrial or community literacy agency must have specific literacy competencies. These populations will be organized in a schema identified as macrostructures (Figure 9). Each macrostructure will be further identified by specific processes unique to programming needs of developmental clients. Macrostructures, as a term, is used to amplify the complexity of addressing the reading needs of developmental clients and the massive structures which teachers/trainers need to consider. Programming across these massive structures will help in meeting reading challenges and issues in the twenty-first century.

Defining Developmental Education and Reading Issues

It is only after true definition of a concept that one can gain control over the concept and make it work to the advantage of teacher, trainer or learner. In establishing a reading agenda for the year 2000, the subsets (macrostructures) of developmental education must be clearly identified and understood. This section serves to clarify the macrostructures and to add definition to developmental education and reading instruction. Hashway (1989) has defined developmental education as that which occurs when a person wishes to enhance his/her skills to meet some here-to-fore unattained goal. Developmental education has several subsets if the definition is to have clarity. The macrostructures that set the tone for educational and training programming include:

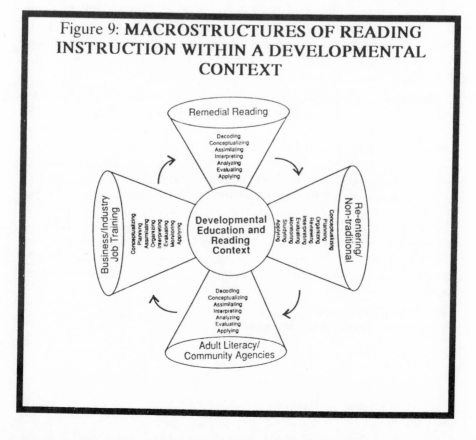

Figure 9: **MACROSTRUCTURES OF READING INSTRUCTION WITHIN A DEVELOPMENTAL CONTEXT**

- remedial education
- non-traditionall (older students)
- business/industry/job training
- adult literacy/community agencies

Remedial education has been defined by Hashway (1989) as occurring when a person enters a training program to enhance his/her skills to meet some here-to-fore unattained goal and finds that he/she does not possess the minimal entry level skills for that training program and must enter another training module prior to executing the process defined by whatever institution is offering that training as the route to completing the primary training and reaching the desired goal. The non traditional student and re-entering students as profiled by John Roueche and Jerry J. Snow (1977) as well as Patricia Cross (1987) are those adult students over the age of 22 who are seeking a second chance at an education. Many such individuals are white and blue collar. Rapidly growing are the number of ethnic minorities that will match the profile of those over 22 and seeking a second chance at a college education. The business/job training subset includes those learners, usually over 22 who are in need of specific literacy training (oral, writing and reading) in order to optimize performance on jobs that might range from mail clerk through middle management in a major Fortune 500 company. Adult literacy (basic literacy) refers to the instructional reading needs (0 reading level to approximately 8th grade) of adults. Such programming frequently takes place in community agencies as well as on site in business and industry.

Developmental education, clarified, becomes a concept that includes programming for those learners who have educational needs that were unmet in previous educational settings due to a myriad of factors. The concept also implies that, developmentally, the learner should be at a certain level. However, due to numerous factors, the learner has not acquired certain skills or learnings consistent with the stage of expected competency . This is particularly the case in basic skill areas of reading, writing, oral communication and even self esteem. In the *Journal of Developmental Education*, September, 1988, Carlette Hardin has made the following assumptions which were interpretations of the work of Abraham (1987), Cross (1971), Moore (1970) as well as Roueche and Snow (1977). Hardin formulated the following assumptions about developmental students.

- Developmental students are underprepared. This underpreparedness does not equate with incapable or uneducable

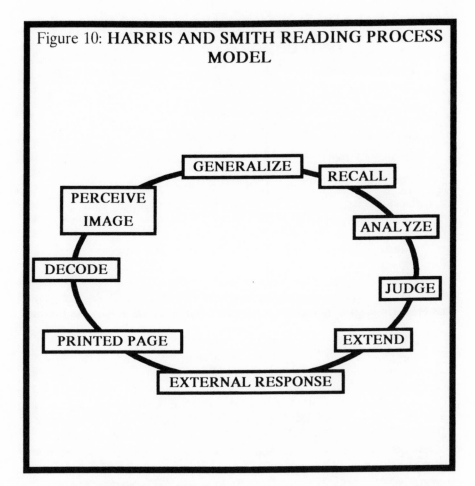

Figure 10: **HARRIS AND SMITH READING PROCESS MODEL**

- The reasons for underpreparedness are complex and often out of the control of the developmental student.
- Developmental students can overcome their deficiencies when placed in appropriate remedial or developmental courses.
- Assistance and personal development is often as critical to the success of developmental students as academic interventions.

In the area of remedial education, reading must be conceptualized as developmental and placed on a continuum from the simple to the complex. There are, instructionally, many processes and skills making up the total reading process. Harris and Smith's model (1980) of the reading process (Figure 10) is an excellent model for viewing the instructional gaps often found in readers needing remedial instruction. Table 7 illustrates traditional materials and activities that have been used to facilitate instruction of the

TABLE 7: POTENTIAL METHODS, TECHNIQUES AND INSTRUCTIONAL ACTIVITIES

METHODS	TECHNIQUES & ACTIVITIES
Basal	Cloze
Individualized (Veatch)	Questioning
Language Experience	Directed Reading
Programmed Readers	Word Banks
Packaged Kits	Learning Centers
Multi-media Kits	SQ3R
Individualized (IGE)	Concept Bombardment
	Gaming, Oral Reading, Workbook Activities

reading process. Remedial readers are usually at least two years below the expected reading level for age and educational level. Often times there are glaring "process gaps" in such learners ability to move fluidly through the reading process. Data from the National Assessment of Educational Progress (NAEP) studies would support the position that major "gaps" are found in the upper-level comprehension/thinking skills areas rather than in the more mechanical and low-level skill areas of word identification and analysis. Remedial education, common in the elementary and secondary schools, is prominent in many colleges, particularly junior colleges. However, frequently the remedial reading courses are offered under learning assistance or developmental education course titles. Such "remedial courses" are characterized by pre/post testing, prescriptive learning, self-directed learning and awareness of self-type exercises. More specifically , instruction in developmental remedial reading courses includes work on specific word attack/analysis skills as well as comprehension skills. Some writing activities are used to reinforce the reading skills. The major goal of remedial reading instruction at the college level is to bring the reader to a level of reading proficiency in order that he/she might succeed in the regular college curriculum. Too often, remedial instruction is subversive and not clearly identified as such to developmental client. Even those programming for such students are often off target because of the "ambiguities and subversive" nature of identifying remedial students. Ambiguity is the nature of learning and teaching but the programmer and learner must acknowledge the ambiguity (Garman, 1984).

Reading instruction for the re-entering/non-traditional student usually moves beyond the Harris and Smith model of the reading process. Reading instruction, for the re-entering/non-traditional student, is often prescriptive. The higher comprehension levels are also major instructional areas for the re-entering/non-traditional student population. Instruction moves rapidly into content area reading type activities(reading in social studies, science, math, literature, etc). Study skills, notetaking and information processing type skills become important. Reading at this point is viewed as more interactive. Addtional instructional attention is given to language processing skills. Metacognition (What do I know about my own reading and thinking?) and metatools (self help tools like a dictionary and a thesaurus) are of grave concern. The re-entering/nootraditional student might need the reading basics, but usually reading basics are not thought to be necessary for the majority of such students. Reading instruction for this population is also often "subversive" in that client and programmer of services are often reluctant to deal with the real needs of this population, especially if such needs appear to fall into the remedial macrostructure. Hardin (1988) addresses the issue of "brushing up" the skills of adults who have a solid college-prep program in high school but have not used the knowledge in an academic setting for a number of years.

Reading instruction for business/job training can span the community setting, the environment and the college setting. At this point, reading can mean basic literacy level of 0-8th grade reading level. The more sophisticated reading skill requirements of analyzing and interpreting complex material are also included. Reading as described for job training is heavily tied to higher order thinking/comprehension or reasoning skills. Reading, in this context, is also viewed within a "training context" rather than a teaching context. Training or corporate education as defined by Blomberg (1988) are those systematic means used by a business to instill new skills, knowledge, or attitudes in employees, thereby increasing the employee's worth and serviceability (Bass and Vaughan, 1966). The reading definition is tied to outcomes in terms of "benefit" to the company, firm or business providing the reading instruction. As reading outcomes become critical, reading instruction for job training is "redefined" as more dynamic and interactive rather than passive and static. Rush, Moe and Storlie (1986) have defined occupational literacy as the ability to competently read required, work-related materials. They continue with the following observations based upon research:

- reading tasks are part of virtually all occupations studied;
- workers perform reading tasks for major portions of the work day;
- reading materials and processes observed in work settings are distinctly different from those found in school settings; and

- occupational materials are successfully read by workers who seem to lack the necessary reading abilities

Reading in the workplace is a concept which appears clear on the surface. However, how to teach and train for this concept is still in question and will be explored further as the agenda for reading instruction is developed. As macrostructures, job training and adult literacy/community agencies are considered separately as has been the case in practice. Community-based organizations have traditionally served the needs of low income communities (Merrill, 1988).

Merrill (1988) cites the following statistics as related to community based organizations.

- The Association for Community Based Education (ACBE) has59 institional members serving 105,000 adults in 31 states (Kangiser, 1985)
- From a survey of 3,500 non member community based programs, it was estimated that 600,00 to 700,000 people were served (Business Council for Effective Literacy, 1984)
- There are over 200 Literacy Volunteers of America in 30 states with 15,000 tutors and 21,000 clients
- Literacy Volunteers of America affiliates are both self-standing and others are located in correctional facilities, libraries, schools, business and industrial facilities
- 80 percent of funding for Adult Basic Education is allocated for individuals with skills below eight grade level

Community agencies/adult literacy is a huge reading macrostructure wrought **with instructional intricacies and low budgets.** This macrostructure is also complicated by definitional problems as well as classification/label issues. Remedial reading has historically been linked with illiteracy and thus consequently with community agencies and literacy programs. Community agencies rarely utilize the term remedial reading in describing their services. Also, often such agencies utilize volunteers who are not trained for true remedial instruction.

The macrostructures of reading instruction have been discussed as separate entities for the sake of clarification. However, the blurring of lines between the macrostructures, in practice, is obvious. Also, as specific reading issues are dealt with the lines become even more blurred between the macrostructures and the process skills that might be used for instructional programming.

ISSUES AND DIRECTIONS FOR READING IN DEVELOPMENTAL EDUCATION

Issues abound in the area of developmental education and reading instruction. The issues can best be understood as viewed within the macrostructures of reading discussed in the prior section. Like "big business" these macrostructures become conglomerates and "take overs" appear on the horizon. It becomes increasingly difficult to determine, who is responsible for what, who is doing, what is being done and what should be done.

Adult Literacy

Adult literacy is one macrostructure of developmental education. Twenty-ven, forty-five or seventy-five million Americans can not read a bedtime story, decipher traffic signs, directions on a medicine bottle or interpret information from an Internal Revenue Form. Depending upon the standard for literacy or illiteracy, adult literacy is big business in the area of developmental education. One topic of discussion at the Fall, 1987 Conference by University of Pennsylvania Literacy Research and U.S. National Advisory Council on Adult Education was a standardization of terms. Richard Venezky recommended basic literacy for improving skills through reading and other materials. Required literacy was the term for reading level required in any social context (*Journal of Reading*, March, 1988). The varied definitions of literacy and illiteracy raise a major issue as it becomes more difficult to identify a truly illiterate population. The lack of standardization perpetuates the hodgepodge of methods, materials and strategies. The lack of clear definition also creates difficulty for literacy advocates. Those needing help in the United states are often lost in a numbers games based up the way that they are classified in terms of literacy.

Basic literacy implies a definition of reading which includes the process of learning to decode and comprehend at least sixth-grade printed material. This definition continues to undergo change as the "war on literacy/ illiteracy" continues. Archie Lapointe, executive director of the National Assessment of Educational Progress (NAEP) has repeatedly emphasized in written reports and oral reports that the definition of literacy is not static but dynamic and must continue to change with the demands of society and technology. Merrill (1988) has indicated that generally it is agreed that functional illiteracy is the difference between an individual's current level of literacy and the level demanded by the individual's environment. Kozol (1985) has reported in Illiterate America that 25 million American adults cannot read the poison warning on an insecticide spray can or a letter from their child's teacher.

Table 9: READING ISSUES IN DEVELOPMENTAL EDUCATION

ISSUE	POTENTIAL ACTION/THEORETICAL CONSTRUCT	RESEARCH BASE
Redefinition	Practical International Literacy Scale	Sticht Project
of literacy	Jean Chall's Stages of Reading National Assessment Reading Proficiency Scale	REALISTIC
Higher	Universal Theoretical Framework	Cognitive
Order Thinking	Information Processing/National Assessment of Educational Progress/Piaget, Vygotsky, Bruner, Aristotle and James	(Glaser) (Frederickson)
Competen- cies in Reading	International Literacy Scale & Process Skills	Farr, Popham and Klare
	National Assessment of Educational Progress	
Strategies and meth- ods for adults	Process Skills	Center for Human Information Processing
	Smith, Goodman, Vaugh, Estes and Rumelhart	Center for the Study of Reading
Collabo- ration/Busi- ness/ Universit- ies/Com- munity	Collaborative to work on problems of literacy for all macrostructures	ASTD National Report (1984)
		Adler (1951)
Is there a state of the art reading instruction?	Research and Research Dissemination in the 21st Century	Center for the Study of Reading
	Technology Center - Vanderbilt University Center for Human Information Processing	

Chall, Heron and Hilferty (1987) reports that adult illiteracy has been around for a long time with the first campaign against illiteracy occuring during the Great Depression. An additional large scale effort to eradicate illiteracy occurred with The U.S. Right-to Read Effort in 1969. Currently illiteracy is being discussed and several community programs funded by the federal government. Universities in urban areas have developed ties to state literacy efforts. Also many community agencies have joined forces with literacy advocacy groups to promote reading instruction for the adult illiterate population.The Correctional Education Association(CEA) founded in 1946 for educators and administrators serving educational needs of clientele in juvenile and correctional institutions has also joined the Coalition for Literacy. The Coalition for Literacy is a national group attempting to organize the many groups concerned with literacy and to focus the attack on literacy. Anabel Newman, in *Reading Today,* December 1988/January 1989, has written that before the inception of the coalition in 1981, there were no:

- U.S. Office of Education Adult Literacy Initiative
- State literacy initiatives or coalitions
- Business Council for Effective Literacy
- American Newspaper Publishers Association drive on literacy
- Project Literacy U.S. (PLUS) campaign uniting ABC and PBS to promote awareness of the needs of adult illiterates

Even with the massive initiatives described above, literacy is a problem. Additional problems with the issue of illiteracy are the high number of dropouts from such programs. Maintaining accurate records and consistent data on literacy project participants is also a difficult task as many of the literacy projects are manned and operated by many volunteers who are often as transient as the literacy student. Chall and others (Phi Delta Kappan, 1987) reported on data from the American Council on Education and the National Alliance of Business with the following statement:

> Demographic figures for 1987 from the American Council on Education suggest that both the number and the percentage of adults likely to be seeking help with literacy will increase consistently, well into the twenty-first century. (12) The problem is likely to be compounded by projected changes in the nature of work and in the kinds of jobs available by the year 2000. These changes will lead to job obsolescence, the restructuring of jobs towards higher levels of skill and increased requirements for technical training beyond high school (13).

Chall and others continue by addressing the issue of the large numbers of Americans needing literacy training. They indicated that not all adults needing literacy training presented themselves at the doors of literacy agencies, such agencies would be ill equipped to deal with the massive numbers. Smith in *Phi Delta Kappan* (January, 1989) raises the issue of universal literacy with the following statement:

> I am by no means sure that universal literacy can be attained.
> Too much is wrong with the way our schools and out if
> literacy is to flourish, it will be in schools. And if literacy dies,
> it will also be in schools. So I would like to see schools
> become places more hospitable to true literacy. (P. 358)

The above statement raises the question not only of definition, but also the assertion that the macrostructures in developmental education are all intricately involved in the literacy and reading for the learner. One challenge for the twenty-first century is for developmental educators to systematically address the issue of literacy definition and programming for adult learners. This issue must be addressed through rigorous research and consolidation of efforts of the many businesses, agencies and universities working in the area of adult literacy. This issue must be addressed whether funding is forthcoming or not. Heretofore, literacy has been focused on in concert with federal, state and corporate funding levels for the war on literacy. As literacy is defined, so must the materials, strategies and methodologies which make a difference.

HIGHER-ORDER THINKING SKILLS

Higher order thinking skills and the lack thereof, is an issue which cuts across all of the macrostructures of reading for developmental learners. The basic issue is that our students, young and old, re-entering or non traditional, on the job and even corporate level have difficulty with thinking (information processing).In the Spring of 1987, the Illinois Association for Educational Research and Evaluation devoted an entire conference to exploring thinking skills (Communique, 1985). At this conference participants dealt with the following questions: (1) Is there a BEST model? (2) Does the research support an integrated or separate program? (3) Do you need to teach specific skills? (4) How do you measure success? and (5) Does the test drive the instruction and, (6) How do you know that students are thinking better as a result of a thinking skills program? Such questions continue to be addressed as educational issues across the country. The thinking skills issue is intricately woven in the reading process of taking and bringing meaning to the printed page. Critical to the issue of lack of thinking skills is the manner by which thinking skills are measured and the theoretical framework from which specific skills are identified. The National

Assessment of Educational Progress (NAEP) is rapidly becoming an "educational ly acceptable manner" in which to assess thinking skills (1986). Many developmental educators' view of the thinking process is theoretically framed by psychologists Piaget, Vygotsky and Bruner as well as philosophers Aristotle and James. These classical thinkers studied and wrote on the developmental stages of thinking and the goals of thinking/reasoning since the time of Plato.

Programming for developmental clients should be based upon the work of the classical thinkers. However, when using the many theories and materials on thinking, confusion results as to what type of instruction in the area of thinking/comprehension for the developmental education client.

Hashway (1988, p. 151) has written the following relative to thinking and learning:

> Regardless of whether programs are designed for remediation or development, these programs must rest upon firm foundations. The foundations of educational programs should have their roots planted in the soil of human learning. ... Consequently, it is important that all educational programs emphasize human processes for cognitive growth and development.

Miles(1986) has explored thinking from a practical level and questions the difference between "it" and "they." "It" relates to thinking a single unit. With the single unit mindset, product becomes important and one target is our aim. Rightness becomes a major influence in teaching thinking skills. On the other hand, in the "they" framework, process and reasonableness becomes the cornerstone of teaching thinking. In a "they" framework, thinking capacity is freed up. Several targets become appropriate. Process is built on the interplay of several forces. Miles continues by suggesting seven factors in thinking:

- Communications Competence
- Style
- Technique
- Self-Concept
- Awareness and Management
- Resources
- Feelings

He posits that thinking is molded by these seven factors.

Another aspect of developing higher order thinking skills in the developmental population is the question of studies which confirm that

	Re-entering	Community	Business
Remedial	**Non-traditional**	**Adult Literacy**	**Industry/Job Training**
Decoding	Conceptualizing	Decoding	Conceptualizing
Conceptualizing	Planning	Conceptualizing	Planning
Assimilating	Organizing	Assimilating	Assimilating
Interpreting	Reviewing	Interpreting	Organizing
Evaluating	Interpreting	Analyzing	Interpreting
Applying	Evaluating	Evaluating	Evaluating
	Monitoring	Applying	Monitoring
	Studying		Applying
	Applying		

Table 10: PROCESS SKILLS IDENTIFIED FOR EACH MACROSTRUCTURE

teachers who were assessed at more conceptually advanced levels were considered more effective as classroom teachers. Most of the challenges to developing higher order thinking skills have rested on the shoulders of the student population. Killion (1988) raised the question of the professional development of trainers and teachers. The issue here becomes that of who is attempting to develop higher order thinking skills/comprehension skills? What is their level of expertise to accomplish this task? Theis-Sprinthall (1980) reported that teachers who are higher conceptually, utilized more indirect teaching methods. This also raises the question of what type of methods should be used to develop higher order/comprehension facility.

As higher-order thinking skills are viewed across the macrostructures of developmental education, the issue of who, what and how emerges. *Higher level comprehension/thinking is of concern in reading instruction. These skills must be taught. However, the trainer/teacher must know what is to be taught and how to assess the outcomes of what is taught. This is still a problem to be contended with in developmental reading across remedial reading, re-entering, community literacy and business/industrial training programs.*

COMPETENCIES IN READING MINIMUM AND MAXIMUM SKILLS

The reform movements have emphasized standardized, criterion referenced and mastery testing. The National Assessment of Educational Progress(NAEP) and widespread publicity has further expanded the vision of competencies "for all" in reading. The educational achievement of American youth, of concern to the nation, lead to the National Assessment of Educational Progress (NAEP). This federally funded testing program, now 20 years old, was intended as a tool for giving a broad picture of the educational achievement of United states students of varied age groupings. With widespread testing across the country and the many assessment task forces at universities and in public schools addressing the issue, we still are not on solid ground when determining minimum and maximum reading competencies for adult learners. In addition, reading competencies and mastery issues are tied in with the varied literacy definitions.

A common scene during reading instruction across the macrostructures is as follows:

> Assessment or testing occurs early on in the clients entry into a reading program. The test might be standardized or criterion referenced(mastery based). Usually depending on the sophistication of client, test items might be standardized or criterion referenced (mastery based). Test items might range from basic word attack skills through literal comprehension tasks. Sophisticated assessment might go into higher level thinking skills and some study skill items as well as attitudinal assessment.

> Some instruction occurs, but frequently testing or assessment data is ignored until the end of treatment or instructional period. Then the question of competencies becomes super important. We return then to a test bank or assessment items and look at what we believe the client should leave with--now we are truly interested in competencies.

The above scene might be an exaggeration of the competency picture. But too frequently, competencies become more important as we move toward the end of the instructional period. Also we often have little faith in the competencies that we are assessing. The question continues to linger: competencies for what?

Farr and Carey (1986) in *Reading: What Can Be Measured?* have defined reading as comprehension. This book deals with the many issues in reading assessment and competencies. They also raise the question of accountability via the corporate metaphor. The central issue is discussed as accountability rather than minimum competency tests. They have written:

> The possibility exists that "accountability," as part of the corporate metaphor, represents an important, unexamined assumption which guides our perception of schools, clouds our judgement of what should(and does) happen in schools and implicitly requires us to apply criteria for excellence that are simplistic, misinformed, corporate era. We live in a period characterized by huge multinational conglomerates, by OPEC, by intense labor struggles, by a thousand frightening economic scenarios. Is it any wonder that the twentieth century mind makes use of the similes, metaphors, and big time business and finance?

They question also the lack of concern for subjective judgement and *how the reader gets where he is going.* The highest number of points appears to be the major concern. This concern is critical to minimum and maximum reading competencies. A high score or a large number of points on a reading test seems tangential to process and being able to read to get a job done.

READING INSTRUCTION AS PROCESS

Reading for the remedial macrostructure is defined as a process of decoding, bringing meaning and taking meaning from the printed page. This definition which meshes with the Harris and Smith Model in Figure 9 can be used as a foundation for looking at the varied reading processes expected of readers across the reading macrostructures. It should be noted that skill hierarchies have appropriately been used to address instruction utilizing the Harris and Smith model. Not many reading educators are questioning the use of process skills. Even though it would appear that the use of process skills (Table 9) has gained acceptance, *such is not as evident when observing reading instruction and viewing reading prescriptions in the developmental arena.*

It is necessary to move from the Harris and Smith reading process model to an interactive model. Rumelhart's reading process model is an interactive model. Rumelhart (1976) views reading as an interactive process with continual interaction of reader with text and text with reader. Probst (1984) has captured the essence of the interactive reading process as he describes the experience of reading:

> As we read, we find ourselves changing perspectives, revising impressions, accumulating information and insight, and

passing through a series of emotional states.

In order to organize the process skills which appear to be inherent in reading theory in the 1980s and moving towards the 1990s, Figure 8 and Table 9 illustrate the process skills that might be attributed to each macrostructure. *The major issue in terms of process skills are the developmental reading instruction tasks that take place across the macrostructures with emphasis on minimal skill attainment.*

It should be noted that the process skills are similar from one macrostructure to another and could very easily be identified or compiled into one basic list of process skills. The process skills were developed by various readings and research across the various macrostructures. This is important to note as we move to a reading agenda for the twenty-first century.

COLLABORATION FOR UNIVERSITIES/BUSINESS/ COMMUNITY

There have been take overs in training and teaching, but without the publicity normally accorded big business. These takeovers have been in the area of reading and the basic skills. Many businesses and corporations have developed programs to train their own employees. Morse has summed up this issue by the following:

> Despite the endless debate on who should be doing what to educate the American workforce, all players must be involved. The economy is becoming oriented more toward human capital, our system of postsecondary education and the participants are changing and demands for education and training are increasing. How to develope a synergistic, positive relationship between the academy and the corporation is the question (Morse, P. 63, 1984)

Educational partnerships have been proposed and implemented during the past decade. Still embarrassing data and remarks flow as to basic skill needs of many industrial/business workers. It is not unusual for trainers in industry and business to lack an understanding of developmental education and reading instruction. Cornell (April, 1988) reporting on data from several authors/researchers wrote the following (Lauterborn, 1981;Mikulecky, 1982):

> Of 800 companies surveyed by the Conference Board 35% felt they had to supplement the basic education received in school. The Mutual Insurance Company of New York estimated that 70% of dictated correspondence had to be retyped and JLG Industries reported spending over one million dollars to correct worker literacy mistakes

(Lauterborn, 1981). For the future, occupations requiring little or no literacy are likely to disappear according to U.S. Department of Labor projections. (Mikulecky, 1984)

Reading instruction in the business/industrial environment differs from that in college and community agencies. The term occupational literacy becomes critical. Rush, Moe and Storlie (1986) have defined occupational literacy as the ability to competently read required, work related materials. They further clarify occupational literacy as a subset of functional literacy and as important concept for prevocational. Some of the characteristics of business/industry type reading instruction and comparative variables include:

- Outcomes based instruction
- Technologically advanced teaching aids
- Individualized teaching methods(Knowle's work on andragogy, 1984)
- Cost-benefit criteria
- More diverse materials and greater indepth reading (Mikulecky, 1982).

In *Reading Today* (December 1988/January 1989), Patricia S. Koppman, President of the International Reading Association wrote the following:

> My father always taught me that teachers taught, parents parented and business engaged in business. Nowadays, that is no longer the case. Businesses are getting more and more involved in our profession. Several businesses have decided to get on the literacy bandwagon. It is my strong opinion that if we want to make sure that these groups are on the right track! How? By offering our expertise so that their ideas, projects and often money, will be directed in ways that are best for students.

Business leaders are in agreement that they should not be in the business of providing reading instruction. However, the general position is that if there is a need, it must be met whether on the job, in the community or in the schools. *The issue here is whether developmental education can clearly identify the role of teachers, trainers and clients? Can developmental education serve as the catalyst for effective reading instruction within the business/job training macrostructure?*

STATE OF THE ART DEVELOPMENTAL READING STRATEGIES AND MATERIALS

Are there state of the art developmental reading strategies and materials? At this point the literature would support little change in the way that reading has been taught since the 1950s and 1960s. Basal readers, skill drill workbooks and varied skill drill computer type programs are still in widespread use. The materials and strategies have changed cosmetically, but not in terms of revolutionary changes. Research, however, is showing and pointing the way to change for the twenty-first century(Center on Reading, University of Illinois; Learning Technology Center, Vanderbilt University(Peabody College), Nashville, Tenn.; Center on Human Information Processing, University of California at LaJolla and San Diego). Reading as a thinking process and true interaction of reader with text will be emphasized. Additional changes will be in the delivery of reading services by home, school, community and business. Much of this instruction will be tied in with modern technology, television and computers. The responsibility for effective strategies will no longer rest simply on the shoulders of schools. The responsibility will be a joint undertaking as all of the macrostructures become integral and integrated members of a team working on literacy and reading needs of a population which can be more productive on the job and in the community as a result of the training/teaching. Emphasis in reading will also be on constructing and extracting meaning.

Several companies and universities are pointing us in the direction of state of the art methods and materials--even though we acknowledge that we are still not there. IBM has developed a reading program which capitalizes on the reading and writing connection. This computer software package is a systematic approach to reading and writing. It is receiving widespread use in business literacy programs as well as many public and private schools across the nation. It should be noted that rarely is this program used as the core in public and private schools. It usually complements the basal reading program.

The Learning Technology Center, at Vanderbilt University (Peabody College) in Nashville, Tennessee is working on microcomputers, optical discs and interactive video discs in teaching thinking, reading and content area thinking/reading. The Vanderbilt approach is unique in that they are cutting across content areas in their research. The Learning Technology Center is also soliciting the help of other researchers in trying out the vast array of technologically related instructional strategies and equipment. They readily admit that they are moving towards state of the art, but are not there yet. The center also distributes research reports, technical reviews and working papers.

Laptop computers, video discs and hypercards are in evidence at educational conferences and exhibits. However, even with the research being done by various universities and companies, such devices have not reached many practioners, trainers and teachers. At best, such devices are potential tools to consider for the twenty-first century. Today, it would be professionally unethical to call such devices state of the art in terms of reading instruction. *A Guest Edited Issue* of the *Journal of Reading* (April, 1989) illustrates the lack of state of the art in terms of new technologies and reading. Most of the articles which come from authors based in Australia touch only tangentially on CD ROMS, laser discs, telephone and satellite networks. As related to reading instruction, the Australia scene is not unlike that of the United States and international scene as related to reading instruction and state of the art programs, methods and materials.

The University of Illinois Center for the Study of Reading, Urbana, Illinois has developed a knowledge base of research on reading and has started answering many questions which will change the way we view the reading process and the type of materials selected to facilitate this process.

The interactive view of reading described above would support the elimination of mindless reading tasks, where the beginning reader and often more sophisticated reader is expected to answer literal comprehension questions. In the year 2000, materials for reading instruction will emphasize greater text structure, coherence and depth. In addition, materials will more closely simulate real life reading tasks. In addition, as the information age explodes so will the number of concepts in instructional materials.

READING AGENDA FOR THE TWENTY-FIRST CENTURY

Brentlinger (Jan, 1986) noted that current students will spend approx. 75 percent of their professional lives in the twenty-first century. The future is wrought with change and unexpected experiences. He proposes teaching students how to think and analyze for the twenty-first century rather than concerning them with facts and information. He writes of "adaptive modes of living" and learning during a period when jobs will change every five to ten years. Reading of necessity must be big business because, in part, our economic, social and emotional survival rests upon thinking, reasoning, problem solving and conceptual filtering (Probst, 1984). Without reading these processes would be limited. By limiting these processes we would be dooming the mind and conceptualization of our world to mediocrity. Probst (1984) continues with a conception of reading thus setting the stage across macrostructures for the twenty-first century:

> Our conception of reading is slightly different....we view the reader not as submissive, bending to the author's will, but as creative, making meaning rather than finding it. Thus, the text is not all important. The reader's task is to build meaning out of the confrontation experience and each work read should be seen as part of this process; not only a valuable experience in itself, but a contribution to something larger. (p. 66)

Fogarty in an unpublished view of a proficient reader sets the stage for outcomes of effective reading/developmental education in the year 2000. The thinking and theories of Vygotsky, Knowles, Cross, Roueche, Chall, Sticht and others are implicit in the that portrait.

Developmental reading for the twenty-first century will include developmental education at the hub of activity, training and instruction (Figure 9). The scholarly works of Cross, Rouech and Snow as well as Malcolm Knowles will continue to set the stage for working with adult learners across the macrostructures. The classic works of Vygotsky, Bruner and Adler will be used as mediating works between developmental education and reading education. The research and writings of Chall, Sticht, National Assessment of Education Progress technical reports, research from the Center on the Study of Reading at University of Illinois, the Technology Center at Vanderbilt University (Peabody College) and the Center on Human Information Processing at Unversity of California will set the stage for resolving some of the major issues facing developmental educators in the area of literacy.

Lines of demarcation and responsibilities for literacy across the macrostructures will be blurred as reading process skills are emphasized through life-long learning. Society in general will become more sensitive to reading as a process. Society will also acknowledge that refining this process is a lifelong commitment. Occupational and workplace literacy will be of concern as well as "deskilling and dumbing down" of reading tasks. Developmental educators will be used as trainers to conduct evaluations and to program for occupational literacy in the workplace. Developmental educators will have an international literacy scale to work with and thus each employee will have such information available if he/she has graduated from high school. Reading disabilities will still exist, but will be treated more clinically and less in the area of remedial reading. Community agencies sponsoring reading instruction will be in tune with reading instruction across macrostructures as developmental educators will once more assume leadership roles in such agencies. The war on literacy will rely less on volunteers and more on trained developmental educators with expertise in process reading and writing.

Minimal and maximum reading competencies will receive little attention as the international literacy scale has established a minimum reading level. Maximum reading attainments and goals will be academic or career related with reading process skills being refined regardless of instructional setting. In addition, thinking skills are tied to reading process skills. In fact lines will be blurred between reading and thinking skills as the reading process will be viewed as making and using meaning from the printed word. Based upon the thinking focus, the work of Anderson, Hiebert, Scott and Wilkinson (1985) will be used to view reading rooted in a cognitive model. Reading instruction will be intricately interwoven into the construction of meaning and the environment in which reading task is expected to be optimized. In addition the reading process will not be far removed from the writing process where mental processes of planning, translating, reviewing and monitoring are emphasized (Pea and Kurland, 1987 in Rothkopf). Collaboration between business, school and community will be an accepted practice rather than a novelty. Businesses will rely upon community agencies for basic literacy training and once more the international literacy scale as well as emphasis on reading as a process will yield higher gains and a larger number of literate individuals moving in and out of the workplace. Related to collaboration is the blurring of lines between the macrostructures and constant motion as the process skills become a part of reading instruction regardless of learning environment. The twenty-first century information age will place great demands on learners , educators and trainers. However, the challenge will be firmly planted on a foundation of problem-solving skills and thinking processes. These processes will be critical to learners, educators and trainers if this agenda is to be actualized.

REFERENCES

Abraham, A. A. (1987). *A report on college developmental programs in SREB states.* Atlanta: Southern Regional Education Board.

Adler M. J. (1951). Labor, leisure and liberal education. *Journal of gender education,* 6, 43.

Adler, M. J. (1986) Why 'Critical Thinking' programs will not work. *Education week,* September.

American Society for Training and Development. (1983) *Models for excellence.* Washington, D.C.: American Society for Training and Development.

Anderson, R. C., E. H. Hiebert, J. A. Scott and I. Wilkinson. (1985). *Becoming a Nation of readers: The report of the commission on Rrading.* Washington, D.C.: National Institute of Education, U.S. Department of Education.

Armbuster, B. B. and R. Anderson (1980) *The effect of mapping on the free recall of expository text.* (Technical Report Number 160). Urbana-Champaign, Illinois: Center for the Study of Reading, University of Illinois.

Blanchard, J. S., et. al. (1987). *Computer applications in reading.* Newark, Delaware: Internatonal Reading Association, 1987.

Bloomberg, R. (1988). Cost-Benefit analysis of mployee Ttaining: A literature review. *Adult education quarterly,* 39, 9-98.

Brentlinger, W. B. (1986). *Curricula for the Twenty-First entury.* (Paper presented at the regional conference on university teaching, 2nd Las Cruces, New Mexico), January 8-10.

Bruner, J. S. (1962). *On knowing.* Cambridge: Harvard University Press.

Bruner, J. S.(1960). *The process of education.* Cambridge: Harvard University Press.

Burnett, R. W. and T. R. Schnell (1983). A look at the future: Teachers in non-traditional reading programs. *Reading horizons,* 24, 33-38.

Carroll, J. (1988) The NAEP reading proficiency scale is ot a fiction: A reply to Mclean and Goldstein. *Phi Delta Kappan,* 69 761-764.

Carvn B. (1988) Ideas in practice: Plan-making: taking effective control of study habits. *Journal of developmental education,* 12 ,26-29.

Chall, Jean. (1983). *Stages of reading development.* New York: MCGraw-Hill.

Chall, J., E. Heron and A. Hilferty (1987). Adult literacy: New and enduring problems. *Phi delta kappan*, 69, 190-196.

Cooper, E. (1989). "Toward a new mainstream of Instruction for American schools." *Journal of negro education*, 58, 102-116.

Costa, A. (1984). Mediating the metacognitive. *Educational leadership*, 9, 57-62.

Cross, K. P. (1971). *Beyond the open door.* San Francisco: Jossey-Bass Publishers.

Cross, K. P. (1981). *Adults as learners: Increasing participation and facilitating learning.* San Francisco: Jossey-Bass.

Cross, K. P. (1981). "Adult learners: Characteristics, needs and interests." In *lifelong learning in America.* San Francisco: Jossey-Bass, Inc..

Cross, K. P. (1987). *Adults as learners.* San Franciso: Jossey-Bass, Inc..

Enzensberger, H. M. (1987). In praise of the illiterate, *Adult education and development*, 28, 96-105.

Farr, R. (1980). Minimum competency testing the appropriate solution to the SAT Decline? *Phi delta kappan* 61, 528-30.

Farr, R. and R. F. Carey (1986). *Reading: What measured?* second edition. Newark, DE: International Reading Association.

Fields, E. L. (1986). Industry-based programs: A growing source for adult literacy development. *Lifelong learning*, 10, 7-9.

Fogarty, R. (1988). *Portrait of the reader.* Chicago: Loyola University of Chicago (Unpublished manuscript).

Frederiksen, C.H. (1975). Representing logical and semantic Structure of knowledge acquired From discourse. *Cognitive psychology*, 7, 371-458.

Garman, N. R.(1984). *The heart of clinical supervision: A modern rationale for professional practice. Readings: clinical supervision reflection in action.* Geelong, Victoria: Australia: Deakin University.

Glasser, W. (1981). *Stations of the mind.* New York: Harper and Row Publishers.

Glasser, W. (1984). *Take effective control of your life..* New York: Harper and Row Publishers.

Glaser, R. (1984). Education of thinking, The role of knowledge. *American psychologist* 39l 93-104.

Glazer, S. M., Searfoss, L. and Gentile, L. M. (1988). *Reexamining reading diagnosis: New trends.* Newark, DE: International Reading Association.

Gutherie, J. (1983). Equilibrium of literacy. *Journal of reading,* 26, 668-670.

Gutherie, J. (1987). Literacy as multidimensional: Locating information and reading comprehension. *Educational psychologist,* 22, 279-299.

Hardin, C. (1988). Access to higher education: Who belongs. *Journal of developmental education,* 12, 2-6.

Harman, D. (1987). *Illiteracy: A National dilemna.* New York: Cambridge Book Company.

Harris, L and C. Smith (1980). *Reading instruction.* New York: Holt, Rinehart and Winston.

Hashway, R. (1989). *Foundations of developmental education.* New York: Praeger Publishers.

Hayes, E. (1988). A typology of low-literate adults based on perceptions of reterrents participation in adult basic education. *Adult education quarterly,* 39, 1-10.

Hyde, A. and M. Bizar (1989). *Thinking in context.* White Plains: Longman Inc.

Illinois Association for educational research and education (1987). *The communique,* Spring.

Killion, J. P. (1988). Parallels between adult development and trainer development, *Journal of staff development,* 9, 6-10.

Irwin, J. (1986). *Teaching reading comprehension processes.* Englewood Clffs: New Jersey.

Kirsch, I. K. and Gutherie, J. T. (1984). Adult reading practices for work and leisure. *Adult education quarterly*, 34, 219-2

Knowles, M. S. (1980). *The modern practice of adult education: Andragogy versus pedagogy.* New York: Associated Press.

Knowles, M. S. (1984). *The adult learner: A neglected species* (3rd ed). Houston: Gulf Publishing Company.

Koretz, D. (1989). The new National assessment: What it can and cannot do. National Education Association, *NEA TODAY* (Special Edition) January, 32-37.

Kozol, J. (1985). *Illiterate America.* New York: Anchor Press/Doubleday and Company, Inc.

Lapointe, A. and N. Larrick (1987). Illiteracy starts to soon. *Phi delta kappan,* 69, 184-189.

Lauterborn, R. F. (1981). *Reading: Why industry cares and what one company is doing about it.* Paper delivered at the International Reading Association annual convention, New Orleans, LA, April.

Merrill, M. (1988). A helping hand: Educational programs for the functionally illiterate. *Lifelong learning* 11, 25-27.

Miles. C. (1986). The fourth R: seven determinants of thinking. *Journal of developmental education,* 10, 22.

Mikulecky, L. (1984). Preparing students for workplace lieracy emands, *Journal of Rrading,* 28, 253-57.

Mikulecky, L. (1982). Job literacy: The relationship between school preparation and workplace actuality. *Reading research quarterly,* 17, 400-419.

Mikulecky, L. and D. Winchester (1983). Job literacy and job performance among nurses at varying employment levels. *Adult education quarterly,* 34, 3-5.

Moore, W. (1970). *Against the odds.* San Francisco: Jossey-Bass Publishers.

Morse, S. W. (1984). *Employee educational pograms: Implications for industry and higher education.* Washington, D.C. : Association for the Study of Higher Education.

National Assessment of Educational Progress. (1986). *The reading report card: Progress toward excellence in our schools: Trends in reading over four National assessments, 1971- 1984.* Princeton, New Jersey: Educational Testing Service.

National Assessment of Educational Progress (1985). *The reading report card.* Princeton, N.J.: Educational Testing Service.

Palincsar, A. and A. Brown (1983). *Reciprocal teaching of comprehension monitoring activities, Technical Report No. 269.* Champaign, Il: University of Illinois, Center for the Study of Reading.

Paris, S. (1987). Introduction to current issues in reading comprehension. *Educational psychologist,* 22, 209-213.

Philippi, J. (1988). Matching literacy to job training: Applications rom military programs. *Journal of reading,* 11, 658-666.

Popham, W. J. (1987). The merits of measurement-driven instruction. *Phi delta kappan,* 68, 679-682.

Probst, R. (1984). *Adolescent literature: Response and analysis.* Columbus, Ohio: Charles E. Merrill.

Resnick, L. (1987). *Education and learning to think.* Washington, DC: National Academy Press.

Richardson, R. C., E. C. Fisk and M. A. Okun (1983). *Literacy in the open-access college.* San Francisco: Jossey-Bass Publishers.

Roueche, J and J. J. Snow (1977). *Overcoming learning problems.* San Francisco: Jossey-Bass Publishers.

Rumelhart, D. E. (1976). *Toward an interactive model of reading* (Technical Report, No. 56). San Diego: Center for Human Information Processing, University of California.

Rush, R. T., A. Moe and R. L. Storlie (1986). *Occupational literacy education.* Newark, Delaware: International Reading Association.

Rothkopf, E. (1987). *Preview of educational research.* Washington, D.C.: American Educational Research Association.

Sinnott, J.D. (1975). Everyday thinking a piagetian operativity in adults. *Human development,* 18, 430-443.

Smith, F. (1988). *What the brain does well.* Victoria, B.C.: Abel Press.

Smith, F. (1989). Overselling literacy. *Phi delta kappan,* 70, 352-359.

Smith. R. (1982). *Learning how to learn: Applied learning theory for adults.* New York: Cambridge Books.

Sticht, T. (1983). *Literacy and human resources development at ork: Investing in the education of adults to improve the Educability of children.* Alexandria, VA: Human Resoruces Research Organization.

Sticht, T. (1975). *Reading for working: A functional literacy anthology.* Alexandria, VA: Human Resources Research Organiation.

Sticht, T. .G. and L. Mikulecky (1984). *Job-related Basic skills:Cases and conclusions.* Columbus, Ohio: National Center for Research in Vocational Education.

Theis-Sprinthall, L. (1980). *Promoting the conceptual and principled thinking level of the supervising teacher.* (Unpublished Manuscript).

Vaughn, J. L. and T. Estes (1986). *Reading and reasoning beyond the primary grades.* Boston: Allyn and Bacon, Inc..

Vygotsky, L. S. (1962). *Thought and language.* Cambridge, Mass: MIT Press.

Whimbey, A. (1987). A 15th Grade reading level for high school seniors? *Phi delta kappan,* 69, 207-208.

Wilson, B. (1986). When technology enhances teaching. *American educator*, 8-13, 46-47.

12

Developmental Reading in College

Robin W. Erwin, Jr.

In modern times society has come to expect that at least its educated citizenry be skilled readers, ordinarily capable of full comprehension and, as needed, able to follow the structure of arguments, synthesize ideas across texts and evaluate arguments in what is read. A democratic society is always in need of citizens who will make decisions as informed and rational thinkers.

The adults of the twenty-first century will require substantial intellectual skills in order to contribute to tomorrow's information-choked civilization. We can confidently predict a strong and growing need for advanced literacy, clear-headed reasoning and the capacity to think deeply and critically about crucial issues in tomorrow's society. Surely the ethical and moral dilemmas, the political impasses and the battles for the mind will be at least as intense in the next few decades as they are today.

An illustration of the complexity of the challenges facing coming generations is the plague-like nuclear arms issue: How can mankind be certain to avoid the horror of a nuclear confrontation? Deterrence seems to have "worked" for the forty-odd years of the nuclear age, but is this the best long-term solution? Jonathan Schell argues in *The Fate of the Earth* (1982) for disarmament and radical rethinking of international affairs, going beyond war and into a more enlightened world society. And how to achieve this? Schell says with great understatement, "I have left to others those awesome, urgent tasks, which, imposed on us by history, constitute the political work of our age" (p. 219). Whatever the composition of the group of people who do "work out" the details of this particular moral imperative and whatever their other qualifications, they will surely have acquired the ability to think deeply, clearly and critically on the issues of the day.

The sobering reality is that these problem-solving saviors of the future are students in our schools now. Are they being challenged to think deeply and critically as they progress through the schools today? Some evidence suggests they are not. A report by the National Assessment of Educational Progress regarding reading performance (1981) indicates that many of our students are quite successfully mastering decoding and basic comprehension skills, but far fewer are skillful in higher-order comprehension, an phenomenon that is especially noticeable at the high school level. Similarly, among the spate of commission reports on the state of schooling in the 1980s, none had positive analyses regarding the schools' success in developing critical thinkers. According to *A Nation at Risk* (National Commission on Excellence in Education, 1983), many 17-year-olds could not demonstrate higher order thinking skills called for by test questions and 40 percent could not draw logical inferences from written materials. In the popular press, a pair of non-fiction best-sellers of 1987 (*The Closing of the American Mind* by A. D. Bloom and *Cultural Literacy: What Every American Needs to Know* by E. D. Hirsch) seemed to tap the public's suspicions about limited intellectual performance among young Americans.

In spite of these negative appraisals of the status of schooling for critical thinking, an incredible amount of professional attention has been directed toward critical thinking and other descriptors of so-called higher-order thinking. For example, one researcher reports identifying 1,894 citations related to critical thinking over a recent seven year span of ERIC database entries (Paul, 1985). Indeed, a search over the 23 year span of the ERIC database from 1966 through 1988 reveals that there have been 3,966 entries under the descriptors "critical thinking" or "critical reading," an average of 172 entries per year over this period. Professional conferences in education regularly call for presentations on critical thinking and keynote speakers repeatedly draw attention to higher-order thinking skills. Whole issues of professional journals in education are devoted to thinking skills and related instruction [see *Review of Educational Research*, 54 (4), 1984 and *Education Leadership*, 42, (1984-1985, issues 1, 3 and 8)] and significant volumes on topics in critical thinking are being published each year (e.g., Chipman, Segal and Glaser, 1985; Segal, Chipman and Glaser, 1985; Baron and Sternberg, 1987).

This literature tells us that critical thinking is regarded as one of the highest and most sophisticated of thinking behaviors and is crucially involved in many of the most valued and civilized of human activities -- careful writing of every genre, serious reading of any genre of writing, debating of positions, individual and group decision-making, functional and aesthetic design and many other intellectual activities. With this value placed on critical thinking behaviors, the notion that all students -- especially college students -should develop their powers of critical thought has formidable public support.

The college graduate as a critical thinker is a valued "product" of the undergraduate experience and the ability to think critically is often listed as one of the supremely important educational goals of the college degree. A National Institute of Education report in 1984 urged the fostering of critical thinking ability as an essential aspect of the college experience and the mastery of the language skills of critical reading, effective composition, clear speech and careful listening as the fuel of thought. Some writers assert that successful college students spend as much as one half of their reading time reading critically (Yellot, et al, 1985). Employers seek this kind of analytical thinker among college graduates and there is ample evidence that the higher education experience does have a positive effect on the critical thinking performance of students (Dressel and Mayhew, 1954; Lehmann, 1963; Perry, 1970; Keeley, Brown and Kreutzer, 1982; McMillan, 1987; Pascarella, 1987; Whitla, 1977).

While these concerns certainly represent the college-wide commitment to develop the maturity and sophistication of all college students' thought processes, they are also the concerns of college developmental reading educators. Consider those students who arrive at college not ready to independently comprehend required freshman reading: will these college level developmental readers genuinely succeed in college without direct reading instruction? In many cases, the answer is no (see New Jersey Basic Skills Council, 1986, for a thorough state-wide study of the effects of developmental studies on retention). And what do these college developmental readers need most in order to be proficient in their college reading tasks? One clear need is the need to acquire a mature, skilled reading ability that allows these readers to critically evaluate new information presented in text material.

Thus, the curriculum for developmental college readers is at its core a plan to help these readers eventually become critical, more sophisticated readers, who read for deeper understanding and application, who read with greater awareness of affect in the writer and self, who more accurately follow the structure of arguments in their reading and are more likely to engage in evaluative thinking about their reading.

In this context, what is the difference between the developmental reader and the traditional college freshman reader? The developmental reader begins college with an apparent academic disadvantage in that his general reading achievement is at something less than the college level. A typical developmental reader has not been a serious high school student, has not read widely and consequently, often does not have a wealth of school-based knowledge (Longman and Atkinson, 1987). However, he is more likely to be aliterate than truly illiterate. The typical developmental reader does not have overwhelming sight word problems or gross word analysis problems.

He more frequently has limited meaning vocabulary, limited skills in comprehending complex sentences and paragraphs, little experience in analyzing the underlying structure of ideas in text and few strategies for dealing with difficult texts (Cohen, 1988). Perhaps just as academically debilitating is his less-than-average world knowledge, at a time when average is already defined to be a state of relative ignorance of civilization (Hirsch, 1987; Cheney, 1985).

So the very goals of the academy insist on critical reading by college students, yet this skilled reading behavior is not one that the developmental reader has customarily practiced. With such an important need among developmental readers, critical reading is an obvious focus of many developmental reading courses.

Some observers may question whether critical reading instruction is appropriate for such academically disadvantaged college students, suggesting that developmental students need basic skills instruction rather than instruction in thinking. Miles (1981) counters by arguing that developmental students need both kinds of instruction and in reality the two categories of instruction are inextricably woven together -- the distinction is artificial, for the two should be seen as inseparable. All domains of instruction should include "thinking instruction."

When critics have suggested that critical thinking or reading instruction takes too much instructional time or that this is not the appropriate territory of developmental educators, Miles has offered that the time devoted to critical thinking instruction is well spent and that developmental students who have learned to think in more sophisticated ways need less reteaching. He argues that even though no one would claim to have the best ways of teaching critical thinking, we have some ways that work and can serve as a starting point. Miles implies that if there is a class of teachers who bear the major responsibility for teaching youngsters to think critically, these teachers need help from any willing quarter, including developmental educators! A narrow viewpoint that claims developmental students should stick to the basics and postpone any concern about thinking skills does not hold up to the realities of developmental reading instruction -- these students are ready to think about the idea structure, the veracity, the worth of what they read and this is the very experience they have often lacked and need so desperately.

DEFINITIONS

Definitions of critical reading and critical thinking are very similar, the major distinction being the involvement in an act of reading as an additional and obvious aspect of critical reading.

Marshall (1985) traces two distinct models of critical thinking: one derived from the work of Dewey (1933), who saw critical thinking as a problem-solving process in which thinking proceeds in an orderly, reasonable and especially, in a reflective manner; the other derived from the work of Blank (1952), and, later Ennis (1962 and 1979), who saw critical thinking as a form of logical analysis that results in evaluation and concerns itself with deductive and inductive reasoning and with language usage. This latter model appears to have had more influence on researchers' and writers' working definitions for critical thinking over the years.

Watson and Glaser (1980) conceived of critical thinking as a composite of attitudes, knowledge and skills. Elaborating on this, Erwin (1985) identified in the construct of critical thinking a metacognitive factor (awareness of writer's and one's own affect), a knowledge factor (the crucial role of background knowledge in the evaluation of arguments) and a skills factor (a practice/experience effect in the analysis and evaluation of arguments).

Paul (1984) distinguishes between two kinds of critical thinking: a weak sense and a strong sense. Critical thinking in the weak sense involves "discrete, micro-logical skills ultimately extrinsic to the character of the person; skills that can be tacked onto other learning." Critical thinking in the strong sense involves "a set of integrated, macro-logical skills ultimately intrinsic to the character of the person and to insight into one's own cognitive and affective processes" (p. 5).

In the *Dictionary of Reading and Related Terms* (Harris and Hodges, 1983) critical reading is defined as

> The process of making judgments in reading: evaluating relevancy and adequacy of what is read; an act of reading in which a questioning attitude, logical analysis and inference are used to judge the worth of what is read according to an established standard. Critical reading is the judgment of validity, or worth of what is read, based on sound criteria or standards developed through previous experiences. (p. 74)

REVIEW OF RESEARCH FINDINGS WITH GENERAL POPULATIONS

In spite of substantial publication on the topic of critical thinking and critical reading, almost all of the related literature could be described as essays on the importance or the methods of teaching critical thinking; only a very small proportion of the literature reports original research findings (see also Marshall, 1985; Greenewald, Dulin and Anders, 1973, for similar comments about the research base of critical thinking/reading). Of those few research studies, only a small handful involve college developmental readers. Of the 3,966 critical thinking or critical reading entries in the ERIC database, indexing both journal articles and microfiche documents between the years 1966 and 1988, only four entries were found to be reports of research concerning critical reading and college developmental readers. Because so few studies have investigated critical reading instruction and college developmental readers, it is valuable to examine some of the research findings with other populations as well.

One important investigation on this question was the Wolf, King and Huck (1968) study of teaching critical reading to elementary students. This relatively large-scale study used 24 intact elementary classrooms in grades one through six with a total of 651 subjects. Four classrooms at each grade level were divided into two control groups and two experimental groups. Students' progress was tracked over the course of an academic year. All differences favored the experimental group exposed to critical reading instruction. The investigators concluded that critical reading can be taught, even at grade levels one through six; that intelligence and reading achievement were strongly related to critical reading performance, but that personality traits, as measured in this experiment, were not associated with critical reading performance; and that teacher verbal behavior had an effect in eliciting critical response from children (questions of an analyzing and evaluating nature elicited more critical responses).

Patching, Kameenui, Carnine, Gersten and Colvin (1983) investigated the effectiveness of teaching three specific critical reading skills to a sample of 39 fifth-grade students over a three day period of instruction. The skills taught were detecting faulty generalizations, false causality and invalid testimonials. The subjects were r andomly assigned to one of three equal groups: control (no instruction), experimental 1 (direct, systematic instruction) and experimental 2 (workbook with corrective feedback). Student performance was measured by researcher-designed tests: one main measure, a domain-referenced test over the material taught and two supplementary measures. Significant differences were found on the main measure only between the experimental group 1 and the other two groups. The investigators concluded that some critical reading skills can be learned by middle-grade students. These conclusions, while perhaps warranted, must be qualified by the the extremely limited instructional content, limited exposure to the training and small sample size.

In a much earlier investigation of teaching critical thinking, Hyram (1957) equated 33 pairs of seventh-grade students from an initial pool of 200 subjects and taught the experimental subjects selected principles of informal logic, using a "Socratic" method of classroom discussion and requiring much reading from his students. The controls participated in regular instruction among nine control classrooms over the duration of the experiment. After four months of fairly intense instruction (250 minutes per week), all results on the researcher-designed critical thinking measure strongly favored the experimental group. After this experience, Hyram advocated the direct teaching of critical thinking skills, especially the principles of informal logic. He further commented that "a seventh grade reading level does seem to be the only prerequisite ability for success in learning how to think logically from the type of instruction given in this experiment" (p. 130).

Frank (1969) reported an experiment to teach critical thinking within a high school speech course for eleventh and twelfth grades. With 103 experimental and 103 control subjects distributed among 10 classrooms and five teachers (each teacher taught one experimental class the first semester and one control group the next semester), students were either taught public speaking skills with an emphasis on correct reasoning and critical thinking or they participated in a typical (control) class with an emphasis on public speaking. Students were pre- and posttested with the *Watson-Glaser Critical Thinking Appraisal* and then administered a delayed posttest with the *CTA* three months after the end of instruction. While the experimental design offers little control for a Hawthorne effect, all differences favored the experimental group, even with the delayed posttest data.

After analyzing approximately fifteen programs to teach thinking skills (including critical thinking) at various school levels and examining related evaluation studies, Nickerson, Perkins and Smith (1985) state:

> Despite the fact that the majority of programs we have discussed lack adequate empirical evaluations, enough evaluative data have been obtained and enough of these investigations have yielded positive results to conclude that instruction can enhance thinking skills. (p. 324)

Nickerson, Perkins and Smith argue (p. 59), in a form of Pascal's wager, that even if we are not sure critical thinking can be taught, we have nothing to lose in attempting to teach it.

McMillan (1987) arrives at a similarly weak endorsement of the notion that instruction in thinking skills, especially critical thinking, is worthwhile. In his thorough and valuable review of 27 investigations of critical thinking instruction with general populations of college students, he concludes that even though the available research findings are not compelling in favor of the teaching of critical thinking and though the reported research is often weak in design, "it seems best not to accept the null hypothesis" [that critical thinking instruction has no effect] (p. 14).

Does growth in reading skill somehow assure growth in critical reading performance? Hyram's 1957 study claimed that a seventh grade reading ability was a discriminating factor in critical thinking performance and the Wolf, King and Huck (1968) study found a strong correlation between reading and critical thinking performance. While these findings are certainly plausible, they do not imply that critical reading develops naturally along with general reading comprehension.

Do critical reading skills develop naturally, without instruction, in non-proficient readers? While not concerned with developmental readers, McMillan (1987) reviewed numerous studies that found that critical thinking performance increased significantly in regular college students over the four years of a typical degree program. This finding is heartening, but the studies surveyed above provide evidence that direct instruction can accelerate the development of critical thinking skills over non-instructed control groups.

Do gains in critical reading persist after the formal instruction is over? The investigation reported by Frank (1969) is one of the few studies that follows subjects' critical thinking performance over an extended period of time. Frank assessed subjects' performance three months after the end of instruction and found substantial retention of the gains that occurred during the instructional phase.

An interesting, if unremarkable, pattern emerges in a study of instructional experiments in teaching critical thinking: teaching styles, course content and classroom atmosphere are important to learners' critical thinking growth! Wolf, King and Huck's (1968) study found that students' critical thinking performance was related to the quality of classroom questions. Higher student achievement on measures of critical thinking was associated with open-ended, higher-order questioning. Smith (1977) found that critical thinking performance in the 12 college classrooms he investigated was consistently related to student participation, encouragement and peer-to-peer interaction. Moll and Allen (1982) argue that the positive results obtained in their study of critical thinking instruction were largely due to the nature of the experimental course and the students' conscientious application to their coursework. Annis and Annis (1979) found differential effects of college philosophy courses on critical thinking performance; some courses appeared to develop critical thinking performance while others seemed to have no effect. These studies provide empirical support for the ideal classroom envisioned by many critical thinking advocates -- one with a more democratic approach to classroom interaction and with a student-centered teaching style.

RESEARCH FINDINGS WITH DEVELOPMENTAL READERS

There is very little published evidence that critical thinking can be taught to non-proficient college readers. However, considering the range of learner characteristics in the studies surveyed above, there is no reason not to expect similar critical thinking growth among non-proficient college readers as a result of direct instruction.

Most college-level studies of critical thinking or reading performance use the *Watson Glaser Critical Thinking Appraisal* (1980) as the main measure of critical thinking. McMillan (1987) discovered that 16 out of 27 investigations reviewed in his synthesis of research depended on the WatsonGlaser test. Because it is so widely used as the sole measure of critical thinking performance in research and program evaluations, any flaws in this test have substantial consequences to these numerous studies using the instrument. While McMillan lists many attributes of the *CTA* with which to be dissatisfied, one of his most important arguments is that the *CTA* is too broad scale a measure to reveal the kinds of finer-grained results of a single intervention program. Yet in spite of this accurate criticism and other substantial weaknesses, the *CTA* appears to function for many as the single strongest commercially available measure of this construct, an opinion supported by a comparison with other available instruments (Arter and Salmon, 1987). McMillan recommends that researchers and instructors devise their own critical thinking tests and in doing so, make sure these tests are closely linked to the course objectives and make sure that future research efforts use more than one measure of critical thinking.

Typical of evaluation studies performed on many of the recent thinking skills programs is the report on Project SOAR (Stress on Analytical Reasoning) by Whimbey, Carmichael, Jones, Hunter and Vincent (1980). The theoretical basis for this particular study is the Piagetian theory of stages of intellectual development and the claim that many college freshmen do not typically function at a formal reasoning level. Strong emphasis was given to the so-called "learning cycle" of three phases: an unguided exploration phase, an invention phase and an application phase (see Nickerson, Perkins and Smith, 1985, p. 240) and learners were carefully guided from concrete to abstract concepts over the five-week intensive program. Activities involved study and practice with "components of problem solving" and regular use of a "think aloud" problem-solving activity as well as material from a student text by the investigators. Students scored average to slightly below average on measures of high school performance as they began the program. After the five-week program, students were tested by a measure of formal reasoning, a reading achievement test and a test of general aptitude. No control group was used, but participants' posttest scores were significantly higher than pre-test scores.

An informal study by Robbins (1981) reported the critical reading criteria used by college remedial reading students. The 22 non-proficient readers were presented with three 1000-word passages to read on topics in sociology, then asked to select the one passage they believed was the best source of information on the topic. Students were then asked to list any criteria they had used in making that judgement. The listed criteria were categorized into six areas: author-related, reader-related, content-related, presentation related, personal-subjective and miscellaneous. Of the responses, 63 percent were content-related, 19 percent were personal-subjective and 8 percent were presentation-related. Even though a cloze test using the passages indicated they were written at a frustration level for these students and their evaluative criteria were unsophisticated, students were able to make judgments about the veracity of the readings and justify their choices.

Blum and Spangehl (1979) investigated the achievement of students enrolled in developmental studies courses based on methods of programmed instruction. Programmed instruction students ($N=94$) were similar to control subjects ($N=63$) not enrolled in any developmental studies courses. Nine hierarchies of higher order cognitive processes were carefully sequenced in a programmed learning fashion with incremental steps through the activities. Pre-test and posttest scores were collected from all subjects, using the *Watson Glaser Critical Thinking Appraisal* as the dependent measure. Differences were found between the two groups, with the programmed instruction group making significantly more growth in critical thinking test scores than the controls.

From these representative investigations, we see evidence to support the claim that critical reading can be taught and that it can be taught to students at varying levels of attainment including non-proficient college readers.

Clearly, more and better research on the issues of critical reading instruction is needed, especially studies involving college developmental readers.

CONCLUSIONS FROM RESEARCH FINDINGS

Critical thinking performance as measured by these research investigations can be developed by direct instruction. The thinking instruction can be made a part of any content instruction by the inclusion of higher-order cognitive skills objectives and activities, but it also deserves a place in the college developmental reading course. A classic statement from Glaser (1941) merits special attention:

There is no evidence that students acquire skill in critical thinking as a necessary by-product of the study of any given subject. On the other h and, almost any subject or project can be so taught as to put pupils on guard against hasty generalizations, contradictory assertions and uncritical acceptance of authority. In general, the research indicates that if the objective is to develop in pupils an attitude of "reasonableness" and regard for the weight of evidence and to develop ability to think critically about controversial problems, then the component attitudes and abilities in thinking critically about such problems must be set up as definite goals of instruction. (pp. 69-70)

CURRENT PRACTICES IN THE DELIVERY OF CRITICAL READING INSTRUCTION FOR DEVELOPMENTAL READERS

Even though the research base in critical reading instruction is not robust and is especially limited for studies involving college developmental readers, there is an apparent need for critical reading instruction for this population. And even to the casual observer, critical reading instructional objectives and critical reading textbooks abound in developmental reading courses.

How then is critical reading taught to this population? While there are a great variety of approaches for teaching critical reading in college, there are two reference points on a continuum of instructional approaches that help contrast how the learning is structured in various classrooms; these reference points help construct a context for this range of instructional approaches. These points should not be considered as absolute positions; rather, they describe relative positions on the continuum.

Like the distinction between a hierarchical skills instruction model versus a whole language instructional model in the elementary school, some developmental courses for teaching critical reading are built on a hierarchical skills model while others have a more holistic learning model at their philosophical foundation (McGlinn, 1988). This is not to suggest that a skills approach does not allow concern for content and whole texts, nor that a holistic approach does not allow concern for specific skill development. What is the difference? It is a matter of degree, emphasis, priority or focus, relative to the competing instructional model.

For example, in a hierarchical skills approach, the decisions about instruction are based on certain assumptions about effective instruction -assumptions that structure the learning from simple to complex, part to whole, in carefully chosen steps, proceeding in sequence. Learners do not work with the whole until they have completed the parts. After the skills have been laid out in the hierarchy, reading material appropriate for practice of the targeted skill are chosen or contrived. The content of the reading material is a tool to develop the target skill and often does not hold lasting meaningfulness or literary quality.

Traditional basal-based reading instruction is an example of this approach in the elementary schools. At the college level, student texts like Whimbey's *Analytical Reading and Reasoning* (1983) and *Mastering Reading through Reasoning* (1985), Miles' *Thinking Tools* (1985), Chaffee's *Thinking Critically* (1988), or de Bono's *The CoRT Thinking Program* (1988) could be seen as textbooks whose structure and content match well with a hierarchical skills approach to critical thinking and critical reading instruction.

On the other hand, in a holistic approach to critical thinking or critical reading instruction decisions are based on a model with different assumptions about effective instruction. Here, learners are required to work with messy, real-world content; to go from whole to part with little concern for carefully chosen steps and sequence. Learners are faced from the beginning of instruction with a whole and may or may not work with constituent parts. Reading materials are chosen for their quality of content or literary beauty and in most cases whole texts, uncut and uncontrived, are used. Skills may be directly taught, but skills are presented as a tool to more fully underst and the targeted content.

In the elementary schools, the recent interest in literature-based and whole-language instruction provide examples of this approach. For the college level developmental reading course, student texts like Epstein and Nieratka's *The Proficient Reader* (1985), Pacheco's *Academic Reading and Study Skills: A Theme Centered Approach* (1985) and more challenging texts provide ready materials for use in a holistic model of critical thinking and critical reading instruction.

An important point to reiterate here is that references to a skills model versus a holistic model as contrasted above describe relative positions, emphases and orientations to instruction and do not describe pure or absolute positions. In reality, we can only claim that a particular method or textbook content has a more holistic quality or a more skills-oriented quality than another, rather than claiming, for example, that a particular method or textbook content is an example of a purely skills-based approach.

Which approach is better? This is probably like being asked who is the most attractive member of the opposite sex in your hometown: there is no single best answer equally well suited for all individuals and all circumstances. Similar to the conclusion from the First Grade Study (Bond and Dykstra, 1967) that found no single method of first grade reading instruction to be superior to all others all of the time, we should probably compose a more useful question than the question of which approach is best. It is probably most useful to set the table with the instructional menu choices so each one can be seen clearly and fully and then encourage instructors to choose the approach that suits their teaching style, their particular curriculum and the apparent needs of their students.

Indeed, among the scant number of research reports and program descriptions on the topic of critical thinking using developmental students as subjects, we see evidence of successful programs based on essentially a hierarchically based model (Blum and Spangehl, 1979; and Whimbey, Carmichael, Jones, Hunter and Vincent, 1980) and successful programs based on a more holistic model (Bartholomae and Petrosky, 1986).

The final questions are not, "Should we teach critical reading to developmental readers?" or even, "How will we teach critical reading?" but rather, "How shall I teach my students to read more critically?" for as Paulo Freire (1985) reminds us, we have not truly read until we have read critically.

REFERENCES

Annis, L. F. and D. B. Annis (1979). The impact of philosophy on students' critical thinking ability. *Contemporary educational psychology,* 4, 219-226.

Arter, J. A. and J. Salmon (1987). *Assessing higher order thinking skills: A consumer's guide.* Portl and, OR: Northwest Regional Educational Laboratory.

Baron, J. B. and R. J. Sternberg (eds.) (1987). *Teaching thinking skills: Theory and practice.* New York: W. H. Freeman

Bartholomae, D. and A. Petrosky (1986). *Facts, artifacts and counterfacts: A basic reading and writing course.* Upper Montclair, New Jersey: Boynton/Cook.

Black, M. (1952). Critical thinking. Englewood Cliffs, NJ: Prentice-Hall.

Bloom, A. D. (1987). *The closing of the American mind.* New York: Simon and Schuster.

Blum, M. and S. Spangehl (1979). *The role of programmed instruction for sequential skill development in higher education.* Louisville: University of Louisville. (ERIC Document Reproduction Service No. ED 197 670)

Bond, G. L. and R. Dykstra (1967). The cooperative research program in first grade reading instruction. *Reading Research Quarterly,* 2, 5-142.

de Bono, E. (1983). The direct teaching of thinking as a skill. *Phi Delta Kappan,* 64, 703-708.

de Bono, E. (1988). *The CoRT thinking program* (2nd ed.). San Diego, CA: Dormac, Inc.

Chaffee, J. (1988). *Thinking critically* (2nd ed.). Boston: Houghton Mifflin.

Cheney, L. V. (1985). *American memory: A report on the Humanities in the nation's public schools.* Washington, D. C.: U. S. Government Printing Office.

Chipman, S. F., J. W. Segal and R. Glaser (eds.) (1985). *Thinking and learning skills (Volume 2: Research and open questions).* Hillsdale, NJ: Lawrence Erlbaum Associates.

Cohen, S. F. (1988). Direct explicit reading instruction for unskilled college students. *Research and Teaching in Developmental Education,* 4(2), 50-56.

Dewey, J. (1933). *How we think.* Lexington, MA: D. C. Heath.

Dressel, P. L. and L. B. Mayhew (1954). *General education: Explorations in evaluation.* Westport, CT: Greenwood Press.

Ennis, R. H. (1962). A concept of critical thinking. *Harvard Educational Review,* 32, 81-111.

Ennis, R. H. (1979). Logic, rational thinking and education. In J. Coombs (Ed.) *Philosophy of Education 1979: Proceedings of the 35th Annual Meeting of the Philosophy of Education Society.*

Epstein, I. D. and E. B. Nieratka (1985). *The proficient reader.* Boston: Houghton Mifflin.

Erwin, R. W., Jr. (1985). Research in critical reading. *Research and Teaching in Developmental Education,* 1(2), 49-54.

Frank, A. D. (1969). Teaching high school speech to improve critical thinking ability. The *Speech Teacher,* 18, 297-302.

Freire, P. (1985). Reading the world and reading the word: An interview with Paulo Freire. *Language Arts,* 62, 15-21.

Glaser, E. (1941). An experiment in the development of critical thinking. In *Contributions to Education,* n. 843. New York: Teacher's College, Columbia University.

Greenewald, M. J., K. L. Dulin and P. L. Anders (1973). *Good, average and poor eleventh grade readers' affective responses to positively-connotative and negatively-connotative adverbs in simulated newspaper articles: A critical reading study.* La Crosse: University of Wisconsin. (ERIC Document Reproduction Service No. ED 189 552)

Harris, T. L. and R. E. Hodges (1983). *A dictionary of reading and related terms.* Newark, Delaware: International Reading Association.

Hirsch, E. D., Jr. (1987). *Cultural literacy: What every American needs to know.* Boston: Houghton Mifflin.

Hyram, G. M. (1957). Experiment in developing critical thinking in children. Journal of *Experimental Education,* 26, 125-132.

Keeley, S. M., M. N. Brown and J. S. Kruetzer (1982). A comparison of freshmen and seniors on general and specific essay tests of critical thinking. *Research in Higher Education,* 17, 139-154.

Lehman, I. J. (1963). Change in critical thinking, attitudes and values from freshman to senior year. *Journal of Educational Psychology,* 54, 305-315.

Longman, D. G. and R. H. Atkinson (1987). Improving recreational reading habits: Using entertainment schemata to make predictions about text. *Research and Teaching in Developmental Education,* 4(1), 47-50.

Marshall, J. P. (1985). Teaching critical thinking in higher education. *In Basic skills: Dealing with deficiencies.* Las Cruces: New Mexico State University. (ERIC Document Reproduction Service No. ED 271 087)

McGlinn, J. E. (1988). Essential education in the reading class. *Journal of Developmental Education,* 12(2), 20-24.

McMillan, J. H. (1987). Enhancing college students' critical thinking: A review of studies. *Research in Higher Education,* 26, 3-29.

Miles, C. (1981). The 4th R revisited. *Journal of Developmental and Remedial Education,* 5(1), 2-4.

Miles, C. and J. Rauton (1985). *Thinking tools.* Clearwater, FL: H and H Publishing.

Moll, M. D. and R. D. Allen (1982). Developing critical thinking skills in Biology. *Journal of College Science Teaching,* 12, 95-98.

National Assessment of Educational Progress (1981). *Three national assessments of reading: Changes in performance, 1970-1980.* Denver: National Assessment of Educational Progress.

National Commission on Excellence in Education (1983). *A nation at risk.* Washington, D. C.: U. S. Government Printing Office.

National Institute of Education (1984). *Involvement in learning: Realizing the potential of American higher education.* Washington, D. C.: U. S. Government Printing Office.

New Jersey Basic Skills Council (1986). *Effectiveness of remedial programs in New Jersey Public Colleges and Universities.* New Jersey Basic Skills Council, Department of Higher Education.

Nickerson, R. S., D. N. Perkins and E. E. Smith (1985). *The teaching of thinking.* Hillsdale, NJ: Lawrence Erlbaum Associates.

Norris, S. P. (1985). *Synthesis of research of critical thinking.* Educational Leadership, 42(8), 40-45.

Pacheco, B. (1985). *Academic reading and study skills: A theme-centered approach.* New York: Holt, Rinehart and Winston.

Pascarella, E. T. (1987). *The development of critical thinking: does college make a difference?* Paper presented at the annual meeting of the Association for the Study of Higher Education, Baltimore, MD. (ERIC Document Reproduction Service No. ED 292 417)

Patching, W., E. Kameenui, D. Carnine, R. Gersten and G. Colvin (1983). Direct instruction in critical reading skills. *Reading Research Quarterly,* 18, 406-418.

Paul, R. W. (1984). Critical thinking: Fundamental to education for a free society. *Educational Leadership,* 41(1), 4-14.

Paul, R. W. (1985). Critical thinking research: A response to Stephen Norris. *Educational Leadership,* 42(8), 46.

Perry, W. (1970). *Forms of intellectual and ethical development in the college years.* New York: Holt, Rinehart and Winston.

Robbins, L. (1981). Critical reading skills of non-proficient readers in college. *Journal of Reading,* 24, 300-303.

Schell, J. (1982). *The fate of the earth.* New York: Alfred A. Knopf.

Segal, J. W., S. F. Chipman and R. Glaser (eds.) (1985). *Thinking and learning skills, Volume 1: Relating instruction to research.* Hillsdale, NJ: Lawrence Erlbaum Associates.

Smith, D. G. (1977). College classroom interactions and critical thinking. *Journal of Educational Psychology,* 69, 180-190.

Thompson, L. and A. Frager (1984). Teaching critical thinking: Guidelines for teacher-designed content area lessons. *Journal of Reading,* 28, 122-127.

Watson, G. and E. M. Glaser (1980). *Watson-Glaser Critical Thinking Appraisal.* Clevel and: Harcourt, Brace, Jovanovich (Psychological Corporation).

Whimbey, A. (1983). *Analytical reading and reasoning.* Stamford, CT: Innovative Sciences.

Whimbey, A. (1985). *Mastering reading through reasoning.* Stamford, CT: Innovative Sciences.

Whimbey, A., J. Carmichael, L. Jones, J. Hunter and H. Vincent (1980). Teaching critical reading and analytical reasoning in Project SOAR. *Journal of Reading,* 24, 5-10.

Whitla, D. K. (1977). *Value added: Measuring the impact of undergraduate education.* Cambridge, MA: Office of Instructional Research and Evaluation, Harvard University. (ERIC Document Reproduction Service No. ED 195 175)

Wolf, W., M. L. King and C. S. Huck (1968). Teaching critical reading to elementary school children. *Reading Research Quarterly,* 3, 435-498.

Yellot, R., L. S. Dilks, J. Dick and C. L. Ware (1985). Critical thinking: Theories and strategies in reading, English and mathematics. In O'Hear, M. F. and Knowles, R (eds.) *Journal of College Reading and Learning,* 18, 48-56.

13

Effective Counseling

Cynthia Jackson Hammond

Counseling in its traditional definition - giving advice - might be traced back to the Old Testament and to Greek philosophers. The early social philosophers, Plato 427 - 347 B.C. and Aristotle 384 - 322 B.C., the hedonists, the philosophers of the British associationist school Locke (1632 - 1704), Berkeley (1685 - 1753), Hume (1711 - 1776) and James Mill (1773 - 1836) were influential in the history of counseling for "they sought to define the nature of man and the nature of society and the relationship between the individual and society" (Shertzer and Stone, 1968, p. 29).

Many factors contributed to the growth of counseling in the United States. Those factors giving rise to counseling were: "the American concept of individualism, the lack of rigid class lines, the incentive to exercise one's talent to the best of one's ability . . . or it was the affluence of America's economic system which supported the counseling dimension." (Shertzer and Stone, 1974, p. 29).

Counseling, since the early 1900's, has developed as a discipline supported by research, professional organizatios and other related fields. Counseling is defined by Lester N. Downing (1975) as follows:

> Counseling is a process and an activity engaged in by a qualified counselor and an individual seeking assistance. Its purposes include aiding the person in resolving his problem, making plans, reducing conflicts, achieving better adjustment and effecting needed behavior changes. (Downing, 1975, p. 7).

When counseling involves one counselor and one client it is called individual counseling. When the counseling approach involves more than one client per counselor, it is called group counseling. Many theorists and counseling practitioiners differ in their conceptual understanding of the similarities and differences in the two approaches.

Downing (1975) sees the principles and concepts of group and individual counseling approaches as being the same, with the major differences being in the number of participants. Lewis (1970) asserts that "individual and group counseling are complementary rather than opposing facets of the same general process and can effectively supplement rather than duplicate each other" (Downing, 1975, p. 126).

Group counseling was first initiated as a means for counselors with limited time to attend to more clients. Therefore, group counseling was viewed as a substitution for individual counseling. Counselors assumed that the goals for both approaches were the same and that group sessions should be composed of clients with a common problem (Zimpfer, 1962). Because of these dual assumptions, little attention has been given to whether or not the concerns usually addressed by individual counseling could effectively be addressed by group counseling. The academic concerns typically addressed in individual counseling are "improvement of students" grade-point averages, congruence of real and ideal self concept and realism of vocational choice" (Zimpfer, 1962, p. 327). If group counseling is based on the same theoretical principles as individual counseling, then group counseling is contradictory to the principle of individual "permissiveness." Encouragement of individual permissiveness is inherent in individual counseling. This "permissiveness" allows the individual to be free of stereotypical constraints such as judgmental attitudes and allows the client to emote freely and produce alternatives for solving problems in his or her own time frame.

No single accepted theory of group counseling has been found in the literature. Although there are volumes concerning the function of group counseling, there is no systematic treatment of procedures, objectives and criteria for evaluation. Researchers pose many questions concerning this lack of theory in group counseling:

- Should the counselor focus on the individual within the group or on the dynamics of the total group?
- Should group approach limit the number of clients to be serviced? Does the number of clients in the group affect effectiveness?

Should the emphasis in group counseling be of cognitive or affective concern?

The lack of theory and adequate conceptualizations of the group counseling approach lends itself to the question of merit, if any, of this approach. Does this approach have any more effectiveness than no-structured counseling. non-structured counseling is "help" received without the assistance of a trained counselor. The setting is without the traditional walls of a counselor's office or counseling center.

The Criterion Problem

Eysneck (1952) reported on more than 8,000 cases treated by an assortment of psychotherapeutic techniques. His control data were hospitalized neurotics and neurotics treated at home by general practitioners. He concluded in his investigations of the effects of psychotherapy, that "roughly two-thirds of a group of neurotic patients recovered or improved to a marked extent within two years of the onset of their illness, whether they are treated by means of psychotherapy or not." Eysenck claimed that any results of counseling or psychotherapy were due to spontaneous remission or to the placebo effect. Eysenck's (1952) study has been criticized by Rosenzweig (1954) as lacking validity because the criteria of success varied widely in Eysenck's studies. There were no valid comparisons of rates or percentages of success.

Levitt's (1957) findings were similar to Eysenck's. He studied clients between the ages of preschool to 21 and revealed that improvement gains resulted in three-fourths of the population. The population showed signs of improvement although they had not been treated by a professional therapist.

Levitt's (1957) results were questioned by Bixler (1963). The degree of "improvement" was not defined nor was there a careful examination of the diverse counseling methods utilized. Bixler posed questions concerning "spontaneous remission" and the "placebo effect." Both spontaneous remission and the use of placebos suggest improvement void of professional help and improvement by the power of suggestion. Bixler asserted that counseling and psychotherapy should also consider the rate of recovery which occurs without treatment.

Strupp (1963) recognized the difficulties in measuring "success and/or outcomes" in general, regardless of the type of therapy used. He says that:

> the outcome problem in psychotherapy has been receiving relatively scant attention in recent years - not because the problem has lost its importance but rather because of a realization on the part of researchers that a new approach to the issue must be found and that more pressing matters must be dealt with first before we can address ourselves meaningfully to the question of the effectiveness of psychotherapy. (p. 10)

Silverman (1962) attempted to define "success and or outcomes." He postulated that any change occuring in the person in counseling or therapy, regardless of its duration, is an outcome and may even be a "cure" if it helps the client deal more effectively with his present life situation.

Rogerts (1961) in referring to his "research findings" of the late 1940s and early 1050s drew these conclusions about the "outcomes" of counseling:

> ... profound changes occur in the perceived self of the client during and after therapy; that there is constructive change in the client's personality characteristics and personality structure, changes which bring him closer to the personality characteristics of the well-functioning person; that there is a change in directions defined as personal integration and adjustment; that there are changes in the maturity of a client's behavior as observed by friends. (p. 231)

Rogers also finds a prevailing problem in defining "success" in terms of measured outcomes by pointing out that what a client may view as comfortable behavior (after therapy) may not be viewed as acceptable behavior from outside observers. The concern of individual uniqueness versus social norms complicates the evaluation of counseling approaches.

Previous evaluation of counseling services fall short of establishing well-defined units of outcome measurement (O'Dea and Zeran, 1953; Patterson, 1960). O'Dea and Zeran (1953) reviewed 80 references pertaining to the evaluation of counseling effectiveness. The literature revealed that more than 16 different criteria have been used for the purposes of evaluating the effects of counseling. Ten criteria were considered by these investigators in evaluating counseling effectiveness. For the final evaluating critera, three criteria were selected as being most acceptable: counselee satisfaction, counselee understanding of test data and before-and-after tests of personality and social adjustments. Social adjustment and personality became one criterion. The writers evaluated the effects of the counseling with 36 counselees using these three criteria. O'Dea and Zeran's (1953) review of the literature indicated that the cirterion problem was significant. Of the final three selected criteria, it was concluded that the criteria should be in part about establishing self-concept. O'Dea and Zeran cite the small numbers of counselees involved and the crudity of instruments as drawbacks to their study.

Rothney and Farwell (1960) reported that some researchers used as many as 12 diverse criteria of counseling effectiveness including: persistence in school or job, performance and grade point average, satisfaction with job, self-knowledge and level of affect. Researchers simply used some criteria based on tasks which do not serve as standard guidelines.

Jenson, Coles and Nestor (1955) stipulate that a criterion should be definable, stable and relevant. Dressel (1954) further states that in regard to criterion relevance, "much research appears to have been done to satisfy the curiosity of the moment without regard to whether it has real implications for practice." (p. 285)

The **criterion factor** presents several problems for the evaluatio of counseling. The lack of standarization of pertinent criteria is a major concern. The criteria for evaluation of techniques is another concern. The evaluation criteria used to measure client behavior is problematic.

In Search of a Criterion

Despite numerous recommendations, very little investigation has occurred concerning the use of client ratings as criteria for measuring counseling effectiveness. In 1957, Grigg and Goodstein stated:

> "Some appraisal of the client's reaction to the counselor and to counseling should be obtained before we can say that we have any comprehensive understanding of who makes a good counselor and what constitutes successful counseling technique." (p. 32)

Anderson and Anderson's (1962) *Interview Rating Scale* (IRS) was devised to be the instrument clients and researchers would use to gather data concerning the clients ratings as a criterion for counselor effectiveness.

Zunker and Brown (1966) in comparing effectiveness of student and professional counselors used the following criteria: growth in study skills, counselor reactions to the program, counselor retention of information given during counseling and counseling productivity as measured by earned course grades. The counselors were the evaluators. A different instrument was used to measure each criteria. The findings of this study concluded that student counselors were as effective as professional counselors on all criteria of counseling productivity employed in this study. Secondly, student counselors received greater acceptance from counselors than did professional counselors and were thus able to evoke better retention of information; and, finally, freshman counseled by student counselors made greater use of the information received during counseling. This was reflected by course grades and residual study problems.

Callis, Polmantier and Roeher (1957) also conducted investigations in developing criteria. After five years of research, client's satisfaction and expert judgement were assessed. This tudy yielded the following: Counselors respond differently depending on what topic is being discussed; clients respond differently depending on topic but not nearly as different as counselors. Counselor's responses (style) became a criteria for possible evaluation. Counselor style was analyzed into two basic units. One unit was called "affective." Affective units included interpersonal relations other than family, family relations and self-reference. The other type of unit was called "cognitive." Cognitive units included educational and vocational problems and planning as well as study skills and habits.

Merenda and Rothney (1958) in their 8-year longitudinal study measuring counseling effectiveness used the categorical criteria: (a) satisfaction with and adjustments to past high school status, (b) measures of optimism in outlook toward the future, (c) measures of reflection of high school training received-how it helped and failed and (d) measures of persistency in post high school endeavors. Four scales were developed for evaluating the effectiveness of counseling in terms of the criteria. The criterion which appeared to be the best over-all single discriminator between the counseled and uncounseled subjects was the self-report measure of Satisfaction-Adjustment. The subjects of their study in 1948 were 870 sophomores. Those students were alternately assigned to two distinct groups: experimental and control. During the three remaining years of high school, the experimental group received intensive counseling from qualified counselors. The control group received no formal counseling. At the end of the three years there were 690 subjects. The follow-up research was gathered primarily during 1956-57, after the subjects had been out of school for a period of five years. The data suggested that preferred outcomes reflective of adult behavior was more prevalent among the counseled subjects. There was not a large difference on criterion variables between the two groups. This small difference was attributed to the short time span of five years; the effects of counseling may be more evident in a more extensive time span. Although the statistical treatment was thorough, little description was given to the randomization of the subjects to the control and experimental groups.

Linden, Stone and Shertzer (1965) state that suitable counseling evaluative criteria should include non-intellectual variables such as understanding, sensitivity and friendliness. Ratings by expert judges, supervisors and/or peers are other criteria considered useful although possessing limitations.

Arthur Dole (1964) suggested that the simplest and most efficient way of predicting the effectiveness of school counselors would be the gathering of comparative ratings from a number of observers who have had a variety of experiences with the candidates. In his 1964 study using comparative ratings of school counselors, the principal's rating was the final criterion measure. Ratings from other observers were secondary to the principal. One of the major difficulties noted by Dole was that principals may be tempted to rate counselors based on their effectiveness as administrative assistants rather than in their effectiveness as counselors.

Metzler (1964) summarized the previous literature on effective counseling and guidance programs. He stated: "There were no agreements as to what constitutes the goals of a guidance program. Without goals, proper criteria cannot be determined; research to determine the effectiveness of guidance programs had been minimal. ... Expert judgement and opinions are the primary acceptable criteria for evaluation; and more emphasis should be placed on longitudinal studies and establishing suitable criteria.

The Effectiveness of Counseling

Speilberger and Weitz (1964) noted in their study that the voluntary group counseling program was ineffective in dealing with non-achievers. The freshman underachiever was most likely not to seek help or volunteer for services which may eliminate the underachievement pattern. The internal motivational attribute which is inherent to directing final outcomes was not apparent in underachievers. Roth, Mauksch and Peiser (1967) support educational programs such as orientation classes, seminars in study habits and the like as being advantages in reaching the reluctant underachiever. They view the "most promising avenue" for reaching the underachiever as being the "group setting."

Shaw and Wursten (1965) cite inconsistent and weak evidence which supports the efficacy of group therapy in academic settings. Reasons for the weak studies are inadequate controls, inadequate statistical procedures, inadequate outcome criteria and insufficient numbers of subjects.

The study which will not be discussed had as its measure of effectiveness the students resulting grade-point average (GPA).

Baymur and Paterson (1965) compared three treatment conditions with each other and a non-counseled control group: individual counseling, group counseling and one session of motivation. Their subjects were eight high school underachievers. There were significant grade-point average increases between those in individual and group counseling versus those in the one motivational session and the non-counseled controls. However, the bulk of the differences was attributed to the group counseling participants. One obvious discrepancy in this study is the definition of the underachiever. Not all underachievement can be defined by GPA.

Winborn and Schmedt (1965), in their study with matched groups of underachieving college students, found that the 59 counseled students had significantly worse grades after therapy than did their 59 uncounseled controls. Sheldon and Landsman (1965) found a significant relationship between counseling and increased GPA with underachieving college freshman as compared to the uncounseled controls. A non-directive group therapy climate was employed in this study. Broedel Ohlsen, Proff and Southard (1965) could cite no significant differences in grades between counseled and non-counseled groups.

In all four studies previously cited, the number of subjects were relatively low which gave weak support to generalizatins of counseling effectiveness. In addition, those studies failed to report any type of subject selection beyond the variable of underachievement. The dysfunction of underachievement was ambiguous, because the underlying dynameics of underachievement were not specified.

Mezzano's (1968) study was designed to answer questions about the effectiveness of two different types of group counseling that might be used with low-motivated students. Ninety-six students ranking in the lower half of their high school junior class on the Michigan M-scales were asked to participate in a counseling program. Seventy-four accepted the invitations to become subjects. Six experimental groups having seven members each were formed. Three of these groups were randomly assigned to the group-individual counseling treatment while the other three groups were assigned to the groups counseling treatment only. The third level of the design, the control group, received no treatment. The group process emphasized the discovery of the students' underlying personality dynamics and its relationship to the lack of achievement. One basic assumption of the study was that maximum effect could be harnessed if group and individual counseling were used in combination. The results of the study indicated a positive change in GPA when using group counseling in comparison to a no-treatment group which used group-individual counseling. It was also noted by the counselees as a limitation that a strong cohesiveness was never truly achieved in group sessions nor in individual sessions. The design of group and individual counseling done concurrently failed to achieve the same type of cohesiveness, which may have impacted on more effective counseling. Affective counseling which stresses the element of cohesiveness was limited.

Roth, Mauksch and Peiser (1967) along with Lefcourt (1982) give major impetus to the correlation of personality and motivation. Motivation reflects an individual's sense of ability to control his or her destiny. Roth, Mauksch and Peiser (1967) investigated the effects of group counseling in maladaptive achievement behavior of college nonachievers. They selected 174 failing students at Illinois Institute of Technology and provided group counseling as a condition of their remaining in school. Focus of the approach was based on the dynamics of non-achievement syndrome (NAS). These cyclical characteristics of NAS were disparagement, anxiety, functional disability, hopelessness and frustration. An underlying assumption based on those characteristics was the students choice to do poorly in school so as to remain a dependent on family; thus he was protected from taking risk and asserting independence. The counseling technique used was designed to resolve these problems by dealing with poor study habits. Although their population was limited by male homogeneity the results are generalizable to other similar populations. The determined criterion for the effectiveness of groups counseling was improvement of grades. Results of this study revealed that the application of NAS therapeutic approach of Roth and Meyensbury (1963) in group settings yielded significant changes in academic functioning. Further, it was demonstrated that probationary students not receiving counseling either maintained their poor academic status or regressed even more.

Measuring Effectiveness

Lubarsky, Singer and Luborsky (1975), Bergin and Lambert (1978) and Frank (1979) noted in their summaries of psychotherapy that the effectiveness of outcomes was limited. However, by the 1980s with the meta-analytic methods applied to the integration of research findings, psychosocial therapies evaluations were described as large and positive (Smith, Glass and Miller, 1980; Shapiro and Shapiro, 1982). These conclusions were met with much controversy and were objectional for two reasons. First, they were based only on a new statistical method and on better methodology. Second, some investigators were suspicious of the positive findings because of the integration of all types of psychotherapies into one category for measurement. Kendall (1984) has asserted that this lumping together of therapies, problems, patient populations and measures negates useful discriminations and relationships. Another criticism of meta-analyisis methodology is that major categories of problems are systematically underrepresented while milder problems such as phobias are overrepresented. Therapists were novices in their field of experiences and the duration of the therapies were short-termed behavioral approaches. Meta-analysis has also been criticized for including studies of inadequate designs, such as non-random assignment of cases to therapy and to control groups, non-blind assessments, high or differential dropout rates or poor outcome measurements (Strube and Hartman, 1983; Wilson and Rachman, 1983).

Parloff, London and Wolfe (1986) cite research designs with high degrees of internal validity as being important because it is only those studies that confident infrerences may be reported in response to treatment.

Studies on educational attainment have identified a personality construct called "locus of control" and have linked this construct to achievement. The degree of internal academic locus of control is an interesting and viable criterion for the evaluation of counseling effectiveness. In the next section the concept of "locus of control" and its related literature will be discussed.

LOCUS OF CONTROL

The expectation of success is often a predictor of success itself. Students who perceive their destiny as being controlled by external forces do not believe in their own ability to make "changes." Students who believe that their destiny is largely controlled by their own initiative tend to be more motivated and success-oriented. This section will review these two types of conditions, otherwise identified as internal (I) - external (E) locus of control. The belief in control can exist in varying degrees. There is a major link between behavior and its conseqeunce and the relationship between outcomes and personal effort. The externalist sees no cause and effect between behavior and its outcomes. The externalist takes little or no responsibility for life events. The internalist expects a certain outcome or event to occur based on personal behaviors. The internalist assumes responsibility for the consequences of s/he actions.

Learning and Locus of Control

The construct, locus of control (LOC) appeared in psychological literature as early as the 1960s. Rotter (1954, 1960) provided the general theoretical background. He compiled extensive data on the social learning theory of the effects of reinforcement on expectancy and behavior. Other psychologists such as Veblen (1899) and Merton (1946) addressed similarly related concepts of LOC. Veblen (1899) viewed the individual who had belief in luck or chance (external factors) as being less productive and that belief in luck was synonymous to believing in fate. Merton (1946, 127) presented the views that belief in luck was more or less a defensive attitude people utilized "to preserve their self esteem in the face of failure."

Merton (1949) stressed another asocial concept linked with locus of control. The concept of alienation, sometimes referred to as powerlessness, is significant to the study of human behavior. The individual who "feels" alienated has no sense of control over his future. Regardless, of his internal ambitions he seems futile in establishing a comfortable place in the large scheme of life. The construct, locus of control, was introduced as a component of societal learning theory and has been integrated into counseling strategies (Phares, 1973). It is "the single most popular topic in current personality research" (Carlson, 1975). Frank (1976) suggests that a major goal of all counseling and psychotherapy is to assist the client to "gain increased mastery" over the social environment. Ballif (1976) injects that internal locus of control is essential to motivation.

Phares (1976) discussed the relationship of generalized and specific expectancies and the coexistence of these expectancies within an individual.

He states "belief in personal control (or lack of it) is both a general disposition that influences individuals' behavior across a wide range of situations and a rather specific belief that may apply to a limited number of situations" (p. 25). explanations as to how these expectancies coexist are abstract which leads to problems in measuring the locus of control (Gregory, 1978; Collins, 1974).

Coan (1974) and Rotter (1975) support the theory that locus of control expectancy is relative; that is, locus of control expectancy is not one generalized expectancy about life, rather it is a group of generalized expectancies from various life function areas. Rotter (1975) points out that counseling strategies whose emphasis is to alter locus of control should consider both the psychological situation of the client and the value of reinforcement when assessing the ramifications of locus of control.

The psychological situation usually means the classification of expectancies by vesbally expressing inner thoughts and feelings. The value of the outcomes should also be verbally expressee and explained.

Seligman (1975) developed the conept of learned helplessness. He contends that if an individual experiences a repetition of helplessness in his life events, he/she learns to be helpless, thus discounting any personal efforts to overcome. This concept is similar to external locus of control expectancies.

Phares (1976) sees as one of the roles of teachers and counselors the responsibility to influence locus of control. He states, "To enhance individuals' capacity to cope with the world successfully, one must influence their generalized expectancy of control" (Phares, 1973, p. 170). Lefcourt (1966) suggests internal locus of control is a prerequisite of competent behavior.

Connolly (1980) utilized a counseling model designed to help the externalist move in an internal direction to facilitate behavior change. The first step in the model develops observation and listening skills to help counselors identify by the clients responses, externalism. Counselors listen for responses categorized as: *Expressions of blame, weakness, regidity, belief in fate or change, or wishful thinking.* The second step in Connolly's model is the counseling process. The main strategies include: facilitating awareness and/or responsibility, identifying deficit and using options.

Carkhuff (1972) considers responding skills as the most effective way to facilitate the counseling process. Carkhuff (1972) advised counselors to identify the client's feelings and relate those feelings verbally in relation to the causes of those feelings. He also advises personalizing the behavior, "*you* feel helpless ... when *you* ..." This personalizing skill encourages the reorientation to internal locus of control. Carkhuff continues his format by advising counselors to take time to identify the behavior deficit or lack of skill and concludes by using counseling options. Questioning and feedback techniques are integrated into the responding strategies. Thurber (1972) suggested that students who have classroom experiences with professors who are powerful sources of reinforcements tend to be more externally defensive. Prociuk and Breen (1975) concluded "the specific external forces to which responsibility for reinforcement is defensively attributed are powerful others." They further assert "defensive externals may be identified as those individuals who believe that powerful other (e.g., professors) are responsible for their reinforcements (e.g., grades) but who tend to behave somewhat similarly to internals, regard reinforcement as primarily obtained through their own effort."

Prociuk and Breen (1975) continue to define characteristics of externals. Congruent externals are different from defensive externals, in that they believe that their academic performance is determined by fate or luck. These congruent externals tend to be less effective in academic pursuits in comparison to defensive externals or internals.

In addition, Thurber (1972) noted other variables associated with defensive externals (DE). These DEs tend to be more sensitive to the demands of powerful others, thus more responsive to powerful others in hopes of obtaining desired reinforcements (e.g., grades). One other variable which was discussed by Thurber was gender. Females who were defensive externals were more successful academically than male defensive externals.

Experimental Studies of Locus of Control

The Locus of Control construct is a personality trait that is closely linked to various general psychological adjustment constructs. This portion of this chapter will review experimental studies with locus of control as a determinant variable.

Butcher and Hebert (1985) utilized an intensive design case study for their investigation. Baseline observations of I-E expectancy (A) were followed by a 10-week treatment period (B) during which regular assessments of I-E and counselor effectiveness were recorded. A one-month follow-up produced overall estimates of locus of control expectancy and counselor effectiveness as perceived by counselor, client and an independent rater reviewing audiotapes of the sessions of the client's treatment. Two clients were selected from among undergraduate men seeking counseling at a public university. Selection was based on three criteria:

- matching by sex to avoid possible confounding on this variable;
- matching of scores on the Rotter I-E scale (Rotter, 1966) with the counselor's

score to identify both an identical and a highly dissimilar locus of control expectancy; and,

● an intake interview with the senior investigator to determine severity and client motivation to remain in treatment for a minimum of eight weeks.

The Rotter I-E Locus of Control Scale (Rotter, 1966) was administered before baseline recordings and again in follow-up assessment to estimate I-E expectancy of each client and the counselor. Additional surveys were given in follow-up: *Structured I-E Interview* (Lefcourt, Reid and Ware, 1976), *Counseling Evaluation Inventory* (CEI) (Linden, Stone and Shertzer, 1965) and the *Counselor Evaluation Rating Scale* (CERS) (Myrick and Kelly, 1971). The purpose of this study was to investigate locus of control similarity of client and counselor to counselor effectiveness. The results of the research did not demonstrate a causal relationship between matching I-E and subsequent counselor effectiveness; but differences do exist across dissimilar pairs. Single case studies for inferring causation should not be used (Bordin, 1974). Nevertheless, the methodology was very precise and offered credibility in examining the many phases of the counseling process and in examining the outcome data.

Edwards and Waters (1981) investigated the moderating effects of achievement motivation and locus of control for 223 college students, on the relationship between scores on the verbal subtest of the *College Qualification Test* (CQT) (Bennett, Bennett, Wallace and Wesman, 1957).

The CQT (Bennett, et al., 1957), the *Prestatic Motivation Test* (PMT) (Herman, 1970) and the Rotter I-E (Rotter, 1966) were administered to 223 undergraduates enrolled in lower-division psychology courses (107 males and 116 females). Cumulative grade-point average (CGPA) over at least two quarters of coursework were obtained from university files. Median splits were made in score distributions on both the PMT and the I-E scale. The correlation between CQT scores and CGPA was computed for groups defined by each split and for groups defined jointly by the splits on the two variables.

The data from this study indicated that achievement motivation did moderate the relationship between academic ability and CGPA for objective as well as subjective estimates of ability. The relationship of LOC to academic ability was correlated by using the Rotter (1966) I-E scale with scores on the verbal subtest of the *College Qualification Test*, cumulative grade-point average and attributions of performance to ability, effort, course difficulty and luck. The I-E scores were unrelated to either verbal ability or grade-point average.

Fagan, Aiken, Gilliam and Kuehl (1983) sought to assess the impact of qersonality variables: ability, locus of control and self esteem on academic performance and attributions. In their study, 212 college students in a required lower-division course were given a questionnaire composite of Rotter's LOC scale, Coppersmith's *Self Esteem Inventory* and an item ability test. This questionnaire was given during the second week of class.

The second questionnaire was designed to assess expectation and attributions of grades. Given immediately after an exam, students were asked to reveal if their grades on the exam matched their expectation. Fifteen attributions were measured using a five-point Likert scale. The items on the questionnaire included teacher ability, course organization, individual attention by instructor, fairness of the exam, student ability, student background, student interest, study time, motivation to do well, luck, meeting time of the class, classroom setting, textbook, difficulty of the exam and circumstances during the exam. The attribution items for those respondents who were pleased with their exam grades were worded in a positive way; for those respondents who were not pleased with their exam outcome, the questions were worded in a negative manner. The questionnaires indicated in regard to personality measures that students with lower ability expected to receive higher grades than they actually did. The students with lower abiltiy may be more likely to receive lower grades, be unrealistic about their capabilities and disappointed in the discrepancy between their expectations and actual achievement. Locus of control was unrelated to either expectations or attributions; self esteem was important in predicting attributiosn, but not expectations. In regard to grades, those with average and low grades were more likely to be unrealistic in evaluating their performance; they expected their scores to be higher. Those with higher grades were more likely to endorse teacher items whereas those with lower grades were more likely to blame themselves. This observation contradicted the general belief (Rodin, 1982) that a student receiving an unexpected lower grade would place the blame on the teacher or some external variable.

Goldston, Zimmersman, Seni and Gadzella (1977) investigated the perceptions of study habits and attitudes analyzed by sex and internally and externally oriented college undergraduates. Their subjects were 239 students enrolled in psychology classes. The Rotter I-E scale was given to differentiate degrees of LOC and the *Brown and Holtzman Survey of Study Habits and Attitudes* inventory was administered thrice during the semester to detect variations among the groups over time. Data showed that both variables, locus of control and sex did effectively differentiate subjects on their study habits and attitudes. Females reported higher scores than the males and internally oriented subjects reported higher scores than the externally oriented ones. There was also a downward trend displayed by the Study Habits and Attitudes past scale. One limitation in this study was the over exposure (three times) of the scales so as to cause a lackadaisical attitude on the part of the subjects in the self-reporting measurement.

Hall, Jaesting and Woods (1977) attempted to assess the relationship between Rotter's I-E scale and Levenson's IPC scales of locus of control for Black and White students. The subjects were 104 White students at a branch unit of a major university and 114 Black students at a church-related college. Both of the previous questionnaires were given along with the 12 Coleman, Campbell, Hobson, McPartland, Mood, Weinfeld and York (1966) items which measured sense of personal control. Results indicated sex and race on the Levenson IPC scale was no more highly correlated with I-E score for Black students than for White students. The Rotter I-E scale was moderately related to the Levenson scales and seems to measure belief in control by chance and internal control. The Coleman items which targeted success and mobility were relatively related to Rotter and Levenson scales. These findings support Lefcourt, Reid and Ware's (1976) theory that locus of control is multidimensional.

Hohmuth and Ramos (1973) investigated the value of Rotter's I-E-LOC scale as a predictor of academic success. This scale was administered to 69, mostly Black high-risk, low-income college students. Two hypotheses were being tested in this study: internally oriented students would have higher grade-point averages (GPA) at the end of their first year; and of those students who were failing as of the end of the first semester, those who were internally oriented would be more likely to show improvement during the second semester. Sixty-four subjects completed the study. There was no significant correlation between Rotter's scale and GPA at the end of the first-semester ($r = -0.16$) or between this scale and cumulative GPA at the end of the second-semester ($r = -0.26$). Although the hypothesized relationship between I-E scores and GPA was not verified, more of the internal than of the external scores improved their performance following failure. The second-semester grade performance improved by a half a letter grade over the first-semester. This suggests that the I-E scale may be a valid predictor in determining the success and failure of an academically high risk student. The small sample size was a limitation in securing verification between the I-E scores and GPA.

The relationship between goal attainment and locus of control was the purpose of the Johnson and Bukacek (1979) study. One hundred twenty seven university volunteer students were randomly distributed into four independent groups and assigned to take the *Life Planning Workshop Questionnaire* and Rotter's I-E scale. The purposes of the research were to provide a more substantial test of the *Life Planning Workshop* (LPW) using a design which would improve the workshops inherent weaknesses and to evaluate the use of the Rotter I-E scale as a measure of change resulting from the LPW experiences. The design was the Sample Pretest-Posttest Design. The results indicated strong support for the hypothesis that the workshop significantly facilitates achievement of life planning goals. However, results measured by Rotter I-E scores showed little pre-post comparisons. The appropriateness of the Rotter I-E instrument for within participants comparisons in life planning was questionable.

Locus of control as a predictor of college success has warranted much attention. The study by Crandall, Katkowsky and Preston's (1962) found it to be a strong determinor of achievement for males but not so for females. Chance (1965) conducted a similar study as Crandall and found significant relationships between locus of control and achievement for males as well as females.

Johnson (1987) examined locus of control and the ACT as predictors of success for Black college students. The success variable in this study was grade-point average. A sample of over 300 freshmen (142 male and 180 female) Black students were randomly selected from students enrolled in a required orientation class. The locus of control scores obtained during the first week of school were correlated with the samples ACT and composite GPA. Pearson correlation coefficients for the three variables were computed with GPA as the dependent variable and various combinations of locus of control and ACT as independent variables. Analyses revealed no significant relationships betwen locus of control and GPA for males ($r=0.03$) or females ($r=-0.05$). The ACT composite score was significantly related to GPA.

The Coleman report and other literature indicated that locus of control played a causative role on achievement. This study contradicts those findings. The contradiction may lie in the sample size. The data indicate that locus of control is a poor predictor of achievement and Black students appear to be more externally oriented than those students who were studied 20 years ago.

Kernis (1984) had previously sought to investigate the importance of internal and external attributions as determinants of performance. Kernis conducted two studies. In the first study 80 female undergraduates worked on a series of mazes with a partner (external variable). All subjects accepted successful feedback and were led to believe their success was attributed either to self (internal) or partner. Half of the subjects were then tested on other maze puzzles and the others were assigned another task. The second study of 92 female undergraduates followed the same procedures as the first study with slight variations. Data was entered into 2 (attribution) by 2 (self-awareness) by 2 (test text) analysis of variance designs. The results showed that internal subjects performed better when tested on the same task (maze) than on a different task. Poor performance was reflected by partner attribution condition subjects. When externals (partners) worked independently, their performance on task was not as great. This investigation provided substantial evidence that the causality of locus for one's achievement is a significant determinant of subsequent performance.

Because locus of control is a multidimensional personality construct, researchers (Joe, 1971; Phares, 1973) have examined variables such as anxiety and depression among college students, which often affects academic performance. Molinari and Khanna (1981) examined the relationship between locus of control and depression and anxiety. From a pool of 300 male and female undergraduates who had been administered the Levenson Internal, Powerful Others and Chance scales, 60 subjects (30 males and 30 females) were chosen to participate in the study. They were equally divided into internals, defensive externals and congruent externals, on the basis of whether their highest standard score occurred on the I, P or C scales, respectively. Scales rating depression and anxiety were administered to each subject. Pearson correlation coefficients between locust of control and the depression and anxiety scales indicated a positive low correlation for congruent externality, while internality and depression were negatively correlated. Additional results indicated that internals have significantly less debilitating anxiety than both external groups and that congruent externals had equal or greater amounts of anxiety than defensive externals. Another conclusion indicated that internals do not show more facilitating anxiety than the external locus of control groups.

Weiner (1980) categorized attributions (causality) into three modalities - locus, stability and controllability. Students of different cultures have different levels of motivation and locus as they strive for academic success. Powers and Rossman (1983) compared the attributions of Native Americans and Anglo (non-Hispanic Caucasian) community college students and investigated correlates of these attributions. The subjects were 211 community college students (112 Native Americans and 99 Anglos). All were subjects in remedial reading classes and 48 percent of the subjects were male and 52 percent were female. Students were given the *Multidimensional-Multiattributional Causality Scale* (MMCS), the *Achievement Motivation Scale* (AMS) and the *Academic Expectancy Scale* (AES). Students were administered the MMCS in the spring of 1983. Random surveying of 102 students (56 Native Americans and 46 Anglow) and 109 students (56 Native Americans and 53 Anglos) were administered the AMS and AES. The four 6-item subscales (Effort, Ability Contex and Luck) of the MMCS were analyzed with a 2 x 2 analysis of variance design with culture and sex as factors. Native Americans and Anglos were compared using t-tests. Only the comparisons of Native Americans and Anglos on the Effort subscale was meaningful ($t = 2.74$; $df = 209$; $p < 0.007$). Native Americans attributed their academic achievement more to effort than did Anglos.

The generalizability of this study was limited in that the sample was drawn from a population who had experienced a high degree of low self-esteem culturally as well as in the academic setting. The definition of remedial class was not clearly defined in the study (i.e., the mean readability level was not specified).

Galper and Luch (1980) noted that success for males is more often attributed to skill whereas success for females is attributed to luck. The analysis was based on a five factor ANOVA consisting of a 2^5 design. The results indicated that when applied to the genders, there was a definite masculine bias. Male applicants and masculine characteristics both received higher ratings on the skill variable and females were more biased on these ratings than males. This study endorses the previous findings that the quality skill is more associated with men than women despite the attitude changes that have occurred because of the women's movement. The skill variable was also more closely linked to a person attempting a nontraditional program of study for his or her sex. The perception of luck was more variable with feminist beliefs of the rater impacting on attributions.

SUMMARY

The criteria problem is pervasive in just about every aspect of measuring counseling effectiveness. The crux of the problem appears to be in how standarized measurements could be used across the counseling domain. Another aspect of concern is the lack of standardized evaluative measurement for the counselor and his or her techniques. When affecting locus of control through the counseling process, the above-mentioned concerns are warranted. Counselors are struggling with determining strategies which may enhance academic progress among high-risk students. High-risk students as revealed through the literature have often experienced failures that may have been legitimately caused by their own initiatives; on the other hand, many of these students may have been victimized by their social, economic and cultural environment. Regardless of the causal ascription of thier academic malady, these students are faced with many problematic situations which hamper their academic progress. Continuous failure by these students in different aspects of their lives generates a lack of perceived control about their life expectancies. This lack of perceived control manifests itself as "hopelessness," belief in fate, belief in luck and chance. These characteristics are not viewed by society as positive attributes, because they negate one's ability to be independent, self-motivated, goal-oriented and in control.

Externals, those believing in the power of forces other than self, are high risk students. Counselors must develop methodologies and strategies to move these externals toward internalization, the belief in control of one's desirable outcomes.

What is to be done? Perhaps the foremost suggestion is also the most obvious one. Counselors must become more aware of the locus of control construct and the impetus it has on the client's psychological perception of himself and the world around him. The "helping" personnel must see the altering of externality as a continuous effort which must be integrated into the client's multifaceted experiences. That effort extends past the immediate counseling setting into support services which include collaborative curriculum planing, providing interactions for externals to experience success in social as well as academic settins and providing methodological in services for various personnel who have direct contact with externals. Being aware of the locus of control orientations should lead the counselor to establishing interventions which would lessen the client's inhibitions about his inadequacies in obtaining successful outcomes.

College counselors whose primary role is academic counseling should actively seek strategies which induce academic success. Such strategies might include extended individual counseling, group counseling sessions, peer counseling, parental involvement, cognitive and psychological assessments, collegiate orientation programs, experiential seminars and any other method that prepares the client for successful integration into "real life."

The process of internalization for externals is a long-term task. The process is not usually completed in the standard minimum time frame as in traditional limited sessions. Therefore, it is imperative that counselors assess their willingness and capabilities in facilitating the type of help which is needed. Although willingness and capability are essential, other considerations are equally important. Counselor style is one such consideration. counselors who are non-directive and less authoritarian tend to have better results with externals. This style of counseling allows for self-actualization and self-direction without the hinderance of time restrictions; and, of course, if externals are to move toward internalization, they must be allowed the freedom of time to move at a comfortable pace. Counseling services might consider counseling style when matching an external counselee with a counselor.

The trend in higher education is to perceive the college student as a full matured adult, motivated to integrate into the collegiate environment. This integration includes seeking help from appropriate sources that the colleg offers. Unfortunately, high-risk students are not internally motivated to seek help when help is needed. Often they are unaware that they may even need assistance. thus, many counseling services are not utilized to their fullest potential and potential clients continue to exist in spheres of "hopelessness" and "inadequacies" about their abilities. To curtail these pitfalls, colleges would be wise to establish a fixed number of mandated counseling visitations through orientation courses for entering freshmen, especially those who may be categorized as high-risk. These counseling visitations would provide the student with clarity of what services are provided as well as dispelling the myth that counseling is only for those with disturbing maladies. At the same time, these counseling settings would permit counselors to observe students who may exhibit personal externalization. From this observation, counselors would be in a better position to offer more specialized services to those students.

Because open admissions does not restrict admission, colleges and universities which are committed to the open admissions policy must incorporate the counseling component into as many areas of college life as possible. The college must be about the business of not only permitting students to enter higher education, but also exiting the academic towers with a degree of self control, independence and an intact belief that they can be successful in the "real world."

REFERENCES

Anderson, R. and G. V. Anderson (1962). The development of an instrument for measuring rapport, *Personnel guidance journal*, 41, 18 - 24.

Ballif, B. C. (1976). *A multi-dimensional model of human motivation.* Paper presented at the annual meeting of the Texas Personnel and Guidance Association, Fort Worth, Texas.

Baymur, F. and C. Paterson (1965). A comparison of three methods of assisting underachieving high school studcents. In M. Kornich (Ed.), *Underachievement.* Springfield: Charles C. Thomas, 501 - 513.

Bennett, G. K., M. G,. Bennett, W. L. Wallace and A. G. Wesman (1957). *College Qualification Tests.* New York: The Psychological Corporation.

Bergin, A. E. and M. J. Lambert (1978). The evaluation of therapeutic outcomes. In. S. L. Garfield and A. E. Bergin (Eds.), *Handbook of psychotherapy and behavior change.* New York: Wiley, 139 - 189.

Bixler, R. H. (1963). The changing world of the counselor: Training for the Unknown, *Counselor education and supervision*, 2, 168 - 176.

Bordin, E. S. (1974). *Research strategies in psychotherapy.* New York: Wiley.

Broedel, H., M. Ohlsen, F. Proff and C. Southard (1965). The effects of group counseling a gifted underachieving adolescents. In M. Kornich (Ed.), *Underachievement.* Springfield: Charles C. Thomas Publishers, 514 - 428.

Butcher, E. and D. Hebert (1985). Locus of control similarity and counselor effectiveness: a matched case study. *Journal of counseling and development*, 64, 103 - 108.

Callis, R., P. Polmantier and E. Roeher (1957). Five years of research on counseling, *Journal of counseling psychology*, 4, 2, 119 - 123.

Carkhuff, R. R. (1972). *The art of helping.* Amherst: Human Resource Development Press.

Carlson, R. (1975). Personality. In M. R. Rosenweig and L. W. Porter (Eds.), *Annual review of psychology.* Palo Alto: Annual Reviews, 393 - 414.

Chance, J. E. (1965). *Internal control of reinforcements and the school learning process.* Paper presented at the annual meeting of the Society for Research in Child Development, Minneapolis, Minnesota.

Coan, R. (1974). *The optimal personality: An empirical and theoretical analysis.* New York: Columbia University Press.

Coleman, J. S., D. Q. Campbell, C. J. Hobson, J. McPartland, A. M. Mood, F. D. Weinfeld and R. L. York (1966). *Equality of educational opportunity.* Washington, D. C.: United States Government Printing Office.

Collins, B. E. (1974). Four components of the Rotter internal-external scale: Belief in a difficult world, a just world, a predictable world and a politically responsive world, *Journal of personality and social psychology,* 29, 381 - 391.

Connolly, S. G. (1980). Changing expectancies: A counseling model based on locus of control, *Personnel and guidance journal,* 59, 176 - 180.

Crandall, V. C., W. Katkowsky and A. Preston (1962). Motivational and ability determinants of young children's intellectual achievement behaviors, *Child development,* 33, 643 - 661.

Dole, A. (1964). The prediction of effectiveness in school counseling, *Journal of counseling psychology,* 11, 2, 112 - 122.

Downing, L. N. (1975). Counseling theories and techniques. Chicago: Nelson-Hall.

Dressel, P. L. (1954). Implications of recent research for counseling, *Journal of counseling and psychology,* 1, 100 - 105.

Edwards, J. and L. K. Waters (1981). Moderating effect of achievement motivation and locus of control on the relationship between ability and academic peerformance, *Educational and psychological measurement,* 41,'585 - 586.

Eysenck, H. (1952). The effects of psychotherapy: An evaluation, *Journal of counsulting psychology,* 16, 319 - 324.

Fagan, N., L. Aiken, B., Gilliam and D. Kuehl (1983). *Self esteem, expectation and attribution of responsibility for academic performance.* Paper presented at the annual meeting of the American Psychological Association, Anaheim, California.

Frank, J. D. (1976). Psychotherapy and the sense of mastery. In R. L. Spitzer and D. F. Klein (Eds.), *Evaluation of psychological therapies.* Baltimore: Johns Hopkins Unversity Press, 47 - 56.

Galper, R. and D. Luch (1980). Gender, evaluation and causal attribution: the double standard is alive and well, *Sex roles, A journal of research,* 6, 2, 273 - 283.

Goldston, J., N. Zimmerson, E. Sini and B. Gadzella (1977). Study habits and attitudes characteristic of sex and locus of control groups, *Psychological reports*, 40, 271 - 274.

Gregory, W. L. (1978). Locus of control for positive and negative outcomes, *Journal of personality and social psychology*, 36, 840 - 849.

Grigg, A. and L. Goodstein (1957). The use of clients as judges of the counselor's performance, *Journal of counseling psychology*, 4, 31 - 36.

Hall, E., J. Jaesting and M. Woods (1977). Relationships among measures of locus of control for Black and White students, *Psychological reports*, 40, 59 - 62.

Hohmuth, A. and R. Ramos (1973). Locus of control, achievement and failure among disadvantaged college students, *Psychological reports*, 33, 573 - 574.

Jensen, B. T., G. Coles and B. Nestor (1955). The criterion problem in guidance research, *Journal of counseling psychology*, 2, 58 - 61.

Joe, V. C. (1971). Review of internal-external control construct as a personality variable, *Psychological reports*, 28, 619 - 640.

Johnson, C. and S. Bukacek (1979). Goal attainment and locus of control: Life planning impetus, *Journal of college student personnel*, 20, 353 - 357.

Kendall, P. C. (1984). Behavioral assessment and methodology. In G. T. Wilson, C. M. Franks, K. D. Brownell and P. C. Kendall (Eds.) *Annual review of behavioral therapy: Theory and practice*. New York: Guilford Press, 39 - 94.

Kernis, M. (1984). *Internal versus external attributions are important determinants of subsequent performance*. Paper presented at the annual meeting of the American Psychological Association, Toronto, Canada.

Lefcourt, H. M. (1982). *Locus of control: Current trends in theory and research*. Hillsdale: Lawrence Erlbaum Associates.

Lefcourt, H. M., R. Reid and C. Ware (1976). Interview questions assessing locus of control. In H. M. Lefcourt (Ed.), *Locus of control: Current trends as theory and research*. Hillsdale: Lawrence Erlbaum Associates, 186 - 187.

Levitt, E. E. (1957). The results of psychotherapy with children: An evaluation, *Journal of consulting psychology*, 21, 189 - 196.

Lewis, E. C. (1970). *The psychology of counseling*. New York: Holt, Rinehart and Winson.

Linden, J. D., S. C. Stone and B. Shertzer (1965). Development and evaluation of an inventory for rating counseling, *Personnel and guidance journal*, 44, 267 - 276.

Luborsky, L., B. Singer and L. Luborsky (1975). Comparative studies of psychotherapies, *Archives of general psychiatry*, 32, 995 - 1008.

Merton, R. (1946). *Mass persuasion*. New York: Harpers.

Merton, R. (1949). Social structure and anomie. In R. Merton (Ed.), *Social theory and social structure*. Glencoe: Free Press, 125 - 149.

Metzler, J. H. (1964). Evaluating counseling and guidance programs: A review of the literature, *Vocational guidance quarterly*, 12, 285 - 289.

Merenda, P. and J. Rothney (1958). Evaluating the effects of counseling - eight years after, *Journal of counseling psychology*, 5, 3, 163 - 168.

Mezzano, J. (1968). Group counseling with low-motivated male high school students - comparative effects of two uses of counselor time, *Journal of educational research*, 61, 5, 222 - 224.

Molinari, V. and P. Khanna (1981). Locus of control and its relationship to anxiety and depression, *Journal of personality assessment*, 45, 308 - 319.

Myrick, R. D. and F. D. Kelly (1971). A scale for evaluating practicum students in counseling and supervision, *Counselor education and supervision*, 10, 330 - 336.

O'Dea, J. D. and J. R. Zeran (1953). Evaluating effects of counseling, *Personal and guidance journal*, 31, 241 - 244.

Parloff, M., P. London and B. Wolfe (1986). Individual psychotherapy and behavior change, *Annual review of psychology*, 37, 321 - 349.

Patterson, C. H. (1960). Methodological problems in evaluation, *Personnel and guidance journal*, 39, 270 - 274.

Phares, E. J. (1973). *Locus of control: A personality determinant of behavior*. Morestown: General Learning Press.

Powers-Alexander, S., G. Galvin, D. Lambert, C. Speth and B. Plake (1983). *Attributions of success in college women: Effort or lack*. Paper presented at the annual meeting of the American Educational Research Association, Montreal, Canada.

Powers, S. and Rossman, M. (1983). Attributional factors of native Americans and anglo community college students, Research/Technical report number 143 (RC 014 440), Washington, D.C.: United States Department of Education, National Institute of Education.

Prociuk, T. J. and L. J. Breen (1975). Defensive externality and its relation to academic performance, *Journal of personality and social psycholgy*, 31, 549 - 566.

Rodin, M. J. (1982). By a faculty member's yardstick, student evaluations don't measure up, *The chronicle of higher education*, 24, 10, p. 64.

Rogers, C. R. (1961). *On becoming a person.* Boston: Houghton Mifflin.

Rosenzweig, S. A. (1954). A transevaluations of psychotherapy: a reply to Hans Eysenck, *Journal of abnormal and social psychology*, 49, 298 - 304.

Roth, H. and H. A. Meyensbury (1963). The nonachievement syndrome, *Personnel and guidance journal*, 41, 535 - 540.

Roth, R., H. Mauksch and K. Peiser (1967). The non-achievement sybndrome, group therapy and achievement change, *Personnel and guidance journal*, 46, 4, 393 - 398.

Rothney, J. and G. Farwell (1960). The evaluation of guidance and personal services, *Review of educational research*, 30, 2, 168 - 175.

Rotter, J. B. (1954). *Social training and clinical psychology.* Englewood Cliff: Prentice Hall.

Rotter, J. B. (1960). Some implications of social learning theory for the prediction of goal decided behavior from testing procedure, *Psychological review*, 67, 301 - 316.

Rotter, J. B. (1966). Generalized expectancies for internal versus external control of reinforcement, *Psychological monographs*, 80, 1, Whole Number 609, 1 - 28.

Rotter, J. B. (1975). Some problems and misconceptions related to the construct of internal vs. external control of reinforcement, *Journal of counsuting and clinical psychology*, 48, 56 - 67.

Seligman, M. E. P. (1975). *Helplessness.* San Francisco: W. H. Freeman.

Shapiro, D. A. and D. Shapiro (1982). Meta-analysis of comparative therapy outcome studies: A replication and refinement, *Psychological Bulletin*, 92, 581 - 604.

Shaw, M. C. and R. Wursten (1965). Research on group procedures in schools: a review of the literature, *Personnel and guidance journal*, 44, 27 - 34.

Sheldon, W. and Q. Landsman (1965). an investigation of non-directive group therapy and students in academic difficulty. In M. Kornrich (Ed.), *Underachievement.* Springfield: Charles C. Thomas, 652 - 661.

Shertzer, B. and S. C. Stone (1974). *Fundamentals of counseling*, 2nd. edition. New York: Houghton Mifflin.

Silverman, H. L. (1962). Psychotherapy: a survey and evaluation, *Psychiatric quarterly supplement*, 36, 116 - 135.

Smith, M. L., G. V. Glass and T. I. Miller (1980). *The benefits of psychotherapy*. Baltimore: John Hopkins University Press.

Speilberger, C. D. and H. Weitz (1964). Improving the academic perfomrance of anxious college freshmen, *Psychological monographs*, 78, Number 14, Whole Number 590, 1 - 20.

Strube, M. J. and D. P. Hartmann (1983). Meta-analysis: Techniques applications and functions, *Journal of counsulting clinical psychology*, 51, 14 - 27.

Strupp, H. H. (1963). The outcome problem in psychotherapy revisited, *Psychotherapy: Theory, research and practice*, 1, 1 - 12.

Thurber, S. D. (1972). Defensive externality and academic achievement by women, *Psychological reports*, 30, p. 454.

Veblen, Q. (1899). *The theory of the leisure class*. New York: Mac Millan, Modern Library Edition, 1934.

Weiner, B. (1980). *Human motivation*. New York: Holt, Rinehart and Winston.

Wilson, G. T. and S. J. Rachman (1983). Meta-analysis and the evaluation of psychotherapy outcome: Limitations and liabilities, *Journal of consulting clinical psychology*, 51, 54 - 64.

Winborn, B. and C. Schmedt (1965). The effectiveness of short term group counseling upon the academic achievement of potentially superior but underachieving college freshmen. In M. Kornrich (Ed.), *Underachievement*. Springfield: Charles C. Thomas, 663 - 670.

Zimpfer, D. (1962). *An analysis of certain factors contributing to outcomes reported in studies of multiple counseling*. Unpublished manuscript.

Zunker, V. and W. Brown (1966). Comparative effectiveness of student and professional counselors, *Personnel and guidance journal*, 62, 738 - 742.

14

Student Retention and Attrition in College

Patricia Hawkins Rogers

The trend in American education for more and more people to attend college is supported by the literature. As early as 1825, Thomas Jefferson advocated the concept of free public education for all during his inaugural address as president of the University of Virginia. That institution became the first truly public university. Jefferson advocated democratization and liberalization of higher education (Brubacher and Rudy, 1978). He stated that education should meet the needs of society and be accessible to everyone. Gallup polls from 1973 to 1982 confirmed that the Jeffersonian belief that college is essential for individual and societal success continues to live in the minds of the public (Morgan and Mitchell, 1985).

Renner (1977) stated that access to college does not always guarantee success in college or later life. American colleges and universities lose, on an average, approximately 50 percent of their population in the four years after matriculation. The immediate and long term costs of student attrition prompted university researchers to focus studies on factors that may influence student retention and attrition in an effort to gain a greater understanding of the process.

What are the characteristics that reliably predict the successful the unsuccessful student? Predictor variables can help universities ascertain ways of improving student retention and providing necessary programs. This was supported by Lenning (1982) when he identified ten purposes of prediction studies among which were to (1) determine the causes of retention/attrition; (2) identify correlates of retention; (3) develop an early warning prediction system to identify students who are potential drop-outs; (4) increase understanding of the withdrawal process; and (5) identify those students who will survive only if special support is provided and to determine what support is needed.

This chapter will discuss the literature pertaining to retention and attrition rates and theories. Those studies that have investigated the impact of selected preadmission academic and non-academic variables on student success in college ,also, will be discussed.

RETENTION AND ATTRITION RATES IN COLLEGE

Individuals entered college with a variety of attributes (e.g., sex, race, ability, age), pre-college experiences (e.g., high school grade point average, academic and social attainment) and family backgrounds (e.g., social status attributes, values climates, expectional climates). Each attribute impacts upon student attrition and retention (Tinto, 1975, 1987).

The extent of attrition in American colleges and universities was reported in several major studies. The National Longitudinal Survey of the High School Class of 1972 conducted by the National Center for Education Statistics indicated that nearly 60 percent of first-time entrants to four year colleges left them insitutions of registration without completing their degree program for various reasons. Though nearly 65 percent of those first-time entrants eventually received a degree, only approximately 44 percent came from the institution of initial entry.

Ramist (1981) reviewed the research on college attrition and retention and found that only 35 to 40 percent of the entering freshmen graduated in four years from their college of original entry. An additional 30 to 50 percent graduated in more than four years, or from a different college or both. The remaining 10 to 35 percent of students never received a degree. Noel, Levitz, Salvri and Associates (1983) analyzed the data provided to the American College Testing (ACT) Program by 2,432 United States colleges and universities. The data reflected the percentage of full-time freshmen who entered college in the Fall, 1981 who returned to the same college in the Fall, 1982. The attrition rate across all types of surveyed institutions was 32 percent.

Rounds (1983) compiled a profile of student characteristics which were common among unsuccessful students and which could be used as predictors of attrition. Potential drop-outs were characterized as having poor academic records, inappropriate goals, poor study skills and habits and limited background experiences.

Reasons for dropping out of school were studied by Astin (1975). He surveyed 101,000 students in 1972 to determine what factors influenced students decisions to drop-out of school. Reasons cited were (1) class boredom, (2) financial problems, (3) family responsibilities, (4) poor academic achievement, (5) institutional dissatisfaction, (6) change in career preference and (7) inability to enter a specific program of study.

More recently, Tinto (1985) found various factors contributing to attrition among college students. Those factors were academics, goal or need fulfillment, personal and psychological. Because of these factors, American universities lost, on an average, approximately 50 percent of their students in the four years after matriculation. The immediate and long term costs of student attrition prompted university researchers to focus studies on factors perceived to influence student retention in an effort to gain a greater understanding of the retention-attrition process. Researchers hoped to identify characteristics of those students who succeeded at their institution and those who did not succeed.

RETENTION AND ATTRITION THEORIES

Several theories have contributed to the understanding of student attrition and retention. Those theories linked success to the student's level of social integration into the institutional setting and to pre-enrollment academic and non-academic factors. Tinto (1985) categorized theories of student departure from college into five types. His categorization was based on their focus and level of analysis. The five types listed were psychological, societal, economic, organizational and interactional. Interactional theories were viewed as the most theoretically sound. A more detailed review of these theories follows.

Spady's Sociological Model of the Drop-Out Process

Spady (1970) was first to develop an explanatory model of the college drop-out process that emphasized the impact of social and academic integration on student persistence and success in college. Spady viewed persistence/withdrawal decisions largely as the results of a longitudinal process of associations between the student and the academic and social systems of the institution.

Spady based his model on a synthesis of the literature and the concepts of Durkheim's Theory of Suicide (Durkheim, 1961) which stated that suicide is more likely to occur when individuals are insufficiently integrated into society. In Spady's model college was viewed as a social system with its own values and social structure; and drop-out from that social system was viewed in a manner similar to that of drop-out from larger society. Other variables that were reported to be associated with persistence and withdrawal were included in an effort to explain attrition as a conditional phenomenon.

Tinto's Theoretical Model of Student Departure

Using Spady's conceptual model, Tinto (1975) constructed an expanded model to explain how and why students drop-out of college. His model posited that individual characteristics, prior experiences and goal commitments along with the individual's integration into the academic and social systems of the institution directly impact upon student retention and success. Tinto viewed dropping out of college as a continuous process that involved aspects of the student's life, both past and present. He related this process to Durkheim's *Theory of Suicide* (Durkheim, 1961) which stated that suicide is more likely to occur when individuals are insufficiently integrated into society. When viewing college as a social system with its own value and social structures, one should treat dropping out from that social system in a manner analogous to that of dropping out from the wider society. Those social conditions affecting drop-out from the social system of college would resemble those resulting in suicide in society in general (Tinto, 1975). In this model, Tinto delineated other factors that, along with integration or malintegration into the social environment of the college, impacted upon student attrition and retention. These were external factors such as costs and benefits, individual characteristics and goal commitment.

Several studies have been conducted to validate the dimensions of Tinto's model. Each of these investigations tended to support the predictive validity of major parts of the model. Pascarella and Terenzini (1983) conducted a longitudinal study from 1976 to 1978. The first purpose was to provide a comprehensive test of the validity of Tinto's causal model of voluntary withdrawal from an institution. The second purpose was to test Tinto's hypothesis of compensatory interactions between social and academic integration and between institutional and goal commitment.

Pascarella and Terenzini concluded the following: (1) The variables in Tinto's model discriminated between persisters and voluntary withdrawals with 80 percent accuracy. (2) The model would be very useful in helping to understand the dynamics of freshmen-year persistence/withdrawal decisions. (3) Although pre-enrollment characteristics and commitments influenced students' interaction with the social and academic systems of the institution, it was social and academic integration that directly affected persistence/withdrawal behavior.

Munro's Reduced Path Model of Drop-Outs

Munro (1981) used the theoretical model conceptualized by Tinto to study students who persisted and those who withdrew. From Tinto's model Munro derived a reduced model. Munro used path analysis to investigate the interaction effect of the student with the college environment and the processes that interplay in the decision to remain in school or drop-out. The model viewed the academic and social integration of a student into the university and the student's interaction with these systems as the primary determinants of persistence. The model also delineated the relationship of antecedent variables such as precollege schooling, personal attributes and social background.

Pascarella's Causal Model of Student Learning and Cognitive Development

Pascarella (1985) constructed a hypothesized causal model to explain the cognitive and other outcomes of college. In Pascarella's model, learning and cognitive development in college were directly and indirectly influenced by five major dimensions: institutional environment, organizational characteristics of institutions, student pre-college traits, interactions between social agents and quality of student effort.

Institutional environment, organizational characteristics and student pre-college traits directly impacted the interaction of major social agents such as peers and faculty. The quality of student effort was directly influenced by student background/pre-college traits and also by the demands of the institutional and social environment. Learning and cognitive development were directly influenced by student background characteristics, interactions with major agents of socialization and quality of student effort.

Bean's Model of Student Departure Syndrome

Bean (1985) conducted a study that sought (1) to describe a conceptual model of student drop-out that emphasizes student selection for or socialization to certain behaviors and attitudes that were expected to have a direct effect on attrition; (2) to estimate the model empirically; and (3) to answer three questions related to the model - Do peers or faculty have a greater influence on attrition decisions? Does retention result from selecting students or their socialization after entering? Do the relationships vary by grade level?

Bean hypothesized that academic factors should positively influence college grades and that social-psychological factors should positively influence institutional fit and institutional commitment. Environmental factors should negatively influence institutional fit and commitment but positively affect decisions to drop-out.

Bean concluded the following from his study, that:

- College grades, institutional fit, institutional commitment and environment factors were positively related to drop-out syndrome.
- Academic and social-psychological variables were not significantly related to drop-out syndrome (academic variables did significantly impact college grades).
- Institutional fit and institutional commitment had the greatest net affect on drop-out syndrome.

Peng and Fetters' Model of College Withdrawal

Peng and Fetters (1978) conceptualized a model to investigate the influence of various background characteristics, personal attributes and environmental influences on withdrawal behavior utilizing a national sample of 5,917 students from more than 1,800 institutions Peng and Fetters' model posited withdrawal behaviors, financial support and college performance and an ordering of variables by the hypothesized causal structure linking one variable with another or by time considerations.

Each of these models served to explain the role of the student, environment and university characteristics on student retention and attrition in college. They helped to explain whether entry-level characteristics or institutional characteristics were more important in influencing students to stay in college or leave. Other studies were conducted to determine the predictive ability of selected variables on college students' academic outcomes. These studies did not necessarily produce causal models. Never the less, they have produced valuable data concerning college success and failure.

COLLEGE SUCCESS STUDIES

The remainder of this chapter will focus on studies of selected variables that impact upon collegiate success such as the American College Test (ACT), high school grade-point average (GPA) and high school curriculum, race, sex and high school size. How effective were these variables as predictors of success? A discussion of that literature follows.

Academic Variables

High school curriculum, high school grade-point average and rank in class are reported to be the most important criteria for college admission. Nevertheless, the Scholastic Aptitude Test (SAT) and the American College Test (ACT) are the most widely used. Approximately 1.6 million SATs and about 1 million ACTs are administered to high school students every year (Boyer, 1987).

The American College Test

Many studies have investigated the validity of these tests in predicting college success. Coker (1968) investigated the diversity of intellective and non-intellective factors that distinguished persisters from non-persisters in college and reported significantly higher mean scores on the sub-scales of the ACT for persisters than non-persisters.

In another study Price and Suk (1976) investigated the relationship between college performance and high school grades and ACT scores using a sample of 92 randomly selected junior and senior business students. It was revealed that both high school grades and ACT were directly associated with college performance. But, ACT was reported to be more significant and important in influencing the variation in college performance than were high school grades.

Smith (1980) examined selected demographic variable profiles and questionnaire responses of students in regard to student persistence. The results indicated that the ACT composite score did discriminate between student persisters and non-persisters.

While many researchers (Schade, 1977; Stiggins, 1978; Rounds and Anderson, 1985) concluded that composite scores on college entrance examinations were the best predictors of academic success, others disagree. Groenke (1979); and Lach (1971) reported that high school grades and aptitude scores did not effectively predict academic success in college. Particularly, Groenke (1979) compared the ACT scores of 959 freshmen at Mesa Community College in Arizona with their college success as measured by college GPA. He found ACT scores to be significantly more predictive of freshmen under the age 21 than over.

Halpin, Halpin and Schaer (1981) compared the relative effectiveness of the SAT, the ACT, the CAT (California Achievement Test) and high school GPA in predicting college GPA. Even though high school GPA was the best single predictor, they reported each test to be equally as predictive of college grade-point average. Rounds and Anderson (1985) examined research concerning the predictive value of the ACT, SAT and Comparative Guidance and Placement Program (CGP). In regard to the ACT, they concluded that, "overall, the ACT, while not making a particularly effective showing, has nevertheless appeared to do as well or better than other tests with which it was compared" (pp. 55).

Hashway (1988) reported a steady decline in ACT and SAT scores. SAT scores declined by 50 points from 1962-1982. ACT scores showed a similar decline form 1962-1982. Those test scores continue to show a decline of about 2 percent per year.

In conclusion, the relationship between ACT scores and college performance was discussed in the literature. Though the findings are mixed, the prevalent finding was that ACT scores were valuable as predictors of academic achievement in college. Successful students achieved higher scores on all of the subscales than did unsuccessful students. The ACT subscales and composite scores were positively correlated with college GPA with the composite score having a better correlation. Correlations for subscales ranged from .35 to .42 and composite score .47. Researchers, nevertheless, recommended the consideration of other variables in the prediction of college performance because statistical prediction increases when other variables are considered (Astin, 1971; Brazziel, 1977; Reyes, 1979).

High School Performance

Research involving high school grade-point average as a predictor of college success continually reported it to be a better single predictor. Cope (1971) reviewed the literature pertaining to student attrition. The four categories of variables were: biographical; pre-college educational; psychological; and institutional environmental variables. Within the pre-college educational variable studies that investigated high school grades as a predictor of success concluded that there was a constant relation between performance in high school and college persistence/attrition.

Panos and Astin (1968) conducted a study to investigate the relationship of various student characteristics to dropping out of college and to estimate the impact of the university environment on student persistence. Panos and Astin found that high school grade-point average was predictive of persistence in college. Persistence was measured as completing four or more years of college.

In a study of Black, Mexican-American and Anglo college students, Perry (1981) also found high school grades along with SAT to be the best predictors of college performance.

Breland (1981) reviewed the literature on 45 variables (student characteristics) considered in admission to higher education to determine which was the best predictor for a given outcome in a given sample and what magnitude of relationship was attained for the prediction of the outcome of interest. In those studies that reported predictions of academic outcomes, Breland concluded that the best predictor of academic outcomes was high school grades with correlations ranging from .22 to .78 and a median correlation of .60.

Allen (1986) utilizing a national sample of 1,583 randomly selected Black students attending six predominantly White state-supported universities in 1981 and those attending eight historically Black state-supported universities in 1983, investigated the ability of seven variables to predict student performance as well as racial attitudes and college satisfaction. Results revealed high school grade-point average to be the strongest predictor of college grades for all groups of students except the Black women on the White campuses. Similar findings were reported by Pedrini and Pedrini (1986) in a study of 104 economically disadvantaged students enrolled at the University of Nebraska.

In conclusion, the literature supported the influence of high school performance on college persistence and performance. The correlation of high school academic record with persistence ranged from .25 to .50

(Ramist, 1981). Astin (1971) reported that ACT and high school grade-point average should be combined with other variables to increase their predictability.

High School Curriculum

Another academic variable associated with success or lack of success in college was high school curriculum. In a study conducted to evaluate the undergraduate experience in America, Boyer (1987) reported that by 1979, only 56 percent of the four-year public colleges nationwide required English for admission. Only about 51 percent required math, biological science, social studies and physical science. Those requirements continued until the early 1980s when colleges once again began to demand core courses and standardization in college entrance requirements. Navarro (1984) reported changes in state standards which were viewed as an effort to improve the quality of education. Two changes reported were an increase in high school graduation requirements and an increase in college admission requirements. Navarro stated that in 1985, 48 states considered legislative proposals to increase high school graduation requirements. Thirty-five of those forty-eight states received approval and are implementing those new requirements. Those requirements designated a particular pattern of courses to be taken by the students. Generally, they included four years of English, two or three years of mathematics, etc., with vast differences among states in specific courses required. Additionally, Navarro stated that approximately 35 states raised their college admissions requirements. Those colleges required particular high school courses, admission test scores, high school GPA or class rank.

The validity of the high school curriculum in predicting student retention and withdrawal has been addressed in the literature (Bistreich, 1977; Peng and Fetters, 1978; Yess, 1979; Lenning, 1982). Bistreich (1977) investigated the validity of seven criteria used along with personal interviews and School and College Ability Test scores in the selection of applicants for admission to four allied health programs. The variables were high school GPA, the number of high school courses, rank in high school graduating class and college GPA at the time of selection. Those variables found to be significant were college grade-point average at the time of admission into a program, high school grades in English and high school grades in natural science.

Similar findings were reported by Yess (1979) in a study to investigate the influence of selected variables on graduating grade-point average of community college students in various programs of study. Predictors which consistently accounted for variance in GPA were high school English average and SAT-Verbal and SAT-Math scores.

Lenning (1982) reported somewhat mixed findings. He found that those students who took a college- preparatory program and those who took more courses in English, mathematics, foreign languages and physical science tended to persist more than those who did not. But the number of courses in social studies and biological sciences were not found to have a significant correlation with persistence.

Edge and Friedberg (1984) investigated a set of academic and biographical variables of which included high school algebra grades as predictors of success in college calculus. The study revealed no significant impact of high school courses on students' subsequent success in college.

Changes in admissions requirements support the importance of high school curriculum on subsequent success in college. The literature also supports the relationship between high school curriculum and college success. Yet, empirical studies based on a theoretical foundations to validate this impact are lacking. Navarro (1985) voiced concern over the lack of impact data or any type of analysis undertaken to look at the effectiveness of the new curricular requirements.

NONACADEMIC VARIABLES

Nearly half of all American college students leave college before graduation and 85 percent do so for non-intellective reasons (Astin, 1976). Adding non-academic variables increases statistical prediction capability (Astin, 1976).

Reyes (1979) conducted a study to predict academic success using selected non-academic characteristics. Of the variables investigated, sex, major, age, number of years to graduate and location of high school attended were found to be correlated to college GPA. Reyes reported that the student most likely to succeed was female, a high school graduate approximately 27 years old, a transfer liberal arts major, a graduate from a high school in a state other than California and a graduate who took about four years to graduate from the community college.

Boyer (1987) stated that personal characteristics of students and out-of-class activities in which the student engaged are hard to describe and assess. Nevertheless, there is growing evidence that such factors are linked to college success. This is supported by Willingham (1985) who reported four variables other than high school rank and test scores to be related to student performance in college. They were high school honors, successful follow-through in extracurricular activities, a well-written personal statement and a strong reference from the high school. These variables improved prediction of student success in college by 25 percent over school rank and test scores alone. Additional support is provided by Wing and Wallach

(1971) who labeled non-academic variables as "accomplishment characteristics". Boyer recommended that colleges give more consideration to non-academic variables in their admission process. In doing so, colleges would gain valuable information about the potential for success of its students.

Non-academic variables affect student success in college and must be taken into account when modeling student success. The non-academic variables investigated in this study were high school size, race and gender. A synthesis of the literature follows.

High School Size

Studies of the effect of high school size on college student success are limited and yield conflicting results. Dwyer (1938) synthesized the literature concerning the relationship between size of high school attended and success in college and found inconsistencies. Dwyer concluded that:

1. No relationships exist between the academic success of students in college and the size of the high school class which are definite enough to serve as the basis for individual prediction.

2. There is a group relationship which is characterized by:

   A. A positive correlation coefficient of high school size with first semester record of not more than .25.

   B. A correlation coefficient between high school size and scholastic record which decreases as the student progresses through college and becomes insignificant by the end of two or three years.

   C. A larger attrition rate for students from small schools than for students from large schools in the first and second semester.

   D. The scholastic equivalence of all groups in the later college years.

Coker (1968) reported differences among persisting and non-persisting students in regard to the size of high school class. Bayer (1968) reported only a slight difference between students from small and large high schools in regard to rate of college completion.

On the other hand, several studies reported that high school size had no significant impact on college success. Slocum (1956) in a follow-up study of drop-outs from three freshman classes found that there was no relationship between high school size and either academic achievement or attrition. Similarly, Chase (1965) concluded that there was no difference between the number of students from small or large high schools in regard to rate of graduation and drop-outs. Also, Panos and Astin (1968) in a large-scale study of over 60,000 students from a national sample of 246 colleges and universities reported that size of high school class was not predictive of dropping out of college.

In summary, the literature is inconclusive concerning the relationship between high school size and student success in college. Cope (1968) concluded:

> Studies relating high school size to academic achievement appear to permit no easy generalization. School or community size may be closely related to such factors as: levels of socioeconomic status, differences in facilities, teacher salaries, class size, available curricular and differences in communities. For instance, who can say that a large high school in an academic community is similar to a school of comparable size in the heart of a large city? (pp. 43-44)

Corroborative findings were also reported in Cope (1971).

Race Differences

Peng and Fetters (1978) used a national sample to investigate the process of withdrawal from four-year and two-year institutions. In regard to race, Peng and Fetters concluded that Black students at four-year institutions showed greater persistence than White students when past academic achievement, aspiration and socioeconomic status were controlled. When such controls were applied to data from students attending two-year colleges no difference in attrition rates was found between Black and White students. White students were more likely to be in an academic high school program and have higher class rank and test scores, but Whites were reported to have lower education aspiration than Blacks. Peng and Fetters stated that race differences were largely accounted for by variables such as rank in class, high school program and socioeconomic status. Race itself had little effect on college persistence or on entry.

Lenning (1982) addressed the relationship between race and college attrition and concluded that although Black students showed a lower rate of retention than White students, Black students exhibited a higher rate of retention when high school grades were statistically controlled.

Munro (1981) used the theoretical model conceptualized by Tinto (1975) to study students who persisted and those who withdrew from college. In regard to race, Munro found that the effects of socioeconomic status, race and sex on persistence in higher education were mainly indirect, transmitted through intervening variables. Race was directly related to high school grades and high school grades were directly related to persistence.

Gosman, Dandridge, Nettles and Thoeny (1983) conducted a study of the influence of race, SAT composite scores, financial aid, mean family income and institutional characteristics on college performance. White students consistently outperformed Black students in terms of their attrition rates, tendency to follow the prescribed progression pattern and length of time to graduate when bivariate analyses were used. However, racial differences in performance disappeared when other student and institutional characteristics were introduced in the the prediction models using multiple regression techniques.

Allen (1986) investigated the ability of seven variables to predict the performance of Black students as well as racial attitudes and college satisfaction. For males on Black campuses, the variables that had statistically significant correlation with high college grades were high school grades (.23), educational aspirations (.196) and campus activities (.10). On Black campuses, female high achievers were those who had high grades in high school (.364) and who set high educational goals (.148).

Gender Research

These studies reflected a definite gender difference in college grades. Reyes (1979) reported that sex was correlated to student performance. The mean grade-point average of females (2.85) was higher than the grade-point average of males (2.68). Reyes reported that the student most likely to succeed was a female, a high school graduate approximately 27 years old, a transfer liberal arts major, a graduate from a high school in a state other than California and a graduate who took about four years to graduate from the community college.

A gender difference was also reported in a study by Pascarella and Terenzini (1983) which investigated student persistence. The first purpose was to provide a comprehensive test of the validity of Tinto's causal model of voluntary withdrawal from an institution. The second purpose was to test Tinto's hypothesis of compensatory interactions between social and academic integration and between institutional and goal commitment.

With regard to gender, social integration, for women, had a stronger effect on persistence (.22) than did academic integration (.14). Conversely, academic integration, for men had a more important influence on persistence (.27) than social integration (.14).

Bean and Bradley (1986) investigated the relationship between two endogenous variables (student satisfaction and cumulative grade-point average) and eight exogenous variables (institutional fit, academic integration, perceived utility of education, academic difficulty, satisfaction with social life, membership in organizations, class levels and high school performance). Their results indicated a correlation between all the exogenous variables except class level and one or both of the endogenous variables. The researchers reported that gender was related to college grades.

CONCLUSIONS AND RECOMMENDATIONS

In critically evaluating the literature, several inconsistencies were noted in study design, sampling methods, data collection and analysis. One inconsistency occurred in the mathematical modeling procedures which were used. Some researchers used first order correlation coefficients between single variables and grades, while others used multiple correlations between several predictors and grades (e.g., comparisons between average group test scores and average group grades).

Few attempts were made to determine the magnitude of the interaction affect among variables or the probable causality. Future studies need to be conducted that link high school academics and personal variables to college grade-point average in causal models. Especially, the link between high school curriculum and college GPA needs further investigation. The magnitude of the linkages should be estimated and validated using multiple regression equations and path analysis. The use of multivariate statistical analyses is supported in the literature but seldom used.

Another reflected inconsistency was the lack of a theoretical base. The literature reflected a tendency on the part of researchers to attempt to link numerous variables to success, but made little attempt to identify the theory or theories which generated the link between variables. Theory is important in prediction studies for it guides the researcher. The theory describes which variables should be examined and how those variables are believed to relate to the subject of study (Bean, 1982).

Kerlinger (1973) defined theory as:

> A set of interrelated constructs (concepts), definitions and propositions that present a systematic view of phenomena by specifying relationships among variables, with the purpose of explaining and predicting the phenomena, p 3.

Theory is helpful in explaining why things happen and in guiding the selection of certain variables and the elimination of others (Bean, 1982).

More studies should be conducted based upon a synthesis of the related literature and the theoretical models formulated by Tinto (1975), Pascarella (1985), Munro (1981), Bean (1985) and others. Those theoretical models viewed the academic and social integration of an individual into the institution and the student's interaction with the social and academic systems as the primary determinants of student retention and attrition. Those models also pointed out the importance of antecedent attributes such as precollege schooling, personal attributes and social background. Those attributes contributed to the academic and social integration of the student into the university. Those models should serve as guides in formulating models which test the relationship between pre-enrollment variables and college GPA.

Sampling methods proved to be sources of inconsistency. In many of the studies no distinction was made between full- or part-time students, no control groups were utilized for comparison and many focused on specific types of students; all of which limited the generalizability of the findings. Though several studies used national samples, a detailed explanation of how data-base subjects were selected was lacking. Also lacking were samples representative of the total college population.

Samples for future studies should be reflective of the full-time undergraduate population from various majors on college campuses. They should contain Black and White graduates of public and private high schools.

The questionnaire was the method used to collect the data in several of the studies and was seldom described. Some researchers failed to follow up questionnaire mailings. The data collected was limited to those respondents who chose to return the questionnaires. The use of self-reported questionnaires was also criticized in the literature. More accurate sources of information is needed. Data should be collected from student files in the college admission office, which includes biographical profiles and student high school transcripts. Student files provided more valid information than self-administered questionnaires.

Another inconsistency was in the definition of successful and unsuccessful students. Success was defined by many researchers as retention in college after one semester of enrollment and lack of success was withdrawal from college. No distinction was made between the types of withdrawal and the types of persisters. Many researchers grouped all withdrawals together and used their mean aptitude test scores or high school performance to compare with the scores of the persisters. College GPA after one semester, one year, four years and graduation were used as measures of success. Several studies measured success by grades in college courses.

The criterion variable for future studies should take into account student performance as well as student persistence i.e., obtaining a 2.0 college GPA after two or more consecutive semesters of full-time enrollment).

REFERENCES

Aitken, N. (1982). College student performance, satisfaction and retention: Specification and estimation of a structural model. *Journal of higher education,* 53, 32-50.

Allen, W. (1986), *Gender and campus race differences in Black student academic performance, racial attitudes and college satisfaction.* ERIC Document Reproduction Service. No. ED268 855.

Anderson, C. (1980). *1980 fact book for academic administrators.* Washington, D. C.: American Council on Education.

Asher, H. (1976). *Causal modeling: Quantitative applications in the social sciences.* Bevelry Hills: Sage Publications.

Astin, A. (1964). Personal and environmental factors associated with college drop-outs among high aptitude students. *Journal of Educational Psychology,* 55, 219-227.

Astin, A. (1971). *Predicting academic performance in college.* New York: Collier-Macmillan Limited.

Astin, A. (1975). *Preventing students from dropping out.* San Francisco: Jossey Bass.

Astin, A. (1977). *Four critical years: Effects of college on beliefs, attitudes and knowledge.* San Francisco: Jossey-Bass.

Bayer, A. (1968). The college drop-out: Factors affecting senior college completion. *Sociology of education,* 41,305-316.

Beal, P. and L. Noel (1980). *What works in student retention.* ERIC Document # ED 197 635.

Bean, J. (1980). drop-outs and turnover: The synthesis and test of a causal model of student attrition. *Research in higher education,* 12, 155-187.

Bean, J. (1982). Conceptual models of student attrition: How theory can help the institutional researcher. In E. Pascarella (ed). *New directions for institutional research: Studying student attrition, no. 36.* San Francisco: Jossey- Bass.

Bean, J. (1985). Interaction effects based on class level in an explanatory model of college student drop-out syndrome. *American educational research journal,* 22, 35-64.

Bean, J. and R. Bradley (1986). Untangling the satisfaction- performance relationship for college students. *Journal of higher education,* 57, 393-412.

Beard, R. and I. Senior (1980). *Motivating students.* ERIC Document Reproduction Service. No. 196388.

Bistreich, A. (1977). *Predicting grade-point average, withdrawal and graduation from four allied health programs at Miami-Dade Community College Medical Center campus.* ERIC Document Reproduction Service. No. ED140925.

Boyer, E. (1987). *College: The undergraduate experience in America. The Carnegie Foundation for the advancement of teaching:* New York: Harper and Row. pp. 26-42.

Brazziel, W. (1977). *Non-intellective predictors of student persistence/ attrition and performance: Implications for college and university research and planning.* ERIC Document Reproduction Service. No. ED139319.

Breland, H. (1981). *Assessing student characteristics in admission to higher education.* New York: The College Board.

Brice, M. (1957). Comparison of subjective predictors with objective predictors of college achievement. *College and University,* 32, 347-353.

Brigham, C. (1926). The scholastic aptitude test of the college entrance examination board. In T. Fiske (ed.) *The work of the college examination board 1901-1925.* New York: Ginn and Company.

Brubacher, J. and W. Rudy (1978). *Higher education in transition.* New York: Harper and Row.

Carnegie Commission on Higher Education. (1973). *A chance to learn--An action agenda for equal opportunity in higher education.* New York: McGraw-Hill Book Company.

Chase, C. (1965). *The University Freshman drop-out.* Indiana Studies in Prediction #6. Bureau of Educational Studies and Testing: Indiana University.

Coker, D. (1968). *Diversity of intellective and non-intellective characteristics between persisting students and non- persisting students among campuses.* Washington, D.C. Office of Education Report. ERIC Document # ED 033-645.

Cope, R. (1968). Academic performance in higher education: A review and critique of the literature. *Journal of College Student Personnel.* 386-392.

Cope, R. (1971). *An Investigation of Entrance Characteristics Related to drop-outs.* Washington, D.C. Office of Education Report. ERIC Document # ED 052-749.

Cope, R. and W. Hannah (1975). *Revolving college doors: The causes and consequences of dropping out, stopping out and transfering.* New York: Wiley.

Crowl, T. (1986). *Fundamental of research: A practical guide for educators and special educators.* Columbus: Publishing Horizons, Inc.

Dobbins, H. (1969). The relationship of the variability of the subtest scores on the American College Test and prediction of academic achievement of college freshman. *Dissertation Abstract,* 30A.

Durkheim, E. (1961). *Suicide* (J. Spaulding and G. Simpson, trans.). Glencoe: The Free Press.

Dwyer, P. (1938). Some suggestions concerning the relationship existing between size of high school attended and success in college. *Journal of Educational Research,* 32, 271-281.

Edge, O. and S. Friedberg (1984). Factors affecting achievement in the first course in calculus. *Journal of Experimental Education,* 52, 136-40.

Elam, S. (1983). The Gallup education surveys: Impressions of a poll watcher. *Phi Delta Kappan,* 64, 26-32.

Fadale, L. and Others. (1977). *Post-secondary developmental studies programs for occupational students: An impact study.* ERIC Document Reproduction Service. No. ED152344.

Fenske, R. (1980). Historical foundations. In U. Hanson (ed.) *Student Services.* San Francisco: Jossey- Bass.

Fuess, C. (1950). *The college board: Its first fifty years.* Princeton: College Entrance Examination Board.

Gallup, A. and D. Clark (1987). The 19th annual poll of the public attitudes toward the public schools. *Phi Delta Kappan,* 17-30.

Garcia, S. and H. Seligsohn (1978). Undergraduate Black student retention revisited. *Educational Record,* 59, 156- 165.

Gosman, E. and Others, (1983). *Predicting student progression: The influence of race and other student and institutional characteristics on college student performance.* ERIC Document Reproduction Service. No. ED220058.

Groenke, G. (1979). *The relationship of entrance examination scores to grade-point average of Junior college freshmen when classified by age, sex and curriculum.* ERIC Document Reproduction Service. No. ED041242.

Hair, J., R. Anderson, R. Tatham and B. Geablowsky (1979). *Multivariate data analysis.* Tulsa, Oklahoma: Petroleum Publishing Co.

Halpin, G., G. Halpin and B. Schaer (1981). Relative effectiveness of the California Achievement tests in comparison with the ACT assessment, College Board Scholastic Achievement Test and high school grade-point average. *Educational and Psychological Measurement,* 41, 821-827.

Hashway, R. (1988). *Foundations of developmental education.* New York: Praeger.

Heise, D. (1975). *Causal Analysis.* New York: Wiley.

Huberty, C. (1988). Discriminant analysis. *Review of Educational Research,* 45, 543-598.

Huck, S., Cormier, W. & Bounds, W. (1974). *Reading statistics and research.* New York: Harper & Row.

Iffert, R. (1957). *Retention and withdrawal of college students.* U.S. Department of Health, Education and Welfare Bulletin. No. 1, Washington: U.S. Government Printing Office.

Irvine, D. (1966). Multiple prediction of college graduation from pre-admissions data. *The Journal of Experimental Education.* 35, 84-89.

Jefferson, T. and Cabell, J. (1856). *Early history of the University of Virginia as contained in the letters of Thomas Jefferson and Joseph Cabell.* Richmond: J. W. Randolph.

Johnson, N. and R. Mottley (1986). Predictors for academic retention for college freshman football players: An analysis offindings. *Educational and Psychological Research,* 6, 181- 190.

Kerlinger, E. (1973). *Foundations of behavioral research.* New York: Rinehart and Winston.

Kerlinger, E. and Pedhazur, E. (1973). *Multiple regression in behavioral research.* New York: Holt, Rhinehart and Winston, Inc.

Knoell, D. (1960). Institutional research on retention and withdrawal. In E. Sprauge (ed.) *Research on College Students.* Boulder: Western Interstate Commission for Higher Education. p.41-65.

Knoell, D. (1966). A critical review of research on the college drop-out. In L. Pervin, L. Reik and W. Dalrymple (eds). *The College drop-out and the Utilization of Talent.* Princeton: University Press.

Lach, I. (1971). *The predictive ability of entrance testing of a survey of socio-economic characteristics of Lakeland College.* ERIC Document Reproduction Service. No. ED058866.

Lavin, D. (1965). *The prediction of academic performance.* New York: Russell Sage Foundation.

Lenning, O. (1982). Variables-selection and measurement concerns. In E. Pascarella (ed.). *New directions for institutional research: Studying student attrition, no. 36.* San Francisco: Jossey-Bass.

Levine, A. (1980). *When dreams and heroes died: A portrait of today's college student.* San Francisco: Jossey-Bass.

Lucas, J. (1986). *Longitudinal study of performance of students entering Harper College, 1974-1984: Research report series volume XIV, No. 6,* ERIC Document Reproduction Service. No. ED264931.

McNeeley, J. (1939). College student mortality studies. *Journal of American association of college registrars.* 15, 119-124.

Miller, R. (1979). *The Assessment of College Performance.* San Francisco: Jossey Bass.

Monroe, C. (1977). *Profile of the community college.* San Francisco: Jossey-Bass.

Moore, R. (1986). Predicting performance of underprepared freshman with high school GPA, ACT scores, learning styles, psychological type and learning skills. *Dissertation Abstract International,* 47(2A), 406-407.

Morgan, A. and B. Mitchell (1985). The quest for excellence: Underlying policy issues. *Higher Education: Handbook of Theory and Research,* 1, 309-348.

Munday, L. (1965). Predicting college grades in predominantly negro colleges. *Journal of Educational Measurement,* 2, 157- 160.

Munro, B. (1981). drop-outs from higher education: Path analysis of a national sample. *American Educational Research Journal,* 18, 133-141.

Navarro, M. (1984). The quality education movement: New state standards and minority access to college. *Educational Standards, Testing and Access.* 15-23.

Nelson, A. (1966). College characteristics associated with freshman attrition. *Personnel and Guidance Journal.* 44, 1046- 1051.

Nettels, M. and Others. (1984). *Comparing and predicting the college performance of Black and White students.* ERIC Document no. ED245615.

Noel, L. (1985). *Improving student retention.* San Franscio: Jossey Bass.

Noel, L., R. Levitz, D. Saluri and Associates. (1986). *Increasing student retention.* San Francisco: Jossey-Bass.

O'Conner, C. and B. McAnulty (1981). The predictive ability of ACT scores for student success at an engineering school. *Measurement and Evaluation in Guidance*, 14, 54-60.

Panos, R. and A. Astin (1968). Attrition among college students. *American Educational Research Journal*, 5, 57-72.

Pantages, T. and C. Creedon (1978). Studies of college attrition: 1950-1975. *Review of Educational Research*, 48, 49- 101.

Pascarella, E. (1980). Student-faculty informal contact and college outcomes. *Review of Educational Research*, 50, 545-595.

Pascarella, E. (1985). College environmental influences on learning and cognitive development: A critical review and synthesis. *Higher Education: Handbook of Theory and Research*, 1, 1-61.

Pascarella, E. and D. Chapman (1983). Validation of a theoretical model of college withdrawal: Interaction effects in a multi-institutional sample. *Research in Higher Education*, 19, 25-48.

Pascarella, E. and P. Terenzini (1977). Voluntary freshman attrition and patterns of social and academic integration in a university: A test of a conceptual model. *Research in Higher Education*, 6, 25-43.

Pascarella, E. and P. Terenzini (1980). Predicting freshman persistence and voluntary drop-out decisions from a theoretical model. *Journal of Higher Education*, 51, 60-76.

Pascarella, E. and P. Terenzini (1983). Predicting voluntary freshman year persistence/withdrawal behavior in a residential univesity: A path analytic validation of Tinto's model. *Journal of Educational Psychology*, 75, 215-226.

Pedrini, B. and D. Pedrini (1986). Attrition/persistence: Stepwise multiple predictors for disadvantaged and control freshmen. *Journal of Instructional Psychology*, 13, 131-134.

Peng, S. and W. Fetters (1978). Variables involved in withdrawal during the first two years of college: Preliminary findings from the National Longitudinal Study of the High School Class of 1972. *American Educational Research Journal*, 15, 361-372.

Perry, F. (1981). Factors affecting academic performance and persistence among Mexican-American, Black and Anglo students. *College Student Journal*, 15, 53-62.

Price, F. and H. Suk (1976). The association of college performance with high school grades and college entrance test scores. *Educational and Psychological Measuremen*. 36, 965- 970.

Ramist, L. (1981). College student attrition and retention. *Findings*, 6, 1-4.

Renner, S. (1977). *College reading programs: What is success?* (ERIC Document Reproduction Service No. ED190178).

Reyes, A. (1979). *Academic success of San Jose city college students using selected student characteristics.* (ERIC Document Reproduction Service. No. ED165836).

Riesman, D. (1980). *On higher education: The academic enterprise in an era of rising student consumerism.* San Francisco: Jossey-Bass

Rounds, J. (1983). *Admissions, placement and competency: Assessment practices in California Community Colleges.* ERIC Document Reproduction Service.

Rounds, J. and D. Anderson (1985). Assessment for entrance to community college: Research studies of three major standardized tests. *Journal of Research and Development in Education*, 18, 54-58.

Rubin, D. (1977). Comparing high schools with respect to student performance in university. *Journal of Educational Statistics*, 2, 139-155.

Schade, H. (1977). *The ability of the ACT and MCPT to predict the college grade-point average.* ERIC Document Reproduction Service. No. ED188683.

Sexton, V. (1965). Factors contributing to attrition in college population: Twenty-five years of research. *Journal of General Psychology*, 72, 301-326.

Sharp, L. and L. Chason (1974). Use of moderator variables in predicting college student attrition. *Journal of College Student Personnel*, 19, 388-393.

Slocum, W. (1956). *Academic Mortality at the State College of Washington.* Pullman: State College of Washington.

Smith, A. (1980). A study of selected variables among student persisters and nonpersisters enrolled in the general and the community and technical colleges. *Dissertation Abstract International*, 41, 963A.

Spady, W. (1970). drop-outs from higher education: An interdisciplinary review and synthesis. *Interchange*, 1, 64- 85.

Stalnaker, J. and H. Remmers (1930). *What Kind of High Schools Contribute to College Failures.* Bulletin of Purdue University # 30, p. 5.

Summerskill, J. (1962). drop-outs from college. In N. Sanford (ed.). *The American college.* New York: Wiley, 627 - 657.

Terenzini, P. (1982). Designing attrition studies. In E. Pascarella (Ed.), *New directions for institutional research: Studying student attrition.* San Francisco: Jossey-Bass, 55- 71.

Thornberg, L. (1924). College scholarship and size of high school. *School and Society,* 20, 189-192.

Tinto, V. (1975). drop-out from higher education: A theoretical synthesis of recent research. *Review of Educational Research,* 45, 89-125.

Tinto, V. (1982). Defining drop-out: A matter of perspective. In E. Pascarella (ed). *New directions for institutional research: Studying student attrition, no.36.* San Francisco: Jossey-Bass, 3 - 16.

Tinto, V. (1985). Theories of student departure revisited. *Research in Higher Education,* 2, 359-384.

Tinto, V. (1987). *Leaving college: Reth)nking the causes and cures of student attrition.* Chicago: The University of Chicago Press.

Tom, A. (1982). *Non-traditional predictors of academic success for special action admissions.* ERIC Document # ED 256 268.

Tracey, T. and W. Sedlacek (1985). Noncognitive variables in predicting academic success by race. *Measurement and Evaluation in Guidance,* 16, 171-178.

Willingham, W. (1985). *Success in College.* New York: College Entrance Examination Board.

Wilson, H. (1978). *An investigation of intellectual and non- intellectual variables as predictors of academic success of high risk college freshman at Southern Illinois University at Carbondale.* (Masters Thesis) (ERIC Document Reproduction Service. No. ED171195).

Wilson, K. (1981). Analyzing the long-term performance of minority and nonminority students: A tale of two studies. *Research in Higher Education,* 15, 351-75.

Wing and Wallach (1971). *College Admission and the Psychology of Talent.* New York: Holt, Rhinehart and Winston.

Wolfle, J. (1980). *The tests of General Educational Development in differential prediction of two-year college academic performance.* ERIC Document #ED185491.

Yess, J. (1979). *Predicting the academic success of community college students in specific programs of study.* (Doctoral Dissertation) ERIC Document Reproduction Service #ED172900.

15

The Developmental Educator's System of Values

Andolyn V. Brown

As we wake to the beginning of a new day, it becomes evident that various life situations will be encountered. Those situations can necessitate actions that range from offering opinions to making decisions. Whatever the case, beliefs, attitudes and values are sure to be apparent in the action(s) taken. If this is the case, how, then, do we define these terms and how do they relate to developmental education?

Webster defines these terms as follows:

1. **Belief**: a state or habit of mind in which trust or confidence is placed on some person or thing; conviction of the truth of some statement or the reality of some being.

2. **Attitude**: a feeling or emotion toward a fact or a state.

3. **Value**: to consider or rate highly; relative worth, utility or importance.

Just as people and professionals in general arrive at conclusions and make decisions on the basis of beliefs, attitudes and values (Simon, 1972), so do developmental educators. That unique group of professionals must put forth a concerted daily effort to devise the best means and methods possible to work effectively with the non-traditional learner. More importantly, they must not only recognize the necessity of understanding the nature and needs of this type of learner, but also the learning style of each. That knowledge, in turn, requires the utilization of pertinent instructional styles. However, acquiring that knowledge and properly employing the correct methods can only be effective when the developmental educator comes to terms with his/her system of values. (e.g., whether or not he/she believes that this type of learner *should* be served; an attitude about a particular learner). Such feelings - negative or positive - are exemplified by the actions, teaching and counseling of the developmental educator.

Raths (1966) suggested seven sub-processes of valuing:

● **Prizing one's beliefs and behaviors:**

  1. prizing and cherishing; and,

  2. publicly affirming, when appropriate.

● **Choosing one's beliefs and behaviors:**

  3. choosing one's beliefs and behaviors;

  4. choosing after consideration of consequences; and,

  5. choosing freely.

● **Acting on one's beliefs:**

  6. acting; and,

  7. acting with a pattern, consistency and repetition.

It is thereby the intent, for the developmental educator to be taught ways in which the processes can be used to claify his/her beliefs, attitudes and values about both the person (non-traditional learner) and the instruction of this type of learner.

In a summary of Chickering's (1969) vectors of development, Miller and Prince (1976) suggest methods for incorporating the values/qualities of the environment with the behaviors of those who consitute the environment. This proposed model can be adapted to that which is required of the developmental educator and effective assistance and instruction given to the non-traditional learner:

1. **Valuing:**

   a. **Achieving Competence**: the developmental educator must learn to develop a coping mechanism that will allow patience while working with the non-traditional learner, in an effort to achieve proposed outcome(s).

   b. **Managing Emotions**: the developmental educator must constantly be in control of personal feelings so as not to portray negativism or lack of trust in the non-traditional learner.

    c. **Becoming Autonomous**: the developmental educator must strive to serve as a role model to the non-traditional learner by encouraging the student to feel comfortable seeking assistance and advice, but at the same time, not becoming dependent upon the educator. The developmental educator must also strive to keep the 'dependency' attitude out of his/her mind.

    d. **Establishing Identity**: the developmental educator must have an inner sense of "sameness and continuity" when working with the non-traditional learner. This means that roles and behaviors should be appropriate.

    e. **Freeing Interpersonal Relationships**: the developmental educator must exude more friendliness and warmth toward the non-tradtional learner and show a degree of tolerance.

    f. **Clarifying Purposes**: the developmental educator must believe in the necessity of having purpose.

    g. **Developing Integrity**: the developmental educator must show the non-traditional learner that he/she can be trusted and is true to his/her word.

2. **Goal Setting**: the developmental educator must set realistic goals that can be achieved by the non-traditional learner. The institutional climate contributes to goals that are set, in general, about the total program.

3. **Programming**: those goals and objectives set by the developmental educator and the institution determine various programs and activities needed by the non-traditional learner.

4. **Fitting**: the developmental educator has to recognize individual needs of each nontraditional learner and prescribe learning on that basis.

5. **Mapping**: the developmental educator must utilize institutional programming as he/she develops learning activities for the non-traditional learner.

6. **Observing**: the developmental educator must constantly monitor each non-traditional learner and develop the proper instructional style(s) as needed.

7. **Feedback**: the developmental educator must be sure to provide each non-traditional learner with information about achievement, necessary improvement or other data describing what needs to be done in order that learning occurs.

What does this mean? It means that once the developmental educator comes to terms with these vectors of development, how these vectors relate to their own system of values with respect to teaching the non-traditional learner and how it is necessary to ensure that the mission and philosophy of the program - eminent, optimal student growth and development - can be realized. More important, however, is the fact that mastery of these activities allows the educators to operate in a more effective and non-partial manner by learning to manage his/her values.

Barr and Upcraft (1988) indicate that one must learn to manage situations, events and circumstances that are in the best interest of the students, staff and institution. Thus, we can say that the same holds true for the developmental educator. S/he has to resolve the conflict between his/her system of values as they relate to working with the non-traditional learner and the implementation of the programmatic thrusts. These authors indicate further that personal values that are to be managed in such situations are:

Honesty the developmental educator should be truthful at all times to the learner.

Genuineness the developmental educator should deal with the learner in a non-prejudiced manner.

Integrity the developmental educator must exemplify a relationship between "beliefs and actions."

Predictability the developmental educator must show the relationship between being fair, honest and full of integrity.

Courage the developmental educator must show the learner that he/she can not only make a decision but also stick to it.

Confidentiality the developmental educator must show the learner that information given is held in the strictest confidence and cannot be breached.

SUMMARY

Values are those goods, events and activities that are of extreme importance to us all. What becomes necessary, however, is the day-to-day means by which we can arrive at conclusions or make impartial decisions on our jobs and in our everyday lives.

Developmental educators must also come to grips with their values and develop ways to alleviate the threat of allowing those values to interfere with their working effectively with the non-traditional learner. In order for this to occur, developmental educators must achieve competence; manage emotions; become autonomous; establish identity to the extent possible; be free with interpersonal relationships; clarify purposes; develop integrity; set goals; do programming; fitting, mapping, observing and feedback when it comes to working with the non-traditional learner.

REFERENCES

Barr, M. J. and M. L. Upcraft (1988). *Managing student affairs effectively.* San Francisco: Jossey-Bass.

Bellanca, J. A. (1975). *Values and the search for self.* Washington, D.C.: National Education Assoication.

Bullmer, K. (1975). *The art of emphathy.* New York: Human Sciences Press.

Chickering, A. W. (1969). *Education and identity.* San Francisco: Jossey-Bass.

House, M. L. (1973). *Human relation activities - A handbook in group dynamics.* Tula, Oklahoma: Department of Human Relations, Tulsa Public Schools.

Johnson, D. W. and P. Frank (1976). *Joining together.* New Jersey: Prentice-Hall.

Kvaraceus, W. C., J. S. Gibson, F. K. Patterson, B. Seasholes and J. D. Grambs (1965). *Negro Self-Concept: Implications for school and citizenship.* New York: McGraw-Hill.

Miller, T. K. and J. S. Prince (1976). *The future of student affairs: A guide to student development for tomorrow's higher education.* San Francisco: Jossey-Bass.

Raths, L., M. Harmin and S. Simon (1966). *Values and teaching.* Ohio: Charles E. Merrill.

Scheibe, K. E. (1970). *Beliefs and values.* New York: Holt, Rinehart and Winston, Inc.

Silver, M. (1976). *Values education.* Washington, D.C.: National Education Association.

Simon, S. B. (1972). *Values clarification.* New York: Hart Publishing Company, Inc.

16

Research in Developmental Education

Kimberly Kinsler and Andrew Robinson

Each year in the United States, developmental education programs enroll large numbers of students who seek to access this society's professional careers and life styles. As these students progressively reflect educational and cultural backgrounds different from those assumed in traditional adult learners, program personnel and support systems increasingly are faced with obstacles to the satisfactory completion of their training and education. In this challenging yet problematic evolution, developmental education is emerging as an important arena for the study of the interaction between culture, cognition and instruction. Accompanying this process is a growing need to link inquiry critical in the field to appropriate research and evaluative methods. More and more, developmental educators need to consider theoretical as well as practical questions, to explore process as well as product issues and to conduct formative as well as summative and monitoring evaluations. To advance developmental education to a disciplinary level and to provide knowledge-based programmatic service, educators in the field need to anchor decisions, instructional methods and support services in research and evaluative findings.

As a result, developmental educators need to acquire formal research and evaluation techniques as essential tools in their problem-solving and decision making processes. Through their use, these educators can obtain answers and information that are objective, valid and transferrable to others in the field. This chapter seeks to assist in this process by acquainting developmental educators with the basic principles and procedures for conducting research and evaluation to warn against some common pitfalls in executing research and to offer ways in which research and evaluation may serve as a productive and integral part of developmental education programs. Discussion of these topics is divided into the following sections: general features of research and evaluation, types of research, conducting research, practical and ethical considerations associated with research and evaluation of developmental populations and suggestions for future areas of pursuit.

RESEARCH AND EVALUATION: GOALS AND GENERAL PRINCIPLES

Educational research is defined as the application of the scientific method to the investigation of problems related to education (Sowell and Casey, 1982). It is the use of a sequential set of procedures designed to achieve greater objectivity in the problem-solving process. Although discussed in more detail later in the chapter the steps in the scientific method include observing and defining the problem, devising possible solutions or hypotheses, experimenting to test these hypotheses; and drawing conclusions. Evaluation is a form of research. Early definitions of evaluation emphasized a highly applied and product-oriented approach. For example, Tyler (1942) defined evaluation as the process of determining whether the objectives of a program had been achieved. Since then other definitions have appeared, many of which stress more rigorous, research-oriented interpretations. Characteristic of this later approach, Berk (1981) defined evaluation as the "process of applying scientific procedures to collect reliable and valid information to make decisions about educational programs" (p.4). This definition illustrates not only the growing contiguity between formal research (paradigms) and evaluation, but the increasing importance of basic research concepts and techniques in the field of evaluation. Consistent with this tradition, research and evaluation are here discussed not as separate entities but, rather, research - being the larger and more rigorous domain - constitutes this chapter's primary focus, and, where appropriate, references and examples specific to evaluation are offered.

Research has three general goals: the explanation, prediction and/or control of phenomenological relationships. Each process requires procedures more rigorous than those constituting the preceding one. Explanation seeks to assess the factors associated with some phenomenon or problem situation by observing events of interest in their natural setting, reviewing the relevant literature and/or conducting informal research. From this information, it may be found that two or more factors tend to occur together; suggesting their association. Moreover, other factors, which may be related to the problem may also be revealed. With this information in hand, researchers and evaluators attempt to explain (i.e., describe the situation in more detail). For example, Pearce (1966) conducted a study to determine those characteristics that students, teachers and administrators considered essential in a developmental instructor. Data was gathered by use of written surveys and oral interviews. Subjects described positive and negative characteristics of existing teachers and described a hypothetical person with the most desirable traits. Data analyses produced a personality profile which allowed Pearce to explicitly describe and explain desired characteristics. This profile was later used to develop a personnel interview schedule to screen future applicants.

From explanatory data, the researcher may seek to better understand the meaning of a phenomenological relationship by predicting how a set of two or more factors, or variables, are related. A variable is any characteristic of a person or the environment that can change under different conditions or differ from one person to the next (Woolfolk, 1987). Change may be quantitative (e.g., test scores, grades, the number of hours per semester a student visits a counselor, etc.) or qualitative (e.g., gender, ethnicity, the instructional methodology to which students are exposed, etc.). To more rigorously assess the existence and the nature of an association between two variables, researchers measure the change in one variable when there is a change in the other. They must, therefore, devise ways to systematically measure variable changes and/or to compare their different levels. By statistically analyzing the degree of correspondence between the states of the two variables, i.e., the magnitude of their association and its direction, researchers can offer predictions about the state of one variable based on the state of another.

Control implies causality (i.e., that change or alteration in one variable brings about a change in another variable). To assess control, researchers directly manipulate the values or states of one variable and then look at the resultant state of the second variable. The variable directly manipulated by the researcher is called the independent variable (IV) and the variable which is expected to change in response to change in the first variable is called the dependent variable (DV). If the amount of change, or variance, produced in the dependent variable by of the manipulation of the independent variable is of a magnitude such that it is highly unlikely to be a chance occurrence, the relationship between the two is said to be "significant" and the independent variable is asserted to control, or to determine, change in the dependent variable. If such evidence is lacking, no causal relationship may be assumed. For example, Hopper and Keller (1966) studied the effects of class size (IV) on learning basic essay writing skills (DV) at a junior college. Each of three instructors wAS assigned a section of 56 students and a section of 26 students. Coursework for all sections was identical. Analysis of pre and post course writing samples indicated that students in both large and small class sections improved over the instructional semester. When analyses were conducted to determine differences between small and large class sections in the degree of student improvement, no significant differences were found. Thus, contrary to general expectations, small class size did not produce significant improvement in students' post test scores above that obtained in larger classes. It was concluded that given the same quality of instructors, program and student involvement, class size up to 56 did not seem to be a major variable in the learning of writing skills.

While the purpose of research and evaluation is to solve problems and provide answers to questions, of major concern is the generalizability of the answers obtained. The concept of generalizability refers to the degree to which information obtained in one situation may be applied to individuals in a similar situation. Thus, if a teacher of developmental mathematics conducts research using two of her classes and a program administrator commissions an evaluation of innovations initiated in his/her program, to what extent can others in the field rely on and use these results? Ideally, researchers and evaluators would like their findings to not only address their own concerns, but to assist others in resolving similar issues. Techniques have been developed to facilitate the generalizability of research results beyond the immediate individuals used in a particular study. This is done primarily through the processes of randomization and variance control.

Randomization. The process of randomization involves both the selection of subjects for participation in a study and their assignment to various treatment conditions. The total (and immediate) pool of individuals to which we would like to generalize the research findings is called the research population. As all of these individuals usually cannot be included in any one study - unless the population is small and readily accessible - only some of them are selected for actual participation. This group is called the subject sample, or subjects. To ensure that the findings obtained from this smaller, more manageable group of individuals is representative of the larger population, their selection from the total population pool must be random. That is, everyone in the population must have an equal opportunity to be chosen for participation. This may be done in several ways. One such procedure involves placing all the names of possible participants into a container and blindly selecting those who will be subjects.

Once the sample is chosen, they are randomly assigned to the treatment conditions, (i.e., to the different states of the independent variable). The same process employed in sample selection or a different one may be used to determine who will receive a particular research experience. Whatever method is chosen, everyone must have an equal opportunity to be assigned to a particular condition.

To illustrate, a remedial program was evaluated to determine whether a seven-week intensive program combining personal and vocational counseling with reading, English and mathematics instruction would facilitate high school underachievers' transition into a two year college program and improve their rates of academic achievement. From the college's total population of entering freshmen in need of academic remediation, 40 subjects were randomly selected (with qualification) for program participation. They were, then, randomly assigned to two treatment groups of 20 students each: the seven-week program with counseling experiences and the seven-week program without counseling. Comparisons of subjects pre and post program data found significant improvement for both groups on intelligence, reading and scholastic aptitude tests from pre to post testing. However, no differences were found between counseled and uncounseled groups on either pre or post test measures (Shea, 1966).

There are several variations on simple random sampling and assignment. Only three variations are discussed below due to their frequency of occurrence in educational research: stratified random sampling, cluster sampling and convenience sampling. Stratified random sampling is used when the researcher wishes to be certain that the sample is evenly balanced or represented by particular groups relevant to the study. Toward this end, the population is first divided into strata, or groups, on some basis (e.g., ethnicity, grade level, sex, etc.) before the sample is picked. Equal or proportionate numbers of subjects are then randomly selected from each group. Cluster sampling is used when the sampling unit is not the individual, but rather a group of people, such as the class, school, program or district. From the total pool of groups, sample groups are drawn by random selection. Subsequently, all relevant individuals comprising the selected groups become subjects in the study. An example of an explanatory survey using a combined stratified cluster design is reported by Roueche and Boggs (1968). This national survey assessed the degree to which junior colleges supported and engaged in institutional research. Of the 837 institutions listed in the *Junior College Directory* (Harper, 1967), ten percent were selected for participation after first dividing them into strata on the basis of control (private or public) and size. Six groups were formed: public institutions with enrollment under 2,000; private institutions with enrollment under 2,000; public institutions with enrollment between 2,001 and 6,000; etc.. A proportionate number of schools from each group were randomly selected. The needed information was then obtained from college presidents, deans and research coordinators by means of structured interviews together with free response questionnaires.

Convenience sampling is used when samples are chosen with no randomization but rather are selected on the basis of their availability. For example, intact classes taught by interested colleagues may be used. While convenience sampling is handy and may be the only subjects accessible to the researcher, when it is used, the results cannot accurately be generalized to the larger population.

Variance and Variance Control

Equally important to the rigor and objectivity of research is the concept of variance. We previously described variance as change. In conducting experimental research and research-like evaluation, there are two basic forms of variance: systematic variance (i.e., change produced in the dependent variable by the manipulation of the independent variable and error variance (i.e., change in the dependent variable produced by chance). To assert that the independent variable) controls, or brings about, change in the dependent variable, we must be able to state that the change obtained in the dependent variable is of such a magnitude that it cannot be explained by error variance alone and, therefore, is due to systematic variance. To do this, the study must be designed to assess the amount of error variance present under conditions that differ only in regards to the experimental treatment (i.e., that the conditions are exactly alike save for the variable(s) in question).

The most common way to assess error variance is through the use a control group. This group is made up of individuals selected from the population pool in the same (random) manner as those selected for participation in the study. These subjects should in all ways be similar to the experimental subjects with one major exception - control group subjects do not receive the experimental treatment. All pre and post treatment data for experimental subjects should also be collected for control subjects. As variance in the scores of control subjects should only be affected by random or non-experimental conditions, their post-experiment data constitutes an index of error variance and the basis for determining if the treatment condition produces a significant amount of systematic variance. Ideally, there should be no difference between experimental and control groups on pre-treatment measures and significant between-group differences on post-treatment scores.

In a study conducted by the first author to assess the effects of supportive peer collaboration in the revision phase of essay writing for college students in remediation, one teacher taught two sections of the same course using identical curriculum materials and class assignments. One section participated in the peer collaboration condition (treatment) and the other did not (control). Students' post-test essays were rated on five criteria: unity, organization, use of examples, grammar and language - only the first three of which were part of the treatment process. Statistical analyses indicated no (significant) difference between experimental and control subjects in their use of language and grammar; however, significant between-group differences were found in students' use of examples and in the organization and unity of their essays. The study concluded that the treatment condition significantly improved the experimental subjects' essay writing in these areas (Kinsler, 1989).

TYPES OF RESEARCH

There are two broad approaches to answering research questions, the first allows us description and knowledge of associations, the second allows us to assert causality. These two approaches are respectively called correlational and experimental research.

Correlational Research

Correlational studies seek to discover the nature of the association between variables by describing how closely and in what direction they are related. Correlational statistics are used to analyze the data, the results of which are expressed as a number which may range from 1.00 to -1.00. The more closely the statistic approaches 1.00 or -1.00, the stronger is the relationship. A correlation of (+ or -) 1.00 implies a perfect one to one correspondence, i.e., a change in the status of one variable leads to a direct and proportionate change in the status of the other variable, while a correlation of .00 implies no relationship between the variables. A positive correlation indicates that two variables both increase or both decrease together. A negative correlation means that when one variable increases the other decreases. For example, Fitch (1966) examined the effects of outside employment on college students' grades. Incoming freshmen were grouped according to the amount of time devoted to wage earning jobs using the following categories: none; 1-10 hours; 11-20 hours; 21-30 hours; and more than 30 hours. Correlational statistics found a negative correlation between students' grade point averages (GPAs of "C" or poorer) and hours of employment over 10 hours per week. That is, there were low correlations between the amount of time worked and GPA for students working less that 10 hours per week. However, as the number of hours worked per week increased above 10, students' GPAs proportionately decreased.

Experimental Research

When researchers are interested in finding out what factors actually will cause a desired change in behavior, a "true" experimental design is needed. Powerful assertions follow from this research and, therefore, design criteria must be more rigorous. To conduct "true" experimental research an independent variable must be manipulated (to see if there is a corresponding change in the dependent variable) subjects must be both randomly selected and assigned to the treatment conditions and a group that serves as control must be used. An analogous model for program evaluation is the randomized field trial. Accordingly, the evaluator must randomly assign individuals to programs and be certain that the programs maintain their integrity.

Quasi-experimental Research

When all the conditions for a true experiment cannot be met, quasi-experimental research may be conducted. Consistent with this design, the independent variable is manipulated, comparison groups are available and treatment conditions are randomly assigned. The difference between "true" and quasi experimental research is that the assignment of subjects to groups is not random (i.e., intact groups are used - although which group(s) will receive the treatment and which will serve as the control are randomly determined). Due to these limitations, quasi-experimental designs do not control variance as well as true experiments. Their control comes from manipulation of the independent variable, the use of comparison groups and random assignment of treatment groups. If any one of these conditions is missing, researchers have a design with even less control (Sowell and Casey, 1982).

Quasi-experimental research is frequently used in educational settings, as research comparing whole classes, whole programs and whole schools is typical and individual students often cannot be randomly assigned to classes or to conditions. In these instances, measures still must be taken to ensure the comparability of the groups. The previously reported Kinsler (1989) study is a example of quasi-experimental research. While intact classes were used; students pre-course essay writing examination scores were similar and the determination of treatment and control conditions was random.

Multiple Baseline Design

An important variation on quasi-experimental research is the multiple baseline design. This design involves the successive application of the treatment condition to one or more children thought to be similar in some way. Prior to the introduction of treatment, the experimenter first gathers baseline data on the dependent variable. The treatment is then introduced for a period of time, withdrawn and subsequently reimposed. Throughout these manipulations, subjects are continuously monitored on the outcome variable. A treatment effect is inferred if behavior changes occur only upon the application of the experimental condition. The primary advantage of this design is that it does not require large numbers of subjects nor that a control group be excluded from the treatment. The individual or the group's baseline information constitutes the comparison, or control data. This method is often used with a subject sample of one. Under these circumstances, it is called a single subject multiple-baseline design.

For research on and evaluation of social service techniques and individualized instruction, multiple baseline designs may prove particularly promising (Bryk and Light, 1981). For while these procedures are individualized and cannot be defined a priori, their activities are not idiosyncratic. Rather, for any given individual, the actual sequence of experiences and activities emerge over time and are the result of an interaction between the program's philosophy and the individual child. That is, teachers, counselors and other program personnel operate within a general theoretical or conceptual framework which guides program goals and objectives. In such cases, the traditional search for significant (mean) differences between groups is often futile. With a detailed assessment of the needs of the individual child and an account of the program's philosophy and goals, multiple baseline designs may be used to assess change in individual performance consistent with program objectives.

Non-equivalent Control Group Design

A second variation on quasi-experimental research is the non-equivalent control group design. It is used when the researcher does not have control over the assignment of subjects to programs, classes or conditions. This model may be applicable when, for example, there is a need to assess the impact of program or instructional innovations, but all students are currently receiving the treatment. Under these conditions, a comparable group of subjects must be found to serve as a control. While possible control data may be obtained from students in the program the year prior to the treatment's introduction, this group may not be similar. That is, students who sign up for a program or a set of courses one year may be different from those who sign up the following year. If data exists to determine the comparability of these groups (e.g., pre-program test scores) it should be used. When no such data exists, a non-equivalent control must be assumed. The weakness of this design is obviously in its lack of control and in the constraints imposed upon the researcher's ability to draw inferences and to generalize to other populations. Its strength lies in students' ability to make natural choices, as they do in real life. The researcher must then try to isolate the program effects as cleanly as possible (Kerlinger, 1973).

Ex Post Facto Designs

Ex post facto means after the fact. These designs are used in studies where the researcher seeks to assess the effect of one variable on another but is unable to impose the treatment condition on subjects (e.g., divorce, orphaned, etc.). Under these circumstances, the researcher must locate people who have already experienced the independent variable and then study its possible effects in terms of the dependent variables. Since there is no manipulated variable, there can be no random assignment of subjects and treatments to groups. As a consequence, variance cannot be as well controlled in ex-post-facto studies as it is in experimental studies. Using a control group is the only way to control variance in this design. Because of these characteristics, ex-post-facto designs are used when explanation or prediction is the goal (Kerlinger, 1973).

CONDUCTING RESEARCH

In actually conducting research, experimenters use the scientific method, which is the systematic, controlled and empirical investigation of hypothetical propositions about the presumed relations among natural phenomena (Kerlinger, 1973). As previously noted, this procedure involves four general steps. Each of these steps is briefly described and illustrated below. The Shea (1966) study constitutes the basis for these illustrations. Where direct data from the Shea study is unavailable, conjectures are ventured but are always indicated as such.

The Observation of Phenomena

The researcher first observes some phenomena in the environment which presents obstacles or problems needy of further study for solution. For example, a hypothetical researcher may observe that academically underachieving high school students do very poorly their first year in college, even when their courses are largely remedial.

Development of a Hypothesis

The researcher develops one or more possible hypotheses concerning the causes of or possible solutions to the problem. Hypotheses may be the result of deductions from theoretical explanations or hunches concerning the behavioral phenomenon under study. Hypotheses should be formulated as conjectural statements which express a relationship between two or more variables and convey a clear implication for testing. These statements are often phrased in the negative (or null), that is, as if no relationship exists. For example, the hypothetical researcher may feel that an intensive seven-week summer program of reading, English and mathematics instruction combined with personal and vocational counseling will facilitate underachieving high school students' transition into college and improve their academic achievement once in college. S/he, thus, formulates the following hypotheses: a) a seven-week summer program of intensive academic instruction will produce no significant effect on underachieving pre-freshmen's academic performance; and b) a seven-week summer experience of intensive personal and vocational counseling will produce no significant effect on underachieving pre-freshmen's academic performance.

The researcher must also determine how the variables in the hypotheses will be defined and assessed in the study. That is, to ensure that the researcher clearly delineates his/her variable(s) and to inform other researchers of their exact meaning in the context of the study, each variable is operationally defined by stating precisely how it is being interpreted and measured. Operational definitions are very important, for researchers may have radically different ideas about the same concept. By stating what interpretation of the concept is being used, as well as how the concept is being assessed, operational definitions facilitate both precise observation and meaningful communication about what is being observed.

In our current example, the independent variables are the intensive seven-week instructional program and personal and vocati/nal counseling. In operationalizing these variables, the researcher must explicitly describe the key characteristics of both program components. The dependent variable of academic achievement was operationalized by Shea as students' pre and post program scores on a battery of aptitude tests: the Iowa Test of Educational Development; the Lorge-Thorndike Test of Intelligence; the Sequential Test of Educational Progress; the Davis Reading Test; and the Scholastic Aptitude Test. Descriptions of these tests are found in the literature and the researcher should refer the reader to these sources.

Experimentation

The researcher then conducts experimentation to test the hypotheses. This is a multiphase process involving the selection of a research design and measurement instruments, the introduction of the experimental treatment, the collection of data and its analysis. Each of the steps is briefly discussed below.

Choice of a Research Design

Decisions concerning the choice of research approach and design largely depend upon the circumstances particular to the study. The researcher must first determine whether assertions related to association or causality are being sought. Association implies the use of correlational research, while causality implies the use of an experimental model. If experimental research is called for, the particular design used may be largely dependent upon the experimenter's ability to control randomization and variance. An effort should always be made to approximate as closely as possible a true experiment. In evaluation, the objectives, needs and questions posed by the hiring agent may dictate the research approach. If detailed explanations and predictions provide valid and reliable responses to the questions, then models appropriate to these objectives should be chosen.

In our current example, the seven-week instructional and counseling programs were intended to increase students' academic performance; hence, the determination of a causal relationship was sought and experimental research was required. What is more, Shea had access to the entire population of underachieving pre-freshmen applying to that institution. It was theoretically possible to randomly select experimental and control subjects from this pool, as well as to randomly assign them to treatment conditions - and, thus, to achieve a "true" experimental design. However, in the actual Shea study a quasi experimental design was used. Potential students were asked to volunteer for the summer program, from which pool 40 subjects were randomly selected. In research, the use of volunteers qualifies the random selection process, for while everyone has an opportunity to volunteer, individual differences and outside circumstances may non randomly influence who will volunteer. Moreover, in a true experimental design, to assess the effects of the academic treatment, counseling and error variance, the following subject groups were needed: 1) academic treatment with counseling; 2) academic treatment without counseling; 3) no academic treatment, counseling alone; and 4) no academic treatment, no counseling. Only conditions one and two were used in the Shea study. While condition three is needed to assess the effects of counseling alone, its omission is not grave. The effects of counseling (in combination with instruction) may be inferred from comparisons of groups one and two. However, the omission of condition four, which constitutes the true control group, is a major shortcoming of the Shea study. Without it there is no basis for assessing error variance.

Instrumentation

This phase involves determining the tools that will be used to measure the status of the variables in the subject samples. Ideally, the researcher should systematically search a variety of resources in order to identify potentially useful tests from which a final selection can be made. The major concern in this process is that the instruments be appropriate to the particular research problem and subject population. Researchers may select commercially published instruments or they may construct instruments of their own. Instruments may include tests, scales, inventories, surveys, observational reports, interviews and apparatuses or materials which subjects are to manipulate. See Cole and Nitko (1981) for an in depth discussion of the instrument selection process.

Regardless of the type or particular instrument chosen, they must be both valid and reliable. The consistency or dependability of data obtained from an instrument is referred to as reliability. Researchers want instruments whose measures are stable over time (Sowell and Casey, 1982). Validity refers to the truthfulness of the results obtained by the instrument, i.e., does the instrument measure what it asserts to measure. There are two forms of validity: construct validity and content validity. Construct validity assesses whether an instrument measures the concept it claims to measure - as defined by the literature; content validity assesses how well the instrument measures the variable specific to the research problem, i.e., the representativeness of the results. When researchers construct instruments particular to the needs and objectives of a study, tests must be conducted to determine their validity and reliability. When published instruments are used, reliability and validi4y data are supplied by the test makers. The Shea study utilized a battery of published tests and scales.

Once the instruments are chosen and subjects selected and assigned to the various groups, pre-treatment assessment(s) may be taken. The experimental condition(s) are then introduced and upon their completion, post-treatment assessment(s) are conducted.

Data Analysis

Mathematical procedures, or statistical tests, are then applied to the "raw" data to assess the association between variables (if it is a correlational study) or the magnitude of the treatment's effects (if it is an experimental study). Many different kinds of statistical tests may be used, depending upon the type of data obtained, the nature of the study (correlation versus experimental), the manner in which the subjects were sampled and other more elaborate criteria. For more information on statistical analyses in educational research see Weiner (1962).

Researchers then scrutinize the results of their analyses to assess the strength of their findings. For correlational studies, correlations over .7 are considered strong associations. For experimental studies, researchers look at the probability that the results obtained could have been obtained by chance. Researchers accept findings as significant when the probability of their being obtained by chance is between (or exceeds) .05 and .01. That is, that there is a likelihood of, respectively, 1 in 500 or 1 in 1000 that the results were caused by random occurrence.

In the present example, a series of t-tests, or pair-wise comparisons were conducted for the subjects who had received instruction alone versus those who had received instruction plus counseling on the different achievement tests. The comparisons revealed that both groups of students significantly improved from pre to post-treatment on the Lorge-Thorndike Test of Intelligence, the Davis Reading Test and the Scholastic Aptitude Test. No significant improvement was found from pre to post-testing on the Iowa Test of Development and the Sequential Test of Educational Progress. More importantly, results of an analysis of variance (ANOVA) found no difference between the counseled and non counseled groups on post-test measures.

Interpretations and Conclusions

The researcher then interprets the results of the statistical analyses in light of the research problem, concept variables and/or the program objectives. Typically, the researcher tells whether the hypothesis was or was not supported and evaluators state whether program objectives were or were not met. In either case, possible explanations for the results are offered. The researcher may explain the findings from the perspective of the particular study's design components or from the perspective of the literature. From the former perspective, the researcher may discuss how various aspects of the particular subject sample, the ways in which the treatment was administered or the data collected, influenced research outcomes. From the perspective of the literature, the researcher may explain the results by referring to other research in which similar or contradictory findings were obtained or in terms of theories that relate to the findings. The researcher would then draw conclusions and make recommendations. The program evaluator may explain findings in terms of program components, subject characteristics, or outside factors impacting upon the program and the participants. Explanations in terms of program components may include discussion of (unrealistic) philosophy and goals, program structure and organization, staffing and human resources. Subject factors may include consideration of their age, expectations and previous experiences. Outside variables may include factors which impacted upon the program (e.g. inability to purchase required materials in a timely manner) and/or the subjects (e.g., their home distance from the program, necessitating car-fare which was unavailable). As with formal research, conclusions are drawn and recommendations made.

VALIDITY AND BIAS IN DEVELOPMENTAL RESEARCH

Unless the research is carefully structured, factors which the researcher did not think of or plan for may influence the outcome. These non random "extraneous" factors may intervene in the process being studied and affect the results, skewing how the problem is conceived, the instruments chosen and the results interpreted. Under these conditions, research findings may be rendered invalid (i.e., unrepresentative of the actual phenomenological state), or biased (i.e., unrepresentative by virtue of a subjective inclination toward or against a particular position, group, or concept). Some of these factors are considered below in the context of developmental education. This list is not intended to be exhaustive, but rather to serve as a source from which to begin more detailed consideration of these factors.

Concepts and Variables

To begin study on a concept variable, the researcher must first develop a reasonable understanding of factors influencing that concept. Initially, the researcher should gather information from reviewing the literature. Articles which present the topic from multiple perspectives should be perused to obtain a broad consensus of the factors impacting upon the variable. For the nature and degree of this understanding will directly determine how the concept variable will be interpreted and the research designed. For example, student attrition in developmental programs is an issue of major concern and an area of current study. While typically defined as the rate at which students leave an instructional setting, attrition is a much more complex phenomenon. Students may leave an educational institution or program to enter to another; leave due to immediate, yet temporary, outside conditions and subsequently return; or leave not to return to an educational setting. Each group is different. The first group, while contributing to a college or program's attrition rate, should not be considered drop outs in the traditional sense; those in the second group are best considered as temporary drop outs, while only those in the last category warrant the label as it is commonly used. The definition chosen by the researcher will impose differing constraints upon the population and the design of the study. Hence, a clear knowledge of the limitations and parameters of any concept variable will facilitate its more exact characterization in the research and improve the representativeness of the results. This should not be taken to mean, however, that unless one advanced knowledge of a concept, research cannot be conducted. Research will often reveal the limitations of many concepts and offer qualifying factors not previously considered.

Context Free and Context Specific Concepts

Educational researchers often attempt to explain concepts in a manner that is independent from the particular situation in which it is being studied. Concepts or characteristics such as achievement motivation, intelligence and creativity are commonly asserted to be general qualities of an individual or group of individuals that are applied to differing material contents and across situational contexts. They are, therefore, treated as "context free" traits or characteristics. Increasingly, however, researchers are coming to realize that there are few characteristics that are context free. Rather, competence is acquired within and tied to specific tasks and interpersonal situations and is, consequently, context specific. Thus, behaviors indicative of a particular concept, when observed or measured in one situation, may not reflect individual concept competence under another set of circumstances. For example, Hare (1977) suggests that achievement motivation differs in the contexts of home, school and community. Individuals who may not seem highly motivated in the context of school may be highly motivated to excel in community related activities, such as sports. Other research indicates that children who fail certain categories of items on IQ tests (e.g., memory and item classification), may be able to demonstrate these same mental procedures in non-laboratory and non-school settings (Rogoff, 1981; Cole, 1975). Thus, when attempting to assess concept variables, it is important to ask what are the contextually imposed constraints that govern access to knowledge within a domain and regulate the deployment of these activities (Miller-Jones, 1989).

Similarly, a subject's demonstration of desired behavior may be heavily dependent upon his/her perception of the task in a social context. A number of studies have demonstrated how decrements in performance on IQ tests as well as on verbal and reasoning tasks may result from negative perceptions on the part of the subject regarding the interpersonal interaction between the tester (researcher) and the subject - rather than specific competence (Labov, 1970; Miller-Jones, 1989; Kinsler and Robinson, Chapter 3 of this volume). Consequently, if the subject perceives the assessment situation as hostile or threatening, s/he may not be motivated to demonstrate existing knowledge or skills.

Subject Sample

In selecting subject groups, care must be taken to ensure their comparability. Before the experimental treatment begins, the researcher should ask: "Are the subject groups equivalent in all regards save for the independent variable?" Minor differences between subjects in the initial population pool will be controlled in the processes of random selection and random assignment. However, if a quasi-experimental design, employing intact classes, programs, or groups is used, a lack of initial similarity between groups could render the results questionable. For example, in studies contrasting developmental and non-developmental students, between-group differences may be so great (e.g., SES, ethnicity, use of non-standard English or English as a second language, community and familial support, etc.) that it is impossible to determine exactly what is causing the results obtained. Increasingly, it is the relative contribution or impact of such intervening variables that is of interest to researchers and educators. While such between-group comparisons are largely prohibitive, when they are required, as in studies seeking to ascertain "standard" or expert problem-solving strategies versus those conducted by novices or students with learning problems, extreme care must be taken in the interpretation of the results (see interpretation errors/experimenter bias section below).

Instrumentation Bias

An instrument is biased if it does not measure the same construct to the same degree in different groups, that is, if it measures or elicits different things (e.g., skills, thought processes etc.) in different groups. Thus, if a test is designed to measure performance in a certain domain, it is fair if it measures performance in that domain the same way in each group of examinees with whom it is used. However, if the test scores of one group are differently and systematically influenced by a factor other than that intended, these results are biased (Cole and Nitko, 1981).

Initially, instruments should be assessed in light of the particular needs of the research or evaluation. If the instruments chosen are insensitive to or inappropriate for the outcome variable, an educational intervention that, in fact, is producing effects may appear to be failing. Problems may, for instance, arise in the format of the test's tasks such that skills and knowledges other than those intended for study are included in the measure and, as a result, the tasks may necessitate a different type of pupil behavior from that intended by the specific objective. For example, a test intended to assess basic skills in mathematics may require the student to read the directions and even to read the problems themselves before any computation can be attempted. Such items lack construct and content validity (Berk, 1981).

Another source of instrumentation bias is found when students lack familiarity with the (post) test items or the assessment criteria is different from that emphasized in the experimental/instructional program. If students have not had the opportunity to learn the material called for on the tests or assessment criteria, then the outcome measure fails to match the assessment to students' actually experiences - and the measure, therefore, lacks content validity. A more accurate assessment of an instructional procedure may require the researcher to develop assessment criteria corresponding to material on which students received instruction - thus permitting a more representative assessment of how the treatment effects students' attainment of the curriculum.

In the Kinsler (1989) study previously reported, developmental students' essays were judged using a standard holistic scoring procedure. Each student's essay was impressionistically read by at least two raters. Each rater assigned the essay one numerical score, which was to reflect the quality of the student's performance on factors such as organization, unity, support, grammar and language. When these scores were subsequently analyzed in term of the relative weight given to the various constituent parts, they were found to most heavily stress language and grammar. However, in many developmental writing courses, language and grammar is not stressed, but rather emphasis is placed on the essay writing process and on the structure and organization of the argumentative essay. These findings suggest that holistic scoring may not judge students on variables consistent with their in-class instruction. While a follow-up study is needed to support these initial conclusions, the results suggest that new assessment measures or scoring procedures need to be developed which are more consistent with the actual content of developmental courses.

Interpretation Error/Experimenter Bias

The problem of inferring internal processes or states from test performance poses particular problems, for a number of non-random, extraneous variables other than those imposed (and controlled) by the researcher may intercede to skew and bias the results obtained. It is the responsibility of the researchers to seek out and offer other possible causal factors and explanations, even though they may challenge the researcher's position. Failure to do so may, inadvertently, lead to errors in interpretation. Take as an example the situation where two intact classes are selected to assess the effects of an experimental instructional methodology. By random determination, the experimental class meets at 10:00 a.m., while the control class meets at 8:00 a.m.. Findings indicate a significant difference in group performance in favor of the experimental course and the researcher, in reporting his results, asserts the superiority of the new approach. In actuality, the differences obtained may not be due to the experimental treatment but due to poor subject attendance or morning fatigue in the control group. Such errors are serious, for they would erroneously support or criticize practices and can lead those who would believe the findings on a "goose chase". Fortunately, the scientific method facilitates the replication of studies and encourages the proffering of contradictory interpretations to correct such errors.

More insidious, however, are when factors or traits are attributed to subjects, groups, programs and institutions that may at best be inaccurate but at worse harmfully characterize the subjects. This is particularly problematic when observations are of populations other than those with which the experimenter is familiar. In such instances, care must be taken to avoid unconscious biases not only on the part of the experimenter, but on the part of the raters and program personnel as well. Covert expectations, not only of correct answers but of the manner in which they should be given, may interfere with any interpretation of the results. On the basis of poor (situationally specific) task performance, researchers may assert not only the lack of learning or improvement, but the inability to learn - both of which may be in error. The consequences of such interpretations can be very costly not only to the credibility of researcher, but to the individuals or groups whose behaviors are being misconstrued and to those who would be misled by these errors in interpretation.

A classic example of such experimenter bias is the 1969 work of Jensen. Jensen compared the IQ scores of underprivileged African-American elementary school children, who either had or had not experienced pre-school compensatory programs. Finding a lack of significant differences between the two groups, Jensen asserted that compensatory programs had been tried and had failed. He further interpreted these data as an indication of the genetic inferiority of African-Americans (i.e., that their basic intelligence as measured by IQ could not be improved by such programs and, therefore, was due to genetic inferiority). Neither researcher considered factors consistent with instrumentation bias nor were other possible explanations offered. Jensen's assertions lead to the stigmatization of a whole group of people for many years to come. Only recently have cross-cultural differences become better understood and are Jensen's conclusions being dispelled. Fortunately, most interpretation errors are not this grave nor so blatantly biased. However, the point is that researchers must keep in mind that few things are entirely what they seem and remain open to the effects of other factors.

RESEARCH DIRECTIONS IN DEVELOPMENTAL EDUCATION

The ability to explain, predict and control phenomenological relationships is a powerful tool to developmental researchers. It can help determine how best to provide instruction and needed support services to an increasing diverse population of students. Recent findings from a number of differing fields have greatly challenged long held notions about traditional classroom instruction and service delivery. To relevance of these findings and challenges to the field of developmental education can only be determined in research and praxis. However, several areas of current research suggests complementary sites of study for developmental educations.

Learners are not monolithic entities, but rather are a complex admixture of factual knowledge, procedural processes, beliefs, feelings and emotions. Culture impacts of all of these factors in ways in which researchers are only beginning to understand. This influence needs to be further explores as well as its interface with traditional and other modes of classroom instruction.

Researchers are increasingly realizing the fallacy inherent in the search for a context free generic instructional methodology. As with subject behavior, teacher behavior it also context specific. Some methodologies are more appropriate with particular contents, students and teachers than others. It is the particulars of a classroom, the interactional give and take of teacher-student and student-student interactions, as well as local conditions and physical circumstances with which teachers work, that influences what is done, how it is done and what needs to be done (Bloom, 1989). Researchers in developmental education must too begin to focus more on this qualitative classroom interaction.

As researchers begin to understand the effects of affective and social factors on cognition, new counseling and other social service models need to be studied. Individual and culturally based belief systems, as well as the need to satisfactorily project in self in the social arena of the classroom, strongly influences academic performance. As a result, educators may need to develop tighter interdisciplinary partnerships, which may include counselors, anthropologists, content area instructors, learning theorists, etc.

Research in the field is new and the area is wide open.

REFERENCES

Berk, R. (1981). Introduction. In R. Berk (ed.) *Educational evaluation methodology: The state of the art.* Baltimore, MD.: John Hopkins University Press. 1-10.

Bryk, A. and R. Light (1981). Designing evaluation for difference program environments. In R. Berk (ed.) *Educational evaluation methology: The state of the art.* Baltimore, MD.: John Hopkins University Press. 11-31.

Cole, M. (1975). An ethnographic psychology of cognition. In R. Brislin, S. Bochner and W. Lonner (eds.) *Cross cultural perspectives in learning.* New York: Wiley and Sons.

Cole, N. and A. Nitko (1981). Measuring program effects. In R. Berk (ed.) *Educational evaluation methology: The state of the art.* Baltimore, MD: John Hopkins University Press. 3263.

Fitch, N. (1966). *The employed student and his achievement level at San Joaquine Delta Junior College.* Stockton, CA.: San Joaquin Delta Junior College. (ERIC Document Reproduction Service No. A ED 011 771)

Hare, B. (1977). Black and white children's self esteem in social situations. *Journal of Negro Education.* 46, 2, 145 - 156.

Harper, W. (1967) *Junior college directory.* Washington, D.C.: American Association of Junior Colleges.

Hopper, H. and H. Keller (1966). *Writing skills - are large classes conducive to effective learning.* Fort Pierce, FLA: Indiana River Junior College. (ERIC Document Reproduction Service No. T ED 012 583)

Jensen, A. (1969). How much can we boost IQ and scholastic achievement? *Harvard Educational Review,* 39, 1-123.

Kerlinger, F. (1973). *Foundations in behavioral research.* New York: Holt, Rinehart and Winston.

Kinsler, K. (1989). *The use of oral discourse and social activity to facilitate written composition in basic writing students.* Unpublished manuscript.

Kinsler, K. and A. Robinson (1990). Cognition and developmental instruction. In R. Hashway (ed.) *Handbook of developmental education.* New York: Praeger Press.

Labov, W. (1970). *The logic of non-standard English. In F. Williams (ed.) Language and poverty.* Chicago, Illinois: Markman, 153-189.

Miller-Jones, D. (1989). Culture and testing. *American psychologist,* February, 360-366.

Pearce, F. (1966). *Dropout patterns in the New Hope project.* Modesto, CA.: Modesto Junior College. (ERIC Document Reproduction Service No. E ED 011 195)

Roueche, J. and J. Boggs (1968). *Junior college institutional research: The state of the art.* ERIC Clearinghouse for Junior College Information and the American Association of Junior Colleges.

Rogoff, B. (1981). Schooling and ghe development of cognitive skills. In Triandis and Heron (eds.) *Handbook of cross cultural psychology: Developmental psychology.* Vol. 4. Boston: Allyn and Bacon Publishers. 233-294.

Shea, J. (1966). *PREP - A program for recovering and extending academic potential for high school underachievers seeking entrance at a regional community college.* BR-5-0569. Greenfield, MA: Greenfield Community College. (ERIC Document Reproduction Service No. S ED 010 120)

Sowell, E. and R. Casey (1982). *Analyzing educational research.* Belmont, CA: Wadsworth Publishing Company.

Tyler, R. (1942). General statement on evaluation. *Journal of educational Research,* 35, 492-501.

Weiner, B. J. (1962). *Statistical principles in experimental design.* New York: McGraw-Hill Publishers.

Woolfolk, A. (1987). *Educational psychology.* Englewood Cliffs, N.J.: Prentice-Hall, Inc.

Selected Bibliography

Anderson, J. A. (1988). Cognitive styles and multicultural populations. *Journal of teacher education,* 39, 2-9.

Astin, A. (1964). Personal and environmental factors associated with college drop-outs among high aptitude students. *Journal of Educational Psychology,* 55, 219-227.

Astin, A. (1971). *Predicting academic performance in college.* New York: Collier-Macmillan Limited.

Astin, A. (1975). *Preventing students from dropping out.* San Francisco: Jossey Bass.

Astin, A. (1977). *Four critical years: Effects of college on beliefs, attitudes and knowledge.* San Francisco: Jossey-Bass.

Astin, A. W. (1985). Involvement: The cornerstone of excellence. *Change,* 35-39.

Baker, G. A. III and P. L. Painter. (1983). The learning center: A study of effectiveness. In J.E. Roueche (ed.), *A new look at successful programs.* San Francisco: Jossey-Bass, 73 - 88.

Basseches, M. (1984). *Dialectical thinking and adult development.* Norwood, NJ: Ablex Publishing Corporation.

Basseches, M., S. Hamilton and F. Richards (1980). *The impact of participatory-democratic work experiences on adolescent development: a methodological report.* Paper presented at the Annual Meeting of the American Educational Research Association, Boston, Massachusetts.

Bereiter, J. (1980). Development in writing. In L. Gregg and E. Steinberbg (eds.), *Cognitive processes in writing.* Hillsdale: N.J.: Lawrence Earlbaum Associates, 73-96.

Bereiter, J. and M. Scardamalia (1987a). An attainable version of high literacy. *Curriculum inquiry.* 17, 1, 9-30.

Bereiter, J. and M. Scardamalia (1987b). *The psychology of written composition.* Hillsdale, NJ: Lawrence Earlbaum

Bereiter, J. and M. Scardamalia (1982). From conversation to compositon: The role of instruction in developmental process. In R. Glaser (ed.), *Advances in instructional psychology.* Vol 2. Hillsdale, NJ: Lawrence Earlbaum Associates, 1-64.

Boyer, E. (1987). *College: The undergraduate experience in America. The Carnegie Foundation for the advancement of teaching:* New York: Harper and Row. pp. 26-42.

Briley, P. (1976). *Planning and implementing learning skills centers in the state of Kansas.* Paper presented at the annual meeting of the International Reading Association, Anaheim, California. (ERIC Document Reproduction Service No. ED 123 603)

Bruner, J. S. (1962). *On knowing.* Cambridge: Harvard University Press.

Bruner, J. S. (1960). *The process of education.* Cambridge: Harvard University Press.

Chall, J. (1983). *Stages of reading development.* New York: MCGraw-Hill.

Chall, J., E. Heron and A. Hilferty (1987). Adult literacy: New and enduring problems. *Phi delta kappan,* 69, 190-196.

Chaffee, J. (1988). *Thinking critically* (2nd ed.). Boston: Houghton Mifflin.

Chipman, S. F., J. W. Segal and R. Glaser (eds.) (1985). *Thinking and learning skills (Volume 2: Research and open questions).* Hillsdale, NJ: Lawrence Erlbaum Associates.

Christ, F. L. (1980). Learning assistance at a state university: A cybernetic model. In K.V. Lauridsen (ed.), *Examining the scope of learning centers.* San Francisco: Jossey-Bass, 45 - 56.

Cross, K. P. (1971). *Beyond the open door.* San Francisco: Jossey-Bass Publishers.

Cross, K. P. (1981). *Adults as learners: Increasing participation and facilitating learning.* San Francisco: Jossey-Bass.

Cross, K. P. (1981). *Adult learners: Characteristics, needs and interests."* In *lifelong learning in America.* San Francisco: Jossey-Bass, Inc..

Cross, K. P. (1987). *Adults as learners.* San Franciso: Jossey-Bass, Inc..

Dewey, J. (1933). *How we think.* Lexington, MA: D. C. Heath.

Enright, G. (1975). College learning skills: Frontier land origins of the learning assistance center. In R. Sugimoto, (ed.) *College learning skills: Today and tomorrow land.* Proceedings of the Eighth Annual Conference of the Western College Reading Association. Anaheim: The Western College Reading Association.

Enright, G. and G. Kersteins (1980). The learning center: Toward an expanded role. In O.T. Lenning and R.L. Nayman (eds.), *New roles for learning assistance.* San Francisco: Jossey-Bass, 1 - 24.

Flamm, A. L. (1984). *Reading Area Community College basic skills program review.* Reading, Pennsylvania: Reading Area Community College.

Glaser, E. (1941). An experiment in the development of critical thinking. In *Contributions to Education*, n. 843. New York: Teacher's College, Columbia University.

Hashway, R. (1988). *Foundations of developmental education.* New York: Praeger.

Henderson, D. D. (1972). *Report on alternatives and considerations for the design of a learning resource center (LRC) at Georgetown University.* (ERIC Document Reproduction Service No. ED 124 121)

Henry, S. and C. P. Omvig (1981). *Learning center handbook.* Kentucky University, Division of Vocational Education. (ERIC Document Reproduction Service No. ED 215 106)

Keimig, R. T. (1983). *Raising academic standards: A guide to learning improvement* (ASHE-ERIC/Higher Education Research Report No. 4). Washington, D.C.: Association for the Study of Higher Education.

Kolb, D. A. (1976). *Learning style inventory.* Boston: McBer and Co.

Kolb, D.A. (1985). *Learning style inventory.* Boston: McBer and Co.

Kolb, D. A. (1984). *Experiential learning: Experience as the source of learning and development.* New York: Prentice-Hall.

Langhoff, H. F. (1980). Learning resource centers: Organizational components and structural models. In K. Mikan (ed.), *Learning resources center conference: Proceedings and evaluation.* Birmingham, Alabama (ERIC Document Reproduction Service No. ED 222 180), 6 - 16.

Lauridsen, K.V. (1980). *Examining the scope of learning centers.* San Francisco: Jossey-Bass.

Labov, W. (1970). *The logic of non-standard English. In F. Williams (ed.) Language and poverty.* Chicago, Illinois: Markman, 153-189.

Lenning, O. (1982). Variables-selection and measurement concerns. In E. Pascarella (ed.). *New directions for institutional research: Studying student attrition, no. 36.* San Francisco: Jossey-Bass.

Materniak, G. (1980). *Developing a learning center from A to Z: Guidelines for designing a comprehensive developmental education program in a post-secondary educational setting.* Unpublished paper. Pittsburg: University of Pittsburg.

Maxwell, M. J. (1966). An individualized college learning laboratory. *Reading improvement*, 4, 5-6.

Maxwell, M. J. (1981). *Improving student learning skills.* San Francisco: Jossey-Bass.

Maxwell, M. J. (1988). Personal communication with Mary Lee Schnuth. McNeil, D. R. (1980). Progress of an experiment. *New directions in continuing education*, 5, 47 - 53.

Mikulecky, L. (1984). Preparing students for workplace lieracy emands, *Journal of Rrading*, 28, 253-57.

Mikulecky, L. (1982). Job literacy: The relationship between school preparation and workplace actuality. *Reading research quarterly* , 17, 400-419.

Mikulecky, L. and D. Winchester (1983). Job literacy and job performance among nurses at varying employment levels. *Adult education quarterly*, 34, 3-5.

McMillan, J. H. (1987). Enhancing college students' critical thinking: A review of studies. *Research in Higher Education*, 26, 3-29.

McPheeters, V. W. (1980). Learning resources centers -- past, present, and future. In K. Mikan (ed.), *Learning resources center conference: Proceedings and evaluation*, 1 - 5. Birmingham, Alabama. (ERIC Document Reproduction Service No. ED 222 180).

Nickerson, R. S., D. N. Perkins and E. E. Smith (1985). *The teaching of thinking.* Hillsdale, NJ: Lawrence Erlbaum Associates.

Pantages, T. and C. Creedon (1978). Studies of college attrition: 1950-1975. *Review of Educational Research*, 48, 49- 101.

Pascarella, E. (1980). Student-faculty informal contact and college outcomes. *Review of Educational Research*, 50, 545-595.

Pascarella, E. (1985). College environmental influences on learning and cognitive development: A critical review and synthesis. *Higher Education: Handbook of Theory and Research, 1, 1-61.*

Pascarella, E. and D. Chapman (1983). Validation of a theoretical model of college withdrawal: Interaction effects in a multi-institutional sample. *Research in Higher Education*, 19, 25-48.

Pascarella, E. and P. Terenzini (1977). Voluntary freshman attrition and patterns of social and academic integration in a university: A test of a conceptual model. *Research in Higher Education*, 6, 25-43.

Pascarella, E. and P. Terenzini (1977). Voluntary freshman attrition and patterns of social and academic integration in a university: A test of a conceptual model. *Research in Higher Education,* 6, 25-43.

Pascarella, E. and P. Terenzini (1980). Predicting freshman persistence and voluntary drop-out decisions from a theoretical model. *Journal of Higher Education,* 51, 60-76.

Pascarella, E. and P. Terenzini (1983). Predicting voluntary freshman year persistence/withdrawal behavior in a residential univesity: A path analytic validation of Tinto's model. *Journal of Educational Psychology,* 75, 215-226.

Powers, S. and Rossman, M. (1983). Attributional factors of native Americans and anglo community college students, Research/Technical report number 143 (RC 014 440), Washington, D.C.: United States Department of Education, National Institute of Education.

Roueche, J. and J. Boggs (1968). *Junior college institutional research: The state of the art.* ERIC Clearinghouse for Junior College Information and the American Association of Junior Colleges.

Rounds, J. (1983). *Admissions, placement and competency: Assessment practices in California Community Colleges.* ERIC Document Reproduction Service.

Rounds, J. and D. Anderson (1985). Assessment for entrance to community college: Research studies of three major standardized tests. *Journal of Research and Development in Education,* 18, 54-58.

Segal, J. W., S. F. Chipman and R. Glaser (eds.) (1985). *Thinking and learning skills, Volume 1: Relating instruction to research.* Hillsdale, NJ: Lawrence Erlbaum Associates.

Sharpe, A. D. (1978). Essentials for an effective learning environment. In J.D. Terry and R.W. Hotes (eds.), *The administration of learning resources centers.* Washington, D.C.: University Press of America, 128 - 139.

Shertzer, B. and S. C. Stone (1974). *Fundamentals of counseling,* 2nd. edition. New York: Houghton Mifflin.

Smith, D. G. (1977). College classroom interactions and critical thinking. *Journal of Educational Psychology,* 69, 180-190.

Tinto, V. (1975). drop-out from higher education: A theoretical synthesis of recent research. *Review of Educational Research,* 45, 89-125.

Tinto, V. (1982). Defining drop-out: A matter of perspective. In E. Pascarella (ed). *New directions for institutional research: Studying student attrition, no.36.* San Francisco: Jossey-Bass, 3 - 16.

Tinto, V. (1985). Theories of student departure revisited. *Research in Higher Education,* 2, 359-384.

Tinto, V. (1987). *Leaving college: Rethinking the causes and cures of student attrition.* Chicago: The University of Chicago Press.

Vygotsky, L. S. (1962). *Thought and language.* Cambridge, Mass: MIT Press.

Whimbey, A. (1987). A 15th Grade reading level for high school seniors? *Phi delta kappan,* 69, 207-208.

Whyte, C. B. (1980). An integrated counseling and learning center for a liberal arts college. In K.V. Lauridsen (ed.), *Examining the scope of learning centers.* San Francisco: Jossey-Bass, 33 - 43.

Yamba, A. Z. (1982). The rescue of Essex County College. *The College Board review,* 123, 9-10, 31-32.

Author Index

Abraham, A. 236, 255

Adler, M. 242, 253, 255

Agrella, R. 160, 164, 175

Aiken, L. 292, 300

Akst, G. 160, 174

Albert, J. 63, 81

Allen, R. 268, 276

Allen, W. 312, 317, 320

Alton, D. 26, 36

Anders, P. 265, 275

Anderson, A. 25, 34, 36

Anderson, D. 306, 310, 326

Anderson, G. 283, 299

Anderson, J. 29, 24, 26, 91, 92, 100, 107

Anderson, R. 253, 255, 283, 299

Annis, D. 268, 274

Annis, L. 268, 274

Arbitman-Smith, R. 69, 79

Archer, J. 205, 212

Archibald, Y. 27, 36

Arkin, A. 28, 36

Armistead, L. 167, 172

Arons, A. 139, 152

Arrigoni, G. 26, 36

Arter, J. 225, 231, 269, 274

Artrobus, J. 28, 36

Astin, A. 20, 86, 107, 306, 312-314, 316, 320, 325

Atkinson, J. 27, 43, 61, 79

Atkinson, R. 29, 36, 263, 275

Au, K. 65, 79

Austin, J. 224, 225, 229

Averill, J. 202, 213

Bailey, C. 182, 192

Baker, G. 133, 152, 155, 156, 161, 162, 170

Ballif, B. 288, 299

Bandler, R. 28, 35, 40

Barata, F. 27, 38

Baron, J. 262, 274

Barr, M. 332, 333

Barshis, D. 162-164, 171

Bartell, N. 223, 229

Bartholomae, D. 273, 274

Bartlet, F. 31, 34, 36

Basseches, M. 4, 5, 7, 8, 12-14, 20

Baymur, F. 285, 299

Beal, P. 133, 152, 320

Bean, J. 309, 317, 318, 320

Beard, S. 205, 212

Becker, J. 26, 45

Beddle, B. 65, 80

Beer, S. 35, 36

Belenky, M. 93, 101, 107

Bennett, G. 291, 299

Benton, A. 27, 36

Benezet, L. 7, 20

Bennett, C. 27, 36

Bennington, J. 199, 212

Berger, T. 26, 49

Bereiter, J. 53, 54, 72-74, 79

Bergin, A. 287, 299

Berk, R. 336, 354

Bezdek, J. 218, 229

Biggs, J. 23, 25, 29, 36, 37

Bistreich, A. 312, 321

Bitterman, M. 25, 37

Black, M. 265, 274

Bloom, A. 262, 274

Bloom, F. 35, 37

Bloomberg, R. 239, 255

Blyth, J. 23, 27

Bogen, J. 27, 37

Bond, G. 272, 274

Bordin, E. 291, 299

Bossing, L. 200, 212

Bouclan, W. 26, 35, 37

Bousfield, W. 26, 35, 37

Bower, G. 26, 29, 34, 36

Bowers, F. 209, 214

Boyer, A. 310, 313, 314, 320

Boylan, H. 158, 162-164, 170

Brain, G. 218, 229

Bransford, J. 69, 79

Bray, D. 169, 170

Brazziel, W. 312, 321

Breen, L. 290, 303

Breland, H. 312, 321

Brier, E. 129, 152

Briley, P. 184, 185, 187, 188, 190-192

Brings, F. 131, 152

Britton, J. 72, 79

Broch, M. 205, 214

Brodzinsky, D. 63, 79

Broedel, H. 286, 299

Brown, A. 62, 70, 72, 79, 82

Brown, J. 65, 80

Brown, M. 263, 275

Brown, W. 283, 304

Brubacker, J. 198, 212, 305, 321

Bruffee, K. 87, 107

Bruner, J. 23, 28, 37, 38, 242, 245, 253, 255

Bryk, A. 342, 354

Bukacek, S. 293, 301

Burgess, T. 72, 79

Burnham, L. 155, 157, 160, 162, 170

Butcher, E. 290, 299

Butterfield, E. 30, 43

Callis, R. 283, 299

Campbell, D. 293, 300

Carey, R. 242, 247, 256

Carkhuff, R. 289, 299

Carlson, R. 288, 299

Carmine, D. 266, 276

Casey, E. 336, 342, 346, 355

Castaldi, B. 188, 191, 192

Cattell, J. 65, 80

Cawley, J. 226, 229

Chaffee, J. 145, 152, 272, 274

Chall, J. 65, 80, 242, 244, 253, 255, 256

Champaign, J. 167, 169-171

Chance, J. 294, 299

Charles, R. 168, 171

Charlesworth, W. 56, 80

Chase, C. 315, 321

Chausow, H. 162, 163, 169, 171

Cheney, L. 264, 272

Chickering, A. 201, 212, 330, 333

Chipman, S. 54, 56, 65, 66, 80, 148, 153, 262, 274, 277

Chobanian, A. 204, 212

Christ, F. 133, 152, 156, 157, 160, 162, 163, 165, 167, 170, 171, 185, 189, 192

Clark, C. 201-203, 215

Clark, E. 168, 171

Clark, R. 27, 43

Clayton, M. 203, 212

Clinchy, B. 93, 101, 107

Coan, R 289, 300

Cobb, S. 202, 212

Coben, S. 202, 212

Cobun, T. 182, 183, 189, 193

Cohen, B. 35, 38

Cohen, N. 27, 38

Cohen, R. 89, 107

Cohen, S. 264, 274

Coher, D. 310, 315, 321

Cohn, R. 220, 229

Cole, M. 56, 65, 80, 83

Cole, N. 350, 346, 354

Coleman, J. 293, 300

Coles, G. 282, 301+

Collins, A. 27, 33, 38, 65, 80

Collins, B. 289, 300

Collins, W. 133, 137, 139, 152

Colonna, A. 27, 38

Colvin, G. 266, 277

Conners, C. 27, 38

Connolly, S. 289, 300

Cook-Grumperz, J. 65, 80

Cooper, G. 91, 92, 100, 107

Cope, R. 312, 316, 321

Coulson, J. 23, 38

Crandall, V. 289, 300

Cremin, L. 129, 152

Crettol, M. 184, 185, 190, 191, 193

Critchley, M. 23, 38

Cross, K. 85, 107, 161, 163, 172, 197, 212, 236, 253, 256

Crosswhite, F. 217, 230

Currey, J. 183, 185, 193

Dahnke, H. 185, 193

D'Atri, D. 200, 214

Davenport, L. 162, 172

Day, D. 63, 81

Dearborn, W. 23, 38

De Bernardis, A. 162, 165, 172

de Bono, E. 272, 274

DeCecco, J. 23, 38

Decker, A. 131, 152

Decker, E. 162, 168, 172

Deichart, K. 182, 192

Delworth, U. 10, 20, 143, 152, 172

Deming, M. 160, 163, 165, 172

Dempsey, J. 160, 161, 167, 172

De Rezi, E. 27, 28, 36, 38

Devirian, M. 155, 172

Dewey, J. 265, 274

Dick, J. 263, 277

Dienes, Z. 31, 38

Dilks, L. 263, 277

Dintman, G. 205, 212

Dodson, J. 200, 215

Doehrizig, D. 27, 39

Dole, A. 284, 300

Donovan, R. 160, 162, 172

Dovalina, R. 168, 172

Downing, L. 279, 280, 300

Drea, J. 167, 172

Dressel, P. 263, 275, 282, 300

Duerden, N. 168, 172

Dulin, K. 265, 275

Dunkin, M. 65, 80

Durkheim, E. 307, 308, 322

Dweck, C. 62, 80

Dwyer, P. 315, 322

Dykstra, R. 272, 274

Dymond, R. 23, 47

Edelman, G. 27, 35, 39, 45

Edge, O. 314, 322

Edwards, J. 291, 300

Edwards, R. 23, 39

Ekstrom, R. 203, 212

Ellis, V. 203, 212

Eliott, I. 168, 172

Ellman, S. 28, 36

Elmore, R. 205, 212

Elner, F. 27, 39

Emery, M. 167, 173

Engehart, N. 179, 193

Ennis, R. 265, 275

Enright, G. 131-133, 152, 155, 157, 172, 173, 193, 183

Epstein, I. 272, 275

Erickson, E. 201, 212

Erwin, R. 265, 275

Estes, T. 242, 259

Eurich, R. 168, 169, 173

Evans, N. 190, 193

Everly, G. 200, 204, 213

Eysenck, H. 281, 300

Fadden, T. 205, 214

Fagan, N. 292, 300

Faglioni, P. 27, 38

Fahlman, S. 27, 39

Farwell, G. 282, 303

Fedderson, W. 25, 37

Fennell, F. 223, 229

Fetters, W. 310, 313, 316, 325

Feuer, D. 169, 173

Field, H. 168, 173

Filmore, C. 34, 39

Fitch, F. 25, 41

Fitzhugh, D. 34, 39

Fitzhugh, L. 34, 39

Flamm, A. 160, 162-164, 173

Farr, R. 242, 247, 256

Flavell, J. 57, 80

Fletcher, J. 226, 229

Flinter, P. 223, 229

Flores, I. 32, 39

Fowler, J. 5, 20

Frank, A. 266, 268, 275

Frank, J. 287, 288, 300

Fredricksen, C. 242, 256

Freedberg, S. 314, 322

Freedman, J. 26, 39

Freire, P. 273, 275

Freud, S. 23, 25, 39

Fry, E. 32, 39

Fuller, J. 157, 170, 173

Gaff, J. 10, 21

Galper, R. 296, 300

Gardner, H. 55, 81

Gardner, J. 160, 173

Garfinkel, B. 203, 213

Garman, N. 238, 256

Garner, A. 183, 184, 193

Garrity, T. 209, 214

Gazzaniza, M. 27, 39

Gerardi, W. 218, 230

Gerber, K. 203, 214

Gersten, R. 266, 276

Giljahn, J. 179, 193

Gilliam, B. 292, 300

Gilligan, C. 92, 107

Girdano, D. 200, 204, 213

Glaser, E. 270, 275

Glaser, R. 57, 83, 148, 153, 242, 256, 262, 265, 274

Glass, G. 287, 304

Glennen, R. 162, 163, 167, 173

Glennon, V. 224, 230

Godzella, B. 292, 301Œ

Goertz, M. 203, 212

Goldberger, N. 93, 101, 107

Goldston, J. 292, 301

Goodlad, J. 88, 107

Gordon, E. 90, 107

Goss, A. 26, 40

Gould, B. 205, 214

Gould, S. 56, 81

Gray, B. 160, 173

Green, E. 23, 32, 40

Greenberg, J. 199, 200, 204, 205, 212, 213

Greenfield, P. 56, 81

Greenholz, S. 219, 230

Greenwald, M. 265, 275

Gregory, W. 289, 301

Greschwind, N. 34, 39

Griffin, P. 56, 80

Grinder, J. 28, 35, 40

Grossman, E. 317, 322

Groves, P. 28, 40

Gubler, R. 227, 230

Guilford, J. 55, 81

Gumperz, J. 64, 81

Gwenke, G. 311, 322

Hale-Benson, J. 91, 92, 100, 106, 107

Hall, E. 293, 301

Hall, M. 25, 41

Halperin, D. 143, 153

Halpin, G. 311, 323

Hamilton, C. 31, 40

Hamilton, S. 5, 20

Hamilton, W. 31, 40

Handelmann, G. 26, 45

Hanson, D. 186, 193

Hanson, G. 172

Hanson, H. 143, 152

Hardin, C. 236, 239, 257

Hare, B. 349, 354

Harlocker, E. 168, 174

Harlow, H. 26, 40

Harper, W. 339, 354

Harris, A. 28, 40

Harris, J. 28, 40

Harris, L. 237, 248, 257

Harris, T. 265, 275

Harrison, M. 32, 40

Hartmann, D. 287, 304

Harvey, O. 35, 40

Hashway, R. 31, 40, 53, 80, 235, 236, 245, 257, 310, 311, 323

Heath, D. 5, 20

Hebb, D. 23, 35, 40

Hebert, D. 290, 299

Hecht, M. 160, 174

Heibert, E. 253, 255

Hencey, R. 168, 174

Henderson, D. 184, 186-188, 190, 191, 194

Henry, S. 157, 174, 187, 189-191, 194

Heron, E. 242, 244, 256

Heron, W. 35, 40

Herz, M. 28, 45

Hicks, L. 26, 49

Higginson, L. 205, 214

Hilferty, A. 242, 244, 256

Hinton, G. 34, 41

Hirsch, E. 262, 264, 275

Hobson, A. 25, 41

Hobson, J. 293, 300

Hockey, J. 200, 213

Hodgen, R. 265, 275

Hofstadter, L. 25, 37

Hohmuth, A. 293, 301

Holland, J. 23, 41

Holmes, T. 204, 213

Homan, D. 219, 230

Honland, C. 25, 41

Honzik, C. 49, 50

Hooper, H. 337, 354

Huck, C. 266, 268, 277

Hughes, J. 23, 41

Hull, C. 23, 25, 41

Humphrey, G. 28, 41

Hunt, E. 26, 27, 41

Hunt, D. 35, 40

Hunter, I. 26, 41

Hutchnson, R. 70, 81

Huxley, A. 28, 42

Hyram, G. 266, 268, 275

Inhelder, B. 28, 46

Jackson, J. 27, 42

Jaesting, J. 293, 301

Janis, I. 202, 213

Jencks, C. 10, 20

Jenkins, J. 225, 231

Jenkins, S. 179, 190, 194

Jenson, A. 55, 81, 352, 354

Jenson, B. 282, 301

Jewler, A. 160, 173

Jody, R. 131, 152

Joe, V. 295, 301

Johnson, C. 293, 294, 301

Johnson, E. 204, 205, 213

Johnson, J. 204, 205, 213

Johnson, N. 34, 42

Jones, D. 185, 193

Jones, L. 27, 36

Jones, T. 220, 230

Jounet, M. 25, 42

Kajan, J. 63, 81

Kameeniu, E. 266, 276

Kaplan, B. 28, 50

Karwin, R. 161, 165, 167, 174

Karwin, T. 182-188, 194

Katkowsky, W. 294, 300

Keating, W. 168, 169, 174

Keeley, S. 263, 275

Keenan, J. 29, 34, 42

Kegan, R. 86, 88, 92, 107

Keimig, R. 148, 149, 153, 158-160, 162, 163, 174

Keller, H. 337, 354

Kelly, F. 291, 302

Kelly, G. 25, 42

Kendall, P. 287, 301

Kenney, T. 34, 42

Kerlinger, F. 343, 344, 354

Kernis, M. 294, 301

Kersteins, G. 155, 157, 173, 183, 193

Khanna, P. 295, 302

Killion, J. 246, 257

Kimura, D. 30, 42

King, M. 266, 268, 277

Kinsler, K. 81, 341, 342, 350, 351, 354

Kintsch, W. 29, 31, 34, 42

Kirby, P. 92, 107

Kirk, R. 161-163, 165, 175

Kirk, S. 32, 42

Knowles, M. 253, 257

Kolb, D. 94, 95, 100, 103-105, 108

Kosc, L. 222, 230

Kosslyn, S. 27, 28, 42

Kozminsky, E. 29, 34, 42

Kozol, J. 241, 257

Kruetzer, J. 263, 275

Kuehl, D. 292, 300

Kunz, L. 160, 163, 174

Labov, W. 56, 64, 65, 82, 350, 354

Lachman, R. 30, 43

Lambert, M. 287, 299

Lamnin, A. 205, 212

Landsman, Q. 285, 303

Lane, K. 189, 194

Lane, M. 189, 194

Lange, S. 205, 212

Langhoff, H. 164, 174, 186, 192, 194

Lansdell, H. 30, 43

Larcombe, T. 227, 228, 230

Larson, P. 203, 213

Lashley, K. 30, 43

Lauridsen, K. 158, 160, 163, 165, 174

Lauterborn, R. 249, 258

Lazarus, R. 202, 213

Lazerson, A. 25, 37

Lefcourt, H. 286, 291, 293, 301

Legrecca, G. 199, 213

Lehman, I. 263, 275

Lenning, O. 305, 313, 314, 316, 324

Levin, J. 27, 43

Levitt, E. 281, 301

Levitz, R. 306, 324

Levy, J. 27, 43

Lewis, E. 280, 301

Light, R. 342, 354

Linden, J. 284, 291, 302

Lissner, L. 136, 137, 139, 142, 146, 149, 153

Llinas, R. 26, 34, 45

Lochhead, J. 70, 84, 139, 153

Loftus, E. 26, 27, 33, 38, 39

London, P. 287, 302

Longman, D. 263, 275

Loveland, K. 226, 229

Lovenger, J. 5, 20

Lowell, E. 27, 43

Luborsky, L. 287, 302

Luch, D. 296, 300

Lushin, B. 164, 168, 174

Lyons, N. 92, 108

Lysaught, J. 32, 43

Maceh, C. 200, 213

MacWhimmey, B. 26, 46

Madden, J. 26, 49

Mahoney, J. 169, 175

Mandler, G. 34, 43, 200, 213

Marshall, J. 265, 276

Martin, E. 26, 44

Martin, N. 72, 79

Marx, M. 209, 214

Maslow, A. 23, 25, 43

Mason, I. 185, 193

Materniak, G. 157, 161, 165, 165, 175, 190, 192, 194

Matheney, T. 179, 193

Mauksch, H. 285, 286, 303

Maxwell, M. 53, 82, 129-131, 153, 157, 160, 162-165, 167, 170, 175, 197, 214

Mayes, A. 205, 214

Mayhew, L. 263, 275

Mazzaniga, M. 27, 37

McCarley, R. 25, 41

McClelland, J. 27, 34, 41, 43

McDermott, R. 65, 83

McDonald, F. 23, 43

McGlinn, J. 270, 276

McKoon, G. 29, 34, 42

McLeod, A. 72, 79

McLeod, P. 25, 46

McLeskey, J. 224, 231

McMillan, J. 263, 267-269, 276

McNeil, D. R. 167, 175

McPartland, J. 293, 300

McPherters, V. 165, 167, 170, 175, 183-187, 194

McWilliams, S. 203, 214

Melingo, B. 204, 214 Melton, A. 26, 44

Mentkowski, M. 86, 108

Merenda, P. 284, 302

Merrill, M. 240, 241, 258

Merton, R. 288, 302

Messer, S. 63, 82

Metzler, J. 285, 302

Meyensbury, H. 287, 303

Meyers, C. 86, 88, 105, 108

Mezzano, J. 286, 302

Michaels, S. 64, 82

Migdoll, D. 34, 42

Mikulecky, L. 249, 250, 253, 258, 259

Miles, C. 245, 258, 264, 272, 276

Miller, G. 26, 28, 44

Miller, M. 169, 175

Miller, T. 287, 304, 330, 333

Miller-Jones, D. 349, 350, 355

Minkoff, H. 164, 175, 184, 194

Minsky, M. 31, 44

Mitchell, B. 305, 324

Mittelmann, B. 23, 44

Moe, A. 239, 250, 259

Molinari, V. 295, 302

Moll, M. 268, 276

Mood, A. 293, 300

Moore, W. 236, 258

Morgan, A. 305, 324

Morison, A. 65, 83

Morse, S. 248, 258

Moss, H. 89, 92, 107

Mouney, C. 18, 20

Mountcastle, B. 35, 39

Mountcastle, V. 27, 44

Moyer, J. 228, 230

Moyer, M. 228, 230

Muller-Willis, L. 218, 230

Mullinex, S. 205, 214

Murro, B. 308, 316, 318, 324

Myers, R. 27, 39, 45

Myrich, R. 291, 302

Nadel, L. 26, 45

Nason, R. 225, 230

Navarro, M. 313, 314, 324

Neagley, R. 190, 193

Nebes, R. 27, 45

Neimark, E. 57, 82

Neisser, J. 25-28, 45

Nestor, B. 282, 301

Newell, A. 24, 45

Newman, S. 65, 80

Newton, E. 133, 153

Nickerson, R. 143, 153, 267, 269, 276

Nieratka, E. 272, 275

Nitko, A. 346, 350, 354

Nodine, C. 26, 40

Noel, L. 306, 324

Norman, D. 25, 45

Norris, S. 272, 276

Norwick, K. 35, 45

Obler, S. 161-163, 175

O'Dea, J. 282, 302

Ogbu, J. 56, 66, 82

Ohlsen, M. 286, 299

O'Keefe, J. 26, 45

Oliver, R. 28, 38

Olton, D. 26, 45

Omvig, C. 157, 174, 187, 189-191, 194

Opton, E. 202, 213

Ortony, A. 34, 47

Osborne, A. 217, 230

Ostfield, A. 200, 214

Pacheco, B. 272, 276

Painter, P. 155, 156, 161, 162, 170

Paivio, I. 27, 28, 45

Palincsar, A. 62, 70, 72, 79, 82

Palmer, P. 85, 94, 108

Panos, R. 312, 316, 325

Parker, C. 6, 7, 20

Parloff, M. 287, 302

Pascarella, E. 263, 276, 308, 309, 317, 318, 325

Pasual-Leone, J. 83

Patching, W. 266, 276

Paterson, C. 285, 299

Paul, R. 262, 265, 277

Pearse, C. 160, 164, 175

Peeke, H. 28, 45

Peiser, K. 285, 286, 303

Pellegrino, J. 57, 83

Pellionisz, A. 26, 34

Pemberton, G. 93, 108

Pendrini, B. 312, 325

Pendrini, D. 312, 325

Peng, S. 310, 313, 316, 325

Perkins, D. 25, 41, 143, 153, 267, 269, 276

Perkins, M. 168, 171

Perry, W. 6, 13, 20, 21, 106, 108, 146, 153

Peterson, G. 157, 160-165, 170, 175, 183, 185-187, 191, 194, 263, 277

Petrosky, A. 273, 274

Phares, E. 288, 289, 295, 302

Phillips, H. 218, 231

Phillips, W. 63, 81

Piaget, J. 28, 46, 58, 59, 83

Piel, E. 10, 20

Pikaart, L. 221, 231

Pinsker, S. 169, 175

Platt, C. 26, 46

Pollack, J. 203, 212

Polmantier, P. 283, 299

Poltroch, S. 27, 41

Popham, W. 242, 258

Posner, M. 25, 46

Postman, L. 26, 46

Potter, V. 168, 175

Powers, S. 160, 164, 175, 295, 302

Prebram, K. 28, 44

Prendergast, J. 31, 46

Prentice, W. 25, 46

Preston, A. 294, 300

Price, F. 310, 325

Prince, J. 330, 333

Probst, R. 248, 252, 259

Proff, F. 286, 299

Purcell, L. 62, 79

Qazilbush, K. 182, 192

Rachford, D. 69, 83

Rahe, R. 204, 213

Ramirez, M. 91, 100, 108

Ramist, L. 306, 313, 326

Ramos, R. 293, 301

Ramsey, M. 199, 214

Rapley-Evans, S. 200, 214

Rauton, J. 264, 276

Raynor, J. 61, 79

Redden, M. 225, 231

Reid, R. 291, 293, 301

Reitan, R. 27, 34, 39

Renner, S. 305, 326

Resnick, L. 23, 46

Richards, D. 65, 83

Riesman, D. 10, 21

Riesman, F. 227, 231

Riley, V. 200, 214

Robbins, L. 270, 277

Roberts, G. 206, 207, 209, 214

Robinson, A. 350, 354

Roch, D. 203, 212

Rochman, S. 287, 304

Rodin, M. 292, 303

Roeher, E. 283, 299

Rogers, C. 23, 25, 47, 282, 303

Rogoff, B. 56, 83, 349, 355

Romney, L. 185, 193

Romney, T. 185, 193

Rosen, H. 72, 79

Rosenbloom, P. 218, 231

Rosenzweig, S. 281, 303

Rosman, B. 63, 81

Ross, R. 25, 41

Rossman, M. 295, 302

Roth, H. 285-287, 303

Rothkopf, E. 254, 259

Rothney, J. 282, 284, 302, 303

Rotter, J. 288, 289, 291, 303

Roueche, J. 157, 158, 160-164, 175, 176, 236, 253, 259, 339, 355

Roueche, S. 163, 176

Rouff, N. 200, 212

Rounds, J. 156, 169, 176, 306, 310, 326

Rudy, S. 198, 212

Rudy, W. 305, 321

Rumelhart, D. 34, 41, 47, 242, 248, 259

Rush, R. 239, 250, 259

Ryan, T. 174

Salmon, J. 269, 274

Saluri, D. 306, 324

Sanford, N. 5, 10, 21

Savell, J. 69, 83

Scarborough, R. 168, 176

Scardamalia, M. 53, 54, 72-74, 79

Schaer, B. 311, 323

Schell, J. 261, 277

Schmedt, C. 285, 304

Schoenfeld, A. 74, 75, 83

Scholsberg, R. 23, 51

Schooland, L. 168, 176

Schroda, H. 35, 40

Schuell, T. 35, 47

Schultz, R. 221, 222, 231

Scott, J. 253, 255

Scribner, S. 65, 83

Segal, J. 54, 56, 65, 66, 80, 148, 153, 262, 274, 277

Seligmon, M. 289, 303

Selye, H. 199, 200, 214

Selz, O. 31, 47

Shapiro, D. 287, 303

Sharpe, A. 184-187, 189, 194

Shaw, J. 24, 45

Shaw, M. 285, 303

Shea, J. 339, 344, 355

Sheldon, W. 285, 303

Shertzer, B. 203, 213, 279, 284, 291, 302, 303

Shiffrin, R. 29, 36

Shryrokov, V. 26, 49

Siegler, R. 65, 83

Silberman, H. 23, 38

Silver, L. 201, 215

Silverman, H. 281, 304

Simon, A. 24, 45

Simon, H. 25, 47

Simon, S. 329, 333

Simpson, D. 8, 21

Singer, B. 287, 302

Sini, E. 292, 301

Skinner, B. 23, 47

Slaughter, H. 226, 230

Slaughter, V. 160, 173

Slocum, W. 315, 326

Small, J. 164, 168, 174

Smith, A. 310, 326

Smith, C. 237, 248, 257

Smith, D. 268, 277

Smith, E. 143, 153, 267, 269, 276

Smith, F. 242, 244, 259

Smith, G. 155, 172

Smith, M. 287, 304

Smith, P. 168, 176

Smith, R. 242, 259

Smolensky, P. 34, 48

Snow, C. 65, 80

Snow, J. 157, 160, 163, 164, 176

Sogaria, M. 205, 214

Sokolv, Y. 28, 43

Southard, C. 286, 299

Sowell, E. 336, 342, 346, 355

Spady, W. 307, 326

Spangehl, S. 270, 273, 274

Spearman, C. 55, 83

Speilberger, C. 285, 304

Spendlove, D. 201-203, 215

Sperling, G. 26, 48

Sperry, R. 27, 28, 45, 48

Spickler, H. 224, 231

Squire, L. 26, 27, 38, 49

Stake, M. 287, 304

Stein, B. 69, 79

Stein, M. 225, 231

Sternberg, R. 55-57, 60, 70, 83, 262, 274

Sternberg, S. 26, 49

Stevens, R. 205, 215

Sticht, T. 253, 259

Stone, S. 279, 284, 291, 302, 303

Storlie, R. 239, 250, 259

Street, B. 83, 66

Strely, W. 29, 34, 42

Strupp, H. 281, 304

Sullins, L. 167, 176

Sullivan, L. 155-157, 176

Suppes, P. 23, 49

Swogger, G. 199, 215

Syz, H. 28, 49

Tarule, J. 93, 101, 107
Taylor, D. 25, 49
Terenzini, P. 308, 317, 325
Theis-Sprinthall, L. 246, 259
Thompson, R. 26, 28, 40, 49
Thornton, C. 228, 231
Thurber, S. 290, 304
Tinto, V. 305, 307, 308, 316, 318, 327
Tolaas, J. 27, 28, 35, 49
Tollefson, A. 4, 21
Tolman, E. 49, 50
Tomlenson, B. 160, 161, 167, 172
Treisman, A. 26, 50
Trevarthen, C. 27, 43
Trueblood, C. 223, 229
Tulvin, E. 27, 50
Turvey, M. 26, 50
Twohig, P. 69, 83
Tyler, D. 25, 37
Tyler, R. 336, 355

Ullman, M. 25, 50
Underwood, B. 28, 50
Upcraft, M. 332, 333

Valeri-Gold, M. 160, 163, 165, 172
Varenne, H. 65, 83
Vaughn, J. 242, 259
Veblen, Q. 288, 304

Vegso, K. 167, 176
Vye, N. 69, 79
Vygotsky, L. 28, 50, 65, 83, 143, 153

Walker, C. 160, 162, 163, 165, 176, 185, 195, 242, 245, 253, 259
Wallace, J. 204, 215
Wallace, W. 291, 299
Wanner, E. 29, 50
Ware, C. 263, 277, 291, 293, 301
Washburne, C. 23, 50
Waters, L. 291, 300
Waters, M. 160, 176
Watson, G. 265, 277
Webster, R. 226, 231
Weiner, B. 295, 304, 347, 355
Weinfield, F. 293, 300
Weitz, H. 285, 304
Wepman, J. 27, 36
Werner, H. 28, 50
Weschler, D. 55, 65, 84
Wesman, A. 291, 299
Whimbey, A. 70, 84, 269, 272, 273, 277
Whipple, W. 101, 108
White, E. 205, 214
Whitla, D. 263, 277
Whitman, N. 201-203, 215
Whyte, C. 160, 162, 165, 176, 186, 195
Widick, C. 8, 21

Wilkinson, I. 253, 255

Williams, C. 32, 43

Williams, E. 219, 223, 231

Williams, W. 198, 215

Willingham, W. 314, 327

Wilmont, B. 228, 231

Wilson, G. 295, 304

Wilson, J. 221, 231

Wilson, R. 10, 21

Winborn, B. 285, 304

Winchester, D. 249, 250, 258

Winograd, T. 31, 50

Winzenz, D. 26, 34, 37, 50

Witkin, H. 89, 108

Wohlwill, J. 57, 80

Wolf, W. 266, 268, 277

Wolfe, B. 287, 302

Wolfe, R. 147, 154

Wollfolk, A. 337, 355

Wong, E. 160, 164, 177

Woods, M. 293, 301

Woodworth, R. 23, 50

Woolfolk, A. 131, 154

Wursten, R. 285, 303

Yamba, A. 160, 162-164, 177

Yellot, R. 263, 277

Yerkes, R. 200, 215

York, R. 293, 300

Zeran, J. 282, 302

Zimmerson, N. 292, 301

Zimpfer, D. 280, 304

Zunher, V. 283, 304

Subject Index

Academic Competence 54-57

Adult Literacy 241-244

Coding 32-34

Cognitive Organization 13, 309

Cognitive Styles 53, 62-63, 89-92

College Success Studies

    Academic Variables 310

    High School Performance 312

    Gender Research 317

    High School Curriculum 312

    High School Size 315

    Race Differences 316

Competence

    Maturation 58-59

    Predicate Knowledge 60-61

    Performance Factors 61-62

    Belief Systems 62

    Task Effects 63-64

    Situational Effects 64

    Culture 64-66

Comprehensive Systems 149-151

Concepts and Variables 348-350

Concept Formation 30-32

Counseling Effectiveness 285-288

Critical Thinking 8, 53, 78, 142-143, 263-264, 269

The Criterion Problem 281-285

Curriculum 24, 53, 144

Developmental Education

Definition 235-240

Issues 23, 53, 85-86, 197-198

Learning 24-25

Macrostructures 233-235

Thinking 4-7, 24

Dyscalculia 219-226

Emotional Stages 11, 23, 25

Hierarchical Sequence 32, 271-273

Knowledge

    Representation 27-32

    Social Construction 86-89

    Ways of Knowing 92-97

Learning Centers

    Academic Component 160-161

    Assumptions 136

    Definition 156-157

    Functions 157-158

    History 127-128, 137-141, 155-156

    Movement 132

    Process Planning 179-182

    Support Component 161-166

Liberal Arts 1, 14, 15, 17-18

Locus of Control

    and Learning 288-290

    Experimental Studies 290-296

Memory 26-27

Metacognition 66, 143-144

Randomizaton 338-339

Retention and Attrition

    Sociological Model 307

    Tinto's Model 307

    Reduced Path Model 308

    Causal Model 309

    Student Departure Syndrome 309

    Peng and Fetters' Model 310

Stress

    Response 199-200

    Learning 200-202

    Coping 202-203

    Indicators 203

    Sources 204-206

Thinking Skills 53, 77, 244-246

Variance 340-341

About the Editor

Dr. Robert M. Hashway is currently a professor of education at Grambling State University. He holds degrees in electronics and mathematics as well as educational research, measurement and evaluation. Dr. Hashway has been one of the leading researchers in developmental education for the past twenty years. As a professor of physics and electronics at Roger Williams College, he designed and developed multimedia approaches for training engineers in the use of advanced instrumentation. In 1970, he was one of the first professors in the United States to incorporate microcomputers in the classroom at the college and secondary levels. As director of developmental education for the Massachusetts State College System he developed the Nation's first multimodality computer managed developmental program to be implimented on a regionwide basis. As chief executive officer of Microware Inc. and their associated Advanced Concepts Learning Centers he developed processes to facilitate life-long-learning for executives, educators, rift employees and the underprivliged learner. He provided technical assistance to Deans Burnett Joiner and Johnnie Mills who went on to develop the only developmental education doctoral program in the Nation at Grambling State University where Dr. Hashway is the ranking professor. He has published over 200 articles and monographs in the field of developmental education as well as two related books (*Objective Mental Measurement* and *Foundations of Developmental Education*) published by Praeger. Dr. Hashway has received numerous honors for leadership in Higher Education and is included in *Who's Who in America*.

List of Contributors

Andolyn V. Brown, Grambling State University, Grambling, Louisiana

Charles S. Claxton, National Center for Developmental Education, Appalachian State University, Boone, North Carolina

Joan M. Dodway, Mohawk Valley BOCES, Mohawk, New York

Robin W. Erwin, Jr., Niagra University, Niagra, New York

Cynthia Jackson Hammond, California State University at Duminquez Hills, Carson, California

Robert M. Hashway, Grambling State University, Grambling, Louisiana

Kimberly Kinsler, Hunter College, City University of New York

Barney Kyzar, Northwestern State University, Natchitoches, Louisiana

Kenneth Lane, California State University, San Bernadino, California

L. Scott Lissner, Longwood College, Longwood, Virginia

Lawrence A. Quigley, Fitchburg State College, Fitchburg, Massachusetts

George H. Roberts, Northeast Louisiana State University, Monroe, Louisiana

Andrew Robinson, Hunter College, City University of New York

Patricia Hawkins Rogers, Northeast Louisiana State University, Monroe, Louisiana

Mary Lee Schnuth, Northeast Louisiana State University, Monroe, Louisiana

Gwendolyn Trotter, Loyola University of Chicago, Chicago, Illinois

William G. White, Jr., Grambling State Unviersity, Grambling, Louisiana